Rekindling the Fire among the Nations of Pentecost

How the peoples of the Bible became Muslims and why many are now coming to Jesus

Robert L. Brenneman

Acknowledgements

Sherry, my wife of forty-seven years. For hanging in there with me after all I have put you through. I would not want to be married to me! Thank you for following me around the world.

Aaron, Joshua, and Leyla. Our children who put up with constant moving, changing schools, city to city and country to country. You often did without what Americans consider normal, even electricity for two years. What a joy to have watched you grow up and become the adults of you are. Leyla, you are still my favorite travel companion.

My daughters-in-law Mariya and Amber. You have given us the best six grandkids in the world: Rebeka, Lukas, Cole, Ellie, Belle, and Lucy.

Elaine my abla (older sister). We moved on from non-stop fighting as kids to prayer partners and intercessors as we share the joys of being grandparents and the prayer needs that never seem to end! She and her husband, Dr. Leroy Coleman, always make me feel at home in their home.

My colleagues at North Central University, past and present, particularly Dr. Nan Muhovich, with whom I have worked with for over twenty years. She challenges me to be at my best spiritually and academically.

The Friday morning prayer group at Stadium Village church for holding me up in prayer for the last decade or so.

The Juma'a (Friday) prayer groups for Muslims. Begun in 1984 by the late David Irwin, there are Juma'a prayer groups around the world interceding for Muslims. Some of the greatest prayer warriors, including Calvin Olson, Del Kingsriter, and Ron Peck are watching the fruit of their prayers in Heaven, while many others continue to persevere in prayer for the people they love. In the Twin Cities, a special thank you to John Spaulding, Michal Neterer, Clarence St. John, and Dawn Sweiven, the backbone of the Twin Cities Juma'a prayer and many others who join us faithfully.

David Leatherberry and his wife Julie gave me a vision for unreached people groups in the Middle East.

Dr. Sharon Ackerman, professor and human rights lawyer, and those at Azusa International provided the way for me to give assistance to refugees for the past four years.

Thank you to the students who used the manuscript form of this book in my History of Christian-Muslim relations class and helped me clarify my thinking.

Dave Roberts my friend from third grade, and Norm Leatherwood, a friend for forty-five years for their long friendships.

Thanks to Dr. Doug Clark for being my boss for the many years we were in the Middle East. Thanks to Rodney Tilley from whom I learned from his example what Paul meant when he said, "we were delighted to share with you not only the gospel of God but our own lives as well" (1st Thes.2:8).

My Turkish and Kurdish friends, some who are Christ-followers and some who are not (yet!). You remain in my regular prayers. Mehmet Y. a Turkish friend to who is closer to me than a brother.

The hundreds of students in my classes for twenty-two years at NCU. What a great joy to have had a chance to visit some of you in remote parts of the earth making Christ known to Muslims.

All the wonderful cross-cultural workers across the Middle East that I have laughed and cried with over the decades.

The SAT 7-satellite ministry to the peoples that are the focus of this book. Their passion to minister to the entire Body of Christ and those without the gospel, deserve the support of God's people.

Thank you to Fathers Michael Becker, Harry Winter, and Timothy Cloutier, and Drs. Scott Hahn and Derya Little have a vision to see more Catholics reach out to Muslims. Fr Jacob Zaki a gracious Coptic priest from Egypt who has been generous with his time and helping me understand more fully the Coptic Church and its theology. Thanks to them and Dawn Sweiven, Bradley Lawrence, Dr. William Ingersoll, and Michael Sayen for reading parts of the manuscript and making suggestions that were very helpful.

A super special thank you to Dr. Liz Rengel, who edited the entire book and helped it read much better. No one else has invested as much time in this book as she has.

May the rekindling work of the Holy Spirit burn so brightly among the descendants of the people of Pentecost, that Jesus is glorified more at the end of the history of His Church than it was even at the first Pentecost.

Table of Contents

Introduction

The Who, What, Where, When, and Why of this Book

The Bad: As of mid-2021, the war in Afghanistan, the longest war in America's history, winds down with much apprehension about what will happen after the American troops pull out. God alone knows the suffering of millions of Afghan people through the years, and the pain of thousands of American soldiers who have been killed or face permanent physical and psychological injuries, which not only affects them but their families.

The Good: Many Afghans, especially women and children's lives have greatly improved due to outside intervention. Thousands have found new life in Christ. There is a growing underground network of Jesus-followers who are prepared to pay the ultimate price of death to stay faithful to Jesus.

The Bad: Tensions between America and Iran remain high after the assassinations of Iranian General Soleimani by an American drone in January of 2020. Later in the year[1] Mohsen Fakrizadeh, one of Iran's leading nuclear power scientists, was assassinated, leading the Iranian government to accuse the Israelis of carrying out the attack. Iran continues to fund terror cells and fight proxy wars in many Middle Eastern lands, including in Iraq, Syria, Yemen,

---

[1] The assignation took place on November 30, 2020.

I

Lebanon and Palestine. People still hold up signs saying, "Death to Israel" or "Death to America" while crying out threats against Israel the Little Satan and America the Big Satan.

The Good: The vast majority of Iranians do not support their government's policies. Maybe no people in the world are as open to the gospel as the Iranian people are. My Iranian friends inform me that the government hires drug addicts who are desperate for a fix of narcotics to hold up those signs that denounce Israel and the United States. It is not the sentiment of the vast majority of the Iranian people. The fastest growing church in the world is in Iran, and Iranians around the world are worshipping Jesus with great joy. (This is not to deny that many Iranians face great economic hardship due to the American sanctions, as well as much persecution for those who turn away from Islam).

The Bad: The Islamic State (ISIS) rallied Sunni Muslims around the world with the vision of the rebirth of the Caliphate that would usher in the *Mahdi* (the coming Islamic savior) and bring the world to Islam. Countless thousands of people have been killed, women raped, and millions were displaced during ISIS's peak years between 2012-2016.

The Good: While some Muslims from across the world did rush to Iraq and Syria to join ISIS, far more fled from ISIS-controlled regions to Turkey, Lebanon, and Jordan in the hope of a better life. The brutality of ISIS, Al Qaida, and other jihadist groups has led many Muslims to reexamine their faith. Many are reading for the first time the Qur'an's *jihad*[2] verses and violent episodes in the life of the Prophet Muhammad that they had never heard before.

---

[2] The word *jihad* itself is controversial. It is often translated as "holy war" but many Muslims reject that definition in light of a *Hadith* (saying of Muhammad outside of the Qur'an) that the greater jihad is the battle against one's own sinful inclinations, and that the lesser jihad is a defensive war, only allowed when Islam is under attack. Other less conciliatory scholars of Islam, including some who were allegedly extremist Muslims in the past, say jihad does mean holy war and the goal of jihad is to bring the entire world into submission to Islam. This is an

The Bad: Most Muslims around the world have an unfavorable opinion of America and there is much anger against it across the Islamic world Much of the unfavorable opinion is due to the U.S. invasion of Iraq in 2003 and the perceived support for Israel's pro-Zionist anti-Palestinian policies.

The Good: American Christians are scattered around the Muslim world and, in unity with Christians from many nations, demonstrate through word and deed, that their love for Muslims transcends politics. Recently, four more Arab nations (UAE, Bahrain, Kuwait and Morocco) have agreed to normalize relations with Israel even before the Palestinian issue has been resolved as Egypt and Jordan did many years ago.

TBD (to be determined). Will Christians persevere in prayer for the Islamic world and in sharing the Good News with Muslims? Will they continue until the streams of Muslims coming to Jesus become flood-rivers, bringing blessing, peace and joy to millions around the world? Will Middle Eastern Christians from the ancient churches that can be traced back to Pentecost, be willing to forgive those who have often persecuted them, and build bridges of trust with hungry Muslims. Will Christians communicate the Gospel through word and deed "in sincere love, in truthful speech and in the power of God" (II Corinthians 6: 6-7)? Will our love for one another (John 17:23) demonstrate to all people, including Muslims, that God sent Jesus into the world?

Each of the good and bad statements above is true as of the beginning of 2021. The suffering in Afghanistan, the oppression in Iran, and the brutality of ISIS in Iraq and Syria has led to much soul-searching among the 1.7 billion Muslims in the world today. Unprecedented numbers of Muslims have come to faith in *Isa al-Masih* (Jesus the Messiah) over the last couple of decades, far more

---

ongoing debate that obviously has major ramifications in the world today. There are many Qur'anic verses that extremist Muslims cite to justify they type of jihad as carried out by ISIS and Al Qaeda, with Surah 9:29 probably being the most well- known verse.

than at any other time in history. Yet now is not the time to decrease praying, proclaiming, and persevering in making Christ known.

What this Book is About

This book is the story of how the descendants of the first Christians, the people who heard Peter preach on the Day of Pentecost when 3,000 people believed in Jesus and were baptized, later became Muslims. No, not right away, as Islam did not come into the world until six centuries later. However, as we will see, the people and places mentioned in the second chapter of the Book of Acts that records the account of the Day of Pentecost are the very ancestors of the people today who are Syrians, Iraqis, Libyans, Iranians, Kurds, Saudis, Afghans and other peoples who make up the world of Islam. The vast majority of these people are now Muslims. Yet the story does not end on that note. We can see from the accounts of what is going on currently in many places in the Middle East and Central Asia, that God has a plan for the descendants of those who believed on that special day when the Church became a reality.

This book is not only a history of dates and places. It is about a journey. I share some personal stories on my journey of forty years engaging Muslims in many parts of the world, but you will also read stories from the journeys of many people from ancient times until very recently.

This book is intended for those who may be curious about how Islam came to dominate the peoples and lands mentioned in the Bible and why many are returning to faith in Jesus Christ. There are many excellent books available for those who are already focused on sharing the good news with Muslims. I have listed many of them in the resource list. My goal is to help Christian college students and people with a heart to want people come to Jesus around the world, better Understand the past, present, and future of the people and places mentioned in the book of Acts. If many readers of this book begin to intercede in prayer for the people of Islam, and a few sense the nudging of the Holy Spirit to give their lives to making the love of Christ known to Muslims, it will be worth it the countless hours, days, and years it took to see this book through to publication.

A Harsh Encounter

Many years ago, I happened to be in the eastern Black Sea region of Turkey. In all of my years in the Middle East, seldom has anyone very aggressively practiced *dawa* ("call non-Muslims to Islam"), especially without first trying to establish some type of relationship. The Black Sea region of Turkey is the last area where Christians converted to Islam en masse after World War I. Perhaps for that reason, many people in the region feel a compulsion to be the most devout of Muslims, as if feeling that they need to convince their fellow Muslim Turks that they are the best followers of the Prophet Muhammad. In a similar manner, many Americans who have converted to Islam may often feel a need to be especially zealous to demonstrate that they are true Muslims.

The man in his zeal for *dawa,* immediately launched into explaining the beliefs and practices of Islam, and how Islam corrected and completed Judaism and Christianity. He said the Bible that Christians use today is not the Torah and Gospel that descended from God as revealed to Moses and Jesus. The Bible that Christians use today has been corrupted, and that only the Qur'an can be trusted now. Then he went on to denounce the Trinity as belief in three gods, stated that Jesus did not die on a cross, and claimed that virtually all Westerners (which is virtually synonymous with Christians in most Muslims' minds) are sexually immoral and live only for money and pleasure. I assured the man that I did not cheat on my wife, and shared why I believed in Jesus and about how he transformed my life. I also showed an interest in him, his work and in his family.

I gave the man a chance to respond and all he could say was, "Do you have an *Injil*[3] (Gospel) I could have?" It appears that this man

---

[3] *Injil* is the word the Qur'an uses to refer to the Gospel as revealed to Jesus as the Torah (Tawrat) was revealed to Moses. The tricky part is that Muslims generally

had longed for the chance to share Islam with a Christian but had never met one who could speak Turkish, as he could not speak any other language. From hostility to openness in one encounter! I have seen similar encounters many, many times. Most Muslims are shocked when they meet Christians who challenge the stereotype like in the story above.

Too Politically Correct?

Stereotypes work both ways, however. Not long after the terrible events of September 11, 2001, I spoke during the education hour at a large church near Minneapolis. I gave my talk and had a time of questions and answers. After the class, perhaps fifteen or twenty people wanted to ask me still more questions or challenge what I had said. I remembered giving talks on Islam before 9/11, and the only people who showed any interest were the church's prayer warriors. No one else thought Islam was relevant. Now after 9/11 everyone seemed interested. As I was explaining that the majority of Muslims in the world are not violent and are gracious and hospitable people, I sensed a lot of the group thought I was being too P.C. (politically correct) and was guilty of minimizing the dangers that Muslims present to our country. Then a woman spoke up and said, "Dr. Brenneman is right." She said that she had many Muslim friends and that they were fine people and were wonderful friends to her. She encouraged all of the people in the church to befriend Muslims in the Minneapolis-St. Paul area, because many are fearful of retaliatory actions by some Americans in their anger over 9/11.

In the first story, the Turkish man had never met a Christian, and he had based his ideas on half-truths and stereotypes. In the second

---

believe the original *Injil* has been corrupted. That is why there are four gospels, and many epistles and other letters that were written by Paul and others and are not divinely revealed. The standard line is that Allah revealed the Tawrat to Musa, the Zebur to Davud, and the Injil to Isa (Jesus) and the Qur'an to Muhammad. However, the first three were corrupted by the church fathers and only the Qur'an cane be trusted today. More will be said about this in later chapters.

story, most of the good church people had never met Muslims face to face, and they likewise based their thinking on media stereotypes.

From Iowa to Inner-City Chicago

I committed my life to Christ as a college freshman in 1971. Within a year, I never wanted to do anything else but make Christ known to those who did not have access to the Gospel. In those days, Islam was not in the news as it is today, and I knew nothing about Islam nor had I ever met a Muslim. I envisioned ministering in Eastern Bloc countries such as the Soviet Union, where Christians were persecuted by the atheistic Communist leadership. My heroes were those who smuggled God's Word into Communist countries like Brother Andrew who tells his inspirational story in the book *God's Smuggler*. After graduating from Trinity Bible College, a small Assemblies of God college in North Dakota, I began my ministry at Teen Challenge[4] in inner city Chicago. I married my wife Sherry while at Teen Challenge, and it was during our 3.5 years of ministry there that I impatiently waited for the "voice" of the Spirit to let me know when it was time to begin smuggling Bibles into Communist countries. Usually working 70 to 80-hour weeks left little free time, but on our day off, it was my time to read books about and dream of ministering in Eastern Bloc countries. Before actually leaving for the Communist world, however, the Lord led us to our next step, which was planting a church in a multi-racial neighborhood in Chicago. We started the church with my wife and two very small sons, and a small nucleus of faithful people. God was gracious to us, many people came to faith, especially African Americans, and the church grew to where it could stand on its own.

The church presented a tremendous challenge. I grew up in Iowa and if working with inner-city drug addicts at Teen Challenge was

---

[4] Teen Challenge is an international ministry that focuses on reaching drug addicts and street gang members with the love of Christ. The story of how the Holy Spirit led David Wilkerson, a young small-town preacher, to begin this ministry, now with centers all over the world is told in the book, *The Cross and the Switchblade.*

not enough of a challenge, pastoring people who had experienced every type of abuse often overwhelmed me. One thing we did right was to have a strong focus on prayer. The church had all-night prayer once a month and other times set aside for seeking the Lord.

Smuggling Bibles into the Soviet Union

During this time, I longed to take a trip abroad. Short-term mission trips were not as common in the 1970s as they are now, and I had never traveled abroad. I saved up money, and worked as a janitor during the days at Moody Memorial Church while still pastoring to earn the necessary money, along with some sacrificial gifts from the people at our church. Three of us attempted to take Bibles into the former Soviet Union openly as Brother Andrew and other Bible smugglers did, so that God would get the glory for blinding the eyes of the guards. It did not work that way for us, however. The military personnel at the Leningrad (now St. Petersburg) airport found our Bibles. We thought Siberia would be our new home and that we would disappear into the Gulag, but the authorities let us go after a few hours. We embarked on a journey to visit several cities in the Soviet Union. I remember being especially fascinated by the cities of Samarkand and Tashkent in Uzbekistan, despite not knowing anything about the importance of Islam in those cities' history. We also visited a few other Communist countries, and in each one, I asked the Lord if this is where he would have us.

Entering the World of Islam

Our last stop on that pivotal first trip abroad in 1980 was Turkey. Turkey was not Communist, but I was interested in it when I read that most of the New Testament was written in what is today the country of Turkey, and that it was the land of the Apostle Paul's birth and the center of his missionary journeys. I also read that Turkey is almost totally Muslim, apart from a small remnant of Christians dating back to the early days of Christian history. We toured Ephesus and a couple of the other seven churches mentioned in the second and third chapters of the book of Revelation. I was mesmerized thinking about how the land of Paul and other Apostles--the "Bible belt" of the world--could now be among the least evangelized countries in the world. Jesus rebuked the church at Ephesus for losing its first love (Rev 2:4). I wondered if that is why there is no church at Ephesus today. Jesus rebuked the Church in Laodicea for being lukewarm (Rev 3:16). In fact, Jesus rebuked and warned five of the seven churches to repent. Could it be that those churches did not repent, and as a result, Islam was God's punishment and judgment on these churches? How can we understand why most of the lands of the Bible are overwhelmingly Islamic today with only a small remnant of Christ-followers?

Ancient Ruins instead of Churches

Most of the places where Paul and Peter preached and addressed their epistles to the believers have been under Islamic rule for many centuries. Paul's famous missionary journeys all originated in Antioch, a city in southern Turkey where the believers in Jesus were first called Christians (Acts 11:26). In fact, my daughter-in-law is from the less-than one-percent Christian minority in that city, a small remnant that did not flee or become Muslim when recently-converted Arab Muslims overran Antioch in the seventh century.

I have been to the majority of the biblical sites in many Middle Eastern nations that are now populated by mostly Muslims. I have the opportunity in my classes at North Central University in Minneapolis, and in the many other schools and churches in the United States and in other countries to challenge people. I urge Christian to pray that Turks, Arabs, Kurds, Iranians and other Muslim peoples will see a living expression of the body of Christ, not just the historic ruins in their countries.

Ephesus is the best preserved of the seven ancient churches in western Turkey. While on the cross, Jesus admonished John to take care of his mother (John 19:26, 27), and it appears that John took Mary to live in Ephesus. Today, outside of her alleged dwelling place, there is a long wall filled with hundreds of thousands of prayer requests placed into every crevice between the stones by both Christian and Muslim visitors (See chapter 24). This demonstrates the high regard that both Christians and Muslims have of Mary.

The Ancient City of Ephesus

The early church councils which formulated Christian dogma (core teachings and doctrines) took place in Nicaea, Constantinople, Ephesus and Chalcedon, all of which are located in Turkey. The Nicene Creed (See chapter four) from 325 AD is recited every week in churches all over the world. The creed was slightly refined in Constantinople several decades later.

The Chalcedon definition that defines Jesus as fully God and fully human was hammered out through much controversy and conflict (See Chapter 4) That site is situated on the Asian side of Constantinople, the only major city in the world situated between two continents. Since the Turks invaded the city in 1453, Constantinople is now known as Istanbul, one of the largest cities in the world, and probably the best situated, with waterways on every side. I have seen many of the great cities of the world, but for me, none can hold a candle to Istanbul.

Of the five ancient centers of the Christian world-Antioch, Alexandria, Constantinople, Rome and Jerusalem--the first three now contain very small minorities of Christians, and Jerusalem is a major center of the three monotheistic religions of Judaism,

Christianity and Islam. Only Rome can be classified as part of the "Christian World" today.

Forty Years of Studying Islam and Engaging Muslims

For the last forty years, I have tried to help Muslims understand what followers of Christ really believe by building relationships, trying to show love, speak truth, and demonstrate God's miraculous power to Muslims. I have also tried to help Christians see Muslims as people with the same hopes, fears and struggles that they have, rather than aliens of a strange religion.

My wife Sherry and I raised our children, Aaron, Joshua, and our Middle East-born daughter in Islamic culture. In fact, we named her 'Leyla' because it is one of the most popular names common among Arabs, Turks, Persians and Kurds, and not after the famous Eric Clapton song!

The Challenge of Presenting Islam in our Day

Whenever I make a presentation about Islam, hoping to encourage people to reach out to Muslims with the love of Christ, inevitably the topic of radical Islam comes up. I always begin my talks by citing Brother Andrew, who devoted his later years to reaching Muslims after Communism collapsed in much of the world. He spells "Islam" this way:

I.S.L.A.M. = (I Sincerely Love All Muslims). I hope all followers of Christ can agree with that spelling!

Some Foundational Assumptions

1) Christians are commanded to love all people, including Muslims. Christians disagree about how they view Islam and the Qur'an. Some approach it more from a conciliatory perspective, looking for bridges of convergence between the two faiths. Others are more confrontational, challenging the misconceptions that arise when sharing the gospel with Muslims. Without a doubt for 1,400 years Islam has presented the greatest challenge in completing the Great Commission.

Christians might disagree on how to view Islam, but there is no question that we are commanded to love all people, even the minority that do despicable things in the name of their religion as Muslims (and "Christians" for that matter!) have often done.

2) Muslims need to hear the Gospel. It is not religious intolerance or arrogance to want someone to hear the most important message in the history of the world. Dialogue has its place to help clarify what each of us believes about the faith and practice of our respective religions, but it does not replace the need to proclaim the message of the crucified and resurrected Savior. The Apostle Peter commands us to always be prepared to give an answer to everyone who asks you to give the reason for the hope that you have. But do this with gentleness and respect (I Peter 3:15). We must always remember that God was in Christ reconciling the world to himself and has given us the ministry of reconciliation (II Corinthians 5:19).

The Importance of Story

I have included stories within the major story. All history is a story. It has been said that history is His story, because of the way we can see the sovereign hand of God throughout all of human history. The story of how the descendants of people and places mentioned in the biblical account in Acts 2:9-11 became Muslims is one side of the story. The other side is how in our day, for really the first time in history, truly significant numbers of Muslims are coming to know Jesus as Lord and Savior.

Rekindling the Fire

Cooking kebabs over an open fire seems to be universal among the people of the Middle East. Families and friends gather together, stake out a place to build a fire, spread out the other food items, and wait patiently for the kebabs to cook. It takes time to cook kebabs over small pieces of wood and often the fire seems to be about dead when someone waves a piece of cardboard or breathes softly on the flames. The flame roars with new life but then again almost goes out. Eventually, however, the coals are hot enough to roast the kebabs. Middle Easterners claim that kebab roasted over a fire are much tastier than when grilled on a gas stove, even though the latter is far quicker and less hassle.

This book is about how the fire of Pentecost burned so bright after the descent of the Holy Spirit, but several centuries later was almost extinguished. Now in our day, the fire is being rekindled again bringing the joy, love and peace of Jesus to millions that never had access to His grace and mercy before.

Stories beyond the Headlines

Since 1979, when Iranian youth stormed the American Embassy in Tehran, Iran and held 52 hostages for 444 days, Iran has been perceived as an enemy country by the United States. Iran has been accused of being the top supporter of terrorism around the world, and tensions between the American and Iranian governments seem to constantly surface.

A couple of years ago, I was staying in a hotel in Istanbul that was full of people from Arab countries, Iran, or other parts of Turkey. I met a young Iranian couple and we spent time together enjoying the many tourist sites in Turkey that I have seen countless times, but they had not seen before. We did not have a deep talk about faith, but they told me that they had friends coming from Iran the next day and they wanted me to meet them.

The next day, upon meeting them, the woman immediately asked me if I had a Farsi (the language of Iran) *Injil* (Gospel) That very morning a friend had given me a Farsi *Injil* in case I met someone who might need it. I was able to give it to the woman, who wept with joy as if I had given her a diamond necklace. She said she had searched throughout Iran, and she had also tried to find a Farsi Bible during previous visits to Turkey but could not get her hands on a copy.

The next day was Sunday, and the woman told me she and her husband had spent the entire night reading the book. I took the two couples to a church that had a Farsi service on Sunday evenings. The woman who was so eager to have an *Injil* and her husband responded to the altar call, gave their lives to Jesus, and were filled with the Holy Spirit. They joined in with other Iranian believers in singing and dancing with great joy.

So, what is the true narrative? The government of Iran and the government of the United States confronting each other with hostility? Is it this young couple gloriously redeemed, and experiencing new life in Christ along with hundreds of thousands of other Iranians?

Iran was known as Persia from biblical times until the 20th century. It contains many biblical sites including Parthia, Elam, and Susa. Many biblical characters, including Cyrus, Darius, Daniel, Esther, Mordecai, Ezra and Nehemiah dwelt there. Almost 1,400 years ago, Arab Muslims began to invade Persia and the majority of the people became Muslims. Zoroastrians[5], Christians, and Jews were reduced to small minorities over time until gradually they became less than one percent of the population. Now, however, according to *Operation World*, Iran has the fastest growing church in the world.[6]

I will refer to the following text frequently throughout this book, in particular, verses six and seven, which I have put in bold font.

II Corinthians 6:3-11

*We put no stumbling block in anyone's path so that our ministry will not be discredited. Rather, as servants of God we commend ourselves in every way: in great endurance, in troubles, hardships and distresses; in beatings, imprisonments and riots; in hard work, sleepless nights and hunger; in purity, understanding, patience and kindness; in the Holy Spirit and; **in sincere love; in truthful speech and in the power of God;***

---

[5] Zoroastrianism is the indigenous religion of the Iranian/Persian peoples. (See Chapter 5)
[6] Mandryk *Operation World*, p. 916

with weapons of righteousness in the right hand and the left; through glory and dishonor, bad report and good report; genuine yet regarded as imposters; known yet regarded as unknown; dying, and yet we live on; beaten and yet not killed; sorrowful, yet always rejoicing; poor yet making many rich; having nothing, and yet possessing everything.

Truth, Power and Love

When anyone encounters Jesus, whatever their religious background, they will have to encounter him on three levels. The order of these encounters and their specifics will vary as each person has his or her own story of how they encountered Christ.

Encountering Jesus through Truth

Jesus said. *I am the truth* (John 14:6). He said, *the truth will set you free* (John 8:32). Satan is a liar. This world system is dominated by him. Every person on this planet has to fight a continuous battle not to succumb to the lies of the devil. There is much good in the Qur'an and much that is admirable in Islamic culture and society. Nevertheless, Muslims have been lied to in major ways. Most Muslims, since childhood have been told that the Bible has been corrupted, that Christians worship three gods, and that Jesus was a prophet but not the Son of God. In fact, they are taught, *Allah* [7] loved Jesus so much that he took him up to himself, and Jesus was never crucified. The denial of Jesus' death on the cross to redeem humankind is perhaps the biggest lie the world in the history of the world in terms of how many people the lie has influenced.

---

[7] The word *Allah* for God concerns many Christians. Jews and Christians, who speak Arabic as their mother tongue, generally use the word Allah when referring to God. There is no doubt that Christians and Muslims often perceive God differently. In Islam, *Tawhid* the absolute Oneness of God is the essence of Islamic faith, whereas the Trinity seems contrary to the Oneness of God in Muslim minds. Horrendous acts have been done in the name of Allah, but terrible things have been done in the name of every religion. The debate of whether or not Christians worship the same God seems to be a question of whether differing perceptions of God means that Christians and Muslims worship different gods.

Encountering Jesus through Power

Throughout this book, we will see that often the Church substituted political and military power for spiritual power. That is why I have to be careful to make sure the reader knows I am talking about spiritual power, not earthly power, when I say that Muslims must encounter Jesus through a power encounter. We will examine this claim later in the book, but when I write that Muslims must have a power encounter, I mean that they will generally need some type of supernatural confirmation that following Jesus is worth the persecution, isolation, and possible death that they will encounter. Paul said, *I did not come to you with persuasive words but with a demonstration of the Spirit's power* (1 Corinthians 1:4). Dreams, visions, powerful answers to prayer, and miracles that give evidence that Jesus is Lord, are usually essential for a Muslim to believe in Jesus and continue to believe when the going gets hard.

Encountering Jesus through Love

God is love (1 John 4:8). Most Muslims begin to explore the path of Jesus because they have met a Jesus-follower who has loved them and lives a life that impresses them. The Apostle Paul said *the greatest of these*, even more than faith and hope, is love (1 Corinthians 13:13). We need to demonstrate to Muslims that we truly love them whether or not they seem to be interested in the message of Jesus.

As we look at the eternal drama of God's redemptive plan to redeem *persons from every tribe and language and people and nation* (Revelation 5:9), we will come back many times to how truth, power and love have sometimes been applied and, unfortunately, often not applied in relationships between Christians and Muslims. May the Lord give us grace to work toward much better days in helping our Muslim friends realize *that God was truly in Christ, reconciling the world to himself* (2 Corinthians 5:19).

The Layout of the Book

Most chapters will begin with the phrase "Just imagine . . ." In doing this, I tell a brief, imaginary story that I hope can lead the reader to put himself or herself into "the shoes" of the person who is reflective of the time and setting under discussion. This is followed by a historical-theological explanation of the story. Finally, at the end of most chapters, there is a testimony or narrative from a real person or event that illustrates the point of the chapter. Some of these real stories will be from the pages of history, while others are people whom I have known or others have known that are quite current.

The chapters will vary in length, but I have tried to keep each chapter relatively short to be able to read in short increments.

Discussion or Reflection Questions

- Why does the subject of Islam bring out such an emotional reaction in many people?
- Have you had any encounters either positive or negative with Muslims that you can briefly describe?
- The author highlights engaging Muslims with truth, power and love. In your own life, which of these dimensions has played a greater role in how you came to know Christ?

I

The Day of Pentecost and the First Believers

Just imagine you are a Jew from Parthia, a region within the Persian Empire. The year is 30 A.D. You and your family have journeyed all the way to Jerusalem to celebrate Passover. You plan to stay for the Festival of Pentecost as well, which is fifty days after Passover. It was a journey of many weeks, and the trip used up much of your savings, but you want your children to see Jerusalem, the holy city.

When you arrive in Jerusalem, the city is not what you were expecting. The number of Roman soldiers is far greater than it was five years ago when you came by yourself. The soldiers are concentrated near the Temple, that magnificent piece of architecture that your fellow Jews are so proud to visit.

All the talk seems to be about a man named Yeshua (Jesus), whom some people seem to love while others spew out venom when they speak of him. You had hoped to show your children the beauty of the Temple as you celebrate Passover in the City of David. Instead, all you hear is talk by some that this Yeshua is another a false Messiah, while others argue that a false Messiah could not heal people born blind or raise someone from the dead. Not long ago this Yeshua was said to have raised a Jew named Lazarus from the dead after he was four days in the grave.

Suddenly the governor Pilate comes out with Yeshua. He had been debating with some of the Jewish leaders about what to do with this man they so greatly despised. Pilate said he could find no fault in Yeshua and that he would have him scourged and release him. The crowd's reaction against this is so strong that Pilate relents. He offers the crowd two choices. According to custom, one prisoner is to be set free at Passover time. One of the prisoners, Barabbas, is a notorious zealot, a revolutionary whose band of fellow zealots want to liberate the land from Roman rule without waiting for the promised Messiah. His band considers much of the Jewish leadership to be collaborators with Rome. Zealots are not popular with many Jews who may not like the Romans, but neither do they want the wrath of Rome to fall on them because of some over-zealous Jewish nationalists.

The crowd screams out that they want Barabbas to be set free, not Yeshua. They demand that Yeshua be crucified. Others in the crowd are yelling for Yeshua to be set free, but their voices are drowned out. You ask people around you what all of this is about. Some people say that Yeshua blasphemously claimed to be the Son of God. Others tell you about the sick people Jesus healed, and once, when there was no food, Jesus fed thousands of families with five loaves of bread and two fish.

The soldiers lead Yeshua away to be crucified, with hundreds of people following the progression along the Via Delorosa. Some are cursing and spitting at him. Others are weeping and obviously adored him.

You do not follow the mob to the site of the crucifixion. After all, you have never heard the man speak nor seen any of his alleged miracles. You want to enjoy the next fifty days of festival with distant relatives who returned to Jerusalem long ago in the days of Nehemiah and Ezra, even as your family stayed in Persia. You connect with people you met five years ago and make some new friends. You show your children the magnificence of the Temple and other holy sites. Nevertheless, the atmosphere is still charged. Even after the crucifixion of Jesus, there is a strange feeling in the air that the question of this Messiah figure has not been resolved.

Finally, it is the day of Pentecost. On your way to the Temple, you hear a strange noise like a ferocious wind blowing, and people are shouting in many languages. Hundreds of people are pushing and shoving to peek into the courtyard of a large house to see what is going on. You hear someone declaring praise to God in the Parthian language. Someone near you says that they hear perfect Cappadocian, a language known by few people outside that region. Someone else says he hears people speaking the Median language. Everyone is wondering why these hundred or so people within the courtyard are speaking in so many languages at the same time. You hear a bystander from Elam say to a fellow Elamite, "I know some of these men. They do not know a word of our language. Yet they are speaking it perfectly." Others in the crowd, however, dismiss the whole thing and say that the people in the room are all drunk.

Then someone they call Simon Peter stands up and says that no one is drunk, as it is only 9:00 in the morning. He says that this was promised to the People of God by the Prophet Joel, that in the last days the Lord said he would fill men and women with His Spirit and they would prophecy and have dreams and visions. Simon Peter then preaches about this man Yeshua: "Although you crucified him, God has raised him from the dead." That very day, many who had screamed "Crucify him, crucify him" were now calling on Yeshua in repentance. After this, the disciples baptized them. What a celebration it turned out to be--from weeping to overflowing joy!

Later you ask one of the men whom you heard speaking Parthian where he had learned your language. He tells you he does not know a word of Parthian. He did not even know he was speaking the Parthian language when the Holy Spirit came on him. Others ask how the men and women gathered there learned the languages of the people of Mesopotamia, Pamphylia, or Crete. Each one says the same thing. "I know not a word of the language you mentioned. I did not even know in what language I was praising God."

You also believed on Yeshua that day. You repented of your sins and were baptized along with thousands of others. You were planning to go back to Parthia right after the Festival of Pentecost but you do not want to take your family back to Parthia without knowing more about the way of Yeshua. You and your family moved in with one of the many hundreds of witnesses who saw the resurrected Savior. Every day you break bread with other disciples and spend time in prayer and study. Miracles of healing and deliverance occur regularly, and there is a unity among the believers in Yeshua that makes you thinks that this is what heaven must be like.

History and Theology

When the day of Pentecost came, they were all together in one place. Suddenly a sound like the blowing of a violent wind came from heaven and filled the whole house where they were sitting. They saw what seemed to be tongues of fire that separated and came to rest on each of them. All of them were filled with the Holy Spirit and began to speak in other tongues as the Spirit enabled them. Now there were staying in Jerusalem God-fearing Jews from every nation under heaven. When they heard this sound, a crowd came together in bewilderment, because each one heard their own language being spoken. Utterly amazed, they asked: "Aren't all these who are speaking Galileans?" Then how is it that each of us hears them in our own native language, Parthians, Medes and Elamites; residents of Mesopotamia, Judea and Cappadocia, Pontus and Asia, Phrygia and Pamphylia, Egypt and parts of Libya near Cyrene; visitors from Rome (both Jews and converts to Judaism); Cretans and Arabs—we hear them declaring the wonders of God in our own tongues! Amazed and perplexed, they asked one another, "What does this mean?" Some, however, made fun of them and said, "They had too much wine." (Acts 2:1-13).

Tongues of Fire on the Day of Pentecost

The second chapter of Acts is often regarded as a watershed moment in the history of Christianity. The little fellowship of eyewitnesses to the resurrection became a fast-growing movement of thousands, which now numbers well over two billion people worldwide. Yet in all the hundreds of sermons I have heard preached on Acts 2 over the years, I have never heard anyone say what happened to the various peoples mentioned in verses nine through eleven.

The map below shows the locations of the fifteen peoples or places mentioned in Acts 2 as Jews of the diaspora who came to Jerusalem for the Festival of Pentecost. New Testament scholar Craig Keener suggests that Luke has simply updated the names of the places in the table of nations (Genesis 10). Perhaps, Keener says, the miracle at Pentecost reversed the judgement that fell on the nations at the tower of Babel where God made them unintelligible to each other. The event at Pentecost had transcended the language barrier. [8]

The Places and Peoples of Acts 2:9-11

Parthians

The Parthians were a tribal people whose homeland was south of the Caspian Sea in what is today the Islamic Republic of Iran. Before the time of Christ, the Parthians were most likely Zoroastrian in religion, worshipping *Ahura Mazda* as the Supreme Being, and holding to a very dualistic worldview, which focused on the cosmic battle between the forces of light and darkness. The Parthians spoke an Indo-European language of the same family as Persian. Like most of today's Iran (or Persia); Parthia fell under Greek domination during the time of Alexander the Great in the fourth century B.C.

---

[8] Keener, *The Bible Background Commentary: New Testament* p. 327

For Alexander there was no point in going west, which was considered primitive and undeveloped. Instead, Alexander went east and even as he defeated the Persians, he admired their achievements. In many ways, Persia was far ahead of Western Europe in terms of culture, art, architecture, roads. It even had a postal service that preceded America's pony express by thousands of years! Near the capital city of Erbil, which today is the capital of the Kurdish region of Iraq, Alexander defeated the Persian Empire of Darius III. Alexander restored Cyrus the Great's temple and gave him a proper burial after his murder. Alexander married the Persian Queen Roxana and encouraged thousands of his troops to take Persian wives.

In about 250 B.C. the Parthians revolted against Seleucid rule (the successors to Alexander), and they experienced something of a golden age in the second century B.C. before the Romans invaded. Some Jews had been exiled to Parthia during the fall of Judah to Babylon in the sixth century before Christ. Parthia was also listed in the biblical text as one of the administrative units administered by Darius (Daniel 6:1). The Parthians represented on the Day of Pentecost probably included descendants of deported Jews as well as converts to Judaism from Zoroastrianism. Today the land of the Parthians is overwhelmingly Islamic, part of the Islamic Republic of Iran.

Medes

The Medes dwelt south and southwest of the Caspian Sea in the Zagros Mountains. Like the Parthians, they are also an Indo-European people, speaking a language considered to be in the Iranian family of languages. The Medes are one of the indigenous people of the Middle East who can trace their origins back to Madai, son of Japheth and grandson of Noah (Genesis 10).[9]

---

[9] In my book *As Strong as the Mountains: A Kurdish Cultural Journey (2015 2nd Edition)*, I point out that the Kurdish people of Iraq, Iran, Turkey, and Syria consider themselves the descendants of the ancient Medes. If this is so, the Medes/Kurds

The Medes played a significant role in biblical history. It was to the land of the Medes that Assyrian King Shalmaneser deported the Jews from the northern kingdom of Samaria in 721 B.C. (2 Kings 17:6; 18:11). The Scripture says that the Israelites were exiled by the king of Assyria during the reign of Hoshea, deporting them to Assyria, settling them in Halah and Gozan on the Habor River in the towns and villages of the Medes (2 Kings 17:5,6). This area is now called Kurdistan and is located in Northern Iraq.

My family and I know the area very well. We lived in Zakho from 1992-1996 in this very region, and our house was a short walk to the Habor River, where Kurdish women washed their clothes in the river today as their ancestors did over two-and-one-half millennia ago. For two of the four years that we lived in this region, there was no electricity as the government of Saddam Hussein, the now deceased dictator of Iraq, seeking revenge against the Kurds for their uprising against his rule after the first Gulf War, still had control over the electrical grid for our city. Most likely, the Israelite women also washed their clothes in the same river, and over time, they were absorbed into the society of the Medes. In fact, until 1950, when Kurdish Jews were allowed to migrate to the newly founded nation of Israel, many Jews lived in Zakho, and Kurds still call the neighborhood *mahalle Musaviya* (Jewish quarter).[10]

The Medes are mentioned primarily in the Old Testament as the instruments of Yahweh in judgment against the Babylonians who invaded the southern kingdom of Judah in the 6th century B.C. Previously to that, however, the Medes were also involved in the final destruction of the Assyrian kingdom, having warred against

---

played an important role in biblical history although few Kurds knew this, at least not until very recent times due to translation of the Bible into various dialects of Kurdish as well as other sources.

[10] There has been much speculation about what happened to the ten lost tribes of the Israelites in the light of their forced exile by the Assyrians. They have been identified as ancestors of Afghan tribes, American Indian tribes, the British, and others. The possibility that the Israelites were absorbed into the culture of the Medes seems more likely than these other speculations.

their archenemies for centuries. In 614 B.C., the Medes and Babylonians joined forces under Cyaxares, the Median king, and the Babylonian king Naboplassar to invade Assyria and overthrow its famous capital Nineveh (today's Mosul, Iraq).

The alliance between the Babylonians and the Medes did not last long. As Isaiah had forewarned, the Medes and Persians formed an alliance and invaded Babylon. Isaiah also predicted that Yahweh would stir up the Medes and they would reduce Babylon to be like Sodom and Gomorrah (Isa 13:17-19). This is the setting for the well-known story of the handwriting on the wall during the time of King Belshazzar. Daniel translates the mysterious writing that so terrified Belshazzar and his guests, telling them that his kingdom has been weighed on the scales and found wanting, and that it would be divided among the Medes and the Persians (Dan. 5:26-28). The Scripture says that even that very night the Medes and Persians invaded Babylon (Daniel 5:30) and set up a kingdom that would play a pivotal role in biblical events.

In the next chapter of Daniel, we read the famous story of his miraculous escape from the Lion's Den. After Daniel is delivered from the lions, King Darius [11] declares that all of the people of the Medo-Persian Empire should fear and reverence the God of Daniel (Daniel 6:26). Much more could be said about the Medes in relation to the stories of Esther, Ezra, and Nehemiah, all of whom thrived under the Medes and Persians despite the Jews being a conquered people, but who were eventually allowed to return to their

---

[11] Biblical historians have disputed the identity of King Darius in Daniel 6. There were several Medo/Persian kings named Darius, but there is scant evidence that it was Darius the Mede who threw Daniel into the lion's den. Youngblood, Bruce and Harrison say that Darius the Mede has not been identified with certainty and that neither Greek nor Persian sources mention him (Nelson's Compact Dictionary, p. 169). McKenzie gives a lengthy list of possible candidates to the question of who this Darius was since there is little or no history to substantiate him (490-492). Often kings had more than one name, however, and the simplest solution is that Darius the Mede is merely one name of the Medo-Persian kings who after seeing God deliver Daniel from the lion's den, declared that all of the people of his kingdom should revere the God of Daniel (Dan 6:25-28).

homeland under King Cyrus and his successors.

Before returning to the Acts narrative, it is interesting to point out that the Magi, who were drawn by a star to Bethlehem to pay homage to the newborn King, the Messiah, were very likely a Median tribe of Zoroastrian astronomers and astrologers. This is not conclusive, and other theories have been offered to the identity of the Magi, but there is a very good case that can be made that the Magi were Medes, the first Gentiles who acknowledged the Messiah.[12]

The Kurds as Heroes

As I write this, the bravery of the Kurds, defeating ISIS with American assistance while losing 11,000 of their brave men and women fighting the brutal jihadists is becoming well known. I highlighted "women" because the Kurds allow women to fight in battle. In fact, it is widely believed by ISIS jihadists, that if a female *Peshmerga* (Kurdish warriors who faces death) killed them; they would not go to Paradise as martyrs.

Elamites

The third group mentioned in the second chapter of Acts is the Elamites, another people whose homeland was in Persia, who like the Medes trace their heritage to Noah. However, the Medes are the descendants of Japheth, whereas the Elamites trace their ancestry to Shem (Gen. 10:22). Isaiah predicted that the Elamites, like the Medes, would be involved in the destruction of Babylon (Isa. 21:2). After the Medes and Persians dominated the region generally called Mesopotamia, the Elamites were absorbed into the Medes and played a role in the events of the restoration of the Jews to their homeland during the reign of Cyrus the Great. Cyrus, among the

---

[12] Yamauchi says that it is complex to prove that the Magi were Persian Zoroastrians. He points out that Clement of Alexandria believed the Magi were Zoroastrians, and also Chrysostom, Origen, Ephraim the Syrian all believed the Magi were one of the tribes of the Medes who functioned as priests and diviners under the Achaemenian Persians from the 6th to the 4th century B.C. (p. 467).

greatest rulers of all time, is best known biblically as the one who gave the decree to set captives free captured under the Babylonians in 539 B.C. Among those set free were the Jews who had been taken captive in 586 B.C. Cyrus is called the "Lord's anointed one "by Isaiah.[13] In both Chronicles and Ezra, we see the decree of Cyrus that allowed the Jews to return to Jerusalem and rebuild the Temple. (II Chron 36:22-23; Ezra 1:1-4).

There is an incredible move of the Holy Spirit among the Iranians, both in Iran itself and wherever Iranians have migrated. We will explore how and why this is happening later in the book. I have heard from many Iranians that they believe Jeremiah 49 relates to their situation in a unique way. In that chapter, verses 35 to 39, Yahweh declares that he will bring the four winds against Elam and scatter them to the nations. There will not be a nation where Elam's exiles would not go. The Iranian believers say that the Iranian diaspora partially fulfills these verses. Millions of Iranians are scattered around the world, forced to leave their beloved homeland as they seek refuge from the current Islamic regime, Yet the prophecy is not only about judgment. The final verse says, "Yet I will restore the fortunes of Elam in days to come, declares the Lord" (Jer. 49:39). The Iranian believers with whom I have dialogued believe that this current ingathering of people coming to faith in Christ, with estimates ranging from hundreds of thousands to possibly in the millions, is a fulfillment of this prophecy of the restoration of Elam. It is impossible to know how many have come to faith in Christ with any kind of accuracy.

Residents of Mesopotamia

Unlike the specific ethnic groups previously mentioned, residents of Mesopotamia include a variety of ethnicities. The word *Mesopotamia* comes from a Greek word meaning between the two rivers (the Tigris and the Euphrates). Mesopotamia was the home of the patriarchs and the traditional location of the Garden of Eden. Both

---

[13] Isaiah 45:1

the northern kingdom of Samaria (2 Kings 15:29; 1 Chronicles. 5:26) and the southern kingdom of Judah (2 Kings 24:14-16; 2 Chronicles 36:20) went into exile in Mesopotamia. Today most of Mesopotamia is in Iraq, with small portions in southeast Turkey and Syria. All of these regions are predominantly Muslim today. It is hard to visualize that Iraq was once a center of Christianity. However, as Peter Frankopan, the author of *The Silk Roads*, points out, Basra, Mosul and Tikrit (Saddam Hussein's hometown) had thriving Christian populations long before Europe did.[14]

Mesopotamia, which included Babylon, has been the center of much of the human drama over thousands and thousands of years, from Abraham of the "land of Ur" who obeyed the Lord's call to migrate to the Promised Land to the horrors of the wars in Iraq. Babylon is mentioned throughout the Bible from Genesis to Revelation. From the earliest days of human existence to a vital role in the end times, (see Revelation 17 and 18) the peoples and places in Mesopotamia play a major role. Tragically, the number of Iraqi Christians, who trace their religious heritage back to the Day of Pentecost, has been reduced from five percent of the population to under one percent after the American invasion/ deliverance[15] in 2003. Yet as we will see later, many Muslims are coming to know Jesus in this region as well.

Places in Turkey

The next five places mentioned in Acts 2:9-11 are located in modern Turkey. I have visited all of these sites, most of them numerous times. Like all ancient sites, volumes could be written about each place. I will summarize their history very briefly.

---

[14] Frankopan p. 55

[15] It is beyond the scope of this book to enter the debate on whether or not the U.S. should have sent troops to Iraq to remove Saddam Hussein from power. Some good did come out of it, and without doubt, many of the American troops had good intentions of helping the people. Sadly, major blunders were also made, and many if not most Americans ,as well as world opinion in general, has come out against the American war effort.

It must be remembered that the Turkish people who make up the majority of Turkey's population today (along with a large minority of Kurds and smaller minorities of Arabs and many other ethnicities) did not come into the region until hundreds of years after Bible days, mostly in the eleventh century. So, unlike the Persians, Arabs, Kurds, and Egyptians, many of whom had been Christians before their Islamization, the Turks primarily practiced shamanistic rituals and had not yet embraced a world religion. Along the Silk Road, they no doubt encountered Buddhism, Christianity and Islam, but the vast majority of Turks chose Islam and became among its most fervent adherents. In time they replaced the Arabs as the protectors and spreaders of Islam, especially in the former territories of the East Roman Byzantine Empire in what is today Turkey.

Cappadocia

In biblical times Cappadocia was a Roman province, stretching from south of Galatia toward Armenia with the Taurus Mountains and Cilicia to the south. Mark Wilson, a specialist in biblical history and archaeology in Turkey, says the people spoke Cappadocian and only the rulers spoke Greek.[16] When people heard the disciples of Jesus speaking Cappadocian at Pentecost, knowing that none of them came from that region, it no doubt added to the wonder of the miracle on the Day of Pentecost. Cappadocia is mentioned only once after Acts 2 in the biblical text, when Peter addresses God's elect as strangers in the world, and lists Cappadocia as one of the places where they have been scattered (1 Peter 1:1). However, Cappadocia became famous in church history, especially as the home of the Cappadocian fathers, Christian theologians who lived in the fourth century and greatly influenced our understanding of the person of the Holy Spirit in relation to the other members of the Trinity. Chadwick says that the mantle of Athanasius, the great defender of the faith during the Arian heresy (See chapter 4) was passed on to the Cappadocian fathers-- Basil of Caesarea (today's

---

[16] Wilson, p. 141

Kayseri (330-379), Gregory Nazianzus (329-390), and Gregory of Nyssa (335-394), the younger brother of St. Basil[17]

In Cappadocia, not only was the doctrine of the Holy Spirit hammered out, but the Spirit as a living person moving among his people was demonstrated. Basil rejected the idea that the Holy Spirit is a created being inferior to the Father and the Son. [18] His writings on the blessed Trinity are extremely rich in truth, written at a time when many questioned the divinity of the Holy Spirit, and the Spirit was perceived more as a force than the third person of the Trinity. Stanley Burgess, a scholar of Pentecostal movements throughout church history, writes that Basil came to be known as a champion of the Holy Spirit and eventually as "Doctor of the Spirit." Basil was far from an ivory-tower academic, however; he ministered to the impoverished and ill in very practical ways.

Even before the Cappadocian Fathers, however, in the third century, Gregory the Wonderworker (213-270) was known as one who performed signs and wonders in Jesus' name as he evangelized Cappadocia, and times of prophecy and revival were reported even in later periods[19].

---

[17] Chadwick, p. 2
[18] Burgess, p. 63
[19] Irvin, p. 147

Chimney houses of Cappadocia

Cappadocia now is almost totally Muslim and has become a major tourist destination for hundreds of thousands of people who visit the exotic landscape filled with "fairy chimneys." Thousands of these chimney-like houses and churches remain, and in many of them, one can still observe painted frescoes of Jesus, his disciples, biblical figures, and revered Christian saints. There are also many underground cities, some of which have been excavated and opened to tourism. In the city of Derinkuyu, visitors can descend eight stories underground to observe how the early Christians hid underground from first Roman and later Arab persecution. They dug out homes where they could hide for months at a time, and one can see churches, wine cellars, kitchens, baptism tanks, and altars for the priests. In another underground city, three stories beneath the earth, there is even an underground missionary school that trained people in evangelism. Tour guides in the region say that there are hundreds of other underground cities that have not yet been excavated.

Pontus

A city on the southern shore of the Black Sea, Pontus is addressed along with Cappadocia and other places situated in Turkey, in Peter's epistle (1 Pet. 1:1). The city is also mentioned as the birthplace of Aquila, the husband of Priscilla (Acts 18:2). This husband and wife team made tents with Paul and accompanied him on some of his travels. Pontus was also the setting in the drama of Mark Anthony and Pompey and other famous historical events in the Roman Empire.[20]

Asia

Asia refers to the Roman province within western Asia Minor, which covers a much larger area. Pergamum was the first capital of Asia, but later Ephesus became the most prominent city, where Paul spent more time than in any other city. A riot was stirred up by silversmiths who were afraid that Paul's preaching might lead to people no longer revering the goddess Artemis, as recorded in Acts 19. Paul preached in Ephesus on both of his second and third missionary journeys, and it is said that all the Jews and Greeks of Asia heard the Word of the Lord (Acts 19:10). Paul probably spent about three years in Ephesus, longer than in any other city.

The letters to the seven churches of Revelation were written to Christians in Asia. Ephesus is the best preserved of the seven churches and draws the most tourists. Pergamum and Laodicea are also very impressive and many tourists visit these sites as well.

Phrygia

Another province of the Roman Empire, a sub-region of Galatia, Phrygia contained the cities of Colossae, Laodicea, Hierapolis, and Iconium. All of these locations are now found in present day Turkey. Hierapolis is the major tourist center of *Pamukkale* ("cotton castle" in Turkish-see picture), and Iconium is today's Konya, the center of the Mevlana (Rumi) tomb and museum.[21]

Wilson points out that the famous Jewish portions of the Sibylline

---

[20] Wilson p. 331-332

[21] Most large bookstores will have multiple books about Rumi, the 13th century Muslim Sufi mystic whose poetry about tolerance and God consciousness has been packaged for modern spiritual seekers.

Oracles came from Phrygia, and Phrygia was supposedly the first land to emerge after the flood.[22]

Pamphylia

Pamphylia was another province of Asia Minor now in southern Turkey. One of its chief cities was Perga, where Mark left Paul and Barnabas (Acts 13:13). Paul passed through Perga with his companions on his first missionary journey and later sailed off its coast (Acts 27:5). Whether Paul established the church there is unknown, but we do know that Pamphylian Jews from the region were among those gathered at the Upper Room on the Day of Pentecost.

North African Sites

Egypt: Hagar and Ishmael

There is so much about Egypt in Scripture that countless volumes have been written about its role in history. For our purposes, it is sufficient to say that this was the land where Abraham sought refuge and met Hagar. The book of Genesis relates the story. Abraham's wife Sarah was unable to bear children and she encourages Abraham to sleep with Hagar and claim Hagar's child as their son. After the birth of Ishmael, relations between Sarah and Hagar became so tense that Hagar flees from Abraham's home. The Lord appears to Hagar and tells her to return and submit to Sarah. The Lord promises Hagar that he would "increase your descendants so much that they will be too numerous to count" (Gen 16:10).

Tony Maalouf, an Arab Christian and professor, argues that Hagar received what is called a theophany, an appearance of the pre-incarnated Christ. The angelic visitor assures Hagar that not only will Ishmael survive, but also that God will multiply his seed and make of him a great nation. [23] Whether it is a theophany or a special visit by a heavenly being, Hagar experienced a very special

---

[22] Wilson, p. 188
[23] Maalouf p. 63

visitation! Maalouf points out that Hagar is the only person in the Bible that confers a name on a deity.[24] The Bible says, *she gave this name to the Lord who spoke to her, "You are the one who sees me," for she said, "I have now seen the one who sees me". That is why the well was called Beer Lahai Roi.* (Genesis 16:13,14). Maalouf notes that in rabbinical tradition only four people in scripture were named before they were born: Isaac, Ishmael, Josiah, and Solomon. Ishmael's birth was the first birth annunciation in the history of Israel.[25] The Lord tells Hagar to name him Ishmael. He foretells that Ishmael's hand will be against everyone, and everyone's hands will be against him, and that he would live in hostility toward all of his brothers (Gen 16: 11,12).

Fourteen years later, when Sarah is 90 years old, she conceived Isaac. The Lord renews his agreement with Abraham, promising him that his covenant will be established with Isaac as an everlasting covenant for his descendants after him (Gen 17:19). However, the Lord did not forget Ishmael. He promised Abraham, "And as for Ishmael, I have heard you: I will surely bless him; I will make him fruitful and will greatly increase his numbers. He will be the father of twelve rulers, and I will make him into a great nation" (Gen 17:19).

Now that Sarah has her own son, she has little use for Hagar or Ishmael. Ishmael mocked Isaac, no doubt out of jealousy. He had lost his privileged standing as Abraham's only son when Isaac became the major heir of Abraham's status and property. Abraham agrees with Sarah to banish Hagar and Ishmael, and he sends them into the desert with very few rations. The rations run out and Hagar cannot bear to watch Ishmael die. She places Ishmael under a bush and turns away. But the Lord calls her by name, "What is the matter, Hagar? Do not be afraid; God has heard the boy crying as he lies there. Lift the boy up and take him by the hand, for I will make him into a great nation" (Gen 21:17-18). And the Lord provided Hagar and Ishmael with food and water.

---

[24] Ibid., p.78
[25] Maalouf p. 66

Muslims as Children of Abraham

It should not be surprising that Arabs specifically, and Muslims of whatever ethnic background, trace their faith to Abraham and Ishmael and take pride in their connection to Abraham. In fact, the biblical story of when Abraham was about to sacrifice his son Isaac in obedience to the Lord's command but was prevented at the last moment from doing so, is told in the Qur'an. It merely says "Abraham's son," however, without mentioning the son's name. [26] Most Muslims believe that it was Ishmael who as the oldest son of Abraham would have been the one to be sacrificed, but the Lord spared him when he saw Abraham's obedience.

The lengthy story of Abraham, Isaac, Hagar and Ishmael, which dominates chapters 15-25 of Genesis, ends on a more hopeful note as Isaac and Ishmael reunite to bury their father alongside Sarah in a cave, which Abraham had purchased from Hittites (Gen 16:13,14).

The conflict between the descendants of Isaac and Ishmael continues today in what seems like an everlasting struggle as Jews and Arabs have been battling over that small strip of land called Israel, which is known as the most contested piece of real estate in the world. This battle has been especially fierce since the establishment of the nation of Israel in 1948. Fortunately, the Bible gives us hope that there will be a reconciliation one day between the children of Ishmael and the children of Isaac (Isaiah 19:23-25).

Egypt is the land where Moses grew up in Pharaoh's court, but from which he later fled after discovering his Hebrew identity. Forty years later, he returned and was used by God to set his people free from bondage. The Coptic Christians still rightfully claim to be the true Egyptians because the majority of the Egyptian population (around 87-90 percent) converted to Islam and took on Arab identity. Only the Christians have maintained their identity as Copts.

---

[26] Surah 37: 101-108

Parts of Libya near Cyrene

Libya lies west of Egypt and is referred to as Phut or Put in the Old Testament. Simon, who carried Jesus' cross, was from Cyrene (Matt 27:32), the New Testament name for Libya. Libya is now one of the most restricted countries in the world in regards to religious freedom for non-Muslims.

The Arabs

Origin of the Arabs in the Bible

Some translations of Acts 2 use the ethnic name "Arabs," while others use the geographical name of Arabia. There is so much biblical material about the Arabs that I can only touch on it briefly. The origin of the Arabs can be traced to three different times in the Scripture. In Genesis 10 in the Table of the Nations, we see the descendants of Joktan listed who are considered ancestors of modern Arabian tribes to this day. Joktan is from the lineage of Shem, and Arabs and Jews are both considered as Semites (Gen.10: 26-30). Kenneth Cragg, who gave a lifetime of scholarship to all things relating to Arab history, the Qur'an and related topics, says the Prophet Muhammad by tradition was 32 generations from Joktan (Gen 10:26), who was five generations from Noah.[27]

The best-known account about the origin of the Arabs is the story of Abraham, Hagar, and Ishmael, which I previously mentioned. Arabs generally consider themselves descendants of Ishmael, and in a spiritual sense he is the father of all Muslims who trace their ethnic lineage as well as their monotheistic faith back to the Patriarch Abraham.

The third source of Arab origins is Abraham's wife Keturah. After Sarah died, Abraham in his old age married Keturah and had several children with her (Gen. 25:1-4) Their children's names became the names of Arabian tribes thousands of years later. Many Old Testament stories include Arabs, who were often called

---

[27] Cragg, p. 13

Arameans, or by tribal names rather than by the term *Arab*. Arabia in biblical times included present-day Saudi Arabia, Yemen, Oman, the United Arab Emirates, Qatar, Oman, Kuwait, and parts of Iraq, Syria, Jordan, and the Arabian and Sinai Peninsula. Other Old Testament names for people of Arabian descent were the Midianites, Ishmaelites, the people of Kedar, the Amalekites, the Deanites, Temanites, and others[28]. In the New Testament, besides the Day of Pentecost, the only reference to Arabia refers to the time when Paul went to Arabia for three years after his conversion before he launched out on his missionary journeys (Gal 1:17).

Iraqi Christian scholar Dr. John Joseph points out that large numbers of present-day Syrian, Palestinian, and Iraqi Christians are descendants of Arab nomads from the desert who settled among the Aramaic-speaking Syrian population and accepted their religion before Islam[29]

Did all the Regions in Acts 2 Come under Islamic Rule?

Three of the fifteen peoples/places listed in Acts 2 are not predominantly under Islam today: Rome, Jerusalem and Crete. The other twelve once had a Jewish presence but are now in majority-Islam nations. This book will focus primarily on the Islamization and restoration to Christ of those 12 people groups.

The Four Big Ethnic Clusters Today

The twelve peoples/places mentioned above can readily be classified into the four largest ethnic clusters in the Middle East today. The four groups are the Arabs, Turks, Persians (Iranians) and the Kurds. The Arabs are by far the largest group, comprising a majority in over twenty countries. There are several places mentioned in Acts 2, as we will see, located in what are today Libya, Egypt, Mesopotamia, and Arabia along with many ethnic groups that are classified as Arab today because of the influence of the

---

[28] Holman, p. 93
[29] Joseph, (1961) p. 6

Arabic language. Some of these peoples may classify themselves by many names based on location or even by pre-Islamic identity, but are generally classified as part of the Arab world today. Turks are related to many other ethnic kin in Azerbaijan, in the Caucasus region, and the "Stan" republics of Central Asia from west to east: Turkmenistan, Uzbekistan, Kazakhstan, and Kyrgyzstan. (Tajikistan, the other Central Asian republic is Farsi speaking and is generally considered part of the Iranian/Persian world. In the modern nation of Iran (generally called Persia in the Bible and throughout most of history) lie Elam and Parthia. The Kurds are part of the Iranian-Median affinity block, but maintain their distinct identity of around 35 million people. The Kurds do not have a homeland but make up a strong minority in Turkey, Iran, Iraq and Syria. For approximate populations see footnote below.[30]

The Missionary Journeys of the Apostle Paul

Any commentary on the book of Acts will give much space to the three major missionary journeys of the Apostle Paul. In Acts, we see how Paul and Barnabas in Antioch of Syria, during a season of prayer and fasting with the leaders of the church there, the Holy Spirit set Paul and Barnabas apart to take the Gospel to new regions (Acts 13:1-3). The church where Paul and Barnabas received their commission is known today as the Church of San Pierre in Antakya, Turkey. Tradition says that Peter was the founder of the church in Antioch, hence the name. The plaques inside the church mention that Paul and Barnabas received their commission at this place, and that the label *Christian* was first coined in Antioch (Acts 11:26). What remains of the church is a cave built into the side of a mountain with secret tunnels leading to it, most likely used by early Christians as hiding places during seasons of persecution. Over the cave is a more modern edifice that visitors pass through before entering the cave. San Pierre overlooks the modern city of Antakya, which can be

---

[30] *Operation World* estimates 332.1M in the affinity block called the Arab world, 154.3 million in the Iranian-Median affinity block (which includes the Kurds) and 170.7 M in the Turkic affinity block, which includes the Turkic people in Azerbaijan and the four Turkic "Stan" countries listed above (see page 25).

viewed in its entirety from the site.[31]

The first missionary journey of Paul and Barnabas was mostly within what was called Asia Minor in biblical times, but what is today south and central Anatolia in Turkey, which included Pamphylia. They began their journey in Antioch, a Syrian city (now Antakya, Turkey). From Antioch, the two apostles preached in Cyprus, the homeland of Barnabas.[32] They went on to Pamphylia and other locations in what is today southern and central Turkey. During the second journey, Paul revisited many of the places where he preached during the first journey, but in obedience to the call of the Spirit, he crossed over into Macedonia and introduced Europe to the gospel. He also spent significant time in Ephesus and the surrounding areas. During the third missionary journey, Paul covered much of the same ground. It is significant that except for the present-day nations of Greece and Macedonia, and two-thirds of the island of Cyprus, the rest of the locations (see map) where Paul preached are now populated by Muslims, including one-third of Cyprus populated by Turkish Muslims. Paul was converted among the Arabs and spent three years in Arabia before launching his journeys (Galatians 1:17, 18).

Cornelius

The story of Cornelius in the tenth chapter of Acts has become one of my favorite biblical stories. The Bible says that Cornelius was a Roman centurion in the Italian regiment. It says, "He and all of his family were devout and God-fearing; he gave generously to those in need and prayed to God regularly" (Acts 10:2). Cornelius sees an angel who tells him to send men to Joppa to bring back a man called

---

[31] Irvin & Sunquist, p. 179

[32] Cyprus is a divided island with the south populated by Greek Orthodox Christians and the north by Turkish Muslims. Cyprus was the birthplace of Barnabas and his tomb can be found on the Muslim north part of the island, as are the ruins of biblical Salamis. Few people in North Cyprus know the significant role that Barnabas played in the biblical narrative. See Rodney Tilley's book *A History and Guide to Biblical Sites in Cyprus* (2018) about the important role Cyprus played in biblical history.

Peter who is staying with Simon the tanner in a house near the sea. The Lord told Cornelius that his prayers and gifts to the poor were like a memorial offering before God (v. 4). The rest of the story is well-known. While waiting to eat, Peter falls into a trance and sees a large sheet filled with all kinds of animals, birds and reptiles. God tells him to kill and eat. Peter says he cannot because the food is not kosher and that he has never eaten anything that is impure or unclean. The sheet is let down a second and then a third time. Then the Lord says, "Do not call anything impure that God has made clean" (Acts 2:15).

After this, Peter is informed that the envoys of Cornelius have arrived. Peter agrees to go with them to meet Cornelius, who prostrates before Peter until Peter tells him he is only a man. Then Peter preaches about Jesus, saying, "I now realize how true it is that God does not show favoritism but accepts from every nation the one who fears him and does what is right" (v.35). Peter preaches about what Jesus did, how he was crucified and rose from the dead, and was appointed by God to judge the living and the dead (v. 42). While Peter was still speaking, the Holy Spirit came upon them all and they heard Cornelius and his household speaking in tongues and praising God (v. 46). They were baptized in water as well, and Peter stayed with them for a few days. Later when circumcised Jewish believers confronted Peter, he told them how the Spirit fell on Cornelius as he had on them and repeated almost the entire story (Acts 11). The Jewish believers said," So then even to Gentiles God has granted repentance that leads to life" (Acts 11:18). One would think in light of Jesus having told them at least five times that the gospel was for all, it would not have been so hard to grasp!

Contemporary Application

Are Unbelievers more willing to receive Jesus than Christians are to offer him?

In the story of Cornelius, we see that Cornelius was more willing than Peter to obey God. Peter needed to have the message repeated three times before he got it. Cornelius was ready to act on it right away! I believe that scattered throughout 1.6 billion Muslims, there are millions of Cornelius-type people who are looking for a Peter to point them to Jesus.

Questions for Discussion and Reflection

- How do the Turks differ from the Kurds, Persians (Iranians) and the Arabs in regards to their Christian heritage?
- Which of the above peoples/places did you find the most interesting or surprising?
- Why is the story of Cornelius so relevant for ministry among Muslims?

2

St. Thomas: The Doubter who Became the Greatest Missionary

Just **Imagine** you and your family are Zoroastrians living in Persia around 36 A.D. You believe that *Ahura Mazda* is the supreme God, but you also believe there is an evil being in the world named Ahriman, who wars against good and tempts people to do evil. You believe strongly in an afterlife in Paradise or Hell, and that there is a thin rope bridge between Paradise and Hell that people must walk across to determine where they will spend the afterlife. Your prophet Zarathustra (Zoroaster) said that good works, good thoughts, and good deeds are what determine the quality of your life now and where you will spend the afterlife. If you faithfully practice these three virtues, Zarathustra promised, when you cross the bridge you will not fall off into Hell, but beautiful maidens will receive you into a place of peace and indescribable beauty. You also have been taught that the elements of earth, fire, water and air are sacred and to disrespect them leads to punishment in Hell. In your hometown, your temple has a fire that the people never allow to die out.

You are eagerly waiting for the *Saoshyant,* a coming savior, who will restore the world; no one will get old, and all evil and suffering will cease. The *Saoshyant* will destroy Ahriman and Ahura Mazda will reign supreme.

You have heard stories about how some of the Magi, your fellow-Zoroastrians, followed a star, which led them to a town in Judea called Bethlehem (Matthew 2:1-2). There they gave precious gifts to a mother and father whose baby will one day be a great king. Could he be the *Saoshyant*?

As you do your best to practice the three most essential ethical rules of your religion-- good works, good thoughts and good deeds--you hear that a man named Thomas has come to your village. He claims to be one of the disciples of the man whom the Magi worshipped when they went all the way to Bethlehem to honor a baby who would be a king one day. Thomas preaches that this baby grew up and performed miracles and even raised people from the dead. You are waiting for Thomas to tell you how this person became a powerful king, but he tells you instead that he was crucified. You are visibly shaken to hear this. How can the *Saoshyant* have been crucified? Then Thomas preaches about how this man rose from the dead and has opened the door to Paradise for all who believe.

The people in your town have mixed thoughts about Thomas's message. Some say that the man whom Thomas called Jesus must be the long awaited *Saoshyant* whom Zoroaster promised would come and bring peace to the world. Others say that he cannot be the Saoshyant as there is no evidence of lasting, universal peace in the world. Even now, the Persians and the Romans are waging war against each other. You have mixed feelings in your own mind. Is what Thomas preaching the truth? There is much in common with what you have believed all of your life. However, there are some glaring differences as well.

History and Theology: Thomas, the underrated hero

Eastern Christians[33] credit "doubting Thomas" as the one who preached the gospel to the Parthians, Medes, Elamites and residents

---

[33] See Appendix B for a fuller definition of the Church of the East, the Assyrian Church of the East, Eastern Christians and other similar phrases. Historians sometimes use different phrases and it can be quite complex, especially as you

of Mesopotamia on his way to India where he established the church there before his martyrdom. Brian Shelton cites an ancient historian named Hippolytus, who claims that Thomas preached to the Parthians, Medes, Persians, Hycanians, Bactrians, and the Magi before being killed by four spearmen in Calamene in India. [34] Tradition[35] says that he may have planted the first church in Mesopotamia in addition to pioneering in Persia and India. Several places where Thomas would plant churches are mentioned in Acts 2:9-11.

It is ironic that the Apostle Thomas, who is best known for doubting the resurrection of Jesus until he put his hands in the nail prints of Jesus' hands and feet (John 20:25-28), went on to become the most traveled of all the apostles. He is the one who planted the church among the most people groups. While not detracting from Paul as a model of a great church-planting missionary, it should be noted that Paul stayed within the boundaries of the Roman Empire. He did face much opposition, as he informed the believers in Corinth, having to endure beatings, a day and night in the open sea, shipwrecks, imprisonment, false accusations, stoning, hunger and sleepless nights (II Cor.11:23-27). Tradition says in about the year 64 A.D.; he was beheaded in Rome during the reign of Nero.

Unlike Paul, Thomas did not leave us any canonical gospels or epistles[36], but other sources stated that he was severely persecuted

---

will see in the next few chapters when Nestorians and Monophysites and other Eastern groups come into view.

[34] Shelton, p. 182

[35] Ancient churches like to trace their origins back to the original disciples of Jesus. While it may be difficult to prove beyond doubt that Thomas and other disciples preached and established churches in all the places mentioned in this chapter, there is no compelling reason not to give some credence to the claims.

[36] The Gospel of Thomas and the Infancy Gospel of Thomas are two gnostic "gospels" that are not included in the cannon of authoritative Scripture that is contained in the Bible. The Gospel of Thomas was discovered along with other pseudo gospels in a cave near Nag Hammadi, Egypt in 1945. They were most likely written by "Christian" Gnostics who named their gospels or epistles after biblical characters to give them more credibility. There is much material in all of the

and that he learned difficult languages like Punjabi in what is today's India. Did he learn Farsi, or the Median language, or the language of the Elamites, or one of the challenging languages of Mesopotamia? We do not know.[37] We do know that he spent most of his ministry outside of the Roman Empire. He had no right of protection as a Roman citizen, whereas Paul, on occasion would remind the Romans that he was a citizen and had a right to a trial (Acts 16:37). Thomas did not preach in as many synagogues as Paul did, but he had to confront Zoroastrian religious leaders, as well as pagan priests. Eventually as he worked his way east, he faced followers of what has come to be known as Hinduism. It is among these people, so strongly divided by the caste system, where Thomas allegedly was martyred. It is quite unfair to remember Thomas primarily for a moment of doubt that all of the disciples of Jesus also experienced, rather than as perhaps the greatest missionary/apostle of all time.

Other Apostles who went outside of the Roman Empire

Besides Thomas, Simon the Zealot, one of Jesus' original disciples, was also said to have been martyred in Persia. Some of the disciples also preached in in the lands east of the Roman Empire, including Bartholomew, Andrew, Matthew and many of the 72 whom Jesus commissioned in Luke 10:1-2.

Matthew is thought to have gone to Persia and may have been martyred there or in Egypt. Mark, according to tradition, was the memorizer of St. Peter, thereby producing a Gospel based on

---

pseudo writings that contradict the four canonical gospels, which is why they were rejected for the cannon.

[37] Some scholars say Thomas got no further than Persia. Whether Thomas learned difficult languages, performed many miracles among many different people groups, and died a heroic death as a martyr is speculation. However, on the other hand, it is widely believed by the Christians in the places cited above, and there is no reason that Christians cannot admire Thomas as a great hero of the faith or as I call him, "an underrated hero" even if it cannot be "proven" that he performed all of the feats attributed to him.

Apostolic witness.[38] He was a cousin of Barnabas and traveled with Paul and Barnabas during their early journeys. Mark preached in Egypt and Coptic Christians proudly claim him as the Founder of the Coptic Church. Andrew is reputed to have gone to Thrace, Macedonia and the city is later known as Constantinople before being martyred in Greece. There is also a tradition that Andrew went to Georgia in the Caucasus region and preached to the pagan Scythians. James, according to Catholic tradition preached in Spain before returning to Jerusalem where he was martyred (Acts 12:2). Philip is thought to have gone from Galilee to Galatia in present-day Turkey, and was martyred in Hierapolis at the age of 87. Bartholomew also went to Hierapolis, then to India and Armenia, where he was martyred in Derbend on the Caspian Sea. James the Less may have been the first bishop of the Syrian church. Jude (not Judas Iscariot) is thought to have evangelized the region of Armenia around Edessa (modern Urfa in Turkey), but there is also a tradition that he evangelized in northern Persia and was martyred and buried near Tabriz[39].

The Armenians: The First Christian Nation

Thaddaeus and Bartholomew are said to have founded the church in Armenia. Several centuries later, the entire Armenian people embraced Christianity during the reign of King Tiridates III through the ministry of Gregory the Illuminator. [40] The Armenians claim to be the first people to accept Christianity as an entire nation in the early fourth century.

A Parthian-Persian-Iranian Encounter with Jesus

A few years ago, I visited a church in the Kurdish-majority area of Iraq. As I was meeting with the pastor and members of his church, a man came into the office. He said there were two men from Iran who wanted to become Christians. The pastor had a full schedule and

---

[38] *Holman Illustrated Bible Dictionary* p. 1077
[39] Tejirian, Eleanor, H. & Simon, Reeva Spector, p. 2
[40] Bailey & Bailey, p. 6

had no time to meet with the men, so I asked whether either of the Iranian men spoke Turkish. Fortunately, one of the men was from the Turkish- speaking area of Iran and spoke both the Azeri dialect of Turkish and Farsi, the national language of Iran. I was expecting the usual questions asked by Muslims, about the Bible being changed or the doctrine of the Trinity. These men simply said they wanted to receive Jesus right then. We got on our knees, I led the one who spoke Turkish in a prayer of repentance and faith in Christ, and he translated it for his Farsi-speaking friend.

I have Muslim friends that I have known for close to four decades who have still not believed on Jesus. For these two men, it was a matter of ten minutes! Evidently, while still in Iran, they watched a film about Jesus and had heard some of the *Injil.* Due to harsh persecution by the Iranian government against anyone daring to leave Islam, they had come to Iraq hoping to find someone to lead them to Jesus. Truly, God is doing remarkable things among the descendants of the Parthians! We will come back to this topic again later in the book.

Questions for Discussion and Reflection:

- Many people only know St Thomas as "doubting Thomas" and have no idea what a great church-planting apostle he was. Who are other unknown heroes of the faith that you are familiar with, but most people may not know much about them?

- Zoroastrianism is a fascinating religion and many say it influenced Daniel and other biblical writers as well as Islam. (See appendix c). What do you think about the possibility that Daniel learned about eternal heaven and hell (Daniel 12: from Zoroastrians because there is little focus on the afterlife in much of the Old Testament? The Sadducees did not even believe in an afterlife and they were experts in Jewish Theology and Law.

3

Church of Piety versus Church of Power

Just imagine you are a bishop[41], a church leader, during a time of persecution around the year 310 A.D. Your fellow Christians recognize you as a bishop, but there is no honor for your position in the general society. You preach to a group of Christians on Sunday mornings, beginning at sunrise. The group meets in different homes to reduce the chance of detection. You preach from the Old Testament and from fragments of writings from the Gospels and letters of the Apostles that have not yet been collected into one book. You tell the stories of brave martyrs like Stephen, the first martyr. You hope to encourage your congregation by telling how Peter was crucified upside-down because he said he said he was not worthy to die as Jesus died. You tell the story of the beheading of Paul and the other apostles. You remind your flock how Christians were persecuted after being falsely accused by the Emperor Nero for starting the fire that almost destroyed Rome. Nero needed a scapegoat, and he claimed that the Christians started the fire to fulfill their preaching about hellfire for those who do not repent.[42]

---

[41] In the New Testament, the word B*ishop* was interchangeable with presbyter or elder and their qualifications are listed in I Timothy and Titus. By the year 150, bishops were regarded as the successors of the Apostles and generally overseeing a specific geographical region with presbyters (priests, pastors, elders) submitting to his authority. See *Evangelical Dictionary of Theology* p. 157-158).

[42] Most scholars believe that Nero had the fire started, as he wanted to rebuild the city. To deflect the anger of the people from himself, he made Christians the scapegoat. This was easy to do as Christians often preached that the world would

You also recount more recent stories of those who paid the ultimate price, some of whom you know personally. Under Emperor Diocletian, conditions have been very hard. He is determined that every person in the Empire offer incense to the Roman gods, and declare that Caesar is Lord or face execution. You encourage the Christians to stay faithful to Christ whatever may befall them. Then you take communion together, eating the body and drinking the blood of your Lord, even as you remember his sacrifice on the cross.

The persecution has been at its most intense point for several years, and then suddenly it stops. You hear something that astonishes you and the flock of believers you are pastoring that is almost beyond comprehension. Constantine, the new emperor of the Roman Empire, is rumored to have become a Christian! It seems unbelievable to you. Soon your congregation no longer meets secretly at sunrise. Now you meet openly in former pagan temples or on "Main Street" in the shop of a wealthy business owner. You as bishop are now honored, not only by the people of your congregation, but also by government and city officials. Now you don special robes that distinguish you as a bishop, and you are acknowledged whenever you attend public celebrations.

You are concerned that many of the people who now come to your Sunday gatherings do not demonstrate much repentance from their former way of life, or try to live simply as Jesus taught. You hope that with time these new believers will gradually change their ways. Part of you misses the purity of faith that you and your little flock of persecuted believers had experienced before the Emperor's conversion. Another part of you, however, likes the prestige of being a bishop, having a good income, enjoying the respect you get when you put on your clerical robes, and the way people kiss your ring as they leave the church after Sunday worship.

---

be destroyed by fire in the last days. Nero could easily say that the Christians started the fire to vindicate their preaching.

History and Theology: The Influence of Emperor Constantine

In the previous chapter, we briefly looked at the Roman persecution of early Christians. So much has been written about this topic, that I have addressed it very briefly. It is the period after the persecution stopped that concerns us now, as it led to what historians call the "The Constantintization of the Church." During the first three hundred years of church history, the church was persecuted but powerful in spirit. After Constantine, the church was often weak in spirit but powerful politically. Some have called it a transition from the "Church of Piety" to the "Church of Power."

The Roman Emperor Constantine

Diocletian, the Roman emperor before Constantine, among the most brutal of the persecutors of Christians, died in 311. Constantine's father, Constantius I, the heir-apparent, had died in 306 in Britain and the army proclaimed his son as the new emperor. In 312, Constantine led an army to face his rival for the throne, Maxentius, at the Milvan Bridge, which crosses the River Tiber into Rome. Bishop Eusebius, the great historian of the early church and a big fan and biographer of Constantine, claims that the emperor saw vision of a cross flaming in the sky at midday and heard a voice telling him "in this sign conquer." The cross quickly became the symbol of this new empire. From a symbol of torture and capital punishment, the cross was transformed into a decoration to wear around the neck!

Followers of Jesus who had been raised to shun the military as contrary to Jesus's commands to love one's enemies, hear that Constantine defeated his chief rival for supreme power in a great military battle. He then declares the Edict of Milan in 313, granting tolerance for all religions, including Christianity. Catholic historian H.W. Crocker III says that the edict was the first legal affirmation of religious liberty issued 1,400 years before a similar idea would take root in America.[43] Try to put yourself in these early Christians' shoes. One minute you are risking your life to be a Christian. The next moment, not only are you free from persecution, but it is even advantageous to be a Christian. Some Christians went from worrying about being food for lions in the arena to scheming how to get the best seats in the arena to watch gladiators fight to the death![44]

It would be almost impossible to overstate the importance that the "conversion" of Emperor Constantine (272-337) had on the history of Christianity. At the beginning of the fourth century, fewer than one in twenty persons in the Roman world could be counted as Christians, whereas by the end of Constantine's life, one in two was a member of the church.

Was Constantine's conversion genuine? Historians have debated this for centuries. Paul Johnson is a Catholic historian, who are often more affirming of Constantine's legacy than Protestant historians tend to be. Johnson says Constantine was a sun-worshipper and held to a number of late pagan cults that had some loose parallels with Christianity. For example, the followers of Isis venerated a Madonna nursing her holy child. The cult of Attis and Cybele celebrated a day of blood and fasting followed by a resurrection feast. Constantine never totally abandoned sun worship, and he kept the image of the sun on his coins.[45] He even built a triumphal arch to the sun god after his conversion.

Constantine seemed to have sown familial divisions over succession to his throne after his death. He had tried to distribute his power among his sons and nephews, dividing Europe, North Africa, and much of the Middle East among them. It was not long before the five

---

[43] Crocker p. 4

[44] As Christianity became the state religion of the Empire around 380, gradually the gladiator games began to decrease and by the 5th century were increasingly rare.

[45] Johnson, pps. 67,68

heirs had to buckle on their swords as they battled for control of the empire.[46]

Constantine's legacy was mixed, reflecting both the fall and redemption. He executed his eldest son, his second wife, and many others on spurious charges. He did pass laws forbidding concubinage, the forced prostitution of servants, and the seduction of slaves, suggesting that he had a puritan streak in him despite using prisoners of war to fight wild beasts in mortal combat.[47] He also inspired welfare spending for widows, orphans and the sick, abolished some kinds of gladiator shows, and shut down some pagan temples that had become dens of immorality.[48] Constantine was not baptized until just before his death, however, feeling that he could not live out what he professed and remain emperor. It should be noted that he moved toward a more-righteous life as he aged.

Was Constantine the Downfall of the Church?

Many Protestant historians tend to see Constantine as the instrument that destroyed the purity of the early church in which only true believers would name themselves by the name of Christ. After Constantine came the institutionalization of the faith, along with pomp and ceremony, elaborate rituals and hierarchies, and the marriage of church and state. Constantine even moved his imperial capital from Rome to Byzantium, later named Constantinople after himself (today's Istanbul, Turkey). He no doubt chose this location on the eastern side of his empire to make a break with the west and make it particularly his own. This move contributed to the divisions between the Latin speaking Western church and the Greek-speaking Eastern Church. The Eastern Church took on elements of Eastern despotism--elaborate ceremonies; jewel-studded royal

---

[46] Ibid p. 61-62
[47] Ibid p. 68
[48] Crocker, p. 59

garments, and other extravagances--which were not as common in the less ostentatious Western church.[49]

Some historians would agree while others would very much disagree with the following statement:

> *Without Constantine's defending sword, the Church faced the prospect of endless persecution. Without Constantine's taking a hand in Church affairs, providing common sense, the threat of force, munificent sums, and marvelous basilicas, the Arian controversy or any of the virtually innumerable other heresies might, in combination, have fractured the church into near nonexistence...For believers, it was so obvious that the best form of rule was when cross and sword, crozier and scepter, worked in unison. Constantine provided the starting point for the divine right of kings as the guardians of the Christian world until liberal, secular democracy altered the equation by making religious indifference the paramount value.[50]*

We can certainly say that for Constantine, the Jesus he served was not Jesus meek and mild, commanding that his followers must love their enemies and forgive those who sin against them seventy times seven. To Constantine, Jesus was a God of War.

Paul Johnson asks a question that many have asked over the centuries, "Which side benefited most from this unseemly marriage between Church and State?" "Or to put it another way, did the empire surrender to Christianity, or did Christianity prostitute itself to the empire?"[51]

The prominent church historian, Kenneth Scott Latourette, says that even before Constantine, Christianity was growing rapidly, and that persecution had failed to stamp it out. In other words, Constantine did not save Christianity from extinction when he

---

49 Ibid, p. 58
50 Ibid p. 58-59
54 Johnson, p. 69

legalized it. Christianity would have continued to grow whether persecuted or not.

In summary, as Spikard and Cragg state, "Throughout the centuries, Christians have interpreted this change in a variety of ways, from 'the triumph of the church' (Roman Catholics and Eastern Orthodox) to 'the great betrayal' (the Anabaptist tradition) to 'something in between (most Protestants).'"[52]

White Martyrdom

Martyrdom for one's faith seldom occurred after Constantine, and as spiritual laxness increased, many sincere Christians adopted what became known as "white Martyrdom," that is, dying to oneself. Serious Christians increasingly sought to give themselves to God by withdrawing themselves from the spiritual laxness and nominalism that had come to dominate post-Constantine Christianity. For example, many people gathered around St. Anthony (251-356) in the Egyptian desert, who had isolated himself for decades, but was sought out by those who wanted a deeper life of prayer and devotion. Many miracles of healing and deliverance from demonic oppression occurred in his long life of over 100 years. Over two-hundred years later, St. Benedict (480-543) from Italy established many monasteries, and the order's *Rules of Saint Benedict* offered, and still offers, guidance to those seeking a deeper spiritual walk.

A Classic Story of Martyrdom

Beautiful Perpetua (180-203) came from a noble pagan family but had come to place her faith in Christ. Arrested by the Romans, she continued to nurse her child in custody. Her father pleaded with her to renounce her faith by appealing to her to remember her infant daughter. Who would take care of her child if she was killed for her faith? Perpetua's servant Felicitas (Felicity) had given birth just before the gladiatorial games that would lead to both of their deaths. In the arena, after gladiators scourged the two women, a bear, a

---

[52] Spickard & Cragg p. 55

boar, and a wild cow were set on them. The animals, however, were supernaturally prevented from killing them. Finally, a swordsman was sent out to finish the job. Probably due to his conscience, he could not bring himself to kill Perpetua. Therefore, she guided his sword hand to complete her martyrdom. Perpetua and Felicity, noblewoman and slave, embraced each other throughout the animal and gladiator attacks, showing how Christians loved each other despite differences of status. They are honored in Catholic, Orthodox, Anglican, and some Lutheran churches on their feast day in early March.[53]

Martyred Saints Perpetua and Felicity

Questions for Discussion and Reflection

- Reflect on the life of Emperor Constantine and the changes that he made upon his "conversion." The Christian experience was transformed from persecution to privilege. What do you think would have been the most positive aspect of the change? What would be the most negative?

---

[53] There are variant accounts of the story of Perpetua and Felicity, including the exact date and circumstances. There is no question, however, that the story was recited among early believers to inspire the persecuted Christians to great dedication and willingness to suffer or be killed for Christ' sake.

- What do you think about the idea of "white martyrdom"? Can you think of any examples of people or individuals practicing white martyrdom in the world today?

4

The Letter (i) Made all the Difference

Just imagine you are a bishop in the fourth century. You have been hearing about a fellow bishop named Arius who has been teaching that there was a time when Christ was not. He teaches that God created Jesus as the most exalted of all creation; nevertheless, he was still created. During the days of persecution, you never thought much about what the incarnation really meant. You proclaimed that Jesus is Lord and that he has risen from the dead. That was the confession that you expected from those claiming the name of Christ.

There is scripture that suggests that Jesus was less than the Father. After all, Jesus himself said, "The Father is greater than I" (John 14:28). However, the Apostle John said, "In the beginning was the Word and the Word was with God and the Word was God" John 1:1). Conflict over how Jesus could be both God and man is beginning to divide the believers.

As a bishop, you are invited to Nicaea, and with other bishops, and Emperor Constantine overseeing the event, to hammer out what the Church believes about the person of Jesus.

History and theology: Divisions among Christians

In the fourth century, Gregory of Nyssa, one of the Cappadocian Fathers of the fourth century,, reported that, "If you ask anyone in Constantinople for change, he will start discussing with you whether the Son is begotten or unbegotten. If you ask about the quality of bread, you will get the answer: "The Father is greater, the Son is less.[54]

I often tell my students that in the period after Emperor Constantine, people did not have the Red Sox versus the Yankees, or Vikings against the Packers to argue about. Instead, they disputed theology.

> *Christ is truly God, declared Nicaea. Christ is truly man, declared Constantinople. Then between Alexandria and Antioch, they wrestled with how Christ can be both God and man.*[55]

The Arian Heresy

The first of all church councils was conducted in Nicaea, today's Iznik in western Turkey, in the year 325. The Emperor Constantine himself called the council, no doubt hoping to keep his empire united rather than allow doctrinal issues to tear it apart. During this council, the famous Nicene Creed was first hammered out (See at the end of this chapter).. This creed focused on the Christological issues that surfaced due to the Arian heresy. At stake was the very nature of redemption itself. As Duffy says, Arianism "emptied Christianity of its central affirmation, that the life and death of Jesus had power to redeem because they were God's very own actions"[56]

Arius was the Bishop of Alexandria, Egypt, by all accounts a dynamic teacher with a lot of charisma. He made statements such as "If the Father begat the Son, he that was begotten had a beginning of existence; hence it is clear that there was (a time) when the Son was not. It follows then of necessity that he had his existence from the non-existent.[57]Arius focused on distinguishing what Christ said and did from the words and acts of the Father. For example, Jesus said "The Father is greater than I" (John 14:28) and scripture states that Jesus had to grow in each dimension of his life (Luke 2:52). Jesus

---

[54] This is widely quoted in books related to church history
[55] Moffett, p. 170
[56] Duffy, p. 29
[57] Noll, p. 52

even got tired! (John 4:6) Many other verses could be cited to support Jesus' subordination to the Father.

Arius's point was that Jesus was the highest and most exalted of God's creation, but not of the same substance as the Father. It is in Greek, the language of the New Testament, that it gets especially tricky. *Homoousios* translated means same substance. *Homoiousios* means of similar substance. Notice that one little letter *i* separates what the majority of Christians today--Catholic, Orthodox and Protestants who affirm the Nicene Creed, which states that Jesus is of the same substance as God the Father--from the heresy of Jesus being of similar, but not the same substance. Arianism today manifests itself in various sects, including Jehovah's Witnesses and Unitarianism. In fact, there is a degree of Arianism in the Islamic understanding of Jesus, which we will examine in more detail later.

I remember reading a book by an Islamic scholar many years ago, in which he argued that Arius was Allah's instrument to bring the Church back to strict monotheism, but the Church did not heed his message. Then Allah sent Muhammad with the same message of *tawhid* (One God) and many Christians believed in it. Others refused to heed Allah's prophet and became *kafirs* (infidels).

The Council of Nicaea

Emperor Constantine came to Nicea in full pomp and splendor, determined to root out division that would not only split the Church, but could even divide the Roman Empire.

Those who sided with Arius tended to favor direct imperial control of the Church. Those who were Catholic/Orthodox[58] (see important footnote below) preferred a certain degree of autonomy in making decisions related to doctrine and church policy. A former professor

---

[58] It is crucial to remember that the Catholic and Orthodox branches were not divided until the final schism in 1054. For this reason, I generally refer to the Church before that date as Catholic/Orthodox.

at Wheaton College, currently professor of church history at Notre Dame, Mark Noll, words it well:

> *Arians, who believed that the Son was subordinate to the Father, applied the Lord-satrap relationship to God (the lord) and Christ (the satrap). Since the Son was subordinate to the Father, so too the kingdom of the Son (the church) must be subordinate to the kingdom of the Father (the empire). The orthodox rejected this reasoning at every point. They believed that the Son was consubstantial (equal in being) to the Father, and they applied the lord-satrap relationship to the Trinity and the bishops of the church. (Since the Son was consubstantial with the Father, so too the kingdom of the Son (the church) was of equal dignity to the kingdom of the Father (the empire)[59]*

In other words, the Arians would have the church be subordinate to the emperor as the Son is subordinate to the Father. The Catholic/Orthodox position held that because Christ is co-equal with the Father, the Son (the church) can submit to the Emperor in matters of state, but the emperor does not directly rule over the church. Thus the church has a greater degree of autonomy in its governance than under the Arian paradigm.

All 1,800 of the known bishops were invited to Nicea, 800 from the west and 1,000 from the east. In the end, 250 attended, and all but five came from the east.

St. Athanasius: Defender of Orthodoxy

Athanasius was the best known of those who argued for the Trinitarian position that the Father, Son and Holy Spirit are equal in substance. The emperor and his successors embraced his view at the time, but Arianism did not die out overnight and plagued the church long after the Council of Nicaea. The Arians fought back and

---

[59] Noll, pps. 60-61

Athanasius paid a price for his staunch support of what became the core belief of most Christians from then until today.

The Council of Constantinople

The Council of Constantinople in 381 A.D. tweaked the Nicene Creed, using the phrase "I believe" rather than "We believe." About 150 delegates attended. The council condemned Apollinarism, a teaching that denied a human soul and mind for Jesus. The conference also helped to clarify the role of the Holy Spirit.

Fellowshipping with Jehovah's Witnesses?

One of the strangest experiences I ever had was fellowshipping rather than arguing with some Jehovah's Witnesses who passed through the Middle Eastern city where my family and I were living. A man whose family had converted from Islam to Jehovah's Witnesses (JWs) started coming to our house meetings. His parents and some of his siblings were avid JWs, and he wanted me to meet them. In the States, I seldom bother discussing religion with a JW because I know we are only going to argue. However, with our new brother in Christ's family, I wanted to find some points of agreement rather than argue if possible. We discussed what Christ had done for us and how he had transformed our lives. When these JWs shared about their changed lives because of encountering Christ, they had that "glow" about them that you see when Christians share their stories of how Christ has transformed their lives from darkness to light.

I will leave the matter of eternal judgment up to God, and I certainly do not believe that JWs interpret the Bible correctly regarding the Trinity, the divinity of Jesus, and many other points. They at least believe that Jesus died on the cross, although it is more accurate to say that he did not die on cross with a crossbar, rather he died on a one-piece stake. There is also some disagreement whether the Jehovah's Witnesses believe that Jesus rose physically or spiritually from the dead.

Like Bishop Arius in the fourth century, many JWs have a great zeal for their faith, whatever their motivation and they are willing to pay a price for their beliefs. In one sense their beliefs are easier for Muslims to embrace than Trinitarian theology, and in Turkey, the number converting to JWs is at least as high as those converting to Trinitarian Christianity.[60] However, JWs will not perform military service, which in Turkey and other Muslim countries is a huge issue, as military service is thought to be a holy duty to God and to one's country. Many Jehovah's Witnesses face court cases and prison sentences because of their refusal.

Furthermore, as I previously suggested, if the Jehovah's Witnesses are the theological descendants of the Arians, the heresy is still plaguing the church today!

The Nicene Creed

I believe in one God, the Father Almighty, Maker of heaven and earth, and of all things visible and invisible.

I believe in one Lord Jesus Christ, the only-begotten Son of God, born of the Father before all ages. God of God, Light of Light, true God from true God; begotten, not made, consubstantial with the Father; through whom all things were made.

For us men for our salvation, came down from heaven, and by the Holy Spirit was incarnate of the Virgin Mary, and became man. For our sake was crucified under Pontius Pilate, he suffered and was buried, and rose again on the third day in accordance with the Scriptures;

---

[60]The number of Jehovah's Witnesses in Turkey exceeds 7,000, https://en.wikipedia.org/w/index.php?title=Special:Search&search=jehovah%27s+witnesses+in+turkey&fulltext=1&profile=default&ns0=1. The number of Christians in Turkey is hard to calculate because often the historic Christians and followers of Jesus from a Muslim background are categorized differently.

He ascended into heaven, and is seated at the right hand of the Father. He will come again in glory to judge the living and the dead and his kingdom will have no end.

I believe in the Holy Spirit, the Lord, the giver of Life, who proceeds from the Father and the Son, who with the Father and the Son together is adored and glorified, who has spoken through the prophets.

I believe one, holy, catholic and apostolic Church. I confess one Baptism for the forgiveness of sins and I look forward to the resurrection of the dead, and the life of the world to come. Amen.

Questions for Discussion and Reflection

- It seems that Emperor Constantine was more concerned about unifying the Empire than he was about what has become Christian dogma. Briefly, write a couple of theological issues that Christians divide over that you most passionate about. What issues are a matter of orthodoxy or heresy, and what ones are more about personal opinion?
- What did you think of the author's story about having fellowship with the Jehovah's Witnesses because they both could testify about Christ having changed their lives despite major doctrinal disagreement?
- Look at the Nicene Creed. Do you think it summarizes essence of the Christian faith and those who do not accept it should not be recognized as true Christians?

5

Heroes and Heretics from the Middle East to Chicago

Just imagine you are a Church of the East missionary in Persian Empire in the year 431. Your task is to strengthen the local believers and bring new people, many of whom are followers of Zoroaster, to faith in Christ. You and your fellow Church of the East Christians have been preaching the Gospel and seeing much fruit in the Persian Empire. You preach that Jesus was born of a virgin, was crucified on the cross to redeem humankind, and that he rose from the dead. The Lord is confirming the Word powerfully. Sometimes you feel like you are experiencing what the disciples of Jesus experienced—people are healed and set free from demonic power.

You just learned that your mentor in the faith, Bishop Nestorius of Constantinople, has been accused of heresy. Cyril, the Bishop of Alexandria, says that Nestorius does not believe in the full divinity of Christ. Cyril believes that Christ is fully God and fully man, and therefore, one must acknowledge his mother Mary as the *Theotokos* (the God-bearer or mother of God). Nestorius argues that Mary should be called the *Christotokos*, the mother of Christ. You are thinking that when you explain the Gospel to Zoroastrians, pagans, and even to Jews, how do you explain the *Theotokos*? How can they grasp the Creator of the universe having a human mother? If Mary is the Mother of God, does that mean that God cried for his mother, had his diapers changed by his mother, and even was crucified on the cross? You hear that Bishop Nestorius is being called to a council in Ephesus to discuss the issue. Nestorius, whom you know can be a hothead, will debate Cyril, from what you hear, also can be a hothead, especially when he is challenged theologically.

A few months later, word of what has happened filters back to your band of evangelists. Even before arriving in Ephesus, Nestorius was excommunicated and condemned. The Roman/Byzantine Church has declared those who believe what Nestorius believes are heretics. You see the problem as a power struggle between Antioch and Alexandria as much as it is a doctrinal issue between conflicting theologies. You continue preaching, but somehow you sense that the body of Christ has been irreparably damaged.

In addition to being declared heretics, Persians still think you belong to the same religion of their long-standing Roman-Byzantine enemies. In their eyes, you are potential collaborators. If the Byzantines invade your homeland they wonder if would you betray your Persian neighbors and fight with your co-religionists.

Over the centuries, there have been times of decreased persecution, but at other times, tens of thousands of your fellow Christians have been tortured or killed. It is ironic. On one hand, you suffer because you are identified with the religion of the enemies of the Persians. On the other hand, the Byzantines do not accept you as true Christians anymore.

The Founding of the Church of the East

A Wonderful Historic Story

There is a moving legend about King Abgar of Edessa, a region in modern-day Turkey. He must have heard about Jesus' power to heal, and he wrote a letter begging Jesus to come to Edessa and heal his malady. King Abgar offers Jesus asylum and a prominent place in his kingdom. Jesus allegedly replies that he cannot personally come as he was soon to be crucified, but that he would send Addai (also known as Thaddaeus), one of the seventy-two disciples (Luke 10:1), to heal him. Thaddaeus went to Edessa, prayed for King Abgar's healing, and Edessa became one of the centers of eastern

Christianity. While the story is a legend and cannot be proven, there is no doubt that Edessa did become one of the centers of the Church of the East.[61] As we will see the Church of the East, whether heretical or not, was the great missionary church of its day even after the advent of Islam.

Another possibility for the founder of the church of Edessa, besides Addai (or Thaddeus- was the Apostle Thomas, who allegedly preached in Edessa on his way to India, and may have led some Edessans to place their faith in Christ. It is quite possible that both stories are true and that both Addai and Thomas preached in Edessa. Yale historian Samuel Moffett goes on to say that the first New Testament translation and the first hymnbooks were probably published in the Syriac language in Edessa. Another development was a change in the places of worship. After meeting primarily in homes for 200 years, the first dedicated church buildings were built in Edessa. In addition, the first Christian poets, the first Christian king, and arguably the first Christian state developed in Edessa. [62]

The Greatest Missionary Movement the World had ever Seen

Edessa was the place where the clergy trained for service in the Persian Empire, but it was still under Roman administration. From its base at Edessa, and later from Arbella (today's Erbil in Iraqi Kurdistan), the Nestorians became perhaps the greatest missionary force ever seen. They evangelized from these two cities that today are predominately Kurdish, into what we know now as Iran, Azerbaijan, Turkmenistan, Kazakhstan, Afghanistan, and further on into India and China.

The city off Edessa was the center of the Christian movement in the east. From one trade route originating in Antioch, the Gospel went to the west. Through the city of Edessa, it went to eastern lands. Edessa is now called Sanliurfa, or generally simply Urfa, a predominantly Kurdish city in southeastern Turkey. In the first few

---

[61] Moffett p. xiii

centuries of church history, however, it was often referred to as part of Syria. Urfa is designated as the City of the Prophets, allegedly containing the burial places of Abraham, Job, and other holy figures celebrated in the Old and New Testaments and the Qur'an. It is one of the most conservative Islamic cities in Turkey, giving no indication that it was once the center of the eastern Christian world.

Church historian Phillip Jenkins says that in addition to Edessa and Arbella, southeastern Turkey's monastic movement centered on Amida (today's Diyarbakir) and included large Christian centers in Nisibis (Nusaybin) and Mardin in southeast Turkey, where 100 monasteries were once located. The area came to be known as the Mount Athos of the East.[63]

The theological school in Edessa was closed in 489, and most of its members fled to Nisibis, which became the leading theological center for the Church of the East.[64] Today this entire area is almost totally populated by Kurdish Muslims, although there are still two operating monasteries, one in Mardin and one in Midyat, each containing only a few resident monks.

Saint Ephraim

Saint Ephraim (306-373), a well-known saint recognized as a Catholic, Orthodox, and Eastern saint, was born in Nisibis but moved to Edessa, and wrote many great theological works. He wrote only in Syriac and refused to write in Greek. Both East and West Syrians revere him as he lived before the great divide. Pope Benedict XV declared him a Doctor of the Church in 1920.[65] He could be said to be the Charles Wesley of the ancient church, having composed hundreds of hymns. He also wrote much prose against heresy and was a great theologian.

---

[63] Jenkins, p. 61
[64] Ibid p. 52
[65] Rassam p. 50

Beautiful Martyr

During the reign of the second emperor of the Sassanid Persian Empire, Shapur I captured some Byzantine Roman Christians. One of the captives was of such beauty that the emperor, Varahan II, (reign 276-293) took her to be his queen. The emperor promised that if she would give up her faith, he would make her queen over the entire realm. She refused and continued to confess Christ. With a radiant face, she was led away to her death.[66]

The "Heresy" of the Church of the East

In this book, when I refer to the Church of the East, I am referring to what is often called the Nestorian Church. The term "Nestorian," has generally been used in a derogatory way. Sometimes the Church of the East is referred to as *Diaphysite* (two natures) as opposed to *Miaphysite* or *Monophysite* (one nature).[67] Suha Rassam, a very accomplished scholar from Iraq, uses the terms "East Syrian" to refer to the Church of the East and "West Syrian" for the Jacobite Monophysite church.[68] What was the alleged heresy of the Church of the East? (Please see Appendix C that focuses on the many church divisions).

The Council of Ephesus

The Council of Ephesus (431) dealt with the issue of whether Mary, the mother of Jesus, should be entitled *Theotokos* (God-bearer or Mother of God). Bishop Nestorius was not the first person who was troubled by the phrase *Mary, Mother of God.* However, Nestorius faced the wrath of many of the other bishops. In addition to strictly doctrinal concerns, there was also the element of the long-standing Antioch versus Alexandria-conflict for political and spiritual influence. Cyril of Alexandria supported the concept of Mary as the *Theotokos,* and he took major steps to have Nestorius excommunicated. The council condemned him on June 22 before

---

[66] Richard & Jewel Showalter, p. 24
[67] Rassam, xxviii,xxix. See also footnote on page 41
[68] Rassam, p.6

Nestorius and the other Eastern bishops even arrived in Ephesus on June 26. After the papal delegates arrived from Rome, those loyal to Cyril reinstated the condemnation of Nestorius on July 10-11.

What did Nestorians believe? In essence, Nestorius apparently believed that in Jesus Christ the Logos and a human person were joined in a harmony of action, but not in a single personhood. Therefore, he objected to the term *Theotokos*. He thought the term *Christotokos* was more biblical and less confusing for most people. Perhaps if Mary had been titled "the Mother of God-incarnate" instead of "Mother of God," the ugly battles between what became known as Orthodox faith and Nestorianism[69] might have been avoided.

Allegorical or Literal Interpretation?

We saw in the last chapter the important word *homoousios* (same nature) in refuting Arianism. In examining what has become known as Nestorianism, the key phrase is *hypostatic union,* which means that the two natures in Christ are united in his one nature.

Two of the leading *Sees* (ecclesiastical centers of authority) were often at odds with each other; Alexandria, in today's Egypt, and Antioch in ancient Syria (now located in Turkey). In Alexandria, the tendency was to allegorize the Scripture, drawing from Greek philosophy and illustrating truth through the use of allegory. They tended to interpret biblical texts mystically and spiritually. In the Antiochene school, biblical texts were more historically and literally interpreted. These two *Sees* continued to battle head to head even after Chalcedon (See chapter 6), and no doubt included godly people on both sides. In the Antiochene school, Theodore of Mopsuestia (d. 428) "favored dividing Christ, and sharply

---

[69] As we will see, the term "Nestorian or Nestorianism" is considered derogatory by the Church of the East. The people of that church, prefer the term "Assyrian Church of the East" or "The Church of the East" or sometimes they are called *Diaphysite* (two-natures) in contrast to *Miaphysite* or *Monophysite* (one-nature), another way of understanding the divinity-humanity of Christ. Later Miaphysites were also considered heretics, which we will examine in a subsequent chapter.

distinguished between his two natures, over and against the Alexandrian school, which favored a unification."[70]

The danger of Theodore's teaching if carried too far, would be that the two natures of Christ are joined together almost in a sense of mutual cooperation; two individuals joined together, rather than a united being that forms one person as the Church Fathers had traditionally taught. John Harden, the author of a contemporary version of *The Catholic Catechism,* points out a disciple of Theodore, named Nestorius, who rose from his life as a monk to become the patriarch of Constantinople. He was a court appointee of the Byzantine court, which gave him a lot of power. He was also well a charismatic preacher with a no-hold-barred personality. [71] He began to preach that Mary was not Theotokos as God cannot be born of a woman. I can visualize Nestorius perhaps illustrating his preaching as I mentioned in the "just imagine" story by sarcastically proclaiming," If Mary is the Mother of God, did God need his diaper changed?" "Did God need his mommy to tuck him in bed at night?" (I am not implying that Nestorius said it that way, but we do know there was a huge reaction to his preaching, so I would not be surprised if he preached along this line!). Nestorius based his argument mostly on logic, whereas Cyril, his main opponent, appealed to the Church Fathers as the doctrine of the *Theotokis* was well established by this time.

Cyril, bishop of Alexandria, was the major opponent against Nestorius, but also Eutyches, Apollinaris, and the emperor Theodosius (ruled 408-450), were of this school as well. On Nestorius' side were Theodore of Mopsuestia, Flavian and Queen Pulcheria of the Eastern Roman Empire (ruled from 450-457).[72] Noll cites from Cyril's second letter to Nestorius supporting the title *Theotokos:*

---

[70] Hardon, *The Catholic Catechism* p. 133
[71] Ibid, p. 133
[72] Noll, p. 69

The one Lord Jesus Christ must not be divided into two Sons. For the Scripture says not that the Logos united to himself the person of a human being but that he became flesh. And for the Logos to become flesh is nothing other than for him to "share in flesh and blood as we do" (Heb. 2:14). ...He did not depart from his divine status or cease to be born of the Father; he continued to be what he was even in taking on flesh...And this is how we shall find the holy fathers conceived things. Accordingly, they boldly called the holy Virgin "God's mother" (*theotokos*), not because the nature of the Logos...took the start of its existence in the holy Virgin but because the holy body, which was born of her, possessed as it was of a rational soul, and to which the Logos was hypostatically united, is said to have had a fleshly birth.[73]

Hardon cites Cyril further saying, "Emanuel is truly God, and the Holy Virgin is, therefore, Mother of God, for she gave birth in the flesh to the Word of God made flesh"[74]

Now let's look at Nestorius's second letter to his sworn enemy, Cyril:

> *Everywhere in Holy Scripture, whenever mention is made of the saving dispensation of the Lord, what is conveyed to us is the birth and suffering not of the deity but of the humanity of Christ, so that by a more exact manner of speech the holy Virgin is called Mother of Christ, not Mother of God. Listen to the words of the Gospels: The book of the birth of Jesus Christ, son of David, son of Abraham (Matt 1:1). It is obvious that the son of David was not the divine Logos.[75]*

Pre-Islamic Persecution

It is important to point out that global persecution of Christians did not stop with Constantine's conversion. The radical events that

---

[73] Ibid, p. 71
[74] Hardon, p. 135
[75] Ibid, p. 71

ended persecution in the Roman Empire did not extend to the rest of the world.

The persecution of heroic Christians in the Roman Empire is well-known and has taken root in the Christian imagination. Heroic Christ-followers who refused to bow before Caesar were thrown to the lions, crucified, or lit on fire to serve as lanterns for Emperor Nero's gardens. Persecution of Christians under Zoroastrian rule in Persia is not as well-known. Large-scale persecution of Christians in Persia began in the fourth century under King Shapur after the Roman Emperor recognized Christianity as the religion of the Roman world.

Rassam says that punishment for apostasy from Zoroastrianism, had occurred before, but it reached its worst under King Shapur II between the years 339-379.

The king summoned Bishop Simon to force him to collect a double tax from Christians. The Bishop refused, as the people were already impoverished. The king then called for all the bishops and priests, and had them killed in front of the patriarch who also was killed.[76] Moffett says during the persecution in Persia, Christians suffered more than Christians ever suffered in Rome, with fewer Christians apostatizing in Persia despite persecution that was more overt. He says that 190,000 Persian Christians died in the terror.[77]

A Powerful Story of Martyrdom

Rassam tells an intriguing story of one of the martyrdoms during this period. Mar Behnam, a son of the Persian king, was a on a hunting expedition when he became lost and had to spend a night in a cave north of Mosul. There he met a cave dweller named Mar Matta who told him of the new religion (Christianity). Mar Behnam was quite impressed with the saint, who was said to have miraculous powers. He asked Mar Matta to heal his sister Sarah who had a skin

---

[76] Rassam, p. 31
[77] Moffett, p. 145

disease, probably leprosy. As a result, both Behnam and his sister believed in Christ. Their father, King Shapur, asked them to renounce their faith. They refused and he ordered them to be killed. Afterwards the king lost his mind. His wife took him to Mar Matta and he was healed. The king and his wife were baptized by Matta and subsequently opened a monastery named Der Mar Matta.[78]

After Rome fell in the fifth century, persecution decreased for a time, but Moffett says that in 548 at Kirkuk in Northern Iraq, today the center of the Iraqi oil industry, ten bishops and 153,000 believers were killed. Their chief persecutor, Tamasgerd, became sickened by the massacre and was impressed by the faith and courage of the martyrs. He converted to the faith of Christ and was subsequently martyred as well[79].

Not long before Islam burst on the scene, the Persians struck deep into Byzantine territory and took Edessa in 607, Antioch in 611, and Jerusalem in 614. Later in this advance, Egypt and Asia Minor fell into Persian hands and the Persians were within striking distance of Constantinople. In 622, however, the East Roman Empire launched a counterattack, drove out the Persians, and even moved into Persian territory. The last Persian Sassanid emperor, Yazdegerd III, was replaced by the Islamic rulers [80]

From the Middle East to Chicago

The number of the Assyrian Church of the East today number 323,300, with Chicago being one of its main centers. A church similar in doctrine but not in total unity is the Ancient Church of the East, which number 100,000. The Chaldean Catholic Church consists of former Church of the East Christians who are in communion with the Vatican number 628, 405.[81] We will examine later why this great missionary church has declined to number only in the hundreds of

---

[78] Ibid, p. 32
[79] Ibid, p. 161
[80] Irvin & Sunquist, p. 272
[81] https://en.wikipedia.org/wiki/Church_of_the_East

thousands when it might be expected to be among the largest branches in Christianity and number in the hundreds of millions.

Those who adhere to their understanding of Christ's two natures will most likely never reap the seed their members had sown around the world. I have no doubt, however, that their suffering, sacrifice, and prayers for the people ranging from today's Turkey to China, in some mysterious way, has contributed to the harvest of Muslims and other peoples that is taking place in regions where they evangelized so long ago.

Moves toward Reconciliation

In 1994, Pope John Paul II and the Catholicos-Patriarch Dinkha IV of the Assyrian Church of the East, signed the Common Christological Declaration, which ended the long conflict over Christology.[82] The declaration between the Assyrian Church of the East (ACE) and the Roman Catholic Church (RCC) allows the ACE to pray to Mary as the mother of Christ our God and Savior, and the Catholics to pray to Mary as the Mother of God.[83] The statement concludes by saying:

> The Lord's Spirit permits us to understand better today that the divisions brought about in this way were due in large part to misunderstandings. Whatever our Christological divergences have been, we experience ourselves united today in the confession of the same faith in the Son of God who became man so that we might become the children of God by his grace.[84]

We will see later that when Protestant missionaries began to go to the ancient lands where the Miaphysites and Church of the East leaders duked it out, they found Christians who shared their Protestant reluctance to call Mary the Mother of God, despite their absolute belief in the divinity of our Lord. The missionaries may not have not realized that these Christians were part of the ancient

---

[82] Lefebure p. 154
[83] Ibid p. 162
[84] Ibid p. 163

Church of the East. Instead, they thought they had possibly found some long-lost, unknown to the world "Protestants" of the Middle East that in some way had found a faith resembling Protestantism before the Protestant missionaries began to arrive in the 19th century. [85]

The "So What" Question Today

Sometimes when I am teaching about how Islam was able to triumph over the peoples and places of the Bible, I mention how the Christological conflicts weakened the church, a topic we will come back to often throughout this book. I often ask my students who are mostly Evangelical Protestants, "Is Mary the Mother of God?" "Raise your hands if yes." A few hands go up. Then I ask, "Is Jesus God?" Most of their hands go up. Then I ask, "Is Mary the mother of Jesus?" All hands go up. Finally, "Then is Mary the Mother of God?" "Raise your hands if yes." Once again, a few hands go up, as students look around the room to see how their fellow students are reacting.

In their book, *Mary: A Catholic-Evangelical Debate,* the authors, Catholic Dwight Longenecker and Protestant David Gustafson, a book endorsed by both prominent Catholics Cardinal Francis George and Peter Kreeft, and Evangelicals, Timothy George and Michael Horton, the two friends debate issues related to Mary. Here, I will only focus on Mary as *Theotokos.*

Longenecker as a Catholic has no problem with the phrase, despite being a Protestant before his conversion to Catholicism. He points out that Irenaeus used the phrase God-bearer as early as 189. He rightfully says, "It is a fact of history that, if true honor is not paid to Mary as the Mother of God, people put our Lord in her place as the highest of creation rather than adoring him as God incarnate." [86]

---

[85] For a full study of the conflict, I recommend Phillip Jenkin's book, *The Jesus Wars,* subtitled as "How fur patriarchs, three queens, and two emperors decided what Christians would believe for the next 1,500 years."
[86] Longenecker & Gustafson, p. 36

Gustafson the Evangelical, however, has some reservations. First, he acknowledges the syllogism, "Mary is the mother of Jesus; Jesus is God; therefore, Mary is the Mother of God—or as Elizabeth said, 'the Mother of my Lord' (Luke 1:43)."[87] He affirms that Mary was the God-bearer, however, he expresses three reservations. First, he says *Theotokis* should be God-bearer rather than Mother of God. Why was she not called *meter theou,* which would be more literally "Mother of God" in Greek. Second, he points out that in the Council of Chalcedon in 451 (which we will look at in chapter six) she is called Mary, "the virgin mother of God as regards to his humanity." He acknowledges that the phrase "Mother of God" gives Protestants a creepy feeling as I found it does among many of my students. Third, he says the connotations seem to exalt Mary at the expense of Christ. So Gustafson says that if we use the logic that Mary is the mother of Jesus and Jesus is God, therefore Mary is the Mother of God, then we can say that Anna and Joachim (Mary's parents) were the grandparents of God, and John was the baptizer of God and Herod was the king of God.[88]

All of that to say, I have no problem calling Mary the Mother of God. However, I can understand why Nestorius and the Church of the East struggled with it. If I put myself in the place of Muslims today trying to understand how the Creator of the universe became a baby and was totally dependent on her and 33 years later was crucified, I can see why they usually need a type of divine revelation to grasp it! A topic to which we will come back to later.

Increasingly, current theologians seem ready to give Nestorius a fresh hearing. His actual writings did not vary as much from orthodoxy as some people have argued, based on misquotations and misunderstandings. In fact, Martin Luther could find no evidence of heresy in Nestorius' writing, because he never denied the deity of Christ, but stated that his divinity and the humanity must be

---

[87] Ibid p. 37
[88] Ibid p. 39

distinguished. [89] The question is, whether he separated them too far, and Christ was almost like two distinct persons.

In chapter twelve we will look at how the people of the Persian Empire became Muslims and the great influence they had on the way Muslims worship and practice their faith. We will also look at how the great missionary church fared under the onslaught of Islam a couple of centuries after the Christological divisions weakened the Church of the East.

Questions for discussion and reflection

- The Nestorians took the gospel all the way to China on foot or by camel or ship. Yet they had been declared heretical by the Roman/Byzantine Church. The Roman Catholic Church is seeking reconciliation with the Church of the East with many Protestants groups as well. Why do you think the once might church has been reduced to such a small number of members, with Chicago one of its major centers?

- Protestants do not usually refer to Mary as the Mother of God. Yet, if Jesus was God and Mary was his mother, why are Protestants so reluctant to call her the *Theotokos?*

---

[89] Moffett p. 176

6

Clark Kent and Superman and how do we Understand Jesus

Just imagine that you are an Egyptian Christian living in the mid-fifth century. As Egyptians or Copts, you have a rich bible heritage. Abraham came to Egypt when there was a famine in Palestine and took an Egyptian maiden as his wife. Of course Moses and the stories about the deliverance of the Children of Israel from Pharaoh may not put Egypt in the best light, but still it gave you pride that so much of the Holy Book took place in your land. Even the holy family of Joseph, Mary and the infant Jesus sought refuge in your land when Herod sought to kill the one he feared would rule in his place one day. In addition, Saint Mark, who wrote the Gospel named after him, was the founder of the Church in your land. Now you hear that the Byzantine Church feels that your church is heretical in denying Jesus' human nature. You are really baffled by the allegations of heresy. Your bishop goes to Chalcedon, a city on the Bosphorus (today the Asian side of Istanbul) and the patriarchs, bishops, and priests hold a council to determine how Jesus' divine and human natures can be best understood for the entire world of Christians.

When it is over, you hear that your fellow Copts and many other Christians have been declared as heretics. To you, it sounds like the Council's decision was heretical as it declares that Jesus has two natures--one human and one divine. That is what the Nestorians believed, and they were declared heretics at the council of Ephesus only twenty years before. Your church does not deny the *Theotokos* like the Nestorians do. You do not deny the divinity of Christ, nor do you deny his humanity. So why did they have yet another Ecumenical council that declared your beloved church heretical? Will your leaders accept the Chalcedon Definition as it has been called about the two natures of Christ, or will your bishops refuse to accept the ruling?

History and Theology: The Council of Chalcedon (451)

We must remember that heresy is a category imposed by the victors.[90]

There was a time in the fourth century when perhaps one-half of the world's Christians belonged to a group that was considered heretical. As Jenkins points out after the twin shocks of 431 (the renunciation of the Nestorianism) and 451 (the renunciation of Monophysitism) many eastern Christians went "underground", and took on to a degree at least, their more normal posture as a persecuted sect, rather than being part of the power structure of the Byzantine Empire.[91] Neither the Church of the East as we previously saw, nor the Miaphysites as we will see in this chapter, accepted the Christology that was decided at Chalcedon and as a result were branded as heretics.

The challenge of grasping the incarnation of our Lord challenged the Church for hundreds of years. That divine sentence inspired by the Holy Spirit, "The Word became flesh and dwelt among us." (John 1:14), so simple to recite, but so challenging for the people who called themselves by Christ's name to come to grips with. We saw the challenge that Arianism presented, when Bishop Arius preached that Jesus was not of the same substance as the Father. Out of the council in 325 came the Nicene Creed, which many thought would be the final word concerning Christology. Over a century later, however, Nestorius of Constantinople denied the *Theotokis*, and preached that Christ was virtually like two separate beings-one

---

[90] Marcus Plested, in *Heresies and how to avoid them* p. 43
[91] Jenkins, *Jesus Wars* p. 13

divine and one human. Therefore, the Council of Ephesus was called in 431 to deal with that heresy. (See previous chapter).

It is perhaps ironic that the Arians and the Church of the East (Nestorians) were both excellent at evangelizing pagans who did not know about Jesus. The German peoples were initially Arians before embracing what became the Orthodox/Catholic faith. Later, we saw how the Church of the East evangelized people as far away as India and China and was the great missionary church of its day.

Why another Council?

Eutyches, a powerful monk from a leading monastery in Constantinople, formulated a Christology that many feared would lead to compromising Jesus' full humanity, as they had feared that Nestorius' doctrine would lead to a compromise concerning Jesus' full divinity. It was hoped that the council at Ephesus in 431, would be the final one. Once again, however, controversy broke out.

Eutyches, Monophysites and Miaphysites

What did Eutyches believe and propagate? He believed that after the union of the divine and human natures in the incarnation, Christ had only a single nature, a synthesis of the divine and human. Eutychianism states that the union between God and Christ is so complete, that his humanity cannot be separated from his divinity. Eutyches was so strong in his opposition to the Nestorian heresy about the over-separation of the divine and human natures of Christ that he went in the opposite direction and fell into another heresy. What Eutyches taught has been called Monophysitism. *Mono*-single, *physis*-nature. For Eutyches, there were two natures before the union, but there was only single nature after the incarnation. In the words of Justin Holcomb, "Eutyches agreed with Cyril that there was only one person, but unlike Cyril, he adamantly refused to say that there were still two natures in the person of Jesus Christ." [92]

---

92 Holcomb, p. 54

The Importance of Cyril of Alexandria

After the Council of Ephesus in 431, Cyril had so established himself as the authoritative voice regarding Christological issues, that future debates about the two natures of Christ had to line up in fidelity to Cyril.[93] Cyril affirmed Christ's full humanity, with a rational soul and born of the Virgin Mary, and that his "human nature was in no way confused with or totally absorbed into the divinity. He allowed that one could speak in terms of two natures so long as this did not detract in any way from the perfection of the union.

Now it gets a little tricky. Today, the Oriental Orthodox churches, which include Coptic, Armenian, Syrian, Ethiopian, Eritrean ,and Indian Orthodox churches, are often classified as Monophysites. However, people from the Oriental Orthodox Church do not like to be called Monophysite by Western Christians. Oriental Orthodox Christians say that it is a derogatory term and that it misrepresents what they believe. They prefer the term Miaphysite going back to St. Cyril. I have used this term throughout this book, although most historical writings use the term Monophysite. The prefix mono means single or absolute oneness. Miaphysites, use the prefix *mia*, which carries the meaning of plural unity. Oriental Orthodox Christians teach that the incarnate Christ has *mia* nature, but one that is of both a divine character and a human character and retains characteristics of both, with no mingling, confusion (pouring together), or change of either nature. Miaphysites believe not in a single nature in Jesus Christ like the term Monophysite implies, but rather within the *hypostasis* (person) are two *physesin* (natures). Father Jacob Zaki, a Coptic priest in the Twin Cities, is as gracious a man as you can imagine. But when I asked him which word Monophysite or Miaphysite I should use in this book, he was emphatic. "We are Miaphysites not Monophysites."

---

93 Ibid pps. 44, 45

How the Fall of a Horse Changed Our Theology

In 450, if a horse carrying emperor Theodosius II who supported the Miaphysite theology had not stumbled leading to his death, there may not have been a Council of Chalcedon. The Miaphysite understanding may have prevailed rather than the Christology of the Council of Chalcedon if it was not for that stumble! Catholic historian Thomas Bokenkotter says that when Theodosius fell off his horse and died, Pulcharia married his successor, Marcian, and reversed the Miaphysite-friendly policy of Theodosius.[94] Pulcharia was probably the most powerful person in the Empire at the time, but as a woman, she could not rule. She agreed to the marriage as long as she could remain celibate. She and her new husband, the Eastern Roman Emperor, called for the Council of Chalcedon in 451 and enforced its decisions.[95]

The goal of Pope Leo and other prelates at the conference was to find a middle-of-the-road solution between Antioch and Alexandria, between the Nestorians and the Miaphysites. Chalcedon, endorsed by the emperor Marcian and his powerful queen Pulcheria, backed Pope Leo's definition of how to view the mystery of Christ.

So let's now look at the Chalcedon understanding of the two natures of our Lord, as set forth at Chalcedon, much of it as written by Pope Leo and accepted enthusiastically by the other church leaders from both the East and the West. It has been called the Chalcedon Definition and Leo's Tome, since Leo was the architect of much of it in consultation with other of the prelates.

The Chalcedonian Definition

> *Following the holy fathers, we all with one accord teach men to acknowledge one and the same Son, our Lord Jesus Christ, at once complete in Godhead and complete in manhood, truly God*

---

94 Bokenkotter
95 Jenkins, pps. 285-86

and truly man, consisting also of a reasonable soul and body; of one substance (homoousios) with the Father as regards his Godhead, and at the same time of one substance with us as regards his manhood; likewise in all respects, as apart from sin; as regards his Godhead, begotten of the Father before all ages, but yet as regards his manhood begotten, for us men and for our salvation, of Mary the Virgin, the God-bearer (Theotokos); one and the same Christ, Son, Lord. Only-begotten, recognized in two natures, without confusion, without change, without division, without separation; the distinction of natures being in no way annulled by the union, but rather the characteristics of each nature being preserved and coming together to form one person and subsistence (hypostasis), not as parted or separated into two persons, but one and the same Son and Only-begotten God the Word, Lord Jesus Christ; even as the prophets from earliest times spoke of him, and our Lord Jesus Christ himself taught us, and the creed of the father has handed down to us.

Hardon says that when the Nicene Creed and Leo's Tome were read together at Chalcedon, the assembled council exclaimed, "This is the faith of the Fathers. This is the faith of the Apostles. This is the faith of all of us. Peter has spoken through Leo."[96]

Ramifications of the Chalcedon Definition

When we read the Chalcedon Definition (Tome of Leo), it sounds so complex, we might be tempted to ask the "so what" question. Why did Christians split over such minute detail about the two natures of Christ? Why did they denounce each other? Why in some cases did they think that Islam was the judgment against the others who came to a different conclusion about the nature of the Son of God?

Today, Roman Catholic churches, Eastern Orthodox churches, and most Protestant churches affirm the Christology that was carved out at Chalcedon. I know many members of the Oriental Church of the East whom refused to accept it. They love our Lord. Many of their

---

96 Harden p. 139

ancestors have suffered great loss of property, faced much discrimination, and the number of martyrs is beyond calculation at the hands of Muslims. While some converted to Islam or appeared to accept the religion of the Prophet (See chapter on Crypto-Christians), many stayed faithful to Christ as Islam conquered their lands.

It is easy to condemn the battles over Christology that led to so much division that today may seem somewhat irrelevant. We can ask ourselves why the early Christians denounced, oppressed, and excommunicated each other to the point that some welcomed Muslims to save them from their fellow Christians. Before we are too judgmental about the rigidity that led to the Church of the East and the Miaphysite Churches being regarded as heretical, let us think about our situation in the United States. We have thousands of denominations in America alone, and when we examine why these denominations split from one another, it is generally for less important reasons than trying to figure out how God could take on human form in the person of Jesus and still be God!

Marcus Plested, a professor at Cambridge and Eastern Orthodox by membership, summarizes why Eutychianism had to be dealt with. He says, first and foremost, to deny the real distinction between God and man in Christ is to put our salvation in danger. Why? Only God can save but man needs to be saved.

> *The Saviour must, therefore be both God and man if salvation is to be effected. Eutychianism removes the authentically human dimension of Christ's saving work. It makes salvation into a mere fiat, a divine action disconnected from God's free human creation. If Christ does not share our humanity, if he is not consubstantial with us, it becomes difficult to understand how his salvation could be extended to the whole human race.*[97]

---

97 Plestted in *Heresies and how to Avoid Them* p. 47 Ben Quash & Michael Ward, Eds.

Of course, questions remain because Miaphysites also deny that they hold to the doctrine of Eutyches. They do not deny the full humanity of our Lord. In fact, they believe God suffered, bled, and died. The widely respected Greek Orthodox theologian, John Meyendorff, states that the "Monophysites" rejected the Council of Chalcedon and the Christological formula of *"one hypostasis in two natures"* because Cyril never used the phrase, and they interpreted it as a return to Nestorianism.[98] The definition at Chalcedon seemed so close to the Nestorian diophysite *en duo physesin* in two natures) instead of the Cyril's *ek duo physein* (or of two natures) that people were confused.

Miaphysitism Perseveres and Spreads

Iraqi historian John Joseph states that since the sixteenth century the Christian world has been divided into four major groups: Roman Catholic, Greek Orthodox, Protestant, and Middle-Eastern.[99] Miaphysites (or the Oriental Orthodox Church)) like the Church of the East, have suffered great persecution and still do, particularly in Egypt and parts of Syria under Islam The Miaphysites, however, over the centuries have fared better than the Church of the East has, and today they have a much more visible church in far more places. The Oriental Orthodox Churches were able to develop in diverse languages such as Armenian, Georgian, Amharic, Coptic, and Nubian, and retained no common language, whereas the Church of the East was locked into the one Syriac language.

One of the Miaphysite clergy was a Syrian named Jacob Baradeus, who had been a very successful missionary into remote parts of Asia Minor (Turkey).[100] Empress Theodora (500-548), wife of Justinian, although a supporter of the Miaphysites, kept a lid on her group, making sure that they were not too overt in their rebellion against the Chalcedonians. Jacob Baradeus, however, sought an alternative

---

98 Meydendorff, p. 34
99 Joseph (1983) , p. 1
100 MacCulluch p. 237

hierarchy among the Ghassanids, a people from south of the Arabian peninsula and had moved next to the border of Roman Palestine, and even going into the Sassanian (Persian) Empire, ordaining clergy[101] and "church planting." Their monastic life came to dominate the monastic life in Tur Abdin, which is now in a predominately-Kurdish area in the southeast Turkey.[102]

Attempts at Reconciliation

In 1989, within the churches, which call themselves by the name Orthodox, representatives, including bishops, patriarchs, and the head of the Coptic Church, Pope Shenouda, met for four days at a monastery in Egypt.[103] One has to wade through much theological language and Greek vocabulary to grasp the details. Please check out the website below for a fuller account. I have highlighted a few aspects that stood out to me. The twenty-three participants from thirteen countries agreed on many important points. They acknowledged "This division is an anomaly, a bleeding wound in the body of Christ, a wound which according to His will that we humbly serve, must be healed." They acknowledged that centuries of ill will have deeply hurt the cause of Christ. The representatives did say that they "found common ground in the formula of our common Father, St. Cyril of Alexandria: *mia physis* (hypostasis)...it is sufficient for the confession of our true and irreproachable faith to say to confess that the Hoy Virgin is Theotokos." Their agreement goes to say:

> *When we speak of the one composite (synthetos) hypostasis of our Lord Jesus Christ, we do not say that in Him, a divine hypostasis and a human hypostasis came together. It is the one eternal hypostasis of the Second Person of the Trinity has assumed our created human nature in the act uniting it with His*

---

[101] Ibid p. 237
[102] Ibid p. 237
[103] For full statements of the agreement see the following website
https://www.trinityorthodox.ca/sites/default/files/Agreed%20Statements-Orthodox-Oriental%20Orthodox%20Dialogue-1989-1990.pdf

own uncreated divine nature, to form an inseparably and confusedly united real divine-human being, the natures being distinguished from each other in contemplation (theoria) only.

The agreement goes on to states, "The Orthodox agree that the Oriental Orthodox will continue to maintain their traditional Cyrilline terminology of "the One incarnate nature of the Logos." The Oriental Orthodox agree that the Orthodox are justified in their use of the two-natures formula, since they acknowledge that the distinction is in thought alone" So both agreed to accept the teachings of the first three councils (Nicaea, Constantinople and Ephesus) and the seventh council that concerns the veneration of icons. The Council of Chalcedon that most Christian Churches have accepted, is still rejected by the Oriental Orthodox Churches, and still perceived as too diophysite).[104] They furthermore agreed to lift the anathemas and condemnations from each other. Both branches continue to condemn the teachings of Nestorius and Eutyches.

Gleaning from Father Jacob

I mentioned Fr. Jacob earlier in this chapter. Later in the book, I will mention his parish in the Twin Cities which is thriving spiritually as they send out missionary teams across the world. I met with Fr. Jacob recently to try to figure out how the Oriental Orthodox Churches, which include the Copts is considered heretical by other Orthodox Churches which accepted the Chalcedon definition. I have briefly summarized a few of his key points:

1) We must remember that the incarnation is a mystery. As the Trinity cannot totally be understood by the human mind, neither can the incarnation.

2) St Cyril is widely cited by both Chalcedon and Non-Chalcedon theologians. (The above agreement cited above confirms this). Fr. Jacob went on to say that there is

---

104 Diophysite means two-natures, what Nestorians have been accused of, that is of separating the divine and human natures of Jesus so far as Jesus almost becomes two separate individuals-one human and one divine.

disagreement with the Tome of Leo but it is more complicated and relates not only to theology but also to historical infighting and misunderstanding.

3) Oriental Orthodox and Eastern Orthodox use the Liturgy of St. Basil each week in their liturgies, and the Eastern Orthodox use it several times a year along with the liturgy of St. Chrysostom. There is not a major difference in their liturgies.

4) The problem is not so much one of belief, but the ugly history that has gone down between the two major branches of Orthodoxy. They have denied the Eucharist to each other and anathematized each other for hundreds of years. (Hopefully the agreement of 1989 has lifted much of this from off the backs of each other and full reconciliation which would include partaking of the Eucharist in each other's churches would be the end-goal).

5) Miaphysites would say that if you stick a rod of iron into a blazing fire, the iron will absorb the fire. The iron is not changed into fire nor is the fire into iron.

Dr. William Ingersoll, a scientist and a theologian, with whom I discussed this issue, states that Chalcedon was an unnecessary council and it failed to be an instrument of reconciliation. The Miaphysites had rejected Eutyches' Monophysite position. For Ingersoll Chalcedon was a compromise that failed because it attempted to maintain at the same time the crypto-diophysitism of Leo and the Miaphysitism of Cyril. It failed to heal the rift between Alexandria and Constantinople. For Ingersoll, the issue gets back to one key question. Who died on the cross? Can we echo the haunting words of theologian Jurgen Moltmann, in the title of his book, *The Crucified God*? How about the words of Charles Wesley in his classic hymn, "Amazing love, how can it be that Thou my God shouldst die for me?" Was it merely the human Jesus who died on the cross, or was it the divine God the Logos who shed his blood to liberate humankind from sin, death and the devil? As professor and author Leo Donald Davis asks, Could one say with Cyril that the Living Word suffered, died and rose? Davis goes on to point out that the definition at Chalcedon satisfied the West down to our times, "But the East found it wanting in clarity about the hypostatic union, the problems of predication, the single subject of suffering and death in Christ and the deification of the human begun in Christ.[105]

The Sovereignty of God in all of this?

This raises up the tricky subject of God's sovereign hand in all of this. No doubt, adherents of Chalcedon saw God's providence in the horse's fall that led the way for the Chalcedon way of understanding the two natures of Christ to prevail. It is doubtful whether the Miaphysites would interpret the horse's fall in the same way! We know that later both sides felt that Islam might have been punishment for the "heresy" of the other view.

Clark Kent and Superman

George Weigel, a prominent Catholic author of two dozen books, in his book about Catholic renewal Evangelical Catholicism, says that Monophysitism is "the tendency to stress the divinity of Christ to the point that his humanity becomes a mere disguise, as Clark Kent's horn-rimmed glasses disguised Superman.[106] Miaphysites would agree with this analogy as true of Eutyches, but not of themselves. Even if Miaphysitism is accused of being guilty of over-focusing on the divinity of our Lord, does not much modern theology downplay his divinity? Jesus has been portrayed as a Marxist-type revolutionary, a superstar, a homeboy, a sexual partner with Mary Magdalene, a homosexual, and even an Aryan supremacist by the Nazis. Besides these somewhat more recent attempts to portray Jesus in whatever image various cultures or sub-cultures want him to be, he has also been reduced to being an apocalyptic holy man, an Islamic prophet like Moses and Muhammad, a moral teacher, or the highest exalted being but not divine as we saw with the Arians.

---

105 Davis, p. 188
106 Weigel, p. 33

In thinking about the ice cream and the Superman/Clark Kent analogies, do they accurately reflect the Christological issue over which Nestorians, Miaphysites, and Chalcedonians fought? Perhaps as Fr. Jacob says, we much accept that the incarnation is a mystery. Is it possible for Catholics, Evangelicals, Oriental Orthodox, and Chalcedon Orthodox, and even the Church of the East Christians to reconcile based on absolute faith in the crucifixion of the Lord of Glory and His resurrection from the dead and his (hopeful) soon return? Jesus in his high priestly prayer in John 17 certainly prayed that we would be one. It is ironic that it has been divisions over the person of Jesus that has perhaps been the most divisive factor is dividing Christian over the centuries. I pray that the world, and in particular, Muslims, would see a united Church one day, that they might believe that God truly was in Christ, reconciling the world to himself (II Corinthians 5:19). The Holy Spirit inspired Charles Wesley to write these words in the second verse of Hark the Herald Angels Sing that states the wonderful mystery of the incarnation that we far too often sing without really grasping the meaning:

Christ by highest heav'n adored,
Christ the everlasting Lord!
Late in time behold Him come,
Offspring of a Virgin's womb.
Veiled in flesh the Godhead see,
Hail the incarnate Deity,
Pleased as man with man to dwell, Jesus, our Emmanuel.
Hark! The herald angels sing,
"Glory to the newborn King!"

Recent Story: Staying at Miaphysite Monasteries

I had the rare privilege for a foreigner to spend some nights at one of the great monasteries in the region. At one time, hundreds of monks stayed in these monasteries, teaching Aramaic (the language spoken during the time of Jesus) to the children. At that time in the late 1980s, there were only one or two monks at the two main

Jacobite monasteries, at Dar al Zafaran in Mardin and Mar Gabriel in Midyat. I was able to meet with the bishop of the region, and several of the visiting priests. On holidays, many of the remnant of *Suriyani* (the Turkish term of self-identification for the ancient Assyrian believers) would return from Istanbul and the few other places in Turkey where Suriyani Christians lived, while others came from various places in Europe. After the special liturgy, the crowds left, and life returned to a couple of monks holding on to keep the faith alive. The monasteries are caught in the crossfire between the Turkish government and the rebel Kurdish separatist rebels called the PKK. Almost all of the people have suffered from this battle, which has cost the lives of tens of thousands of Kurds as well as Turkish soldiers. It has also led to the small remnant of ancient Christians feeling extremely vulnerable. If they give supplies to the rebels, the government accuses them of being collaborators with the terrorists. If they do not, the PKK often harms them.

The Death of the Old and the Resurrection of the New

I will never forget a summer day in 1988 when a priest who learned his faith in the monasteries of Mardin and Midyat, and I drove around the region. The priest pointed out village after village that used to be full of *Suriyani* Christians that are now either empty or populated by Muslim Kurds. He had tears in his eyes as he discussed his childhood memories from a time long ago. Even his own flock in a bigger nearby city had dwindled down to just a few families who had not migrated to Istanbul or somewhere in Europe. A few, including one of the priest's brothers, had migrated to New Jersey. In their faith tradition, priests was supposed to raise a son to be a priest to ensure the survival of the faith. In his case, he and his wife (Orthodox priests can marry, but once they are ordained they cannot marry, as marriage must take place before ordination) had seven girls together. The priests jokingly told me that he must keep having children until he finally has a boy so the son can become a priest. Finally, child number eight was a boy. When I saw him many years later, the priest informed me that his son chose not to become a priest, but rather he is small business owner.

He told me something else, however, that was encouraging. When one considers how much these Christians have suffered under Muslim domination, it is not hard to understand why they are afraid of rocking the boat, and why most Christians avoid mixing with their Muslim neighbors much besides maybe an occasional seasonal greeting at holidays. But as the priest drove through village after village that was formerly full of Christians, he told me that even if not a Christian remains in southeast Turkey, the Lord would raise up a new people from among the Muslims to ensure the survival of the Christian faith.

True enough, the Lord has raised up some exciting churches in the region of people from a Muslim background, who while not speaking the language or worshipping as the Jacobite Christians did of past centuries, are joyfully worshipping their Redeemer.

Questions for Discussion and Reflection

- Perhaps if it was not for the fall of a horse, we might be all be Miaphysite in our understanding of Christ. How might it make a difference in our lives today if the vast majority of the Church believed in the Christology of the Miaphysites rather than the Chalcedon Definition?
- Does the Superman/Clark Kent analogy make the controversy more clear or more muddled in trying to grasp the Christological issues between Miaphysites and the majority of Christian denominations in understanding the how the human and divine natures of Christ co-exist in one person?
- Do you think you would like to stay in a monastery? If so, for how long?

7

Kebabs around the Campfire: Jews and Islam

Just imagine you are a Jew living in Arabia in a city called Yathrip in the year 612. You are a merchant who trades with the various caravans coming through your city from Persia, Abyssinia, Egypt and many other lands. At night, you and people from across the known world gather around fires and cook kebabs. Jews, Christians, Zoroastrians, and others tell stories and debate about faith. You tell various stories from the Torah and the historical books. Your listeners are fascinated by the story of Abraham and Isaac. Imagine God commanding you to sacrifice the son that you have been longing for, and finally at the age of one hundred has finally become a reality. You tell them about the Exodus, about Elijah and the prophets of Baal, and Samson, the strongest man who ever lived, and the people cannot seem to get enough of your stories. Even those who express skepticism still find them fascinating. The Zoroastrians speak about life as a tiny string bridge that crosses a big gulf. Those who walk across the bridge safely by practicing good thoughts, good words and good deeds will be rewarded with the gardens of Paradise and beautiful maidens. Those who do not will fall off the bridge into hell. Others tell stories about their religions from their shared folklore.

Over the years, you have told many of the listeners the stories about Noah, Moses, David, Solomon, Daniel and other biblical characters. You notice a young man whom people call Muhammad bin

Abdullah is there too, taking it all in. He seems to be listening very carefully but does not say much.

There is a lot of arguing among the Arab tribes in Yathrip, and the tribal elders have called for a man from Mecca to mediate between the conflicts. That man is Muhammad, known for his ability to resolve disputes. He and a small group of followers move into your city. Muhammad is especially eager to meet Jews and Christians. The people of Yathrip know that Jews and Christians disagree about the person of Jesus. The Christians believe that he is the true Messiah, while the Jews do not. They both agree about the stories in the Torah and the historical books, and some are friends despite their deep theological differences.

One day Muhammad gathers the people of Yathrip together and tells them about the revelations he is receiving from Allah through the angel *Jabril* (Gabriel). He begins by saying that Jews, Christians, and Zoroastrians all worship the same God. He tells of God's mercy, about Paradise and Hell, and the need for people to obey the law. The Jews are beginning to get a little restless. They say that many of the laws Muhammad claims to have received by revelation have already been revealed in the Torah. Muhammad says of course they are the same, because Allah's word confirms the message that Allah previously gave to *Musa* (Moses), *Daoud* (David), and *Isa* (Jesus).

Over the next weeks and months, Muhammad continues to share his revelations. He tells what Allah has revealed about Nuh (Noah) and the flood, about how God stopped Abraham from sacrificing his son, about Musa (Moses) and Pharaoh, about Lot and the destruction of his city, and many other stories.

You are careful not to insult Muhammad. After all, many people think that he is a prophet like the prophets in the Torah. In their eyes, he is a messenger who calls people to repent and submit to Allah. However, when Muhammad talked about Abraham being thrown into a fire without being burned, some of your fellow Jews snickered and said, "Hey Muhammad, you got it wrong. Abraham was not thrown into a fire. The three Hebrew children, the friends of the prophet Daniel, were thrown into the fire and were not burned." When Muhammad said that none of the greatest prophets sinned, the Jews pointed out that Abraham lied, telling Pharaoh that his wife was his sister in order to save his neck. Some of the Jews gave other examples of prophets and holy men who sinned but to whom God showed mercy. Perhaps the Jews questioned how Muhammad, a man with such limited knowledge of the Torah, could claim to be a prophet and expect the Jews to honor him as they did the prophets in their holy book.

Meanwhile, Muhammad has more revelations. He marries more wives, including a very young Aisha. His language towards your people began to change--from being honored as People of the Book to saying that Allah changed your people into monkeys and pigs. He changes the direction of the *quibla* (the location Muslims face when they perform their five daily prayers) from Jerusalem to Mecca.

Another Jewish tribe was accused of betraying Muhammad to his enemies the Meccans. Muhammad got his revenge by killing hundreds of your fellow Jews. You saw the men being killed and the women and children divided among the followers of the Prophet or sold as slaves. Could this happen to you and your tribe as well?

History and Theology: A Brief Summary of the Life of the Prophet of Islam

There are many biographies of the Prophet of Islam. The most authoritative is Ibn Hisham (d.219/834)[107] whose edition of Ibn Isaaq's *Sirat Rasul Allah* came out about two hundred years after Muhammad and his followers traveled from Mecca to Yathrib (Medina). That journey, called the *Hijra,* marks the date from which the Muslim calendar begins.

---

[107] When reading Islamic history, many authors will list two dates with about 600 years separating the dates. The first date is based on the date of the *Hijra,* the migration of Muhammad and his early followers from Mecca to Medina. The second dates is based on the Gregorian calendar that is used by Western historians.

In favorable biographies of the Prophet, Muhammad is often called *Kamil Adam* (perfect man), a model for all of humanity. There are also unfavorable portrayals of Muhammad that show him as an immoral man and a power-hungry manipulator. The negative portrayals especially focus on his thirteen wives, his raiding of caravans, and waging wars against the Jews and other tribes that would not submit to his rule.

For about twelve years, Muhammad preached in Mecca and the surrounding areas and encountered great opposition. His followers were persecuted, and at one point, Muhammad was forced to flee to Ethiopia to find refuge. Some leaders among the people of Yathrib, hearing that Muhammad was a trustworthy individual, invited him to their city to settle some disputes. Later the name of the city was changed to Medina, taken from the name of Midian, the fourth son that Abraham had by Keturah (Genesis 25:1-2).

Muhammad and the Jews

During his approximately ten years in Medina, Muhammad established his rule over Yathrip and the surrounding areas, and his revelations continued. When one reads the Qur'an and compares the *surahs* (chapters) written in Mecca with those written in Medina, it is obvious that circumstances had greatly changed. In Mecca, Muhammad was quite conciliatory toward the People of the Book, especially Jews and Christians. For example, a Meccan surah says, *We believe in that which has been revealed to us and revealed to you, and our God and your God is One, and to Him we submit* (Qur'an 29:46). In the later surahs, the tone of the Qur'an toward Jews and Christians is much harsher, especially toward the Jews. A Medina surah, referring to the Jews, says *but Allah hath cursed them on account of their disbelief, so they believe not but a little* (Qur'an 4:46) There were three large Jewish tribes in Medina, and no doubt Muhammad preached to them about the revelations he claimed to have received from Allah. I can visualize him perhaps feeling humiliated by the Jews when he recited biblical stories that varied from the Torah.

In addition to mocking Muhammad for not knowing the biblical stories as they had been revealed to the Hebrew prophets, the Jews challenged Muhammad for a sign to demonstrate that he was a prophet. *Why are not signs sent down upon him from his Lord? Say Signs are with Allah only, and I am only a plain warner*[108] *Is it not enough for them that we have revealed to thee the Book that is recited to them?* (Qur'an 29:50, 51). The desire of the Jews for a sign brings to mind that the Jews had demanded signs from Jesus as well. In the Gospel of John, after Jesus cleansed the temple of the moneychangers, the Jewish leaders demanded, "If God gave you authority to do this, show us a miraculous sign to prove it" (John 2:18).

Eventually ,Muhammad's forces killed a large number of Jews (estimates vary from 600 to 900) from the tribe of Qurayzah, who had allegedly betrayed the Prophet, and divided their women, children, and booty among themselves or sold them in the slave markets.

Muhammad's Later Years

The Prophet led his Arab warriors into at least twenty-seven battles, including the Battle of Badr in 623 which is especially revered as a battle in which the favor of Allah was granted to the Muslims[109]. when he returned to his hometown of Mecca, he came in triumph, showing mercy even to those who had fought against him, and most of the people submitted to Islam. With a few exceptions, Muhammad was gracious toward those who had formerly

---

[108] The word "warner" is not a word used often in modern English. The biblical prophets often warned of the judgment to come. In that sense, they were "warners."

[109] In the Battle of Badr, the Muslims were greatly outnumbered by the opposition forces, demonstrating that the Muslims had supernatural support in their victory. An in-depth study of Muhammad's battles is beyond the scope of this book. A good encyclopedia of Islamic history, or a biography of the Prophet will give greater detail. In the Old Testament, we see God's favor attributed to military victories, especially in the times of Joshua, Samsun, David and others. Jesus, however, never relied on military power nor did the early Christians until the time of Constantine.

oppressed him, which added to his legacy as the *Kamil Adam* (perfect man) by his admirers.

Muhammad died at the age of 62 without leaving a male successor, a point that has led to much conflict in the Islamic world today. The Muslim *ummah* (community) appointed Abu Bakr as the next caliph (political-military) leader of the Muslims. Muhammad was linked to Abu Bakr through his marriage to Abu Bakr's daughter, Aisha, who became his favorite wife. The *Hadith* (a collection of Muhammad's words and deeds) are very clear that Aisha was only six years old when they were betrothed, and nine years old when the marriage was consummated. Muhammad was about fifty-three years of age at the time. Muslim apologists point out that girls at that time reached puberty at younger ages than they do today, and that Abu Bakr gladly offered his daughter to the Prophet. Aisha in turn truly loved Muhammad.

I once respectfully asked a prominent professor of Islam, who is also an Imam[110], about Aisha. He told me somewhat defensively that if their marriage had been scandalous, people would have reacted against it. There is no record, however, that they did. He went on to say that we cannot project 21st century sexual mores to Muhammad's time when girls married at much younger ages than they do today. Muslim apologists, knowing that the issue of Muhammad's wives is troublesome for Westerners, defend the Prophet by saying that Muhammad was faithful to Khadija, his first wife, as long as she lived, despite her being fifteen years older than he was. After the death of Khadija, he married mostly widows to cement alliances with various tribes and to care for those who had no male support networks. Two of Muhammad's wives were Jews

---

[110] Prayer leader in a mosque and often can refer to a head of a community. Among Shi'a Muslims, imams carry more weight and most believe that there are 12 rightly guided imams from Muhammad's son-in-law Ali to the Mahdi, the awaited one who appears at the end of time to destroy the Antichrist and bring justice to the world.

and one was a Christian. Besides Aisha, the most controversial of his wives was Zaynab (Zainap), the wife of his adopted son-in-law. r.

I do not believe it is wise, especially for Western Christians, to attack the person of Muhammad. Our task is to lift up the name of Jesus among Muslims. Muslims who want to learn about the life of their Prophet can learn about it for themselves in authoritative biographies, in the *Hadith,* even in the Qur'an itself.[III]

From where did Muhammad's Revelations Originate?

I know a brilliant Islamic scholar who is one of the smartest people I have ever met. Not only is he a *hafiz* (memorizer of the entire Qur'an) but he has memorized hundreds of Hadiths as well. Whenever we compared our faiths, I suggested that Muhammad would most likely have discussed faith issues with Jews, Christians and Zoroastrians who may not have known their faiths well. That would explain why the Qur'an, which was revealed over 600 years after Christ, differs from the Bible, despite the Qur'an claiming to be a fulfillment rather than a correction of the Biblical text. I pointed out that some docetic[112] Christians did not believe that Jesus was crucified, but only appeared to be, which is how it is stated in the Qur'an.[113] The Islamic scholar would not acknowledge that the story in the Qur'an of Jesus breathing life into clay pigeons, or the baby Jesus defending his mother against charges of adultery, are apocryphal stories circulating in Arabia at the time of Muhammad. The Trinity in the Qur'an, which consists of God, Jesus, and Mary, demonstrates a misunderstanding of the Christian Trinity. It is very

---

[III] There is increasing debate whether the Muhammad is a real historical character. The arguments for and against are interesting, but in this book, I have briefly summarized his life as most historians have written it.

[112] Docetic Christians are those who held to Gnosticism, the heresy that stated that Jesus only appeared to be human and did not really suffer because God cannot suffer. Gnostics believed that only certain people had special revelation knowledge. The Nicene Creed says that Jesus was truly God and truly man, which debunks the essence of gnostic teaching. It is possible that Muhammad may have been influenced by Gnosticism in denying Jesus' death of the cross.

[113] I will examine some of these arguments in more detail later in the book.

likely that the Prophet of Islam observed some Christian sects that inadvertently gave the impression that Mary was almost a divine figure, and that she was being worshipped rather than merely highly honored.

Muhammad in his pre-prophethood days was a caravan trader. I can envision a group of caravan traders making kebabs over an open fire after a day of trading and bargaining. While grilling the meat (to this day, Middle Easterners love picnicking and grilling kebabs over a fire), Muhammad most likely heard many stories about the various biblical prophets. Many of these stories are found in the Qur'an, but in some cases differ somewhat from how they are told in the Bible. For example, the Qur'an does not record the moral lapses of prophets like Abraham and David, whereas the Bible is quite clear about human failures, even among its revered characters. Muhammad most likely would have heard Jews and Christian argue about whether Jesus was the promised Messiah or merely an imposter. He well may have heard discussion about the two natures of Jesus--divine and human. Muhammad may have heard Persian Zoroastrians talk about the narrow bridge that separates Paradise from Hell that all humankind will have to cross over, and that most will fall into Hell. It baffles me why this brilliant Islamic scholar believed that Muhammad never discussed religious issues with those of other faiths as they sat around the campfire. He seemed to feel that everything in the Qur'an came by direct revelation from Allah through the Angel *Jabril* (Gabriel), or the Qur'an would not be the perfect book he believed it to be.

One way to understand the discrepancies between the Bible and the Qur'an is to look at it through a human focus Perhaps the Prophet misunderstood the biblical stories and teachings he heard from Jews and Christians. Or perhaps Allah revealed them as Muhammad received them, but Jews or Christians had tampered with the biblical stories and Allah revealed them as they were supposed to be. We will examine this possibility later.

Let us suppose that the Bible and the Qur'an are in agreement 99 percent of the time. (I am not saying that the percentage is that high, but only for the sake of argument). If the content is virtually the same except for the Qur'an's denial of the crucifixion and resurrection of Jesus, then our Muslim friends have missed the entire plan of God--that God would reconcile sinful humankind to himself through shed blood of his Son. There is another strong possibility to understand the discrepancies between the Bible and the Qur'an. The Apostle Paul wrote, *And no wonder for Satan himself masquerades as an angel of light. It is not surprising, then, if his servants also masquerade as servants of righteousness* (II Corinthians 11:14-15).

There is a reason why some scholars hold to the "angel of light" theory. In the earliest biography of the Prophet, the *jinn or jinni*[114] squeezed Muhammad's neck so hard that he thought he was being strangled. "He could no longer bear the pressure and therefore let the angel take control over him and make him repeat the words."[115] Muhammad feared that he had been influenced by *jinn*. His wife, Khadija, and her cousin, Waraqa, assured him that he was receiving revelation as the prophets of old did. In reality, there is no record of a biblical prophet fearing that he was being deceived by evil spirits or demons when receiving revelation from God.

Core Beliefs and Practices

Over the years I have many lectures on Islam given by both Muslims and non-Muslims. The first thing a Muslim lecturer will point out is that the word *Islam* (s-l-m) can mean peace or submission. A Muslim is one who is submitted to the will of Allah. In informal dialogues as well, Muslims point out the following statements in describing their beliefs and practices. Similar to Judaism, Islam focuses more on right-doing (orthopraxy) than on right beliefs or doctrine (orthodoxy).

---

[114] *Jin, Jinni* refer to spirits who were made out of fire rather than clay like humans were. They often interfere in the lives of humans and are often invoked in folk Islam for magical purposes. *Jin* can resemble demons in the Bible, but can also be more mischievous in Islam rather than totally evil as demons are in the Bible. The English word "genies" probably derives from the Arabic word.
[115] Shayesteh, p. 12

The Five Pillars

1) Shahada: There is no God but God (Allah) and Muhammad is the Messenger (Apostle) of God. This is the entry point into Islam.

2) Salat: The five daily prayers that Muslims perform at certain times throughout the day. They must be recited in Arabic with the right postures, especially the way in the worshippers prostrate.

3) Suam: Fasting from food, liquid, smoking, and sexual relations, from sunup to sundown, especially during the Holy Month of Ramadan.

4) Zakat: About 2.5 percent of what a person owns should be given to the poor or to advance the cause of Islam.

5) Hajj: Muslims must make the pilgrimage to Mecca at least once during their lifetimes if physically and financially able.

The Six Core Beliefs

1) God (Allah) is One (Tawhid): This is the foundation on which Islam is built. It is the continuation of the faith of Abraham.

2) Messengers of God. There are 25 messengers listed by name in the Qur'an, most of whom are also mentioned in the Bible. Tradition says Allah sent 124,000 messenger/prophets to people groups throughout the world. Muhammad was the Seal of the Prophets, the prophet for all humankind, whereas the other prophets were for specific peoples.

3) Holy Books: There are four Holy Books that descended from Heaven--the Tawrat (Torah revealed to Moses), the Zebur (the Psalms revealed to David), the Injil (the Gospel revealed to Jesus) and the Qur'an (revealed to Muhammad). The Qur'an completes and illuminates the previous revelations.

4) Angels: Angels play a very active role. The angel Gabriel was the instrument of Allah to reveal the Qur'an to the Prophet Muhammad. Angels serve and protect humans, but the jinn or bad angels can tempt Muslims to do bad things.

5) The Day of Judgment: All people will give an account to Allah of all of their deeds in this life. Muslims strive to have their

good deeds outweigh their bad deeds, but no one knows for sure how Allah will judge them on the Day of Judgment. The Qur'an focuses heavily on Paradise and Hell.

6) The Decree of God. God has a divine plan for the universe and humankind and it will not be thwarted.

Keep in mind that volumes are written on the specifics of each of the beliefs and practices of Muslims, just as there are volumes written about each belief and practice of Christians. My goal is to give readers a brief summary of what they might likely hear when engaging Muslims about their faith.

Questions for Discussion and Reflection

- Try to imagine yourself around a campfire cooking kebabs and someone starts telling everyone that he is receiving revelations from God. Some of what Muhammad says sounds like what you believe as a Jew, but on other points, what he says does not line up with the Bible. How do you think you might have responded in that situation?

- Some Christians have called Muhammad a prophet in the Old Testament sense, as one who warns of judgment and the need for repentance and obedience to the Law. They point out that many of the people we honor in the Old Testament were polygamous and far from perfect in their moral lives. Others see Muhammad in a much harsher light, especially in regards to his marriages and his military battles, and caravan raiding. Briefly, how do you view Muhammad?

8

Muslims are from Mars and Christians are from Venus

Just imagine you are a Christian living in Arabia at the time of Muhammad. You hear that the Jews mocked Muhammad and paid a heavy price for it--hundreds of men were killed and their wives and children distributed to his followers. Some no doubt ended up in the slave markets or were forced to become concubines or additional wives for Mohammad's followers. You try to stay out of theological discussions with the Prophet. After all, you have a hard time explaining that God is one but also three. You are happy that Muhammad affirms that Mary was a when she gave birth to Jesus. The so-called prophet call Mary the most exalted of all women. You like that Muhammad calls your savior Isa al Masih (Jesus the Messiah). Muhammad tells other stories that are floating around Arabia, such as Jesus making clay pigeons come to life and speaking as a baby to defend his mother against charges of adultery. Some learned Christian scholars say that these stories are from a pseudo-gospel and are not inspired by the Holy Spirit. Nevertheless, at least they honor Jesus. When Muhammad is questioned about why he does not perform miracles as other prophets did, he says the Qur'an is his miracle.

You are hoping that as Muhammad can continue to co-exist with you and your fellow Christians. Then one day, as Muhammad is preaching, he declares Jesus was not crucified, but, Allah made someone else look like Jesus who was crucified. Allah had played a joke on the Jews and taken Jesus directly to Paradise. The recently converted Arabs laughed at how God tricked the Jews. Now you are deeply troubled. The Prophet is determined that before he dies there should be no non-Muslims in Arabia. This land that has been your home for centuries is all you know. Can you say the *shahada* and join the *ummah*? Or should you move your family somewhere else where you know no one and have no source of livelihood? How important is to you whether it was really Jesus on the cross? How essential is it really to believe in the Trinity and that Jesus was divine?

Just Imagine you are a young Muslim man in Mecca. You have been listening to Muhammad as he preaches after recently coming back in triumph from Medina. Everyone around you seems excited that Allah has chosen one of their kinfolk as a prophet. The entire city seems to be saying the *Shahada* and builders are constructing mosques all over the city.

Since early childhood, it was assumed that your uncle's daughter would be your wife when you reached marriageable age. It is ok with you and you think she likes you too. However, your uncle has not said the *Shahada yet*. He seems to doubt that Muhammad is a prophet. The leaders of your clan are trying to convince him that Muhammad is the one that the Gospels promised would come after the Prophet Jesus was taken to heaven.[116] They cannot figure out why your uncle does not see the will of Allah so clearly. It makes so much sense. The prophets came to warn and admonish people to submit to the one God. Jews and Christians are People of the Book but they did not submit to God's will of Allah. Allah constantly punished the Jews because of their disobedience, and Christians have committed the unforgiveable sin by worshipping Jesus as a god.

---

[116] Some Muslim apologists say that the comforter or *paraklit* in John 16:7-8; 12-14 refers to Ahmad, another form of the name Muhammad (Qur'an 61:6), whereas Christian theology points to the Holy Spirit as the one to come after the ascension.

Your uncle stubbornly refuses to say the *Shahada*. As pressure grows against him, he takes his family and flees, leaving most of his possessions behind. You wonder if his daughter if given a choice, would have stayed behind and married you and been the mother of your children. Years later, you still think of her often, although you are now married to another.

History and Theology: Muhammad Encounters Christians

Ibn Ishaq, the first biographer of Muhammad, tells of several encounters between Muhammad and Christians of one type or another. One was with a monk called Bahira, who was looking outside the window of his cell (room in a monastery) when a caravan passed by. He noticed a cloud overshadowing Muhammad, and when the caravan stopped, the branches of a tree stooped to give the Prophet shade. Bahira is said to have recognized the mantle of prophethood as some type of physical mark between his shoulders. [117] He told the caravan guards to watch over Muhammad as God had great things in store for him.

A second encounter occurred with Waraqa ibn Nawfal, a cousin of Muhammad's wife, who had some knowledge of the Torah and *Injil*. Upon hearing of Muhammad's manner of revelation, Waraqa assured him that the source was Allah. Muhammad had been so shaken by the first revelations that he feared that demons were harassing him. Waraqa has often been thought to have belonged to the Ebonite sect, and Khadija, Muhammad's wife, may have as well. The Ebonites accepted Jesus as Messiah, but not as divine. There are certainly parallels between what the Ebonites believed and what Muhammad preached. Because Muhammad believed in Jesus as Messiah but not divine, Muslims sometimes point out that Islam corrects both of the previous revelations. Judaism missed the mark by not acknowledging Jesus as Messiah, while Christians strayed from *Tawhid* (Monotheism) by claiming Jesus is God.

---

[117] Goddard, p. 18

A third encounter with Christians occurred when Muhammad sent a group of his followers who were forced to flee from Arabia to seek refuge in Axum in Abyssinia (Ethiopia). When the King of Axum interviewed these refugees and asked them who their leader was, Jafar ibn Abu Talib replied:

> *O King, we were an uncivilized people, worshipping idols, eating corpses, committing abominations, breaking natural ties, treating guests badly, and our strong devoured our weak. Thus, we were until God sent us an apostle whose lineage, truth, trustworthiness, and clemency we know. He summoned us to acknowledge God's unity and to worship him and to renounce the stones and images which we and our fathers formerly worshipped...He forbade us to commit abominations and to speak lies, and to devour the property of orphans, to vilify chaste women.[118]*

The Bishop then asked them to read any revealed word of their prophet. They read from Qur'an 19, the story of the birth of Jesus, from a surah that is actually entitled *Maryam* (Mary). The Bishop was quite impressed with the story and continued to shelter the refugees, thus saving the Muslim community from being wiped out in its very early stages.

A fourth encounter occurred when some Christians from Najran, most likely either Nestorian or Monophysite, met with Muhammad. He told them that they had not submitted to God if they believed that God had a son and if they worshipped the cross and ate pork. At that, the Christians retreated peacefully and returned home.[119]

The last encounter occurred when Muhammad sent letters to various kings, including some Christian kings, in Byzantium, Egypt, and Persia, to invite their people to Islam.

---

[118] Ibid. pps. 18,19
[119] Guillaume, A (1965) has translated the Ibn Ishaq biography as *The Life of Muhammad*, pps. 270-277

Why did Muhammad not become a Christian?

The Bible had not been translated into Arabic, the language of the Prophet Muhammad, until well after Islam had spread throughout the Middle East and beyond. We can only imagine what might have been if the Prophet was able to hear (I do not say read since the Prophet was allegedly illiterate) the Bible in his own language. We need to remember that much of the appeal of Islam to the Arabs was that in Muhammad the Arabs now had a prophet who was related to them ethnically and spoke their language. His revelations seemed to confirm the faith in one God as preached by Abraham and all of the other biblical prophets, including Jesus, but with Muhammad, the message came from one of their own. Allah spoke their language! A prophet had arisen who was not a Jew like most of the other prophets, but an Arab. Jews and Christians may have looked down on the Arabs as illiterate and uncultured Bedouin nomads. After all, the Jews had the Torah, the Psalms, and the Gospels, which were revealed to Moses, David, and Jesus, but the Arabs had no holy book[120]. Now they had the Holy Qur'an, the culmination of God's final word revealed through an Arab prophet

After Muhammad's victories, Arabic became the most holy of all languages and the Arabs the most blessed of all peoples. Why wasn't the Bible translated into Arabic? I have alluded to the despised status with which the Bedouin Arabs may have been regarded. Most likely, as Aramaic was a universal language at that time, and relatively close to Arabic, the Christian community may have felt that translating the Scriptures into Arabic was not a high priority. After all, few could read Arabic anyway. Furthermore, Aramaic was the language of Jesus.

---

[120] In Islamic understanding, the Torah was given to Musa (Moses), the Zebur (Psalms to Davud (David) and the Injil (Gospel) to Isa (Jesus). The Qur'an completes the three previous revelations. The vast majority of Muslims in the world have never read the other three revelations although virtually all Muslims say they believe in four holy books. As we will see later, the narrative for most Muslims is that the other three holy books have been changed or corrupted; only the Qur'an remains unchanged and uncorrupted.

Muhammad's Thoughts about Christians

Muhammad had quite positive things to say about Christians in the earlier revelations, especially toward the humble monks whose eyes overflowed with tears when they heard the truth (of what has been revealed to Muhammad)[121] Later he wrote more harshly about Christians when they did not recognize him as a prophet:

> *Certainly, they disbelieve who say: Allah, He is the Messiah, son of Mary. And the Messiah said: O Children of Israel, serve Allah, my Lord and your Lord. Surely, whoever associates others with Allah, Allah has forbidden to him the Garden and his abode is the Fire. And for the wrongdoers there will be no helpers. Certainly, they disbelieve who say Allah is the third of the three. And there is no God but One God. And if they desist not from what they say, a painful chastisement will surely befall such of them as disbelieve. (Qur'an 5:72-73)*

When you read the above verses, you will probably want to scream, saying, "Christians don't say that God is the Messiah (the Christ)." Nor do we say, "God is the third of the three." In short, we just do not know how much Muhammad understood about the Christological issues that Christians were debating.

A Story of Conversion in Muhammad's Time

As you continue reading this book, you will see that most conversions from Islam to Christ have occurred within the last few decades, but not all. I am indebted to my good friend, Rodney Tilley,[122] for the following story, which I have condensed.

In the city of Mecca in 615 A.D., a close partner to Muhammad, Ubayd-Allah ibn Jahsh, was one of the early Muslims who fled to Abyssinia (Ethiopia) to escape persecution at the hands of the Meccans. Ubayd-Allah was no ordinary man. He was Mohammad's cousin and the brother of Zainap bin Jahsh, one of Muhammad's

---

[121] Qur'an Surah 5:82-83
[122] Allan Rodney Tilley, *Finding Christ in Muslim Lands*

wives, who was formerly the wife of Muhammad's adopted son, Zayd.

While in Ethiopia, Ubayd-Allah ibn Jahsh became a follower of Christ and was baptized. He testified quite openly about his faith in Christ, saying in Jesus he had found the "Pearl of Great Price," and that he now saw clearly, while Muslims saw only with half-open eyes. Surprisingly, Ubay-Allah was not martyred; the Law of Apostasy that calls for death to those who leave Islam was not carried out on him. After his death, his wife returned to Mecca and became the Prophet Muhammad's tenth wife.

Throughout the history of Christian-Muslim relations, the vast majority of conversions have been from Christian to Muslim, at least until recently. However, throughout history, there have been many brave souls like Ubayd-Allah ibn Jahsh who believed on Jesus, despite great suffering and martyrdom.

Questions for Discussion and Reflection

- In the last chapter you put yourself in the shoes of a Jew hearing Muhammad's revelations. Now, put yourself in the shoes of a Christian who hears the Prophet seemingly misunderstanding your core beliefs such as the Trinity, the divinity of Jesus and his death on the cross. How might you have responded?

- Can you grasp how exciting it was for the early Muslims that the Seal of the Prophets was one of their own kin and the recipient of the Qur'an which completes the previous revelations? Do you suppose that they thought that those who do not become Muslims are crazy or just stupid?

- How might you have interpreted Muhammad's coming into the world in the way he did if you were living in Arabia at the time?

9

How Islam Became Dominant in the Arab World

Just imagine you are a member of one of the few Arab Christian families in Mecca during the time of the Prophet Muhammad. Most of your neighbors are pagans who believe in many gods. Others are *Hanifs*, Arabs who believe in one God but are neither Jew nor Christian. You mix with everyone because good relationships are essential in your business, but outside of work most of your social interaction is with your fellow-Christians.

You heard Muhammad preach about the one God Allah to his fellow Quraysh tribe and other Arab tribes. Few people listened very seriously, and you heard he escaped to Abyssinia for safety. Later he and a small band of followers fled to Yathrib. Muhammad's messages were ok with you. He told stories from the Torah and he said that Allah will accept all who believe in One God and who believe there will be a Judgment Day when all people will give an account to Allah. As long as he leaves you and your family alone, you are not too concerned with Muhammad and his message.

Ten or so years later, Muhammad comes back to Mecca with an army. Those who once mocked him and forced him to flee before submit to this new religion of Islam. People are relieved that, instead of taking revenge, he behaved graciously to all except a few who would not accept his prophethood. In a very short time, everyone around you is saying that Muhammad is a prophet. In fact, he is the Seal of the Prophets. He came to complete what Moses, Jesus and the other prophets preached before him. There were thousands of prophets, they claim, each to his own people, but Muhammad is the prophet for the whole world.

Your business partners, customers, and neighbors are exulting in their new found faith. Allah has chosen a descendant of Abraham and Ishmael, an Arab, as his final prophet! He has commissioned Muslims to bring Islam to the world. They ask why you would remain a Christian after Allah has revealed his perfect will to a fellow Arab.

History and Theology: Identity Issues

The former brilliant Yale historian Kenneth Scott Latourette points out that remnants of Arian Christianity remained in the Middle East, and those who held to it would have converted to Islam with much less hesitancy then Christians who held to Trinitarian theology. The simple reason was that Arian and Islamic theologies both denied the incarnation and divinity of Christ. [123]

Many of the people who were Islamizing were not ethnic Arabs. As they became Muslims, they took on not only the religion of Islam but also its Arabic language, leading many to consider themselves ethnic Arabs. Berbers, Kurds, Copts, Greeks, Assyrians, Armenians, and many others upon conversion were absorbed into Arab society and referred to themselves as Arabs. Later we will look at some of the peoples who became Muslims but have resisted taking on Arab identity.

Arabs today are the majority citizens in twenty-two countries, numbering at least 300 million people. At the time of Muhammad, however, Arabic was a peripheral language divided into many dialects. The Qur'an transformed it into a literary force. Now few people in the world speak Aramaic, the language of Jesus, while Arabic is one of the most widely spoken languages in the world.

---

[123] Latourette p. 306

The Dilemma of Arab Christians

After the Qur'an was revealed, Arab Christians were forced to face major theological and socio-cultural questions as well as issues of identity. Their fellow Arabs were rejoicing that Allah had revealed the greatest revelation ever, the Holy Qur'an, to them. Furthermore, the Arab people, once often looked own upon by others, had been commissioned to spread the message of Islam throughout the world. In their enthusiasm for the new faith, the early Muslims must have wondered why Christian Arabs would cling to a faith that was the legacy of the Jews and Byzantine Christians who had often regarded them as ignorant nomads. Allah had spoken his final revelation through one of their own! The rapid spread of Islam throughout Arabia and beyond gave further credence to the divine favor of Allah to the faith of the Prophet.

The brilliant scholar of Arab history, language and religion, Kenneth Cragg, states: "The unilateral relation of Arabic and the Qur'an is particularly the burden of Arab Christianity."[124] He goes on to say that Arabic was one of many languages mentioned on the Day of Pentecost, but with Islam came the glorification of the Arabic language and identity. Arab Christians must have suffered non-stop questioning about why they would stay Christians when Allah was so evidently favoring Islam. This appeared especially true in light of the Qur'an being revealed in Arabic, making it the most divine of languages, the one in which Allah choose to reveal his final, perfect revelation.

It must have seemed very logical to the newly converted Arabs that the Qur'an fulfilled and corrected the previous revelations given to Moses and Jesus. The Qur'an rebuked the Jews for their pride in assuming that they were the especially chosen people of God and in rejecting Jesus as Messiah. It rebuked Christians for saying that Allah is three and that he begat a son. The tragedy is that most likely the Qur'an was the first holy book written in Arabic. The Bible was

---

[124] Cragg *The Arab Christian* p. 32

finally translated into Arabic in Spain a couple of hundred years later. Cragg further states:

> *Though the Qur'an did have some favorable observations on Christians, it had only reproach for the core of Christian faith and for Christian factions, which as it saw them arose from Christian confusion...It has only impatience for what exercised the Christian mind in the defining councils of the fourth and fifth centuries.* [125]

Islamization did not happen overnight

It should be pointed out that conversion to Islam took longer than is generally assumed. Persia converted faster than Iraq, and Iraq converted faster than Syria. Egypt, which had a much stronger Christian presence than the other three regions, remained predominantly Christian until the tenth century.[126] In most places, the Muslims were a minority when they invaded a region. They invited people to Islam and established Islamic law and rule. If members of pagan tribes or nominally Christian professed Islam, they were exempt from further Muslim raids. As the *ummah grew*, Muslim warriors expanded their conquest further and further away from their home base. Gradually over many years and even centuries, people eventually became Muslims for a variety of reasons.

Factors other than religious zeal motivated the spread of early Arab Islam. Access to plunder and spoils of wealth and women were also great motivations for the early Arab armies as they have been for armies before and after the advent of Islam. To sanitize the early Arab Islamic armies, by saying it was only zeal for Allah and his prophet that motivated the early Muslims to risk their lives as they spread Islam quickly across the known world, would not be an accurate picture. On the other hand, to overly demonize the Islamic armies as interested only in wealth and sex with captured girls or

---

[125] Ibid p. 73
[126] Tejirim & Simon p.. 19

women is unfair. One would be hard-pressed historically to give examples of triumphant armies that did not plunder the defeated.

Richard Bulliet, perhaps the leading authority on the rates of conversion of Christians to Islam in the medieval period, affirms that it was a gradual process. The first to convert were the trendsetters. They converted to Islam when the majority of people were still holding onto their Christian (or pagan or other type of religious identity). When the Christians saw their former Christian brothers and sisters being given favorable positions in the new Islamic administration, the process of conversion accelerated until it became quite frequent. Over time, whether decades or centuries, the majority joined the *ummah*[127]. In the end, only a small minority refused conversion and remained in their former faith.[128] Rodney Stark, the renowned author and sociologist of religion, cites Bulliet's research that shows that it took at least 200 years for Syria, Iraq, Iran, Egypt, North Africa, and Spain for at least 50 percent of the people to convert to Islam.[129] Iraqi Professor John Joseph says that the Jacobite Christians after 500 years of Muslim rule were still a community of two million faithful with 20 metropolitans, and 103 bishops in Iraq, Syria, and Cyprus.[130]

We need to remember that the Qur'an was not yet in written form at this time. Probably the majority of Christians understood Islam to be another Christian sect or viewed Muslims as a group of invaders bent on plunder and booty. It took time for people to realize that a new religion, with much of its roots in Judaism and Christianity, came to supplant the faiths that preceded it. Many Christians thought that the Arabs or (Ishmaelites as they were often called) were the instruments of God to punish the spiritual and moral laxity of the Church. This helps explain why thousands of

---

[127] Bulliet, pps. 31,32. ; *Ummah* the Muslim community
[128] Goddard p. 63
[129] Stark, p. 32
[130] Joseph (1983) , p. 14

Christians sought a deeper spiritual life in monasteries that were scattered throughout the entire region.

As the Umayyad Caliphate passed to the Abbasids, the center of the Islamic world in the year 750 moved from Damascus to Baghdad. Muslims were still the minority among Miaphysite populations in Egypt, Syria, and Mesopotamia, and among the Church of the East Christians in Iraq and Persia.[131] It was not as if one day the Middle East was Christian, the next day Muslim.

When the Arab armies marched across the Middle East, they no doubt would have observed many people who were Christians in name only. They would also have seen many serious Christians seeking a deeper spiritual walk in monasteries. Muhammad himself said about some of the Christians, priests and monks, "Thou wilt find the nearest in friendship to the believers to be those who say, We are Christians. That is because there are priests and monks among them and because they are not proud."[132]

Just imagine you are a Coptic Christian living in Egypt while your homeland is rapidly becoming Muslim in the late seventh century. Your Church rejects the decree of the Council of Chalcedon and holds to its Miaphysite view of Christ (See chapter 6). Now on top of that, Arab invaders are commanding your people to submit to the new religion called Islam. If you remain Christians, you will have to pay the *jizya*[133] and submit to the rules for dhimmis[134], but your own

---

[131] Ye'or p. 63

[132] Qur'an 5:82

[133] The *jizya* was a poll tax that non-Muslims were required to pay as "protected" people under Islamic rule. The primary Qur'anic verse this is based on is 9:29. We will come back to the *jizya* frequently because of its importance in the conversion of many peoples to Islam.

[134] Dhimmis are "protected" mostly Jews and Christians under Islam. I will often be referring to this term and give a fuller explanation. At this point, think of *dhimmis* and *dhimmitude* as Jews and Christians being under their own religious leaders, but ultimately under the control of the Islamic regime in power, who can demand and tax their subjects as they see fit.

religious leaders will administrate your community's affairs as long as it is not contrary to Shari'a law.

At first, the Arab invaders seemed ok, but the *jizya* they are demanding is getting increasingly harder to pay, and they keep raising the amount. You hear that in many villages, the Arab invaders are killing your fellow Copts. In others, they are taxing the people to the point that they convert to Islam because they cannot afford the *jizya*. As a Coptic Christian, you know that you are the descendants of the indigenous people of Egypt, the heirs to the Pharaohs. Now you wonder whether your people will survive if the invaders keep up this level of coercion. You almost want to cry out to God, the words your Lord said while on the cross, "O my God, my God, why have you forsaken us?"

The Islamization of Egypt

The Christian faith was quite lively in Egypt before the advent of Islam. The city of Alexandria was one of the five major sees (centers) of the Catholic-Orthodox faith. St Anthony of Egypt was one of the founders of the monastic movement. After years of isolation, he had to contend with multitudes of Egyptians who joined him in the desert despite his desire to remain isolated. Stories of miraculous healings and deliverances from demons abound during St. Anthony's long life of over one hundred years. Many Egyptian Christians longed for a more demanding expression of faith than the church offered after the cessation of persecution. Often throughout church history, when conditions became "too comfortable" for Christians and persecution was rare, many sought what has been called" white martyrdom," or dying to self as a form of martyrdom, as opposed to "red martyrdom" or shedding blood for Christ's sake. By 300, Christianity had taken root among the Egyptian people in their own language rather than the foreign-imposed Greek language. For another 350 years before Islam, Christianity sank its roots deeper and deeper into the Egyptian soul.

In Egypt, many Coptic Christians considered the Arabs the instrument of God to punish the Byzantines for their corruption and heresy in accepting the decision of the Council at Chalcedon. Initially probably only 100,000 Arabs settled in Egypt, and they did not push hard for conversion of the people. If they had, they would have not been able to collect the *jizya,* which can only be collected from non-Muslims. After about 100 years of relative calm with few Christians converting, the amount of the *jiyza* was increased. By then Arab power over the people was too strong for rebellion. Over the next centuries, many more Christians converted simply because they could not afford the *jizya,* including 24,000 in the year 744 alone.

However, some historians record an even more dismal record of Egypt's Islamization. Mark Gabriel cites Iris al Massri, a highly respected Egyptian church historian, who estimates that four million Coptic Christians were killed in the first one hundred years after the Islamic invasion. They were forbidden to use their native tongue and forced to speak only Arabic. Those that persisted in speaking Coptic had their tongues cut out.[135]

The Coptic Church survived because it had networks of monasteries, village churches, and spiritual leaders to whom the local people could look up to instead of clergy appointed by the Byzantine rulers. The hierarchical nature of the Egyptian church, as well the status of Alexandria as one of the original Patriarchal Sees, also helped it survive. This has given the church a strong sense of identity. Furthermore, Copts had a sense of being the true Egyptians, unlike the Muslims who had converted through the invading Arabs hundreds of years later.

Saint Mark, the alleged founder of Egyptian Christianity, and author of the second Gospel, would probably be proud that even after so much suffering, between 10 and 15 percent of the population of Egypt is still Christian today.

---

[135] Cited in Gabriel *Islam and the Jews* p. 52

Current Issue: The War against the Copts

Throughout the 1,400 years that Christianity and Islam have co-existed in Egypt, there have been ferocious attacks on Christians, like the one carried out in Cairo by the Islamic State in 2016. Suicide bombers attacked the Church of St. Peter and St. Paul and killed 25 people, mostly women. There have been many similar attacks throughout the centuries.

In Egypt, almost all Coptic Christian boys and men and many girls and women wear a small tattoo of a cross on their wrists, a mark of distinction as a Christian minority. Samuel Tadros in *The Atlantic* tells the story of 13-year-old Tony Atef's experience when he attempted to compete in junior soccer tryouts at Egypt's most successful soccer club. He scored two goals, and the coach was about to tell Tony that he was accepted on the team, an absolute dream for the boy. Then the coach noticed the small cross on his wrist. He sent Tony home and gave him no place on the team.[136] Tadros writes that there is not one Copt among the league's top 540 players, which is quite ridiculous in light of the fact that between 10 and 15 percent of Egypt's population is Christian, mostly Coptic. Besides discrimination on the football field, no Copt is allowed in the state security or intelligence services. An unofficial one percent quota for Copts is maintained in the military, police, judiciary and Foreign Service.[137]

As in most parts of the Islamic world, the country's textbooks say little about non-Muslims' contributions to society. Muslims are often misinformed about Coptic beliefs and practices. Tadros tells the story of a Coptic journalist who was asked by a coworker where her soon-to-be husband would spend his wedding night. The question seemed to be based on the movie *Braveheart,* in which the English lords had the right of the first night with the new bride. The Coptic woman's co-worker assumed that this was the norm among

---

[136] Samuel Tadros in *The Atlantic.* December 17, 2016
[137] Ibid.

Christians, including the Copts in Egypt. Rumors abound that Coptic doctors hope to retake Egypt by performing abortions on Muslim women. As a result, no Copt has been allowed to become an OB-GYN professor in any Egyptian university.[138]

Egypt's Loss is America's Gain

Over a million Copts now live in the West where there are over 600 Coptic churches. In 1971, there was one Coptic Church in the United States. Today there are 235. Coptic churches are flourishing in Sub-Saharan Africa and over a half-million Africans have joined it.[139]

In the Twin Cities, there are two Coptic churches that reach out not only to the Egyptian community but to other communities as well. I have had the privilege of teaching at one of the churches and participating in the Divine Liturgy and in special festivals. I believe it may be the best-educated church in the Twin Cities. Almost everyone you meet at the church is a doctor, an IT engineer, a pharmacist, or some other highly educated professional.

Truly, Egypt's tragic persecution and discrimination of the Copts and other Christians both Catholic and those of various Protestant denominations, have forced the "cream of the crop" to leave Egypt to benefit the societies to which they have fled.

Just imagine you are an Arab Christian father raising your family in a region of North Africa where Islam is rapidly expanding in the seventh century. Your people have been Miaphysite Christians for centuries. The Arab invaders are your ethnic kin and they do not care about the Creed of Chalcedon. Your fellow Arabs who believe in the religion of Muhammad have begun to rule according to Shari 'a (Islamic law). Christians are still a slight majority in your village, but Muslims have the power and they administrate the governance of your small city. Your teen-age son has many questions. "Dad," he asks, "Why do the Muslims seem to win every battle when they fight

---

[138] Ibid
[139] Ibid

against us Christians? Why do we have to live as dhimmis and pay the jizya? We have to wear special clothes, we cannot repair our churches, and we have to ride donkeys and not horses. If someone wants to sue us on false charges, they will win every time in court. If a Muslim man wants to marry my sister, he is allowed to do so. But if I fall in love with a Muslim girl, we cannot get married. Muslims can try to convert me to Islam, but I cannot share what we believe with them. If a Muslim should convert to our faith, he would probably be killed, but if one of us converts to their religion, there is a big celebration. Let's face it, Dad. Muslims can plunder their enemies and take their booty and marry their women. Our Bible says to turn the other cheek and to do good to those who mistreat you. A guy made fun of me yesterday. He said, 'Christians have three gods and are allowed to have only one wife. In Islam, we have one God and we can have four wives. We will win and you will lose!' Dad, is he right? Why don't we say the shahada and join the ummah (Muslim community)? We can still secretly believe that Jesus is the son of God."

Dhimmitude

The topic of *dhimmitude* comes up constantly throughout this book due to its pivotal role in Christian-Muslim relations. In his classic work, *A History of the Arab Peoples,* Albert Hourani points out that Islamic law demanded that Jewish and Christian families be differentiated from the Muslim community. They had to wear special clothes and avoid certain colors, in particular green, the color of Islam. They could not carry arms, ride horses, build new places of worship or repair old places without permission. (This has been a big issue in Egypt even in current times where churches have sat in disrepair for decades because its members are unable to make any improvements.) As stated in the story above, a Muslim man could marry a Christian or Jewish woman, but never the other way around. Conversions could only be one way: Jewish or Christian to Muslim, never from Islam to Judaism or Christianity.[140]

Until the 13th century, almost all Christian ministry in Asia, Africa and the Middle East had begun in Syrian or North African churches. We have seen how Edessa was a center of the Church of the East. Later its headquarters moved to Nusaybin, which became a center from which the church spread the gospel throughout the Middle East and Central Asia. Ethnic classification and geography have changed over the centuries. Today Edessa and Nusaybin are in southeast Turkey, and Arbella, another center of the Church of the East, now known as Erbil, is the capital of the Kurdish region of Iraq. Nevertheless, when Islam came into the world, those regions were part of what was called Syria.

Slavery

The jihad slave system included the enslavement of both genders in conformity to treaties of submission. When the emir[141] conquered Libya in 643, Jewish and Christian Berbers[142] were required to give their wives and children as part of the jizya. From 652-1276, Nubia[143] had to send slaves from their own people to Cairo. Under the Umayyads and Abbasids, an annual quota of slaves was demanded. In Ephesus, 7,000 Greeks were deported into captivity, and further east the Seljuk Sultan Alparslan (Alp Arslan) took many Georgian and Armenian slaves while decimating major populations. In 1268, the Mamluks killed the men of Antioch and enslaved the women and youth. There are many other accounts that could be cited.[144]

---

[140] Hourani p. 117

[141] Emir-a military commander

[142] Berbers were among the indigenous peoples of North Africa. Many have been absorbed into Arab identity, while others have resisted Arabization, and are reasserting their distinct identity.

[143] Nubia-a place whose people were mostly Christians at one time before Islamization. They can be mostly found in Sudan

[144] Ye'or p. 108-113. She gives other examples of the treatment of *dhimmis* in these throughout her books.

Islamic law recognizes slavery but states that a freeborn Muslim cannot be enslaved. Slaves were generally non-Muslims captured in battle or the children of parents born into slavery. Some slaves were used in agriculture, but the majority were domestic slaves and concubines.[145]

Islamization of Syria

Damascus, then as now, was a very important city. Most of its Arab inhabitants were in the 7th century were still Christians. Arabs, who had recently become Muslims, then began to invade the region. Perhaps Arab Christians may have felt closer to their ethnic kin who had Islamized than they did to their fellow Christians of Greek, Roman, or Armenian ethnic origin.

Syria remained strongly Christian for quite a time span. Of four million people, perhaps 250,000 converted to Islam soon after the conquest. Under the Umayyad dynasty, Christians faced the destruction of their churches and property in addition to many petty types of discrimination. They were forced also to wear distinctive yellow clothing, a foretaste of how European "Christian" societies in the mid-twentieth century marked the Jews as distinct from the Christian population.[146]

Life was not all bad, however, especially in the earlier days. One Nestorian bishop wrote in 649 that "these Arabs do not fight against our Christian religion, but rather they defend our faith, they revere our priests and Saints, and they make gifts to our churches and monasteries."[147] Unfortunately, this early tolerance did not last as we will see.

When Muslims invaded an area, not all the people, or even the majority, converted to Islam immediately. Egypt and Persia (639-643) were next to come under Arab rule, then the rest of North Africa and much of Byzantium and Persia. Between the years 710-714, the

---

[145] Hourani, p. 116
[146] MaCullough p.262
[147] Ibid p. 263

Umayyad Caliphate established Islamic law from Spain in the West to the Indus valley in the east, ruling from Damascus until 750. With the defeat of Caliph Marwan II by Abbas in 750, Caliph al-Mansur ruled what became known as the Abbasid caliphate, which ruled from Baghdad until 1258 when it fell to the Mongols.[148]

Under the first four caliphs, Abu Bakr, Umar, 'Uthman, Ali and their Umayyad successors, Muslims overcame Persian armies and took Babylon, Mesopotamia, Armenia and Persia. In the West, they conquered Christian provinces of the eastern Mediterranean, including Syria, Palestine, Egypt, and North Africa and on to Spain.[149] In Babylon, some Christian Arabs fought on the Persian side, but others were attracted by the possibility of booty and fought with the Muslims.[150]

Islamization of Iraq

Baghdad replaced Damascus as the center of the Caliphate, which lasted for another 500 years.[151] The eastward shift of the Muslims benefited the Church of the East more than it did the Miaphysites and Melkites. During this time, Christian patriarchs were given official jurisdiction over the Christians from Egypt into Central Asia.

Courbag and Fargues write that judging by the records of *jizya* revenue, about two-thirds of what is today Iraq and beyond converted to Islam within 50 years after the Arab invasion, making Iraq's population consist of six million Muslims and three million Christians.[152] This shows a faster rate of conversion than Bulliet's estimate that it took over two hundred years until Christians were

---

[148] Maalove p. 27
[149] Ye'or p. 43
[150] Ibid p. 46
[151] The Caliphate refers to the administrative head of the Islamic world, both politically and spiritually. The Umayyad Caliphate ruled from Damascus for almost a hundred years from the mid-600s until 750. This was followed by the Abbasid Caliphate, which ruled from Baghdad from about 750 until 1258 with the coming of the Mongols.
[152] Courbage & Fargues, p. 6

no longer the majority of the population. It is difficult to ascertain exact numbers based primarily on the payment or lack of payment of the *jizya*. We do know that the Christian population of Iraq has been greatly reduced from the initial Muslim conquest in the seventh century until today.

It is sad to have to admit what Hourani says, that the coming of Islam improved the position of the Church of the East Christians and Miaphysite churches, freeing the people despite being *dhimmis* into important roles in society under their own patriarchs. That these two branches of Christians felt freer under dhimmitude than they did under Byzantine rule, shows us how tragic division within the Body of Christ can be.

Islamization of North Africa

Christianity gave way to Islam quite rapidly in North Africa. The predominantly Arab-populated North Africa is often included with the Middle East as the heart of the Islamic world. North Africa was once a center of Christian activity, but relatively quickly, the church was greatly reduced, especially outside of the major cities. North Africa was almost completely Muslim by the 12th century. How did this happen?

Early church leaders from North Africa included Augustine, Tertullian, Cyprian, Clement, Origen, Athanasius, and Cyril of Alexandria. These names are among the most prominent of the early Church Fathers who figured largely in the shaping of early Christianity. Even today, Catholic, Orthodox, and Protestant theologians consult their writings for theological clarification. Jenkins points out that the Coptic Church in Egypt has flourished (although not without much difficulty at times) while the rest of North Africa has very little evidence of its Christian heritage. In the late fifth century, North Africa had five or six hundred bishops, but fifty years after the Arab conquests, Muslim rulers were apologizing to the caliphs that they could no longer provide Christian slaves because Christians were so rare. [153]

The Arabs arrived in North Africa in 697. Most of the Latin-speaking church officials and upper classes fled to Italy and Spain. The Berbers, who often preferred to be called *Amazigh* (free people), made up the majority of the population, and most were either non-Christians or nominally Christian. They had little reason to resist conversion to Islam.

Lessons to be Learned from Failure

The failure of Christianity to survive in North Africa was due to the churches' failure to evangelize the people outside of the Romanized inhabitants of the city. The Arab conquerors lived a lifestyle that was similar to the Amazighs, the indigenous people of North Africa. Their way of life was mostly nomadic. This was very different from the urbanized Latin culture in the big cities. Christianity seemed foreign to the Amazigh majority. The last references to Christianity in North Africa go back to 1049 in Libya, 1091 in Tunisia, 1150 in Algeria and 1300 in Morocco. In about 500 years, Christianity had totally disappeared except for a very small remnant[154].

The major lesson we can learn from North Africa is how essential it is for faith to become indigenous, so that people really "own it." It has to become "ours." The Latinized philosophical Christianity of the urban dwellers did not sink its roots deep into the native, indigenous peoples of the region. They would become among Islam's greatest defenders in the days ahead. Egypt and Ethiopia were the exceptions, as they both had indigenous churches that worshipped in the language of the people, and the Christians in these lands embraced Christianity as their own true faith.[155] They both also had translations of the Scriptures in their heart languages.

---

[153] Jenkins, p. 228
[154] Courbage and Phillippe (pps. 39-41)
[155] Jenkins p. 229

Again, this is not the final word. As we will see later, the Lord is doing a fresh work in North Africa among the Berber tribes, and many are returning to the faith that preceded Islam in their homeland. This time, it appears that the people are truly making the faith of Jesus their own.

Early Stories of Martyrdom

An Orthodox Christian historian, Yurij Mazimov, tells of two martyrdoms under Ali, Muhammad's nephew and son-in-law who became the fourth caliph of the Islamic world. One martyr was a Muslim who had come to faith in Christ. When he refused to renounce his faith, Ali killed him and would not give his body to his relatives for burial. Another Muslim believed on Christ and would not recant, boldly declaring "I know that Jesus is the Son of God." Ali and others stamped on him until he died, then burnt his body.[156] Even in the earliest days of Islam, some Muslims embraced Jesus despite knowing that it might very well cost them their lives.

The Syrian Refugee Crisis can have a Silver Lining

A 2017 issue of *Global Post* tells the story of Abu Radwan and his family who are from Homs, Syria. They fled from Syria to Lebanon in the early stages of the civil war that has ravished Syria. Abu Radwan was raised in a Muslim family, and much to his surprise, Jesus appeared to him in a dream. He began to go to church, and seven months later, he became a Christian. The pastor who baptized Abu Radwan and his family says he has baptized around 100 Muslim Syrian refugees since 2011. There are big risks in becoming a Christian. Abu Radwan has been under threat from his own tribe for converting, and he has been stabbed with a knife.[157]

Many other pastors have also seen Syrian refugees come to Christ, but have kept their identities secret, fearing reprisals from Islamist groups like ISIS. No one knows exactly how many Syrian refugees

---

[156] Maximov, J. (2010) *A History of Orthodox Missions among Muslims. Retrieved from https:/orthodoxwiki.org* Thanks to Rodney Tilley for informing me about this site.
[157] Story was recorded on *Global Post* and *Pri.org* 3/3/2017

have become Christians. We will examine the refugee situation further in chapter 26.

Questions for Discussion and Reflection

- What does Cragg mean by the statement, "The unilateral relation of Arabic and the Qur'an is particularly the burden of Arab Christianity?"
- Why do you think the Coptic boys and men and many girls and women insist on wearing the tattoo of the cross? Do you think it might be wiser for them not to display their Christianity so outwardly?
- Put yourself in the position of the Christian young person in last "just imagine" story. How do you think his father might best address the issues that the son has raised, and encourage him not to convert to Islam?
- Comment on life as a *dhimmi*. What do you think would be the most difficult aspect for you if you were a dhimmi?

10

The Persians Become Muslims, But Resist its Language and Culture

Just **imagine** you are a Zoroastrian Persian soon after the Arab Muslims came into your land. It has been said that the Arab Prophet Muhammad himself invited the Persians to embrace Islam. You heard he also invited the Byzantine Romans, your longtime enemies, to do the same. You are a Persian—a people with a proud history. At one time, you had the largest empire the world had ever seen. The rulers and powerful people among you laugh at the gall of uncivilized Arabs to invite you to accept their religion and rule.

However great Persia might have been at one time, it is not so great now. The people pay high taxes. They feel oppressed and neglected by their rulers. The Arabs begin to come into your villages and call you to Islam. At first, many of the people resisted and died fighting. But many of your fellow Persians say that the Arab *jizya* is less than the tax money your own rulers require. At first, the Arabs destroyed some of your fire-temples but now they understand that Zoroastrians believe in only One God, and they treat you as People of the Book as they do Jews and Christians. Some Persians submit to Islam, while others remain followers of Zoroaster. Among Jews and Christians living in Persia, it is the same. Some convert to the Arab religion, while others remain in their own faith and become *dhimmis*. Some of the wealthy people convert to Islam in order not to pay the *jizya*. After all, there are many similarities between the religions, especially about life after death in either Paradise or Hell.

For now, you are keeping the faith of your ancestors. But if the advantages of converting to Islam outweigh the disadvantages, you will convert.

> *...at whatever moment he dies eighty maiden angels will come to meet him with flowers...and a golden bedstead, and they will speak thus: do not fear etc.... And his fruitful work, in the form of divine princess, a virgin, will come before him, immortal...and she herself will guide him to heaven.*[158]

History and theology: Islamization of the Persians

It is not much of a stretch to see the parallels between the *houri*[159] promised to Muslim warriors who die in jihad and the maiden angels and the divine virgin princess who guide one to heaven in Zoroastrianism.

As mentioned in the "imagine story," the Byzantines and Persians had been warring against each other for centuries. Before his death, the Prophet Muhammad invited them both to submit to Islam. The Persians had a proud history. Imagine how the Persian rulers felt when they received a letter or some form of communication from someone named Muhammad inviting them to Islam. The audacity of some unknown self-proclaimed prophet of a god called Allah to implore the Persians, who already honor their own God. After all, Ashura Mazda revealed their religion to the Prophet Zoroaster many centuries before the Arab prophet. The nerve to order them to submit to a new religion called Islam when all over Persia were fire temples to Ashura Mazda, where the fires are never allowed to be extinguished.

---

[158] Cited in Axworthy, pps. 74-75.

[159] A lot of critical media-coverage of Islam focuses on *Houris*, the dark-eyed beautiful virgins who inhabit Paradise, The hope of being rewarded with 70 (some say 72) beautiful *houris* if a Muslim dies in a jihad, has been used to motivate suicide bombers and to urge bravery on Muslim troops in battle. Apologists for Islam, often spiritualize this idea, and say that *houris* are the purified souls in heaven and are not a promise of unlimited sex in the next life.

Michael Axworthy, a British scholar specializing in Persian/Iranian studies, writes that the Arab invasion of Persia in 637 came after centuries of war against the Byzantine Empire. The royal Arab army defeated Persian King Yazdegerd III, opening the door for them to take all of Mesopotamia (mostly in what is today Iraq). The Arabs defeated the Persian king again near Hamadan (in today's Iran) in 641, which set in motion the invasion of the entirety of Persia.[160]

There was not a large loss of life when the Arab Muslims conquered Persia. The people were allowed to practice their Zoroastrian faith. Initially, some fire temples were destroyed, but as the Arabs begin to accept the Persians as believers in one God and not polytheists, they gave local people relative freedom to live as dhimmis under their own religious leaders as did the Jews and Christians. Arabs did demand the *jizya,* but the people were already paying taxes to Persian rulers. In some cases, the Arabs demanded less tax money than their own rulers did, and as is true today, people "voted" with their pocketbooks. If submission to Arab rule was less a hardship financially than submission to their own rulers, why would impoverished peasants not submit to Arab rule and religion? Besides the poor, however, there was also great wealth. Arabic sources say that the treasures of the Persians and their kings were distributed among the conquerors, and the booty, said without shame, included girls.[161]

Comparing Zoroaster and Muhammad

There are many interesting comparisons between the lives of Zoroaster and Muhammad despite the fact that the former preceded the later by at least 1,200 years. Daniel Shayesteh, a Persian scholar, is a former Muslim who is now a Christ-follower. He lists many parallels, which I have reduced to just a few key ones. Both Zoroaster and Muhammad grew up in polytheistic (belief in multiple gods) environments. Both spent much time meditating in caves. They had limited success in their ministries in their early

---

[160] Axworthy, p. 72
[161] Kennedy, p. 124

years until they moved to new cities. They both legitimized holy war against idol-worshippers and pagans. They destroyed idols and established their own belief in one God. They reportedly journeyed to heaven and ordered their followers to pray five times a day after washing ceremonially. They were influenced by pagan beliefs and Judaism, as Jews dwelt both in Persia in Zoroaster's time (569-492 B.C)[162] and in Arabia in Muhammad's time (570-623 A.D.) Perhaps most important, they believed that after death both the righteous and unrighteous will enter hell. Those whose good deeds outweigh their bad will cross over a narrow bridge on a string as thin as a piece of hair and enter heaven (paradise). Those who were unrighteous will plunge into hell and remain there.[163]

Once the Persian army was defeated, the conquerors were quite merciful. They did not massacre townspeople or villagers. In reality, it was loss of identity more than direct persecution that led many Persians to resent Islam. Kennedy points out that in Egypt, no one spoke Arabic in 600 AD, but by 12th century, everyone spoke it. In Persia, no one spoke Arabic in 600, and by 1200, still no one spoke it.[164] That resistance to Arabization continues on to this day, as we will see later.

(150 years later) Just imagine you are a missionary of the Church of the East in the year 800. Your bishop and hero is Timothy, the Patriarch of your church. He oversees hundreds of missionaries, thousands of churches and monasteries, and millions of Christians. He meets regularly with the Muslim caliph and they engage in respectful dialogues. You heard horror stories of what it was like to be a Persian Christian under the Zoroastrian kings, because they associated Christians with their Roman enemies. Now under the Muslim caliphate, neither the Byzantines nor the Zoroastrians threaten you. Yes, you have to pay the *jizya*, and there are other rules that you have to follow as a conquered people, but for now, relations

---

[162] The dates for the life of Zoroaster vary from the 7th century BCE to several centuries earlier
[163] Shayesteh, pps. 17-19
[164] Kennedy, p. 199

are not too bad between the people of the cross and the followers of the Arab Prophet.

Your missionary order preaches up and down the Silk Road where you run into many ethnic, tribal, and religious groups speaking so many languages that you wish that the Tower of Babel could be reversed! Many types of goods, from noodles to exotic silks, are being transported between China and Italy, passing through Anatolia, Persia, Central Asia, India, and China. You run into Buddhists, Hindus, Zoroastrians, Manadeans[165], Jews, Shamanists, Christians, and increasingly people who call themselves Muslims, but whom most people call Arabs, Saracens, or Ishmaelites.

You are implementing what Bishop Timothy encourages you to do--preach the Gospel, live simply, and look for bridges to build relationships with those adherents of other religions. He tells you to try not to argue, and to study their beliefs and practices so that you can better relate the story of Jesus to them. Patriarch Timothy himself has read the Qur'an many times, and he never puts down the Qur'an or Muhammad. He tries to point them to Jesus as the one who can satisfy their spiritual hunger. You and your fellow missionaries are emulating Timothy, whether preaching to Buddhists, Zoroastrians, Muslims, or whomever else you encounter.

---

[165] Manadeans were an ethno-religious monotheistic sect that followed their prophet Mani. They were dualistic in that they believed in the sphere of light and sphere of darkness, somewhat akin to Zoroastrianism. Small communities of Manadeans have remained in Iraq and Persia until the present day and have suffered much persecution.

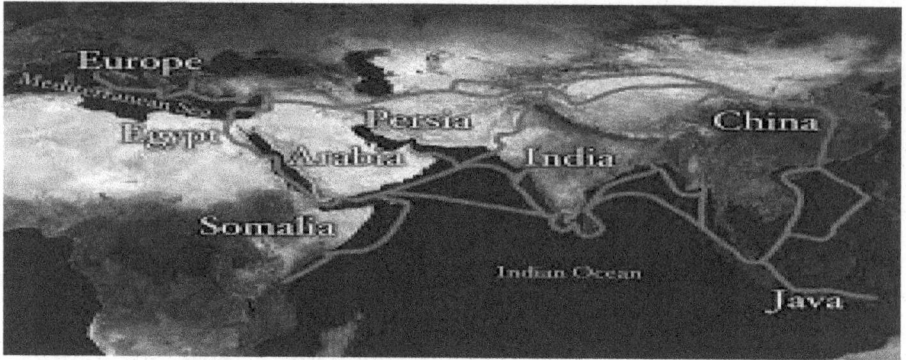

The Famous Silk Road

Christians doing Prostrations? Who is Influencing whom?

A number of years ago, I had a chance to attend a lecture given by then-Penn State University Professor Phillip Jenkins, author of *The Next Christendom,* and numerous other books related to church history. His lecture was based on his recent book, *The Lost History of Christianity* (2008), a book I eagerly devoured as one who has lived in places where Christianity has been "lost." Dr. Jenkins made the statement that if Jesus were to come back today, he would be more at home in a mosque than in a typical evangelical church. He then in a humorous way put up his hands in a defensive position as if to fend off any objects thrown at him for that statement. During the Q&A time after his lecture, I had a chance to say to the audience that I have been to many worship services in churches that date back to the earliest days of the spread of Christianity in the Middle East. From a ritualistic (liturgical) perspective, Dr. Jenkins is right. I still remember the shock I felt the first time I walked into a church that dates back to the third century in southeast Turkey and watched the priest and the faithful remnant in that 99 percent Muslim city perform prostrations that closely resembled the Muslim way of prayer. I asked the priest afterwards if the Christians are emulating the ways Muslims pray in order to attract them to Christianity. He replied that the eastern churches[166] had been praying with prostrations for 500 years before Islam conquered the Middle East. In fact, as Jenkins confirms, the issue that distinguished Christian prayer from Muslim prayer was not prostrations, as they both did that. Christians prostrated before icons and relied on bells to call them to prayer, whereas Muslims do not use icons and were called to prayer by a *muezzin* (the person who calls Muslims to prayer). He went on to say that the month of fasting during Ramadan was a practice that Muslims most likely borrowed from eastern Christians who also performed rigorous fasts during the Lenten season.

Similarities between Eastern Churches and Islamic Liturgy

I designed a chart that demonstrates some of the similarities between worship in the eastern churches, which continues in very limited locations, and Islamic worship. It needs to be remembered that the earliest Christians were Jews who maintained many of the ways of worship that they had learned at synagogues. Most likely, the Islamic pattern of worship was influenced by the liturgical practices that they observed as they invaded the regions where eastern churches existed. Of course, some rituals, Muslim did not adopt. They do not cross themselves, burn incense, or kiss the imam's hand as they leave the mosque. The famous Hagia Sophia in Constantinople was the center of the Orthodox Christian world for 1,000 years until it became a mosque in 1453. Mosques built throughout the Middle East reflect the architecture of that famous church. (See picture in chapter 15). From a liturgical and cultural perspective, Jesus and the early Christians probably would be more comfortable in a mosque than in the contemporary Western church.

---

[166] The Church of the East, Orthodox Oriental Churches, and Orthodox Churches that accepted the Chalcedon declaration all worshipped in ways that Muslims most likely learned from and adapted. My purpose here is to examine the manner in which these pre-Islam Christians worshipped. In this chapter, when I use the phrase "eastern churches" I am referring to any of the above churches.

Worship in Eastern Churches before Islam	Worship in Islam
Fountain to wash before prayer	Fountain to wash before prayer
Bell 3x daily called people to prayer	Muezzin calls to prayer 5x daily
Removal of shoes upon entering church	Removal of shoes upon entering mosque
Separating of genders during worship so as not to distract men. Women's hair covered	Women located in back of men so as not to distract men. Women's hair covered
Scripture is chanted in Aramaic and expounded on in language of the people	Qur'an is chanted in Arabic and expounded on in language of the people
Prostrations performed by all who are able	Prostrations performed by all who are able
Rigid fast for 40 plus days to prepare for Easter season	Fasting from sun-up to sun-down during month of Ramadan

Patriarch Timothy, an Unknown Christian Hero

For over forty years from 780-823, Patriarch Timothy launched a missionary movement that sent Church of the East missionaries as far as China to proclaim the gospel. They travelled up and down the Silk Road across the Middle East, the vast regions of Central Asia, and even further east. They journeyed through what is today India and Pakistan, as far as central China, to spread the gospel. Remember, this was before jet travel or any type of transport beyond animal caravans and on foot.

During the initial spread of Islam from the time of the Prophet through the first caliphs, the Church of the East maintained bishoprics, metropolitans, churches, and monasteries. Timothy was appointed head over all Christians under Abbasid rule. There are still over 200 of his letters that have survived. In one letter, Timothy says that he appointed a bishop in Tibet, while in another he discusses a king among the Turks becoming a Christian. Letters from Yemen and India came to him seeking counsel.[167] Without a doubt, Timothy had more bishops and Christians under his administrative care than the Pope did at that time. During his over forty-year reign beginning in 778, Timothy had good relations with five Muslim sultans, and he entered into Islamic-Christian dialogue with them and Islamic scholars.

What Think Ye of Muhammad? A Conciliatory Approach

Patriarch Timothy debated Caliph Mahdi, the supreme ruler of the Islamic world, in an oft-cited dialogue of mutual respect. When the Caliph asked Timothy what he thought about Muhammad, he commended Muhammad for declaring the oneness of God, separating people from idolatry and polytheism, and teaching them to do good works. The Patriarch further stated, "Muhammad taught about God, His Word, and His Spirit, and since all the prophets had prophesied about God, His Word, and His Spirit, Muhammad walked, therefore, in the path of the prophets." [168] Moffett goes on to cite the Muslim caliph saying to Patriarch Timothy, "If you (only) accepted Muhammad as a prophet, your words would be beautiful and your meanings fine". To this Timothy graciously replied, "May God grant to us that we may...share it (the precious pearl of the faith) with you...We pray God who is King of Kings and Lord of Lords, to preserve the kingdom and the throne of the Commander of the Faithful (the caliph) for multitudinous days and numerous years.[50]

---

[167] Moffett, p. 285
[168] Ibid, p. 351

It was under Timothy's reign that saw the Assyrian[169] missionaries erect their famous monument in China so that in the later years of the eighth century, the Church of the East's reach went as far east as China.[170] Because he was considered a heretic and his ministry was conducted in the east, not in the west, however, he is almost unknown to most Western Christians.

During Patriarch Timothy's time, around a quarter of all Christians saw Timothy as their spiritual leader. [171] A later Assyrian patriarch in Baghdad in the early tenth century counted some 250 bishops and perhaps twelve million adherents out of a worldwide population of 270 million, of which 50 million were Christians.[172]

How did Christians View Islam?

Scottish Historian Hugh Kennedy tells an interesting story concerning the Old Testament Prophet, Daniel. Daniel was highly revered in Persia and was buried in Susa. Some monks and priests taunted the Muslims that no one could take Susa unless the Antichrist was in their army because the city was supernaturally protected because it harbored Daniel's tomb. However, one of the commanders kicked the lock to one of the gates and the gate opened. After that, the monks had to cry out for mercy.[173]

Professor Hugh Goddard says there were three ways Christians understood Islam just before the time of Timothy: 1) fulfilment of God's promise to Abraham and his son Ishmael; 2) judgement on Christians who accepted the ruling of the Council of Chalcedon; 3) as a Christian heresy.[174] Those who saw Islam as a fulfilment of God's promise to Abraham and Ishmael, especially if they felt an

---

[169] Sometimes the Church of the East was also called the Assyrian Church of the East. Sometimes rather than repeatedly writing Church of the East, I have shortened the phrase to simply "Assyrian Christians."
[170] Ibid, p. 52
[171] McCulloch, p. 267
[172] Ibid, p. 376
[173] Kennedy, p. 129
[174] Goddard, p. 36

ethnic connection, would have embraced Islam with much less resistance than those who viewed it as a Christian heresy. For some today, Timothy's dialogues with the Caliph are models of inter-religious dialogue at its best. For others, the Patriarch is an example of a Christian who, for the sake of not offending Muslims, was unwilling to speak the full truth about the essential differences between Christians and Muslims. Throughout the 1,400 years of Christian-Muslim engagement, there are many models of conciliatory approaches like Timothy and the Caliph demonstrated toward one another, and there are many examples of confrontational approaches. We will examine some of each as we proceed. Paul's admonition to "speak the truth in love" (Ephesians 4:15) is absolutely essential in communicating the truth claims of our Savior to Muslims, while also demonstrating God's love.

Patriarch Timothy's Prayers

Several times in this book, I have mentioned that God may well be listening to the prayers of long-deceased saints and their prayers for the people and places where they preached the gospel. In the fifth chapter of the book of Revelation, we see that the Lamb of God has purchased for God persons from every tribe and language and people and nation, and made them to be a kingdom and a priesthood to serve our God and reign with him on earth. The verse before that great missionary verse shows us a picture of the twenty-four elders falling down before the Lamb. Each one had a harp and held a golden bowl full of incense, which are the prayers of God's people. (Revelation 5:8-9). I believe Patriarch Timothy and faithful members of eastern churches have contributed to that great volume of prayer for the people and places we have been discussing throughout this book. In many of the places where Timothy once gave spiritual guidance and pastoral oversight, including the Middle East, Central Asia, South Asia and China, the Lord is doing a new work among peoples who have not had the gospel before. Arabs, Persians, Turks, Kurds, and many other peoples who lived in places for which Timothy no doubt prayed for many times, will join the heavenly throng, singing the songs of the redeemed in praise to the Lamb of God, slain from the foundation of the world.

Questions for Discussion and Reflection

- Do you think that the Patriarch Timothy was too conciliatory toward the Prophet Muhammad after reading about the Prophet's life in previous chapters?
- Comparing the chart concerning the Church of the East with Islamic practice and worship, what stands out to you? Should Christians today draw on some of the ways that Christians used to worship that might appeal to Muslims more than Western styles of worship?

II

The Kurds as Magi, Jews, Christians and Muslims

Just imagine it is the year 1988, and you live in a place you call
Kurdistan,) land of the Kurds), but officially known as Iraq or
Northern Iraq. Despite the Kurds having been Muslims for
centuries, you have been curious for a long time about your history
before Islam. In your city of Zakho, there is a section they call the
Jewish quarter. It is empty of Jews now, but everyone knows Jews
used to live in your city until Israel became a state and the Jews
migrated there. There are a couple of small quarters where
Christians dwell as well. They pretty much stay to themselves and
speak their own language, but most of them speak Kurdish as well.
There are also Yezidis who are shunned by many Kurds, although
they speak Kurdish and their religion predates Islam. They are
sometimes called "devil worshippers" by devout Muslims. The few
Yezidis you know seem like good people who just want to live in
quietly in peace.

Saddam Hussein has ruled your land with an iron fist since coming
to power in 1979. In 1988, Saddam feared the Kurds were going to
rebel against his rule and he launched the Anfal campaign. He
totally leveled 4,000 villages and killed almost 200,000 people. His
pilots dropped chemical weapons on Halabja, and 5,000 Kurds died
in one horrible night. He built prisons in which tens of thousands of
men were killed. Those that he did not kill he forced into collective
villages to so he could control them more easily. Your people have
always been farmers and shepherds, raising sheep and goats in the

valleys and mountains in your beautiful homeland. Saddam reduced you to beggars who are dependent on the government for your monthly rations.

Saddam also forced Arabization on your people. Schools are conducted primarily in Arabic. All official documents are in Arabic. Once when you were in primary school, one of your friends spoke up in class and said that Saladin, your national hero, was a Kurd. The teacher, who was an Arab, beat the kid with a ruler and said that Saladin, the one who took back Jerusalem from the Crusaders, was an Arab. All of your history has been suppressed, and you know almost nothing besides what the Arabic textbooks published in Baghdad want you to know.

You know that the borders between your people were established without your consent. Your people thought that after World War I they would have their own homeland, but the Treaty of Sevres was abolished, and the Lausanne Agreement squashed that hope. You know that across the mountains and rivers, not far from you, are millions of Kurds living in Turkey, Iran and Syria, No official maps, however, have Kurdistan written on them. Your people all mourn that you are the largest people group in the world without their own homeland. How often have you heard the words, "The Kurds have no friends but the mountains." The mountains have been your refuge and security when tyrants rise and seek to harm your people. You flee to the mountains to survive to fight another day. What pains you so much is that your oppressors are fellow Muslims. In Iraq and Syria, it is the Arabs. In Turkey, it is the Turks. In Iran, it is the Iranians. All call themselves Muslims. Yet all oppress your people.

Three Years Later

Just Imagine it is now 1991, after the War in Kuwait, the American President George H.W. Bush encouraged the Kurds and the Shi'a Muslims in the south of Iraq to rebel against Saddam's regime. Everyone thought Saddam had been weakened by the American bombing and military operation to free Kuwait in the first Gulf War.

We Kurds rose up and won some early victories and pushed back Saddam's troops. Then we realized that Saddam was as sly as a fox. He kept back his best troops, the Iraqi Republican Guard, in case the Iraqi people would try to get out from under his rule. His tanks and superior weapons drove a million and a half Kurds to the mountains where they crossed over into Iran or Turkey.

My family lived in the city and were not directly involved in the uprising against Saddam. This does not mean that we supported him, but we tried to stay out of it. We knew that our people were freezing to death in the mountains and that neither the Western powers nor our fellow Muslim Arabs did a thing. Ironically, some aid came from Israel, the only country that denounced Saddam when he launched the Anfal Operation three years ago.

As the American people watched the news about the Kurds suffering on the mountains, they demanded that their government take action. Finally, aid came. Then the United Nations with US backing ordered Saddam out of Northern Iraq. Since 1991, the Kurds have had a degree of autonomy even though we are still a part of Iraq.

I am an engineer and a university graduate who speaks good English. I was able to be hired by an NGO (non-government organization) to oversee a massive construction project to bring Kurds back from the mountains, refugee camps in Turkey and Iran, and the forced collective villages to rebuild their ancestral villages. While we oversaw the distribution of construction supplies to build the simple shelters and village schools, I got to know some of the foreigners who came to help us. Many were Americans, and some were British, German, Dutch and from other western countries. Some of them said they were followers of Christ, and that God called them to Kurdistan to help our people. One of them in particular asked me if I knew that the Kurds can be traced back to the Prophet Nuh (Noah). He mentioned that the grandson of Nuh was named Madai, the father of the Medes. Well, we Kurds always said we are the descendants of the Medes. This man than told me other stories from what Muslims call the Tawrat. He pointed out how the Jews were exiled to the Habor River in the Land of the Medes over 2,700 years ago. Now I understood why we had a Jewish quarter in my city, and why there are tens of thousands of Kurdish Jews in Israel. Maybe that is why the Jews sent us relief supplies in 1988. The rest of the world did not speak out against Saddam for fear he would cut off their supply of oil.

The American also mentioned the story of Daniel in the Lion's Den. After the Lord saved Daniel from the lion's den, King Darius the MEDE called on all the people of his kingdom to honor the God of Daniel. Perhaps many Kurds choose Judaism as a result and intermarried with the descendants of the Jewish exiles? He also mentioned the Magi. I had heard of the Magi, who were a tribe of Kurds from Persia who studied the stars. They were Zoroastrians before they became Muslims. The American told me that the Magi were the first people besides the Jews to recognize and worship the Isa Mesih (the Messiah). Finally, he asked me if I knew why some Kurds are still Christians even though the vast majority are now Muslims. Then he pointed out the story in the Injil about the Day of Pentecost, and how the Apostles spoke in the Median language. Some of them came and preached about Jesus to the Kurds hundreds of years before Islam.

The American did not want to speak against Islam but I told him I know Islam had been forced on the Kurds beginning over 1,000 years ago. I told him my people have had great agony because no Muslim country stood up for us when Saddam was destroying our land and killing our people. All the Muslims in the world speak out against the Jews when they mistreat the Palestinians, but Kurds have suffered far more than the Palestinians have. The Jews have never murdered 200,000 Palestinians or dropped bombs that killed 5,000 in one night.

There was no Bible in Kurdish but I had been educated in Arabic and English, so I was able to read the stories in the Bible the American told me about. When they began to translate the Bible into Kurdish, I was one of the translation checkers, and gave feedback to the team made up of foreigners and Kurds.

There is so much about the faith of that American NGO worker that draws me. We Kurds, however, have been Muslims for a long time. I think my whole family would turn against me if I left Islam. They say they do not like the Arabs, but Islam is still their religion.

History and Theology

A significant body of archaeological evidence points to the Kurdish mountains as the site of the invention of agriculture, approximately 12,000 years ago (Braidwood, 1960). From the Kurdish mountains, the revolutionary technology later spread into the neighboring lowlands of Mesopotamia, the hills of Anatolia, and the plateau of Iran. By about 8,000 years ago, it had further spread into North Africa, Europe, and the Indian subcontinent. As such, Kurdistan is the point of origin for many crops and domesticated animals.[175] Mehrdad, R. Izady, (Kurdish historian)

Conversion of the Kurds to Islam

The city of Haran, where Abraham passed through on his way from Mesopotamia to the Promised Land, is not far from Urfa and the Turkish government has maintained some houses that may resemble what houses looked like in Abraham's time. (See photo in this chapter).

Arab armies who had recently converted to Islam conquered Mesopotamia (today's Iraq) by 637.[176] During the Umayyad (AD 661-750) and the Abbasid periods (AD 750-1299), Kurds at times rebelled against Arab rule. However, with time, it was economically and socially advantageous for Kurds to submit to Islam. Even as late as the thirteenth century many if not most Kurds were trying to maintain their Yezidi (Yazidi) identity. Because many remained in the Yezidi faith, while others stayed Jewish and Christian, Arab governance must not have been overly oppressive, at least not in the earlier days of Islamic rule.

---

[175] Irzady, pp. 23-24
[176] McDowell, p. 21

There are some similarities between the Islamization of the Kurds and the Persians. After all, for centuries the Medes and Persians had been living and ruling together. This is demonstrated in the Bible, especially in the books of Daniel and Esther where it states that the Law of the Medes and Persians cannot be repealed (Dan 6:8; Esther 1:9). We know that it was under King Cyrus that the Persians became the stronger of the two peoples, whereas, before Cyrus, the Medes were the stronger of the "cousins." For the Arabs, Islam provided a strong sense of identity and pride that one of their own was the final messenger of Allah. For the Turks, Islam gave them a faith to believe in, fight for, and the impetus to establish one of the greatest empires of all time, the Ottoman Empire. Both the Persians and the Kurds over time Islamized, but both peoples have resisted absorption into Arabic culture. The Kurds remain stateless and are oppressed to varying degrees by the Arabs, Turks, and Persians. They have maintained a sense of *Kurdayati*[177] from their more powerful neighbors through their language, folklore, dress, and other cultural distinctives. To be a Kurd it to be a Muslim, yet perhaps not to the degree that it is for Turks or Arabs. By maintaining *Kurdayati*, the Kurds have resisted Arabization, yet the Kurds can be among the most conservative Muslims in Turkey and in Iraq.

Who are the Yezidis?

The long-suffering Yezidi people were given a much higher profile as ISIS jihadists invaded the Yezidis' home province of Shinar in 2014. Thousands of Yezidis were killed, especially men, while the girls and women were often used as sex slaves or sold to be exploited by the wealthy. Yezidi boys were often brainwashed into radical Islam. The Yezidis claim to have experienced over 70 genocides in their history, but they have never gotten much global attention except for the recent suffering at the hands of ISIS. Tragically, many thousands of Yezidis are still unaccounted for despite ISIS being

---

[177] *Kurdayati* is the term the Kurds use to express their sense of being distinct from their Arab, Turkish and Persian neighbors who seek to assimilate them into the majority culture. It speaks of resistance but also a positive sense of Kurdish pride.

driven out of their homeland. Yezidism is often considered the indigenous religion of the Kurdish people. (See below footnote for a brief overview of Yezidism.)[178]

Kurdish Jews

From the time of the Neo-Assyrian Empires (1180-609 B.C.), a large community of exiled Jews dwelt in what is today Iraqi Kurdistan. In a book tracing the history of ethnic cleansing, Andrew Bell-Fialkoff affirms the biblical account of the Jewish exile, stating that 27,290 Israelites, mostly of the upper classes, were exiled to Gozan and Media near Zakho in 721 BC.[179] Again confirming the biblical account, about 124 years later, about 10,000 leading citizens from the southern kingdom of Judah were exiled when the Babylonians conquered it. These Jews were successful in converting almost all of central Kurdistan to Judaism. In the biblical account of the well-known story of Daniel in the lion's den, King Darius was tricked into having Daniel thrown into a den of hungry lions. When no harm came to Daniel, the king had those who had tricked him and their families thrown into the den, and lions devoured them immediately. This event may have been one factor that led many of the King's subjects, including the ancestors of the Kurds, to accept Judaism. Remember that the King commanded that all of the subjects should follow the God of Daniel after his great deliverance (Daniel 6:26). The Kurdish historian Izady, while not mentioning the story of

---

[178]Yezidism has been compared with Zoroastrianism, the indigenous religion of the Persians. Both are dualistic and have a lot of focus on angels, but there are many differences as well. In the Yazidi religion, the dualism is between God and *Melek Tawus*, the Peacock Angel, who needs to be placated so no harm comes to the community. *Melek Tawus* will ultimately repent and be restored to divine favor. Sheikh Adi is the patron saint and said to have attained his divinity through transmigration, and is now one with Melek Tawus and a reincarnation of the Peacock Angel himself. The Yezidis have been considered "Devil worshippers" by the Arabs and persecuted by their fellow Kurds as well. There have been some positive steps by Kurdish Muslims to see the Yezidis as fellow Kurds and not to oppress them. Nevertheless, some Yezidis accused the Kurdish Pershmerga troops of not trying as hard to battle against ISIS as they would have if the Sinjar province was predominately Muslim rather than Yezidi.

[179] Bell-Fialkoff p. 7

Daniel in the lion's den, says the Talmud reports that the Assyrian King Shalmaneser III (858-824 B.C.) settled Jewish deportees in Kurdistan 2,800 years ago. The Talmud says that Jew were given permission by the rabbinic authorities to convert local Kurds. [180] Two years after the modern state of Israel was created in 1948, Kurdish Jews by the tens of thousands left Kurdistan to move to the newly created land. I think it is very possible that not just one tribe, but many Jewish people, were absorbed into the Median people as they lived together for centuries and no doubt there was some intermarriage between the Jewish exiles and the local Medes/Kurds.

Further connecting the Kurds and Kurdistan with the Bible, Irzady points out that the tombs of the prophets Nahum, Jonah, Daniel, Habakkuk and Queen Esther and Mordecai, are all buried in various parts of Kurdistan. [181]

Where did blond-haired, blue-eyed Kurds come from?

There is also a bit of mythology about Kurdish origins that Kurds sometimes humorously tell. The famous biblical King Solomon wanted some fair-haired women to add to his harem, which was full of darker-haired women. He sent his angels to northern Europe, but the angels could not resist the fair-haired beauties, and had sexual relations with them. In his anger, King Solomon banished their offspring to the Zagros Mountains, where the Kurds reside today. This bit of folklore explains why a minority of Kurds are blue-eyed and fair-haired among a majority of people who are generally brown-eyed and olive or brown in skin color..

I have discussed the controversies raised by conflicts over Christology in Iraq, Syria, Persia and Egypt. The regions in which the Kurds resided were not isolated from the controversy either. The areas surrounding the heavily Kurdish cities today of Diyarbakir,

---

[180] Irzady p. 162
[181] Ibid p. 162

Mardin and Midyat in southeastern Turkey, were old Jacobite centers (Miaphysite Christian) as early as the sixth century.

Haran, where houses like Abraham's have been restored

Kurds as Victims, Villains, and Heroes

The Kurds have been portrayed as victims in most recent history. As mentioned before the world stood silent during the Anfal Operation in 1988 while Saddam was butchering the Kurds. They were driven to the mountains to seek refuge from Saddam again in 1991, but this time the world became aware of their plight. Since then they have lived within their own piece of Iraq, in what has been called the "Other Iraq." While the rest of Iraq has been torn apart by sectarian violence and destruction, Kurdistan has been transformed into an almost European like country. Shopping malls, five-star hotels, universities, luxury restaurants, and the latest technology is readily available. The transformation from the time my family and I lived there, when there was destruction everywhere and no electricity for two years, is incredible to behold.

The Kurds' recent battle against the ISIS jihadists, that resulted in 11,000 Kurdish deaths, while defeating one of the most brutal fighting forces in recent times, gained the admiration of the world. The way the Kurds fought so bravely was commended by the

American troops who assisted the Kurds with weapons and logistics. The Kurds also allow their women to fight. The bravery displayed by Peshmerga[182] women defending their homeland against the jihadi has gained them deep respect. There is also the issue that many ISIS warriors believed that if they died at the hands of a woman, they would not go to Paradise, which further worked to demoralize some of the jihadists.

Kurdish Female Peshmerga

Historically, the Kurds have often oppressed their Christian neighbors, which usually had been instigated by those in power, especially in Ottoman times. Fearing an Armenian takeover (with the help of the Russians) of their lands and property, the Kurds did much of the dirty work in the slaughter of the Armenians in 1915. As mentioned earlier, some Kurdish *agahs* (tribal leaders) also exploited the Christians and plundered them, and took their

---

[182] *Peshmerga* literally means "those who face death." The Kurdish fighting forces, are called by that name.

girls/women as wives. There are also many accounts of Kurds who risked their lives to defend their Christian neighbors.

A Kurdish Story of Grace

Ishmael (not his real name) is originally from the Kurdish region of Iraq. He is extremely intelligent, a born leader. He was the chief engineer of the non-government organization (NGO) that I worked with during the 1990s. Ishmael oversaw the construction of thousands of shelters, schools, clinics, and roads, and often translated for me as I was trying to learn Kurdish while working with the NGO. Many NGOs were Christian organizations that focused on rebuilding various sectors of Kurdistan after Saddam Hussein's destruction of 4,000 villages and the killing of 180,000 Kurds during the Anfal Operation in 1988. Ishmael was not a very devout Muslim, and he was more than glad to translate not only work-related topics but spiritual matters as well.

One Easter I met with many of our engineers, laborers, guards, and other workers at our NGO as we gathered near the Habur River. Right across the border was the Syria of the Assad family, who have caused so much destruction in that land, and continues to do so today. To the south of us was Iraq and Saddam Hussein, who was still a threat to the Kurds during the early 1990s. To the east was Iran, where Kurds have often also often been severely oppressed. We were also quite close to the border with Turkey, another country that has had major conflicts with the Kurds. I preached that day that every one of those countries' leaders, perceived as enemies of the Kurds, was going to fall or die in the near future, while Jesus is still alive after 2,000 years, and each of them needed to place their faith in the crucified and resurrected Savior.

Ishmael eventually was notified that his long-awaited immigration papers to a western nation had been approved. I hated to lose Ishmael, but no one could blame anyone for leaving, as the situation in Kurdistan seemed hopeless. Not only were the Kurds' external enemies--the governments of Syria, Iran, Iraq and Turkey-- in opposition to any type of autonomy for the Kurds, but the two major

Kurdish parties were in a civil war against each other that was far more disheartening to the Kurds than their external enemies were.

When Ishmael arrived in the western country, he was shocked. The only Christians he had known were the strong believers who had come to Kurdistan to help the Kurds and to share the love of Jesus in a culturally sensitive way. The vast majority of the people in the western nation lived what he perceived as very immoral lives, with little sexual restraint and broken families. In reaction, he became a much more devout Muslim in the West than he had ever been in Muslim Iraq. After a period, however, of doing all the requirements of prayer, fasting, giving of alms, and reciting the Qur'an, Ishmael still felt empty and no nearer to God. What especially drove Ishmael out of Islam, however, was investigating the life of Muhammad. The more he read about him, the more he realized that he could not take him any longer as a spiritual leader or example.

He began to cry out to Allah, "O Allah, I have tried to please you as a Muslim, and I cannot believe you would want me to be like these westerners. Show me what I must do!" Ishmael says that the Lord spoke clearly to him saying, "Son, follow the way of Jesus as a Kurd." Ishmael then realized that following Jesus was the path between western license and Islamic legalism. *Xude* (God in Kurdish) had created him as a Kurd and he would be a Kurd who lived for Jesus. In Ishmael's fellowship there are well over one hundred other Jesus-followers who meet and worship the Jesus who has showed himself to each of them in the context of their Kurdish-Islamic culture.

Questions for Discussion and Reflection

- As the Kurds learn more about their pre-Islamic roots, do you think it will lead to more interest in Judaism or Christianity? Why or why not?
- Do you know other ethnic or religious groups that have been denied learning about their historical heritage? Give any examples you can think of, and whether any efforts are being made to address the issue.

12

The Turks Dominate Islam and Threaten Europe

Just imagine you are a young man of Turkic origin living along the Silk Road in the eleventh century. Your tribe is all-important to you. You were trained for battle at an early age, and you are an excellent archer and swordsman. You believe in Tangri, the great but distant god. You need supernatural help to defend your tribe against your enemies, both human and unseen enemies in the spirit world. Shamans, both men, and women, are consulted in discerning adverse events that happen to people in your tribe. When misfortunes like disease or military defeats occur, your people ask the shamans, "who caused this to happen?" "Did someone curse us?" "Did someone of our tribe commit a taboo?" The Shamans tried to discern where the problem lay, and then reverse the effect of the curse or taboo.

Many of your tribe are saying that your people need a religion that is bigger than just your tribe. Along the Silk Road, you see Buddhist monks. They beg for food, live in monasteries, and spend a lot of time chanting and meditating. You also see Christian monks who live in monasteries like the Buddhists. They also recite their sacred writings and preach about a crucified man who rose from the dead and was God in human form. There are also people who call themselves Muslims. They do not have monasteries, at least not like Buddhists and Christians have, as their religious men marry and have children. In fact, many of them have more than one wife, as your people often do. They also believe that their religion allows them to fight against their enemies, and if they win, they can take the other tribe's plunder of wealth, women and children. The Muslims seem to be growing the fastest, and their God, whom they call Allah, seems to be really working on their behalf. As a young man trained for war, sitting in a monastery chanting when you could be out battling against other tribes, and taking plunder, including beautiful girls, is much more like the customs of your people. With Islam, you have the right to fight in this life, and if you die in battle against infidel forces, you will be assured of going to Paradise, where there are rivers of wine and beautiful virgins to gain. Maybe living with other men, chanting and meditating is ok for some, but for you and your people, the Islamic way is more appealing.

History and Theology: Conversion of the Turks and Turkey

> *Turkish Islam was dedicated from the start to the defense or advancement of the faith and power of Islam, and never lost this militant quality. It was born on the eastern frontier against heathendom, was carried to the western frontier against Christendom, and took control of the caliphate at a time when Islam itself had to be defended against the threefold attack of the Eastern heathen, the Western Christian, and the internal heretic.*[183]

The Turks were a nomadic people, primarily Shamanistic in faith. Some Turks had some exposure to Buddhism and the Church of the East. Patriarch Timothy tells of a king of the Turks who became a Christian and asked for a metropolitan (office higher than a bishopric) for them. Timothy also wrote of ordaining a bishop for the Turks. By the ninth century, Samarkand (now in Uzbekistan, Central Asia) had become a metropolitanate of the Church of the East, and by the tenth century, the Church of the East had reached east Turkestan.[184]

---

[183] Lewis, p. 95
[184] Rassam, p. 39

Most likely, the Turks were searching for a faith to which to devote themselves--a faith that would not forbid them from fighting for honor and booty. It would also unify them around a cause both in this world and in the world to come. Islam was that faith. The Turks did not have a long history of empire or a superior culture that spread to other peoples like the Persians could boast. Along the Silk Road, perhaps the Turks saw that Christianity and Buddhism were world-denying faiths. Both honored celibacy. Both discouraged the pursuit of wealth. Both discouraged fighting and taking plunder from one's enemies. Islam was much closer to the traditional Turkic-Mongol way of life than the other religions along the Silk Road were.

By the 11th century, the majority of Anatolia (today's Turkey) was still Christian. Marco Polo commented that 200 years after the battle of Manzikert, in eastern Turkey which took place in 1071, the Turks were a minority in a land populated by Greeks and Armenians. Close to one-half of the population was Christian in 1200. Latourette says that in the eleventh century, there were massive conversions of Turks to Islam, yet at the end of the twelfth century, there were enough Turkish Christians in Persia and Mesopotamia that Christian literature was prepared for them. Their final mass conversion to Islam did not occur until the thirteenth and fourteenth centuries.[185]

Shamanism, Buddhism, Manicheism[186] and the Church of the East influenced the kind of Islam practiced by the Turks. In the earlier days, Muslims and Christians even shared places of worship, honored some of the same saints, and celebrated the same feasts.

---

[185] Latorette, p. 275

[186] Manicheism was a Persian religion dating back to the third century. It focused on the dualistic battle between the forces of light and spirit against the forces of darkness and the material.

Followers of Jalal al Din Rumi (Mevlana) (1207-1273)[187] who were Sunni Sufis, and the Bekasi order, which was a Shi'ite (Alevi) branch of Islam, saw both branches spread across Anatolia and influenced more people to embrace Islam than the negative factors that we saw in other places, such as the inability to pay the jizya. Mixed marriages between the Christians and the more recent arrival of Muslim Turks probably influenced more Christians to become Muslims than massacres did.

Three major events have contributed much to the condition of the church in what is today Turkey. First, there was the Seljuk invasion beginning at Manzikert in eastern Turkey in 1071. The Seljuks (eventually merging into the Turkish Ottoman Empire) moved west over the next 400 years until the capture of the grand prize of Constantinople in 1453 (See chapter 15). Second, was the Crusades. Third, was the Mongol invasions that deeply divided the Christians and led to much suffering. I will come back to these themes later in the book.

The Seljuks Replace the Arabs

The armies of the Seljuk Turks marched against Byzantine armies, took Jerusalem, and prevented pilgrims from making pilgrimage, which eventually led to the Crusades. By the beginning of the eleventh century, the Seljuk-Turkish army began to take over sections of the Abbasid Caliphate. Eventually they became the real custodians of the Islamic empire rather than Arabs. They also overran Armenia in 1064 and as mentioned above, Manzikert in eastern Turkey in 1071, which paved the way for the total takeover of Anatolia.[188]

One of their early leaders, Imad al-Din Zangi, treated the indigenous Christians with tolerance, but his son, Nur al-Din Zangi,

---

[187] It is interesting to see that Jalal al Din Rumi of Persian ancestry who settled in Konya, Turkey has become incredibly popular. Books of his sayings and poetry sell well in American bookstores.
[188] Latourette Vol 2, pps. 387, 393,394

was very harsh toward them. Dinno cites Michael the Great, a prominent Christian leader of that time about the destruction of Edessa (today's Urfa) that at the time was center of the Church of the East. Its theological school had sent out missionaries around the world. Dinno says what Michael wrote about the fall of Edessa in 1146, resembled a lament of Jeremiah:

> *The Turks with rattling swords and lances entered the city to drink the blood of old men and children, of women and men, of priests and deacons, of monks and anchorites, of nuns and virgins, of children of tender years, and of bridegrooms and brides...The city of Abgar, the friend of Christ, was trodden because of OUR sins (capitols added by this author)....What a calamity! Fathers deserted their own children and mothers lost compassion for their children...others gathered their children like a hen and her chicks. waiting to die or be taken captive. Some older priests carried with them coffins containing relics of saints and martyrs. When they saw this affliction, they repeated the word of the Prophet (Micah 7:9) 'I will bear the indignation of the Lord because I have sinned against him.' They did not escape but kept praying until the sword silenced them. Their bodies were found later stained with their own blood while their hands clung to the coffins of relics of the saints.*[189]

Dinno again cites Michael the Syrian that in the two occupations of Edessa by the Turks in 1144 and 1146, some 30,000 were killed, and 16,000 were taken captive. No women or children remained uncaptured with some killed and others scattered throughout the region. Only a thousand men made it to safety.[190] Wherever the Turks fought, both Islamization and Turkification followed. Greek, Latin, Serbian, Bulgarian, Hungarian, Arabic, and Turkish sources all verify this process[191]

---

[189] Dinno, pps. 13,14
[190] Ibid, p. 14
[191] Ye'or, p. 53

As the first wave of Islamization of Christians and other non-Muslims was primarily Arab, the Turks led the second. After the defeat of the Byzantine armies at Manzikert, the Turks invaded their way west, taking more and more land and bringing more people into subjugation. In the thirteenth century, the Mongol advance brought more Turkic nomads into the region. Osman Ghazi (1299-1326) was the chief of the tribe of Oghuz Turks, from which the Ottoman (Turkish-Osmanli) whose followers established the Ottoman Empire.[192] By the fifteenth century, the Turks had conquered much of Eastern Europe until defeats in Lepanto in 1571 and Vienna in 1529 and 1683, when the Empire began to decline.

Questions for Discussion and Reflection

- The author mentioned that Buddhism and Christianity seemed to be world-denying religions, whereas Islam was more in line with Turkic-Mongol values. What might Christians have done to make their faith more appealing to the Seljuks?
- Think of the terms "world denying" and "world affirming". Could these categories still describe Christianity and Islam today? How?

---

[192] Ibid, p. 53

13

Russia, Central Asia, and Communism

(This chapter connects a number of events over several centuries. For that reason, I have placed the "just imagine" section later in the chapter, after first reporting the conversion of the Slavic peoples to Orthodox Christianity and summarizing the Great Schism when Christianity divided into Catholicism and Eastern Orthodoxy. Then we will look at the conversion to Islam of the 200 million plus Turkic people of the world, and why some have become followers of Jesus Christ, especially after the collapse of Communism in 1991. Each of these topics is related to one another, despite having taken place over a long time in many diverse places).

The Conversion of the Russians

In 988 Prince Vladimir, ruler of the Slavic/Russian people,[193] sent his envoys across the known world to choose a religion for his people. The story goes that his envoys visited Jewish synagogues, Catholic churches and monasteries, and Muslim mosques, but none of them stood out to the envoys. When they arrived in Constantinople, however, they attended the Divine Liturgy at the Church of the Holy

---

[193] Slavic people include Russian, Ukrainians, Byelorussians, Bulgarians, Serbs, Croatians, Macedonians, Czechs, Slovaks, Bosnians, Slovenians, Poles and others. The Poles, Czechs, Slovaks, and Croats are predominately Roman Catholics, whereas most of the other Slavic people have remained at least nominally Orthodox over the centuries, although some have converted to Islam, especially the Bosnians and other minorities.

Wisdom (*Hagia Sophia*)[194]. They viewed the procession of the priests, smelled the holy incense, and were overwhelmed by the magnificent architecture, the golden icons and frescoes, which told the entire biblical story on its walls and ceilings. They were said to have proclaimed in absolute awe, "This is as close to heaven as one can get on earth." Orthodoxy has been the religion of most of the Slavic people ever since (despite the Communist era from 1917-1990 when communist-atheism became the official ideology).

Division between Catholicism and Orthodoxy

Throughout this book, I have often used the phrase Catholic/Orthodox Church. After 1054, however, the two terms must be differentiated. Until that fatal year, the Church was still one Church. What is now the center of the Catholic Church was in Rome, while the political seat of the Empire was in Constantinople, the new Rome. Until 1054, the churches that adhered to the Council of Chalcedon and united by the Nicene Creed were still one church.

What were some of the factors that led to the Great Schism? There were linguistic, cultural, personality, power and theological issues. Latin became the lingua franca of the West, while in the East, the Greek language was dominant. In the West, theology was understood more through the lens of Roman law, whereas in the East, theology was greatly influenced by Greek philosophy. In matters of practice, the Roman church used unleavened bread in the mass, whereas the East used leavened bread. In the West, priests were increasingly required to be celibate, whereas in the East, parish priests could marry, but those aspiring to be bishops or higher in rank had to be celibate. In the West, the power was increasingly in the hands of the Bishop of Rome, the Pope. In the East, there were patriarchs over various geographical regions. Perhaps for modern Christians the most important reason for division may seem trivial, but it was not for the people of that time. That is the matter of the *Filioque* (Latin "and the son"). The Western Church added to the

---

[194] See chapter 15 for a picture of the Hagia Sophia

Nicene Creed the phrase "the Holy Spirit proceeds from the Father and the Son." The Eastern Church resisted changing the phrase, and has stuck to the original phrase "the Holy Spirit proceeds from the Father." According to their understanding, the Spirit proceeds through the Son rather than from the Son. Orthodox theologians say that the *Filioque* compromises the distinct identity of each person of the Trinity, whereas Catholic theologians claim that the Orthodox understanding can lead to the unity of the nature of God being compromised.

There are other differences in regards to the doctrine of purgatory, a somewhat different understanding of the Immaculate Conception, and authority to decide how Scripture is to be interpreted. In later years, there have been attempts at reconciliation, particularly by the Polish Pope, John Paul II. As of this writing, since 1054, there has been no formal union between the two churches. With the beginning of Protestantism in the sixteenth century, Christian unity took another huge hit.

Just Imagine you are from a Turkic tribe in Central Asia called the Kerait. You live by grazing animals and raiding other tribes. Manliness is gained by fighting ability and sexual prowess.

Your tribe seemingly out of nowhere gets word that your king has accepted a religion that you know nothing about. You hear that he was lost and close to death in the high mountains in your homeland, when he had a vison of someone who said he would be spared if he believed in Christ. Who is this Christ, and to which tribe does he belong? You have no idea. Will this Christ help you defeat other tribes in battle? How much will he demand of the plunder you take from other tribes? Will he want the most beautiful girls for his own pleasure?

The Kerait Turks

Around the year 1000, the Kerait Turks from Central Asia became Christians. This happened when the Kerait king was lost in the high mountains and had a vision of a saint who said that if the king would believe in Christ, he would lead him so that he would not perish.

The king returned safely and Christians sent him to the archbishop of Merv, who baptized 200,000 Keraits. They were the first of the Turkic tribes to befriend Yesugei, a small chieftain of an insignificant sub-clan, who became the father of Genghis Kahn.

Genghis defeated the Kerait Turks in battle, but he married the oldest daughter of the brother of the defeated chief. Dr. Richard and Jewel Showalter, as they explored the legacy of the Church of the East along the Silk Road write, "Her younger sister he gave as a wife to his oldest son, and the third daughter, Sorkaktani, he gave in marriage to his fourth son, Tolui. Thus there were three Christian Turkish sisters married to khans of the Great Mongol Empire." [195]

Sorkaktani was a strong believer, and after her husband died young, she raised four sons as a widow. Her first son, Mongke, served as Great Khan and her second son was the great Kublai Khan who ruled the Mongol Empire at its peak (1260-1294). Her third son, Hulegu, ruled the southeastern part of the Empire under his brother Kublai. A fourth son rebelled against his brother and lost his succession to the throne. [196]

The Showalters ask if the great Turkic-Mongol civilization that ranges from Istanbul to Xi'an, China, could be on the verge of reopening its doors to the descendants of Sorkaktani, the godly mother of three of the most influential sons in Central Asian history. We know that China is experiencing great spiritual harvest, and Central Asia stands on the threshold of perhaps a new day. In China the rain has begun, and in Central Asia, the rain clouds are growing. [197] To understand how miraculous a major turning to Christ among the Turkic-Mongol peoples would be, we need to look at both their Islamization and their life under Communism.

---

[195] Showalters p. 98
[196] Ibid pps. 99-100.
[197] Ibid p. 100

The Islamization of the Turkic-Mongol Peoples

The Mongol empire at its height extended from Europe to the Pacific Ocean, and included most of China, Manchuria, Mongolia, Central Asia, northern India, Persia, Mesopotamia and Russia. Dinno says it was the largest contiguous empire in history, ranging from the Danube River in Europe to the Sea of Japan, and from the Arctic to Cambodia, comprising 100 million people.[198]

Genghis Khan, the founder of the Mongol Empire, died in 1227, and named his son as his successor as the Mongol Empire spread across Eurasia from Eastern Europe to China. The Mongolians, coming out of today's Mongolia and Western China, caused great horror throughout Central Asia, the Middle East, and Europe. While they are thought to have been bloodthirsty murderers bent on plunder and destruction of their enemies, in reality, they were very open to knowledge from the people that they conquered. Most Mongol rulers were pluralists in religion, and several flirted with Christianity. They were originally Shamanists who believed that God was the Great Spirit whose presence was active in nature. They mimicked the life of totem animals, much like the Indians of North America. [199] Their Shamanistic beliefs and practices were mixed with Buddhist and even Christian ideas because many Mongols had Christian wives who had been led to the Christian faith by Church of the East missionaries. In many places, Christians were highly placed in the Mongol courts and greatly respected. With Islam seen increasingly as a threat, some Christians looked to the Mongols as their hope of getting out from under the yoke of Islam. So Mongols and Christians teamed together until toward the end of the 13th century when gradually more Mongol rulers became Muslims.

The Silk Road was a crossroads of many peoples and religions in the seventh and eighth centuries. In 651-652, Muslims conquered Khorasan, an area that spans northeastern Iran, southern

---

[198] Dinno, p. 17
[199] Glasse, Encyclopedia of Islam, p. 358

Turkmenistan and northern Afghanistan. After defeating the Chinese Tang dynasty in 751, the Muslims solidified their territory, and the great cities of Merv, Samarkand and Bukhara became centers of Islamic learning and culture.[200]

In 1221, the Mongol hordes swept into the region and in Merv alone, one of the great cities of the world, perhaps one million people were killed.[201]

The Destruction under Tamerlane of the Church of the East

The climax of destructive persecution was under the notorious Mongol leader Tamerlane (Timur the Lame, 1336-1405), who virtually eradicated the church in Central Asia, Persia, India, the Caucasus, and the Middle East. Tamerlane wanted to restore the Mongolian Empire to its previous glory, using Islam as the glue to hold it together. In the 14th Century, he led his armies into Iran, India, Mesopotamia, Syria, Anatolia, and Georgia. Tamerlane did not slaughter only Christians, however. In Estefan, 70,000 heads were stacked up in a pyramid after his conquest. In Baghdad, 90,000 heads were stacked in mountains of skulls. From Russia to India people suffered under his rule. Tamerlane was called the "Scourge of God" and is reported to have slaughtered 100,000 people in North India alone. He fought against his fellow Muslims in Anatolia and Persia as well as in other locations. His motives seemed to be more about the love of conquest than devotion to Islam. In fact, Christians continued to be educators and scholars in the lands in which he ruled.

The Church of the East never recovered from Tamerlane's wave of destruction, however. As British historian MacCulluoch points out, the Church of the East, which previously had taken the Gospel across the Middle East, Central Asia and into India, was reduced to struggling to survive in small somewhat secret enclaves. Even after

---

[200] https://www.islamreligion.com/articles/11398/islam-in-central-asia-part-1/
[201] Ibid

Tamerlane, however, the situation remained dire, as the Ottoman Turks continued to put pressure on non-Muslims.

By the end of the 15th century, only a handful of churches in the East Syrian tradition remained, mostly in what is today Iraqi Kurdistan.[202] Tamerlane may have been responsible for more deaths per capita than either Hitler or Stalin. It is not surprising that many Christians converted to Islam during this time, although some survived as Christians by migrating to Kurdistan.

The Russian Empire

In the 17th century, the Russian Empire under the Tsars began to focus on Central Asia, and within a decade had established control over the region. Until the 19th century, the Russians, who were predominately Russian Orthodox in religion, showed goodwill toward their Muslim subjects, building mosques and schools and printing Islamic literature. By the 19th century, however, Russian Orthodox missionaries were sent into the area, hoping to decrease the Islamic fervor of the people. To this day, most Central Asians have a difficult time disassociating Christianity from Russian imperialism.

After the Tsarist regimes fell to the Soviet Communists in 1917, the five republics of Kazakhstan, Uzbekistan, Turkmenistan, Tajikistan, and Kyrgyzstan became independent Soviet Republics.[203] Under Communism, The Muslims were promised freedom to express their Islamic faith after the oppression of the Tsars. In reality, however, those who resisted the secularizing policies of the Communist governments were often oppressed. For example, there was a big campaign to "liberate" Central Asian women by having them remove their veils. Some women did remove them, but others chose not to. The Soviets also switched all writing to the Cyrillic script,

---

[202] Irvin & Sunquist p. 495
[203] In addition to the five Central Asian Republics, there are many Muslims, in Southern Russia, Tartarstan, Tans-Caucasia, Azerbaijan, Crimea, and even in Siberia. Most of these people have Turkic-Mongol origins, although the Tajiks are Persian, and others have mixed origins.

which made it difficult for Muslims to read the Qur'an, which is written in Arabic script.

Re-Islamization of Central Asian

In 1912, there were 26,000 mosques in Central Asia alone. By 1949, there were only 415 mosques in the entire Soviet Union. By 2004, there were 2,500 mosques and dozens of religious schools in the Central Asian states alone. The re-Islamization of Central Asia continues.

Tamerlane and Hitler

David Garrison in his groundbreaking book, *A Wind in the House of Islam,* tells a fascinating but tragic story. It seems that in 1941, a Soviet anthropologist, Mikhail Gerasimov, exhumed the body of Tamerlane enshrined in his coffin. Inside the tomb, a curse was inscribed, "Whoever opens my tomb shall release an invader more terrible than I." Remember that in World War II, despite his generals' warning against opening up a two-front war, Hitler launched the biggest invasion army in the history of the world. The result was 20 million military and civilian deaths, or three million more than Tamerlane allegedly killed during his bloody reign.[204]

God Used Joseph Stalin

Joseph Stalin, a former seminary student in training to be an Orthodox priest, will by anyone's calculation, go down as one of the bloodiest dictators in the history of the world. The blood of tens of millions of people is on his hands. Yet even Stalin had a purpose in God's plan to bring redemption to the nations. Over a hundred years before the Communist Revolution, Catherine the Great (1729-1796), who was of German descent, ruled in Russia during tsarist rule. She invited German pacifists, including Mennonites and Baptists, to come to Russia to avoid compulsory military service in their home countries. In Russia, many of these Christians witnessed about Christ until the time of Joseph Stalin. Stalin, fearing that the

---

[204] Garrison p. 142

German Christians might be collaborators with the Nazis, forcibly relocated them to Central Asia. He also forcibly relocated up to half a million Koreans who had come to eastern Siberia to work in the mining and timber industries. Although the Koreans and the Japanese were enemies, Stalin was afraid that some Koreans might aid the Japanese if they invaded the Soviet Union, so he exiled them to Central Asia as well. The Koreans who knew the Lord also began to evangelize the local people. Then came the Communist anti-religion era, but in 1991, when the Soviet Union collapsed, there were many Germans and Koreans (and a smattering of European peoples) ready to share the Gospel in Central Asia during a time of great openness. Garrison writes, "For this reason, history may yet identify the atheist Joseph Stalin as the greatest gospel deployment agent in the history of Turkestani evangelization.[205]

The Collapse of Communism

In 1991, Mikhail Gorbachev officially declared the dissolution of the Soviet Union. The Central Asian republics became independent states within the C.I.S. (Commonwealth of Independent States). Independence has proved a mixed blessing, however. Hundreds of thousands of Central Asians have gone to Russia to work, often facing discrimination. Many Islamic missionaries from Turkey, Iran, Afghanistan, and Arab countries, especially Saudi Arabia, have attempted to re-Islamize the region, resulting in a more outward expression of Islam, including the veiling of women. Fear of Islamic radicalism has led some of the Central Asian Republics to crack down on all religious activity. In order to demonstrate "fairness," Christians have had their freedoms limited, even though they do not present any political threat to the Central Asian regimes. Several of the regimes are dictatorial in their governance, despite their leaders professing to be Muslims.

---

[205] Ibid, p. 149

Testimony of God's Work among other Turkic Peoples

I mentioned in the introduction about attempting to smuggle Bibles into the former Soviet Union in 1980. In 1985 after having lived in a county along the Silk Road for several years, a friend and I decided to visit five of the Turkic republics still under Communism in the former Soviet Union. We worked our way west from Azerbaijan, which is actually in the Caucasus area, but Muslim in religion and ethnically Turkic. Then we worked our way east into Turkmenistan, Uzbekistan, and Kazakhstan and ended up in Kyrgyzstan. In each place, we prayed for these countries to be open one day for the Gospel. We did not attempt to take Bibles this time, and we only really had a couple of chances to share much of the gospel with anyone. Most of our trip revolved around intercessory prayer while prayer walking.

Six years later, I had a chance to revisit the countries, which were now no longer under Soviet Communism. Under the Soviets, we felt we were watched constantly, but in 1991, the people seemed to be out from under the yoke of oppression. In fact, I preached at a factory in Uzbekistan, and to a large church in Kazakhstan, which under the old regimes would have been impossible. The friend with whom I had prayer-walked through Central Asia, oversaw the work of scores of missionaries who planted churches in the region. Many witnesses of Christ from around the world have spent years in these lands and they can give a more detailed testimony to God's work among the various Turkic-Mongol people than I can. However, I can give first-hand testimony to the incredible changes that took place between 1985 and 1991. Exact numbers of Turkic peoples who have embraced Christ would be impossible to know for certain, but it is beyond doubt that tens of thousands have experienced new life in the Savior.

Popes, Prayer, Blue Jeans and Rock and Roll

The above sub-title may seem a little strange, but all have been credited with being a major reason for the collapse of the former Soviet Union. Pope John Paul II, himself a Pole living under

Communism, probably played the greatest human role. Along with former American President Ronald Reagan's denunciation of the Soviet Union as an "evil empire," John Paul helped expose how bankrupt economically and spiritually the empire had become. The head of the Communist party, Mikael Gorbachev, opened the country in ways unimaginable a few years previously. Brother Andrew, years before the collapse, called for seven years of 24/7 prayer for the end of Communism, which no doubt paved the way for the Pope and the president to be the instruments of God to bring about its downfall.

I believe it was one of the Rolling Stones who said that the collapse of the Soviet Union could be attributed to Russian young people wanting to listen to Rock music and wear blue jeans, like young people in the rest of the world. You can view Paul McCartney, formerly of the Beatles performing for millions in Moscow and St. Petersburg on DVD, or on YouTube. The DVD contains many interviews with Russians telling how they would give weeks of their salaries just to purchase a Beatles record on the black market. The ramifications of the collapse of Communism both positive and negative is beyond the scope of this book. One thing for sure is that the Lord opened a door for millions of people, including Turkic peoples, to hear the Gospel!

Pope John Paul II

Questions for Discussion and Reflection

- What was the most surprising thing you read in this chapter?

- As we will see throughout, the author states that perhaps the prayers of Sorkaktani, the faithful widow, are being heard today. Can you think of other deceased saints or living prayer warriors whose prayers are having a powerful influence in people coming to faith today wherever it might be in the world?

- The collapse of Communism in 1991 caught much of the world by surprise. It opened the door for Christians to share the Gospel among the many peoples of the former Soviet Central Asia. What do you think of the idea that the iron curtain was brought down by a combination of prayer, denunciation by President Reagan, the popularity of Pope John Paul II, and the global youth desire for blue jeans and rock n roll?

14

Who Really Began the Crusades?

Just imagine you are a wealthy European nobleman in the year 1095. You were there when Pope Urban II described the horrific oppression, rape and killing of Christian Pilgrims in the Holy Land by the infidels. Despite the schism that occurred only fifty years ago, dividing the Western and Eastern Churches,[206] the Pope declares that it is the responsibility of all Christians who are able to fight, to retake the holy sites of your faith from the Turks. He says that for those who go to free the church in Jerusalem for the love of God and not for gaining glory or hope of material gain, the journey would serve as a penance for sin. If you die, you will gain instant access to paradise without purgatory.

You have a family. You have to be sure they will be able to survive while you are away for several years. It is very possible you will not come back at all. You also need horses and servants to accompany you all the way from northern Europe to Jerusalem. Buying horses, food, and other travel expenses, and leaving some money behind for your family in your absence, will take all of your resources and savings. Nevertheless, you want to prove your love for God. You want a guarantee of eternal life. You want to see the Church of the Holy Sepulcher and the other holy sites to be again in the Church's hands. You believe that Christians should be able to make a

---

[206] See previous chapter that explains the Great Schism between the Latin Roman Catholic Church from the Greek Orthodox Church.

pilgrimage to where Jesus lived and not be harassed by the infidels. You join other knights and nobles from established families on their way to join the crusade. You also see those who are less noble on the journey as well. Some are the real riff raff of society with not much to lose if they do not come back. For them it is an adventure and an escape. For you it is not an adventure, and you have everything to lose. But you have followed what your priest proclaimed from the pulpit: that Christians must be willing to give up family and possessions, and lose everything for the sake of the Kingdom of God.

On the way, some of the riff raff beat up, rape and murder many Jews. They justify it by saying that Jews are infidels too, like the Muslims, and they are Christ-killers. Some owe debts to Jewish moneylenders and the Crusades gives them an excuse not to pay the money back. You feel somewhat sorry for the Jews, but you feel too outnumbered to do much to defend them. Even when the pope rebuked those killing the Jews along the way, the scum among you did not stop their evil.

As you journey onward, you see that fewer and fewer people have endured the long, long journey. Many elderly people and children have died on the road before they even reached Constantinople where they agreed to meet before marching to the Holy Land. By the time you get to Jerusalem, maybe one out of four of those who started with you have made it to the target city.

> *I say to those who are present. I command that it be said to those who are absent. Christ commands it. All who go thither and lose their lives, be it on the road or on the sea, or in fight against the pagans, will be granted immediate forgiveness of sins. This I grant to all who will march, by virtue of the great gift, which God has given me (Pope Urban II).*

> *When the Crusaders took back Jerusalem, they killed every Jew and Muslim they could find until the blood flowed to their horse's knees and then thanked God at the Church of the Holy Sepulcher. (Summary of eyewitness accounts)*

Just imagine you are a Muslim fighting with the mighty Saladin. Almost 100 years ago, the infidel Crusaders took the city of Jerusalem from the Muslims, slaughtering every one of your brothers and sisters in Islam. They say blood flowed as deep as the horses 'knees. Jerusalem is the third holiest site in your religion, the place where Muhammad ascended into Paradise and led the other prophets in prayer. After a long and hard battle, you triumph! The Muslim armies beheaded the resistant Crusaders, but unlike the Christians, your army did not slaughter the non-combatants.

Pope Urban II Declares a Holy War

The Crusades that began almost 1,000 years ago have gotten increasing attention in our day. Justifiers of jihad, like Osama bin Laden, the architect of the 9/11 attacks, constantly used the phrase *Crusader-Zionist alliance* to explain why killing Jews and Americans anywhere is justified, and is not contrary to Islam. New books are regularly published about the Crusades, and many writers, like popular author Karen Armstrong, a former nun, attribute most of the problems in the Middle East to the legacy of the Crusades. I will very briefly summarize the highlights of a topic that could easily stretch to volumes.

In the year 1095, Pope Urban II challenged the people in Clermont, France to take back the Holy Places where the Lord Jesus was born, lived, and was crucified by the Turks. Even the Church of the Holy Sepulcher had been defiled and destroyed by the Muslims. He challenged the men of Europe to go and free the lands of our Lord and proclaimed that those who were killed would be guaranteed to have their sins forgiven and go straight to Paradise. The people who heard the Pope's fiery sermon cried out "God wills it!" "God wills it!" Of course, this sounds very familiar, as a similar battle cry of jihad for Muslims over the centuries, ensuring the same promises of forgiveness and Paradise.

Motivation for the Crusades

Often the Crusaders have been portrayed as bloodthirsty savages, bent only on acquiring wealth through plunder and escaping the oppressive way of life during the Middle Ages in Europe. While no doubt that was true of some Crusaders, others were motivated by a sincere desire to please God. Many gave up their wealth and privilege to join in the Crusades, knowing that they might not see their families or resume their privileged lives for many years, if they returned at all. Franks, Gauls, Normans, and Scots, among others, hoped to unite against a common enemy--the Muslim Turks. In short, some of the Crusaders were godly men who sacrificed everything they held dear for the love of God, while others were the dregs of society, with nothing to lose. Still others were somewhere between the two extremes.

When did the Crusades Really Begin?

The prominent sociologist of religion and highly respected author, Rodney Stark, makes the point that the real Crusades did not begin with the Pope's declaration in 1095, but rather when the Muslims invaded the holy sites of Christianity in the seventh century. Soon after the Seljuk Turks became the ruling force in the Holy Land beginning in the 11th century, they began to exploit the pilgrims who wanted to visit the places where Jesus once walked. In the past, pilgrims had been allowed to make pilgrimages to the biblical sites, but the Seljuks, who had only recently converted to Islam, in their newfound zeal, often exploited and oppressed the pilgrims.

Another item of special interest that Stark points out, is that for the most part, Muslims did not make a major deal out of the Crusades until quite recently. Muslims were engaged in many wars from the Prophet's time until the Enlightenment. It was the writings of anti-Catholic European Enlightenment scholars in the eighteenth and nineteenth centuries that put the most of the blame on the Crusaders, who slaughtered the "innocent" Muslims because of their greed and lust for power, plunder and war.

Stark points out that it was the demise of the Ottoman Empire in the early 1900s, and especially the establishment of the state of Israel in

1948, that led to so much anti-Crusader feeling among Muslims. [207] Until this time, the Crusades were looked on as one of the many wars recorded in Islamic history. In actuality, the invasion of the Mongols, not long after the Crusades, led to far more death and destruction of the Muslim world than the Crusaders caused, but without the anger that Muslim radicals use to stir up people against the so-called Crusader-Zionist alliance. One reason for that is the simple fact that most of the Mongols eventually converted to Islam.

The Background to the Crusades

In the mid-ninth century, the great threat to the papacy was Muslim domination. They overran Sicily in the 820s, and became established on the mainland of Italy by 838. In 850, a fleet of Arab Muslims sailed up the Tiber, attacked Rome, desecrated the tombs of Peter and Paul, and robbed the riches from the tombs. [208]

Two hundred years later, the call to crusade by Pope Urban II at Clermont in France in 1095 helped to focus Christians against a common enemy. After years of Christian infighting, Pope Urban II made his famous declaration, as cited previously, that fighting against the infidels to take back the holy sites served as an act of penance for the forgiveness of sin.[209]

Such a clear link between salvation and holy war was something new, and it caught the imagination of Europe. Out of this came the battle cry *"Deus le voit"* (God wills it). The pope encouraged the Crusaders to sew the sign of the cross on their tunics and to take a vow that whoever dishonored the vow would face eternal condemnation. Fulfillment of the vow, however, would bring remission of sins. In a day when there was much consciousness of sin and fear of hell, the Crusades were perceived as a great opportunity for the certainty of forgiveness of sin and salvation. Men came from as far away as Scotland and Ireland to join the

---

[207] Stark, pps. 8-9
[208] Duffy, p. 99
[209] Ibid, p. 136

Crusader army. Eventually, even those who helped finance the Crusades were given indulgences (relief in the afterlife from the penalty of sin).[210]

While Islam has often been portrayed as a religion that was spread by the sword, Christianity was also spread through force at times. It is said that many Saxons, when following their king into baptism, refused to put their right arms under the water. That was the arm most of them used for fighting, and they refused to give up the "glory" of conquest, battle and plunder. The Vikings also converted to Christianity without immediately giving up their love of battle. Before being too critical of the way Islam was spread, we need to remember that the sword also spread the Christian faith at times.

The Goal of the Crusades

British historian Hugh Goddard points out that in the early years of the Crusades, apocalyptic expectation was strong. Peter the Hermit preached that the Holy Land must be recovered for the Church before Christ could come again. The journey would be hard and they would battle against the legions of the Antichrist, but the goal was Jerusalem and God would help them. [211]

The First Crusaders

Beginning in 1095 a peoples' crusade set out from Cologne, Germany under the leadership of Peter the Hermit, and while on their way to Jerusalem began plundering and slaughtering Jews who were also perceived as infidels. Estimates of between 50,000 to 60,000 people set out with perhaps one-fourth actually making it to Jerusalem. A rumor leaked out that the spear that had pierced Jesus' side was buried in Antioch.[212] Convinced that this was the "holy spear," the Crusaders spent five days of fasting and prayer. Then in a religious frenzy they defeated a much larger Turkish army. The Turks broke rank and left their provisions, leaving much plunder. Finally, on

---

[210] Ibid, pps. 136-37
[211] Goddard, p. 76
[212] Gonzalez, p. 347

June 7, 1099, the Crusaders got their first glimpse of the Holy City, Jerusalem. It was actually the Fatimite Arabs from Egypt, named after Muhammad's daughter, Fatima, not the Seljuk Turks, who were defending the city at that time.

Divisions among Muslims led to their defeat at Jerusalem, as the Seljuk Turks adhered to the Sunni sect, while the Fatimites were Shi'ites. Gonzalez cites an Arab chronicler, Ibn Al-Athir, as saying that the Crusaders had come to Syria at the request of the Fatimites who feared growing Turkish power.[213] After four years of travel and war, the Crusaders took Jerusalem on July 15, 1099, after first taking back Antioch. Tragically, the Crusaders proceeded to slaughter all the Muslim residents of the city, and they burnt the Jews alive in their major synagogue. This event still lives infamously not only in Jewish and Muslim mnds, but also among Orthodox Christians. Remember that it was only fifty years before this that the Great Schism between Catholics and Orthodox took place. Many of the Eastern Orthodox clergy were expelled because the Western Latin Church perceived them as heretics like Jews and Muslims. After the slaughter, the Crusaders gave thanks to God for the victory at the Church of the Holy Sepulcher.

The Second Crusade

Imad ad-Din (d.1146) rallied Muslim troops who took Edessa and Aleppo, clearing east Syria of Crusader forces. His son Nur ad-Din, after his father's assassination, united Muslims from Damascus to Edessa. Crusaders held on to Antioch and a few towns in Palestine, including Jerusalem. Nur ad-Din died in 1171, and one of his officers, Saladin, rose from slavery to be vizier of Egypt. He took over the command of the Muslim forces. He led the Muslim armies against the Christian forces in Galilee and retook Jerusalem. Saladin beheaded the soldiers who resisted the recapture of Jerusalem, but unlike the "Christian" crusaders, Saladin did not kill non-combatants, or many of the soldiers who had surrendered (some

---

[213] Ibid, p. 248

soldiers and their officers appeared to want to die as martyrs, and fought even after it was clear that there was no hope of victory). For demonstrating mercy in the midst of a brilliant military victory, Saladin was highly regarded by Jews, Christians, and Muslims alike as a man of honor.

Saladin-more Christian than the Christians?

Saladin was Kurdish in origin, giving the Kurds a well-known historical figure whom they regard with a sense of pride. While he defeated Christian forces, he behaved more like a Christian than the Crusaders often did. Volf tells a story about Saladin when he recaptured Jerusalem in 1187. Unlike the Crusaders who killed all the Muslims and Jews they could find, Saladin offered safe passage to all those who could pay a ransom. The ransom was ten dinars for males, five for females and one for children. The well-off immediately paid the ransom and left the city. Those who could not pay became booty to be sold or killed. As the poor expressed their woe that they were to be sold or enslaved, they became angry, not at Saladin, but at their fellow wealthy Christians who could easily have paid the money to set them free.[214] Later Saladin did release one thousand of the poor without ransom, but about one-half of the city's Christians were marched off to the slave markets. [215]

The Third Crusade

In this crusade, the Pope again promised indulgences for those who crusaded against the infidel Muslims. The famous Richard the Lion-Hearted, well known as the hero-king in books and films about Robin Hood, fought against Saladin. Despite their fierce battles against one other, each man respected the other, and they finally reached a truce in 1192. Jerusalem remained in Muslim hands even as the surrounding areas were taken by the Crusaders. Christian pilgrimage could continue unhindered.

---

[214] Volf, pps. 121-122
[215] Stark, p. 198

Stark points out that Saladin has probably been overly glorified, whereas anti-Catholic Enlightenment-era historians have usually demonized the Crusaders. This has been the narrative passed down to modern-day historians of the Crusades. While Saladin was relatively merciful in Jerusalem, he was not so gracious after the Battle of Hattin, and he participated in the slaughter of captured Knights Templars and the Knights Hospitallers.[216] [217]

One other area that Stark debunks concerns the Eastern Orthodox Church. Enlightenment-era scholars often portray the Orthodox Church as the victim of the evil Catholic Church. There were several times when the Eastern patriarchs did not send the troops and aid that they had promised, and the Crusaders were left under-manned and defeated by the Muslim troops. Tragically, in the thirteenth century, the Crusaders did invade and destroyed much of the predominately Orthodox-Christian city of Constantinople, which contributed to its final fall in 1453 at the hands of the Muslim Turks.

Many more Crusades were fought, finally ending at Acre in 1291. The Holy Land and its Holy Sites remained under Muslim control until the end of World War I.

The Legacy of the Crusades

It is interesting how the *Concise Encyclopedia of Islam* discusses the results of the crusades:

> *The effects of the Crusades upon the Islamic world, on the other hand, were negligible. In the course of the fighting Saladin*

---

[216] Ibid, p. 200

[217] The Knights Templars have been a topic of much curiosity with many books, novels and movies, including one of the Indiana Jones films that portray them. Initially, they were an elite military force. The Templars were named after the Temple in Jerusalem, and the Hospitallers were named from their hospital there. MacCulloch points out that the Templars ignored the fact that the Temple had been destroyed by the Romans (in 70 AD) and built churches modeled after the Muslim Dome of the Rock. After the Crusades, the entire Templar order was suppressed after it was clear that they had no chance of reconquering the Holy Land. (MacCulloch, 386).

consolidated his control and dethroned the Fatimids of Egypt, but the Crusades did not unite the Muslims against a common threat. Indeed, some Muslims allied themselves with the Franks (and some Christians allied themselves with the Muslims). Although in Palestine and Syria the Crusader castles remain as traces of their passage, for Islam, the Crusades were ultimately only a transient and localized episode.[218]

Notice that the author says the effect of the Crusades on Muslim lands was rather minimal. Goddard cites Runciman from his three-volume work on the history of the Crusades:

The Crusades were launched to save Eastern Christendom (particularly Jerusalem) from the Muslims. When they ended the whole of Eastern Christendom was under Moslem rule. When Pope Urban preached his great sermon at Clermont the Turks seemed about to threaten the Bosporus. When Pope Pius II preached the last Crusade, the Turks were crossing the Danube.[219]

As can readily be seen, from a military perspective the Crusades were a total failure. Concerning their spiritual impact, I cite Yale Scholar Joseph Cumming who writes:

I believe that Satan's greatest masterpiece was the Crusades. Why? Is it because the Crusades were the worst atrocity that ever happened in history? I think Hitler was worse. Stalin was worse. Pol Pot was worse. What is so horrible about the Crusades is that it was done under the symbol of the cross, that Satan succeeded in distorting the very heart of the Christian faith. The cross is at the heart of the entire Christian faith, and for the Muslims and Jews of the world, what does the symbol of the cross signify? The cross now signifies, "Christians hate you enough to kill you." It is supposed to signify that "God loved you enough to lay down his life for you, and I love you enough that I would lay

---

[218] *Encyclopedia of Islam* p. 121
[219] Goddard, p. 82

down my life for you." Satan succeeded in taking the very heart of the Christian faith, and turning it around to mean not just something different, but to mean the exact opposite of what it was supposed to mean.[220]

Professor Stark is right in pointing out that the Crusades have been portrayed too often as one-sided—the evil Christian soldiers of the pope against the peaceful Muslims. It is also true that Muslims did not make a big deal of the Crusades until anti-Catholic scholars, who wanted to destroy the grip of Christianity in Europe hundreds of years later, began to focus one-sided attention on it. At the same time, I agree with Joseph Cumming--the Crusades so misrepresented what Christ and Christians should be about that they still serve as an obstacle to sharing the true message of Jesus with Jews and Muslims unto this day.

Some Bright Spots in a Time of Much Darkness

The following portrayals are about people who advocated reaching Muslims through preaching and loving acts rather than with violence and crusades. Most of them did not see much fruit for their efforts at the time. John Tzimisces actually preceded the Crusades, and the motivation of those seeking baptism is questionable. Nevertheless, it illustrates that not all conversions were one way, from Christian to Muslim, as we have seen throughout most of history.

John Tzimisces (925-976)

Tzimisces was a Byzantine emperor who seized territory on the southern border of Syria and Palestine. Between the years 972 and 975, 12,000 Arab Muslim men along with their wives and children sought baptism from Orthodox priests. Their motivation may have been related primarily to tax relief, as the Abbasid Empire was winding down, and high rates of taxes were being extracted from

---

[220] Joseph Cumming Toward a respectful witness, *From Seed to Fruit* J. Dudley Woodberry (2011) (Ed.). pps. 331-332

both Christians and Muslim subjects. There is no record of the movement lasting. Garrison claims this was the only significant movement of Muslims toward Christ that occurred during the first 500 years after the advent of Islam.[221]

St. Francis of Assisi (1181-1226)

So much has been written about St. Francis of Assisi that there is no need for me to add more to the existing literature beyond mentioning his involvement in the Crusades. Francis originally tried to go to Egypt to preach to the Muslims, but he fell ill, and his trip was delayed for several years. Eventually he made it to Egypt, and he saw the Crusaders and Muslims denouncing each other as infidels as they prepared for battle, each convinced that God was on their side. Francis marched up and down the space between the armies rebuking both sides and pleading with both to repent. Then Francis was invited into the tent of the Sultan Al Malik al Kamil of Egypt, and stayed for about seven days. The sultan was so impressed by the holiness of St. Francis that he almost converted to his faith. He allegedly said to St. Francis that if there were a few other people like him, he would quit warring and become a follower of Jesus.

Recently, Pope Francis commemorated this event on its 800th anniversary. There is no doubt that encountering St. Francis drastically changed the Sultan, just as the time spent with the Sultan transformed Francis. Later other Franciscan friars ventured to Egypt and preached the gospel to Muslims generally without much success. Francis said that it was not yet God's time for Muslims to come to the Savior in large numbers, but he believed the day would come. Perhaps the Lord is hearing the prayers of St. Francis, often said to be the most Christ-like person in all of history, as many Muslims begin to discover the Savior that Francis loved.

The orders established by St. Francis and St. Dominic (1170-1221) were sent out to preach the gospel during this time. Friars made the same vows of chastity, poverty, and obedience that monks did, but

---

[221] Garrison, p. 7

they were more focused on outward ministry than inward introspection and contemplation. It was mostly friars who attempted to share the Gospel with Muslims.

Raymond Lull (1232-1315)

Lull was born into wealth and privilege, but upon receiving Christ renounced everything to preach the gospel. He learned Arabic well enough to teach and preach, made many journeys to North Africa, and opened up training schools to prepare Christians for service among Muslims and Mongols. He was truly a great apologist of the faith. Lull eventually died a martyr in Algeria at around the age of eighty. He did not see many converts in his day, but he influenced many Catholics to approach Islam armed with the gospel and not with the sword. He also advocated for learning Arabic and the deep study of Islam.

Raymond Lull was cited as saying, "I see many knights going to the Holy Land and to other lands of the infidel, seeking to acquire them by force of arms. But they never attain that. As for me, the only way of conquest is the old, old apostolic way, namely by love and prayer and the pouring out of tears and blood."

Peter the Venerable (1092-1156)

Peter was a brilliant scholar, the first person to translate the Qur'an from Arabic into Latin. He viewed Islam as a heresy, but advocated for challenging Islam like all heresies by speaking the truth in love. He paved the way for a scholarly refutation of Islam based on its own sources rather than attacking what people often perceived Islam as teaching.

Some Who Experienced Fruitful Ministry in the Middle Ages

William of Tripoli (1220-1275) was said to have baptized over 1,000 Muslims in what is today's Lebanon. [222] Garrison points out that William learned the culture and language of Islam. However, when

---

[222] Latourette, p. 326;

the last of the Crusader outposts of the region withdrew two decades later, none of the fruit remained.[223]

Conrad of Ascoli (1234-1289) was a Franciscan who saw 6,400 people, mostly Muslims, baptized in his time.[224] He lived humbly and preached the gospel, evidenced by signs and miracles.[225] It is ironic that the beloved St. Francis saw almost no fruit among Muslims, whereas the little-known Conrad saw people come to Christ that few others in history came close to matching in fruitful ministry among Muslims.

The 1999 Reconciliation Walk

Beginning in 1996 in Cologne, Germany where the first Crusaders gathered to begin their march to the Holy Land 900 years ago, 2,500-3,000 mostly Western Christians began the long 2,000 mile-march to Jerusalem. They passed through the Balkans, Turkey, Syria and Lebanon, arriving in Jerusalem in 1999, 900 years after the tragic event when Crusaders sacked Jerusalem, killing tens of thousands of Muslims, thousands of Jews and many non-Roman Christians. Along the way, Christians stopped in mosques and synagogues to apologize for the way their ancestors distorted the true meaning of the cross and what true Christianity really is.

Most of the reaction by Jews and Muslims was favorable. Some Christians from the ancient churches, who have lived under Islam for centuries, wished the apologies were not all one-sided. Efforts to bring healing between Christians with Jews and Muslims should be commended. It should not be too surprising, however, that some Jews and Muslims perceived it as new form of proselytizing their co-religionists.

One thing is sure. Every person who goes into the Muslim world with the intention to share the love of Christ needs to be aware that his or her efforts may be perceived through the legacy of the

---

[223] Garrison p. 11
[224] Latourette, p. 325
[225] https://www.roman-catholic-saints.com/blessed-conrad-of-ascoli.html

Crusades. Western Christians, especially Americans, must be very careful to disassociate their actions from the actions of their government. This can only be done by living simple, humble lives, serving the people through word and deed like St. Francis and many others have done throughout the centuries.

Questions for Discussion and Reflection

- Why do some scholars blame the Crusades for many of the problems in the current Middle East? What points do they make that may be valid? Do they lay too much of the blame on the heads of the Crusaders rather than the Muslims?
- What do you think of the Reconciliation Walk?

15

Christendom's Greatest City Falls: Whose Side is God on?

Just imagine you are living in western Anatolia, near Constantinople, in 1452. Your family are Christians who have farmed and raised livestock in the countryside for generations. You are hearing stories about people called the Seljuks, or "Turks," who won a huge military victory in Manzikert hundreds of years ago. They have been steadily marching west ever since. They do not seem to be in a great hurry to invade your town and in some places the Seljuks and the Greeks (and other ethnic Christians) are getting along pretty well. In most villages and towns, some people have become Muslims and speak Turkish as their primary language, while others have remained Christians, continuing to speak their ancestral languages. Everyone has had to learn at least some Turkish in matters pertaining to government and in transactions outside of their *dhimmi* community.

Your daughter is very beautiful, and you do not want her to marry a Muslim. You son is also approaching the age when the Turks might take him and make him into a Muslim warrior in a practice they call *devshirme*. Some Christian families say the devshirme is a way for their sons to get ahead and become powerful members of society rather than mere dhimmi. You, however, want your son and daughter to be Christians. You also do not want to give any more of your hard-earned money for the *jizya*. As the Ottomans come into your town and set up the local government, you decide to take your wife, son, and daughter and flee to Constantinople, one of the few places nearby still under Christian rule.

You feel safe in Constantinople, but you also know that the Seljuks are determined to conquer your city for Islam. Around you, you see signs of godliness--monks and nuns, monasteries and beautiful churches. You also see godlessness-brothels, immorality, and drunkenness in many places as well, and there is a huge economic gap between the lifestyle of the king and his administrators and the majority who are poor. You ask yourself whether the Turks are God's judgment on Constantinople. You have no doubt that the Christian faith is the true faith. You know, however, throughout the Bible that God used wicked nations like the Assyrians and the Babylonians to punish His people for their disobedience and corruption. What if God is angry with the Christians and allows the Ottomans to triumph? What about your family and your beautiful daughter? What if her husband, by choice or not, is a Turk, and your offspring for generations to come are Muslims?

***

Just imagine you are a young Turkish man with a wife and a small son and another child to be born soon. You are religious and practice the Five Pillars of Islam, although you sometimes do not perform all five daily prayers. Sometimes you just cannot endure the Ramadan fast during the long hot days of summer. You hope Allah has mercy on you when you cannot endure without water and a bite of food until *iftar*,[226] which can be as late as 9:00 at night in the summer. You have never made the *Hajj* to Mecca, but you are young and hope to do it one day. You are content living in your village, and you hope to have several more sons and even a couple of daughters would be ok. Then the call comes forth from the young Sultan Mehmet for all young men to join the battle to take Constantinople and make it a Muslim city for the glory of Allah. You have heard that every previous attempt at taking Constantinople has failed, but this

---

[226] *Iftar* the breaking of the fast after sundown during Ramadan.

time will be different! There have been prophecies of victory. You heard that the Sultan has purchased cannons so powerful that they can bring down the mighty city walls, Constantinople's only protection. You give your son a pat on the head, pinch his cheeks hard, something that all Turks do, and call him *aslan* (lion). You tap your wife's very pregnant stomach, and march off to war.

History and Theology: Is God on the Side of the Ottomans?

The Fall of Constantinople

Hagia Sophia in Constantinople

Perhaps it was the taking of Constantinople in 1453 by the twenty-one-year old Sultan Mehmet II even more than the Crusades that made Christians wonder whether God abandoned them or was he on the side of the Muslims. The Turks, working their way west after the battle of Manzikert in 1071 (See chapter 14), approached the gates of Constantinople almost four hundred years later. As painful as it must have been for the Byzantines to lose so much territory, they still had Constantinople, the Rome of the East. Twenty-two previous attempts to take the city, from the early days of Islam until Mehmet II, had all failed.

As I watched *The Ottomans,* a series on Netflix about the epic battle between the Turkish Muslims and the Byzantine Christians, I experienced a wide range of emotions. First, I was repulsed that the Byzantines would fight a war against their Turkish enemies using swords, spears and cannons, and celebrate when the enemy Turks were initially defeated and killed in battle. I wanted to shout at the television and say to Turkish (and other Muslim) viewers, "Hey those are not real Christians who do that. Real Christians love their enemies!"

Yet that is tricky because with the Constantintization of Christianity, the simple faith of the first three centuries, when Christians were a persecuted sect, was no more. The Byzantines had conquered other lands and people. They had an army, a navy, and weapons capable of much destruction and loss of life. They felt safe behind the most impenetrable walls of any city of its time. How contrary this militarism seems to the spirit of their founder and the experience of the first three hundred years of Christian history, when Christians would rather be killed than to kill.

The Walls of Constantinople

Christians had a good chance to win the battle. If the Christian Emperor had been willing to pay the Hungarian weapons-maker what he asked for the most powerful cannon of its day, things might have turned out differently. Instead, the cannon maker, a Christian, sold his powerful invention to the Ottomans. Those cannons could shoot a ball that weighed 600 pounds and the impenetrable walls proved to be not so impenetrable after all.

The continual striking of the walls with those huge cannonballs terrified the people trapped within those walls. Mehmet II, in a brilliant move, ordered his troops to cut down trees secretly at night to make it possible for his troops to carry their ships overland by the way of Pera. They made a path using well-greased logs as a base to drag their ships up the surrounding hills in order for their small navy to bypass the larger Byzantine navy. The Byzantines had linked a chain across the Bosporus Strait that ships were unable to sail past. Mehmet did the unthinkable by bypassing the Bosporus and attacking from the Golden Horn. Like the walls, the Byzantines thought the chain could not be penetrated--another layer of false security. Due to Mehmet's action, the Byzantines lost their sea advantage. Then it was a matter of time for the walls to crumble under the constant barrage of cannon fire, and the Ottoman troops forced their way in and took the city.

Remember that this battle was four hundred years after the split between the Orthodox and Catholic churches. Two hundred years previously, the European crusaders had invaded Constantinople and looted and destroyed much of the city. When the King of Constantinople appealed for troops from the Pope and the Venetians to repel the Ottoman attack, they did not seem to feel responsible for aiding their fellow Christians. The Byzantine King's pleas fell on deaf ears. The Venetian mercenaries delayed sailing to Constantinople to help their fellow-Christians until it was too late.

Devshirme and Janissaries

The application of Devshirme law was carried out during the Ottoman Empire in which one-fifth of Christian youth aged fourteen to twenty years from the conquered Balkan regions were taken from their families. This was usually carried out every four or five years. [227] The young men were forcibly converted to Islam and entered the *Janissaries,* a military militia. Most of the children were from Greek, Serbian, Bulgarian, Armenian and Albanian ethnicities, and many were children of the upper classes. Even priests' children were taken. Many came to be the most fanatical and radical Muslims of their day, often called to war against the people

---

[227] Encyclopedia of Islam, p. 129

from their own ethnic and religious heritage. With time, the need for crack troops grew and the draft was conducted every year. Any Christian boy between the ages of ten and fifteen could be a potential Janissary in training.[228] A great irony is that the Byzantines, although greatly outnumbered, had defeated the Ottomans several times when they battled outside of the walls. Then Sultan Mehmet sent in the crack Ottoman troops, the equivalent of the Army Rangers or Navy Seals of their day, the Janissaries recruited under the *Devshirme* system. So former Christians helped conquer the most important Christian city in the world, which at the time many thought spelled the final doom of Christianity and the ultimate triumph of Islam.

The Hagia Sophia Becomes a Mosque

One of the first acts of the victorious army was to take the most important church in Christendom, the Hagia Sophia, and transform it into a mosque. Both Christians and Muslims in those days looked for signs of God's favor that demonstrated that he was on their side. In the Netflix series, which is quite historically accurate, there is an account of a blood moon that had been prophesied as a sign that the Ottomans would triumph. Furthermore, a *Hadith*[229] predicted that Muslims would take Constantinople when the city was at its peak under Byzantine rule. What a motivating factor for the person who could fulfill the prophecy so widely believed by Muslims, but must have seemed impossible to achieve when allegedly given by the Prophet hundreds of years earlier!

A Historical Lesson

There is a museum in Istanbul that is dedicated to displaying the events leading to the conquest of Istanbul. It shows the various stages of the conquest, especially the role played by Mehmet II. A few years ago when I took a team of students to see the museum, we

---

[228] Ibid p. 129
[229] Hadith are the saying and deeds of the Prophet Muhammad, and are second to only the Qur'an itself in importance to govern the lives of Muslims.

noticed a middle-aged Turkish woman with her *tespih* (Muslim prayer beads that somewhat resemble a rosary) and tears in her eyes, relishing the Turkish victory as she stared deeply at the pictures on the walls portraying the triumph of the Muslims. To her, there was no doubt. Allah gave the twenty-one-year-old Sultan the wisdom, strength and courage to take the city. God was on the side of the Ottomans, not the Christians. So, how do we determine whose side God is on?

I have had the opportunity many times to tour the great former Hagia Sophia Church, the most important church in Christendom for over 1,000 years. At its peak, its beauty must have been unfathomable. The mosaics made of gold were plastered over by the Ottomans due to the Islamic belief that religious figures should not be portrayed in visible form. Big wooden signs in Arabic with verses from the Qur'an hang from the walls, as if to draw attention away from the splendor of the frescoes of Jesus and his mother and other biblical characters. For decades, there have been efforts to scrape off the plaster and recover the beauty of the original artwork.

In addition to the frescoes, there is the matter of the Hagia Sophia's historical importance. Many important church councils had been held at the church, and as seen in the previous chapter, it was the church that awed the envoys of Prince Vladimir, compelling him to make Orthodoxy the faith of the Russian people. It was the most visible church in Christendom for 1,000 years.

Kemal Ataturk, the great "Father of the Turks, had transformed the Hagia Sophia into a museum in 1935 in his campaign to secularize Turkey. (See chapter 22). Recently, on July 24, 2020, Turkish President Recep Tayyip Erdogan allowed Muslim prayers to be said inside the ancient edifice and declared it is a mosque once again. An estimated 350,000 Turks, Kurds and foreign Muslims celebrated the historic event by packing into the Sultan Ahmet area of Istanbul. The Hagia Sophia seems to be the physical symbol of the Muslim triumph over Christianity, confirming that Allah is truly on the side of the Muslims.

For Christians, it symbolizes something very different. Pope Francis stated that he was deeply distressed at the event. One Orthodox bishop declared it should be a day of mourning for all of Christianity. We can hope and pray that the event will lead Christians to pray that God will work in the hearts of many Muslims like Dr. Derya Little, a former Muslim and atheist, now a Catholic scholar. Her excellent article about the fall of Constantinople is referenced below and I highly recommend it. She wrote it before the event of July 2020, but her article gives excellent background material.

In later chapters, however, we will see some battles that went the other way. Was God on the side of the Christians? Does God take sides in military conflict? Those are tough questions to answer!

https://www.catholicworldreport.com/2017/05/29/the-fall-of-constantinople-on-may-29-1453-a-cautionary-tale/

Questions for Discussion and Reflection

- There are probably three ways people can look at the fall of Constantinople to the Ottomans. a) God is on the side of the Muslims because Islam is the true religion; b) God was punishing the Christians by allowing the Muslims to take the city; c) God did not intervene because war and killing are outside of his plan no matter who is doing the killing. Which of these to you think is the most likely?

- Many Christians do not give much importance to buildings, since in the New Testament, believers often met in homes. Do you think the Hagia Sophia becoming a mosque again is a major tragedy if Jesus in in the midst of his people wherever two or three are gathered together (Matthew 18:20)?
- Some Christians, based on Jesus' teachings in the Sermon on the Mount, say Christians can never engage in battle or defend themselves, their families and property, or their homeland from outside forces. Were the Byzantines wrong in the first place to engage the Turks in war?

16

The Reconquista and Lepanto: Now Whose Side is God on?

Just imagine you are a young Berber Muslim living in in the fifteenth century in Andalusia or what Spaniards call Spain. You know the glorious history of how your people, whom the Spaniards call the *Moros* (Moors), conquered Spain 700 years ago. For hundreds of years, Moors, Jews and Christians built a civilization that was glorious, where medicine, education, science, and the arts thrived. Jews and Christians had their own religious leaders who governed them according to their laws as long as they were not contrary to Islamic rule. You believe that Shari'a law is good for everyone. No, not everything is perfect. Sometimes the Arabs look down on your people, and they claimed the best agricultural land after the invasion, and they left your people with less productive lands. But both Arabs and Berbers feel that Allah has made them victorious over the Jews and Christians, those who the Qur'an says are "People of the Book."

However, the Christians are getting more and more restless and have begun to rebel more fervently against Muslim rule. They claim that Santiago Matamoros (St. James the killer of Moors)"[230] had

---

[230] James, one of Jesus's disciples, according to legend, preached the gospel in Spain and founded the church there. The legend goes that in 834 James supernaturally appeared on the battlefield and helped the Spanish to defeat the larger Moor army in battle, leading to 5,000 Moors being killed. This victory led to the soldiers crying out *Santiago Matamoros*, meaning James the Moor-Slayer.

appeared to them. The Catholics claim that James was one of the Apostles of Isa al Masih who came to Spain and converted the people to the Christian faith. Then they claim he went back to Kudus (Jerusalem) and died as a martyr. Now 800 years later, he is supposed to have shown up in a vision and empowered the Christians in battle to kill 5,000 of your brother Muslims. That defeat, coming after Muslim victory upon victory, still causes your community shame. But that was a long time ago. The problem is that now Muslims are again losing battle after battle and having to submit to Catholic leadership. Even Cordoba, the center of Muslim rule in Andalusia,[231] surrendered to the Pope. Finally, only Granada remained of Muslim Andalusia, but it too fell during the reign of Spanish King Ferdinand and Queen Isabella.

Some of your fellow Moors left their centuries-long homeland and crossed the sea back to North Africa. Your family loves Andalusia, where their ancestors have been buried for hundreds of years. Your grandparents say they are too old to move to a new land. Your parents feel obligated to take care of their parents. Already many of the people you know have become what the Spanish call *Morisco,* people who have often unwillingly been baptized and are officially now Catholic. Your family decides to become Moriscos. You submit to baptism, but in your heart, you are asking Allah to forgive you, and secretly you continue to perform *Salat,*[232] and keep the Ramadan fast as much as possible. Every time you cross yourself at Mass, you beg Allah's forgiveness and do Muslim prayer as soon as you can in the privacy of your home. Most of the mosques have been turned into churches. A long time ago, it was the reverse. Churches were turned into mosques. You wonder why Allah has allowed this

---

The legend did not come into writing for three hundred years after the event, but the nature of the legend seemed to have given encouragement to the Spanish to throw off Moorish rule over the next several centuries. https://www.caminoadventures.com/st-james/

[231] The Arabs called Spain *Andalusia.*

[232] *Salat,* the Arabic word for the 5-times-a-day ritual prayers that Muslims are required to do.

to happen. Have we done so much evil that Allah has allowed the infidels to triumph over us?

Your people are Berbers and the Berbers converted to Islam hundreds of years ago. Some of them were Christians before becoming Muslims. You wonder if they pretended to be Muslims but in their hearts were still Christians, as you pretend to be a Christian but in your heart, you are a Muslim. You do not like being a *Morisco*, but at least you have been able to stay in the land that you love.

May the Sword be red with Arab blood (The Knights of Santiago, cited in Crocker III, p. 155).

> *Over time both Christian and Muslim accounts of this event (the taking of Spain by the Muslims) became tales replete with prophetic utterance, spiced with suggestions of lust and betrayal. The myths provided an explanation of how it was that Tariq, with no more than a few thousand men at his disposal, could have defeated "all the Christian fighting men of Spain," numbered by some at 100,000. Why had God turned against his people? The answer was found in moral depravity that had occasioned divine wrath.* The Chronicles of Alphonso III in the year 883. (cited in Wheatcroft, p. 62).

The Iberian Peninsula (Andalusia) in 1100.

The above citation is interesting in that Christians saw their defeat at the hands of the Moors due to the immorality of their Visigothic[233] rulers. Scottish scholar Andrew Wheatcroft[234] says the people likened it to the way the Israelites were punished after David's terrible adultery with Bathsheba, when Nathan declared that the sword "would not depart from his house."

---

[233] The Visigoths ruled southwestern France and the Iberian Peninsula (includes Spain and Portugal) from the 5th-8th centuries
[234] Wheatcroft, p. 62

In 711, Muslims invaded Iberia and pushed inland, marching toward southern France. The Moors launched an attack against France and the door to all of Europe appeared to be open to them. However, a ragtag outmanned army under the command of Charles Martel, grandfather of the famous King Charlemagne, defeated the Moors and saved Europe from Islamic conquest at Tours in 732. This victory spared the rest of Europe from coming under the Crescent rather than the Cross. After that defeat, the Moors focused on bringing Andalusia under control, and they did not seek further conquest in Europe for centuries.

During this time, many Christians converted to Islam. Many who refused to convert moved further north to lands under Christian control. Wheatcroft points out that Jews, Christians and Muslims all saw the people of the other two religions as depraved sexually and grossly immoral. Christians in particular saw the Muslims as given to sexuality and cruelty, and their prophet Muhammad a forerunner of the Antichrist, if not the actual Antichrist himself.[235]

Arab and Berber Muslim armies often fought against each other and called on Christian forces to back them. I have discussed Christian disunity in previous chapters, and how that infighting helped pave the way for Islam to triumph over peoples and places that used to be Christian. The Muslims had their own share of disunity that led to their defeat in Andalusia centuries later. Sometimes outside mercenaries fought on whatever side paid the most, and it did not matter whether the people they fought for were Christians or Muslims.

The Moors ruled over what are today Spain and Portugal for over 700 years. The *Reconquista* (re-conquest) was the retaking of Andalusia by the forces loyal to the pope, which took several hundred years to complete, as gradually more and more of the region came under Catholic control. Eventually, only Granada survived as the sole independent Muslim kingdom. In 1492, the year

---

[235]Ibid, pps. 71-82

Columbus "sailed the ocean blue," King Ferdinand and Queen Isabella completed the Reconquista in the last Muslim stronghold of Granada, and banished Jews and Muslims from Spain unless they were willing to convert and be baptized. The "just imagine" story that began this chapter is about a young man who became a *Morisco* or what we might call a Crypto-Muslim.

Later we will devote a chapter to Crypto-Christians, or those who were outwardly Muslims but remained Christians in their hearts. In Spain, however, it was the reverse, with many Muslims outwardly appearing to be

Catholics, but inwardly were still Muslims.

Our Lady of the Assumption Church in Cordoba, Spain: From church to mosque to church

Crypto Jews

After the Reconquista, Queen Isabella gave Jews the option to convert or be expelled from Spain as she did Muslims. Perhaps 70,000-100,000 chose to become refugees.[236] Many more converted to Christianity and became *conversos*. Some of the converted Jews no doubt sincerely became Catholic both outwardly and in their hearts. Others appeared to be Catholics but practiced Judaism secretly. I had a chance to meet and befriend some of the descendants of the Jews who fled Spain and were received by the Turkish Sultan in the

---

[236] MacCulloch, p. 586

fifteenth century. There is still a small Jewish community in Istanbul, and a small number of Jews scattered in other Turkish cities. Traditionally they have been treated quite well, but with the rise of militant Islam, there was a major bombing of two synagogues in Istanbul in November 2003 that killed 59 people, including the suicide bombers, and wounded more than 750. Al Qaida claimed responsibility for the attacks.[237]

There have been increasing tensions between Turkey and Israel after centuries of relatively good relations between Jews and Turks. Even after Israel became a nation in 1948, Turkey did not cut off relations with the new nation. Under Turkish President Recep Tayyip Erdogan, however, Turkey has been vocally supporting and aiding the Palestinians in their conflict with Israel.

Whatever we might say about the political realm, it pains me to have to write that the Church at times forced people to be baptized against their will, or face being exiled to another land far from family and community. That seems so contrary to everything Jesus taught his followers to do. While there are far more Christians who have had to pretend to be Muslims during times of persecution, there have also been Muslims who had to pretend to be Christians as well.

Just imagine you are a commander in a ship in the year 1571 under the command of the Austrian Don Juan. Your ship is in the waters off southwest Greece, one of hundreds of ships in the fleet of combined Christian forces called the Holy League. You are about to do battle against the Turkish navy led by their much more experienced captain whom they call Ali Pasha. It was over one hundred years ago when the great city of Constantinople fell to the Turks. Doubt about whose side God is on has caused the Christian world much anguish of heart. Is God on the side of the Turkish Muslims because their beliefs are true? Or maybe God is using them as his chastising hand against Christians because of their

---

[237] https://en.wikipedia.org/wiki/2003_Istanbul_bombings

ungodliness and corruption. Either way, the thought of a Turkish victory is horrifying.

You know that if the Turkish forces win the battle, all non-Muslims will be made to serve as slaves on their galley ships or sold in the slave markets of North Africa or Constantinople. The same fate would be in store for Muslims if they lose the battle. They will also be compelled to be galley slaves or sold in the marketplace as slaves. You have heard the horror stories of what happened in Cyprus a year ago when Turkish troops besieged the capital city of Nicosia. They killed 20,000 people and paraded the heads of the city's leaders on their lance points. Of course, the goal was to terrify the rest of the city into submitting to Turkish rule.[238] You hear the stories of how brutal the Turks are to people in the places they conquer, and you motivate your troops by sharing the horror stories of what will happen if they lose this battle. In your mind, you wonder if Ali Pasha is telling his troops a similar horror story of what will happen if they lose this war to the Christians.

The battle rages on throughout the day. Under the protection of a golden image of Christ, the Christian soldiers and sailors fought. They had the assurance from the pope that those who died in the shadow of the battle flag under the figure of Christ would be spared the worst of purgatory.[239] You are aware that Ali Pasha is most likely promising forgiveness of all sins and paradise for Muslims who are killed in the battle.

The battle rages on until the late afternoon. After a few hours, one of your troops holds up the head of Ali Pasha on his spear and shouts a cry of triumph. Your men can begin to taste victory even as the Turks have begun to taste defeat.

After the battle is over and what's left of the enemy troops has surrendered, you celebrate with your men. You had heard much about how the hand of God was with the Muslims when they took

---

[238] Wheatcroft, p. 18
[239] Ibid, p. 4

Constantinople from the Byzantines. You had also heard about signs in the heavens like blood moons that pointed to the supernatural power that assisted the Ottomans in their victory. Now it is your turn to point to some signs in the Christian triumph at Lepanto. The winds that had favored the Ottoman ships suddenly shifted, giving the advantage to the Christians.[240] Your ship's Christian flag was not shot full of holes like Ali Pasha's green Islamic flag was. No Spanish or Christian monk or priest was killed or even wounded, despite being in the thick of the battle. None of the crucifixes on the ships suffered any damage despite musket balls flying all around them.[241] Most of all you attribute the Christian victory to the thousands of faithful Catholics who prayed the Rosary[242] during the battle.

The Battle of Lepanto

This is a very condensed telling of a major victory.[243] It was not that the Battle of Lepanto was such a great military victory that made it significant. Rather it was the assurance that it gave Christians that God had not forsaken them, or that He was not always on the side of the Muslims. Huge celebrations took place immediately after the

---

[240]https://en.wikipedia.org/wiki/Battle_of_Lepanto

[241] Ibid, pps. 26-27

[242] The Rosary is one of the most widely practiced of Catholic devotional practices. Each day focuses on different actions in the life of Jesus from birth to resurrection and beyond. The Joyful Mysteries focus on five events related to his birth. The Sorrowful Mysteries focus on five events related to his death. The Illuminous Mysteries focus on five events during Christ's life. The Glorious Mysteries focus on five events between the resurrection and the second coming. The Rosary begins with reciting the Apostles Creed, the Lord's Prayer and the reciting of the *Hail Mary* ten times while meditating on each of the mysteries of Christ. Many websites demonstrate how to pray the rosary and give its history in more detail.

[243] 7,500 Christians lost their lives in the battle, but Muslims losses were almost three times higher. 15,000 Christian galley slaves were freed as a result. Kathy Schiffer states higher numbers. The Holy League (Christians) lost 50 galleys and 13,000 casualties. The Turks lost 25,000 sailors along with 210 of their 250 ships, including 130 captured by the Holy League.

victory and continue[244] to be celebrated on October 7 every year. Father Steven Grunow discusses how it may seem out of character for the victory at Lepanto to be considered a triumph of the Virgin Mary. Most Western Christians may not think of Mary as one who fights battles on behalf of those who call upon her name and who will intervene in battle on their behalf. We need to remember, however, that Europe was under siege. People lived in fear that Muslims were ready to take all of Europe as they had the Middle East 1,000 years before. Spain had only been free of Muslim rule for about eight decades when the battle of Lepanto took place. The pope had called Catholics to urgent prayer and continuous recitation of the Rosary. The victory at Lepanto was viewed as a triumph of the forces of good over evil--God triumphing over Satan and all the forces of Hell.

Protestant readers may find it disconcerting to hear that the triumph of the Battle of Lepanto was attributed to the intercession of Mary. Yet I am reminded of Protestants uniting together to pray for victory against Nazism in World War II[245] and against Communism during the Cold War. Protestants often gather together for collective, spontaneous prayer just as Catholics often gather together for the collective praying of the Rosary or the Divine Mercy Chaplet. Both Catholics and Protestants, as well as Orthodox Christians, need to be regularly reminded that they are in a spiritual conflict even more than a physical one. We all need to remember that the real enemy we wrestle against is not flesh and blood, but principalities and powers of the Evil One, and we need to be equipped with spiritual armor and pray with all kinds of prayer (Ephesians 6).

The Protestant Reformation had taken place only 54 years previously, and the Catholic Church was struggling with the ramifications of that as well as worrying about the Ottomans taking

---

[244] https://www.wordonfire.org/resources/blog/our-lady-of-the-rosary-and-the-battle-of-lepanto/1220/
[245] I remember binge greatly inspired by reading about Rees Howell, the great prayer warrior, and their intercession for the Allies against the Nazis when I was a Bible school student in the early 1970s.

all of Europe. Lepanto was a great moral victory that Protestants could rejoice in as well, despite their inter-religious conflicts against Catholics. After all, as much as Martin Luther despised the pope, he also lived in Europe at a time when fear of the Turks was pervasive. Protestants and Catholics fought against each other, but neither wanted to fall under Islam.

Remembering the Battle

In 1571 Pope Pius V instituted "Our Lady of Victory" as an annual feast of thanksgiving. Two years later Pope Gregory XIII changed the name of the day to the "Feast of the Holy Rosary." In 1716 Pope Clement XI extended the feast to the whole of the Latin Rite[246] to the first Sunday in October. Almost 200 years later in 1913 Pope Pius X changed the date to October 7.[247]

The Decline of the Ottoman Empire

In 1529 and in 1683 the Turkish armies again sought to conquer Europe but both times were defeated at Vienna. The defeat of 1529 led Suleiman (Suleyman) the Magnificent to give up on conquering Europe, despite having won impressive military battles in eastern and central Europe. In 1683, under the armies of Kara Mustafa, the Turks came closer to taking Vienna, which would have opened the door to all of Europe to succumb. At the last minute, however, King John III Sobieski of Poland came to the aid of Vienna, and again the Turks were defeated. After this loss, the Ottoman Empire went into serious decline and never really threatened Europe again, although they held onto many of their colonies for over another 200 plus years. These battles for Vienna, despite being great triumphs that held back the Islamic armies from invading all of Europe, are not viewed through a spiritual lens as much as is the Battle of Lepanto.

---

[246] In the days before Vatican II beginning in 1962, Mass was conducted in Latin throughout Europe rather than in the national language of the particular country.
[247] Kathy Schiffer https://www.ncregister.com/blog/kschiffer/the-pope-the-rosary-and-the-battle-of-lepanto?utm_source=google&utm_medium=cpc&utm_campaign=ncrtraffic&gcli d=EAIaIQob

John Sobieski has probably never gotten the place in history that he deserves, perhaps because he was Polish rather than German, English, or French.[248]

Application

Whose side is God on? Both Muslims and Christians can point to events that seemed to show divine favor in their military pursuits. They can also blame their defeats in terms of God abandoning or punishing them and allowing their enemies to defeat them to bring them to repentance and to be more faithful to do what their faith demands. As we shall see, the rise of Europe and the decline of the Islamic world, especially after the establishment of the state of Israel, has led to a lot of soul searching in the Islamic world, just as it did to the Christian world after the fall of Constantinople.

Questions for Discussion and Reflection

- Do you think Muslims might have thought about the Battle of Lepanto and the two losses at Vienna in the same way that Christians might have thought after the fall of Constantinople?
- Many Catholics attribute the victory of Lepanto to the united praying of the Rosary. Previously I mentioned Rees Howell and his prayer warriors praying for the defeat of the Nazis. Whether the Rosary or the more conversational style of many Evangelicals, do you think Christians should pray for military victory in certain circumstances?

---

[248] The famous novelist, James Michener, wrote an excellent account of the battle in his novel *Poland* 1983, which I would highly recommend.

17

Millets and Identity Issues

Just imagine you are a Jew living in the mid-nineteenth century in the Ottoman Empire in what is today western Turkey. Your ancestors fled to the Ottoman Empire from Spain in 1492, when Jews were forced out of Spain if they did not convert to Christianity. Jews were accepted as refugees by the Sultan of the Ottoman Empire. Your community is made up of Spanish Jews, as well as Jews from other European lands. Most of your fellow Jews have done well under the Ottomans. They have allowed you to follow your own laws, and they allow you to open synagogues.

Western Christians have been coming to your city and throughout the Empire in increasing numbers. You stay within your own Jewish community as much as possible, but your Jewelry business puts you in contact with other goldsmiths and jewelers who are mostly local Christians. Many of your customers are Turkish Muslims who buy gold for their prospective brides. Most Muslim families insist that the bridegroom give the bride's family a good amount of gold, a type of bride price. If for whatever reason the marriage does not work out, at least the bride and her family get something out of the marriage.

Some of the talk you overhear among the Christians is disconcerting. Even though many of the Christians around you are doing quite well financially, they are getting increasingly restless under the millet system. Europeans from different countries, and even Americans, are opening schools and hospitals, and the children of the Christian millets are getting a really good education. They are learning European languages, which gives them a big advantage in dealing with European countries. Wealthy Muslim families want to send their children to these Christian schools as long as Christian teachers do not try to convert their children.

You think the Christians have an idealized image of how great life was under Christian rule during the Byzantine Empire, and that they focus too much on the hardships of being dhimmis under the Ottomans. As a Jew, you know that the Byzantine Empire was no picnic for your ancestors. Neither was Spain or anywhere else your people lived under "Christian" rule. You hope that this wave of ethnic-Christian nationalism, be it Greek, Armenian, Assyrian, or whatever is only a fad and will fade away. You don't think it will, however. You overhear conversations in Turkish among your Muslim customers that the Christians are pushing too hard and that it is about time for Muslims to remind them what their place is under Islam.

History and Theology: What was the Millet System?

The Ottoman Empire reached its zenith under Suleiman (Suleyman) the Magnificent (d. 1566) and in its heyday, the Ottomans controlled Asia Minor, Syria, Egypt, North Africa, Azerbaijan, the Balkans, Hungary, much of the Arabian Gulf, and parts of southern Russia[249]

The term *millet* essentially means "nation" based on a shared religion within a religious community. The *dhimmi* system that we previously examined goes back much further, and some historians trace it back to Sultan Mehmed I in the early fifteenth century even before the fall of Constantinople. Full implementation of the Millet system probably goes back to the nineteenth century under Sultan Mahmud II. As the highly esteemed historian of the Middle East, Bernard Lewis, states:

---

[249] Encyclopedia of Islam, p. 402

A millet was a religious-political community defined by its adherence to a religion. Its members were subject to the rules and even to the laws of that religion, administered by its own chiefs, naturally in so far as these did not conflict with the laws and interest of the state. In return for this measure of religious freedom and communal autonomy, non-Muslim millets owed allegiance to the state and accepted the limitations and disabilities of dhimmi status.[250]

This meant that tax collection, education, and legal and religious issues could be decided within the millet's own community under the supervision of the Ottoman administration.

The millet system was a unique way of governing the expanding Ottoman Empire. It has won much praise for its tolerance and relatively just way of governing non-Muslim subjects. That is not to say there were no difficulties and that it was always fair, but compared to the way Jews and heretical Christians were often treated in the Byzantine Empire or in Spain after the *Reconquista,* Christians should not be too quick to judge. After all, the Thirty Years War, fought mostly in Central Europe in the seventeenth century, had cost the lives of up to eight million people; and destabilized the region for long afterward. It began as a Catholic versus Protestant conflict; then evolved into a power grab that transcended religious differences. Going into detail about that conflict is beyond the scope of this book, but I mentioned it to point out that many historians blame the Thirty Years War as the catalyst that drove many Europeans away from holding a religious worldview, instead of moving toward a secular and nationalist way of thinking that came into full play after the Enlightenment. In light of this, we should not be overly critical when evaluating the millet system under the Ottomans. Many Jews and Christians became quite wealthy under the system despite its discriminatory policies.

---

[250] Lewis, pps. 321-322

What was especially interesting about the millet system is how it made religion rather than ethnicity the major societal classification. Within the Muslim millet were Arabs, Turks, Kurds, Muslims from Eastern Europe, and even converts to Islam. Most Muslims simply identified themselves by their religion rather than with an ethnic label. The Greek Orthodox millet included Orthodox Christians with Greek, Bulgar, Serb, Romanian, Albanian, and even Turkish and Arabic-speaking Orthodox Christians. The Armenian millet, as Lewis points out, was more ethnically homogenous, and included members of the Jacobite and Coptic churches and Turkish-speaking Armenians. It did not include Catholic or Protestant Armenians.[251] In the 19th century, during thelatterr days of the empire, there were millets for both Catholics and Protestants independent of the Orthodox millet. The Jewish millet included Spanish, Arabic, and Greek speakers, as well as others of Jewish ancestry. The Jews had been forcibly exiled from Spain in 1492 as we saw in the "just imagine" story, landed in the Ottoman Empire and were well received by the Sultan.

As we will examine in more detail later, European ideas of independent nation-states began to infiltrate the Ottoman Empire in the nineteenth century, resulting in people developing their own sense of national identity. Armenian, Assyrian, Greek, Serbian, and even Jewish nationalism began to evolve, although the Jews did not focus on it as much as other millets did.

European powers began to pressure the Ottomans to give their non-Muslim millets equal citizenship with the Muslim millet. This was hard for the majority of the Muslims to accept as the dhimmi system was perceived as divinely inspired by the Qur'an. Furthermore, it was a somewhat hypocritical demand by many of the Western powers who certainly were not giving the Jews in their countries equal treatment.

---

[251] Ibid p. 322

Not only was there more of a demand for equality in the Ottoman Empire, but some of the millets were pushing toward autonomy if not full independence within their regions. Some of the eastern European millets were primarily in one geographic region, but the Armenians were scattered throughout the entire region of what is today Turkey, although in no place were they a majority. What would an autonomous or independent Armenian millet have looked like? Bernard Lewis cites Cevdet Pasha in an 1856 note related to the issue:

> The patriarchs...were displeased... Whereas in former times in the Ottoman state, the communities were ranked with the Muslims first, then the Greeks, then the Armenians, then the Jews, now all of them are put on the same level. Some Greeks objected to this, saying, 'The government has put us together with the Jews. We were content with the supremacy of Islam.[252]

The rivalry between different millets was so strong at times that there was more animosity between millets than toward the Ottoman rulers who subjugated them. There are many accounts of Christians turning in other Christians to the Ottoman authorities, especially when they felt that other Christians were "sheep stealing." As many Armenians converted to Protestantism, Armenian Protestants had complaints lodged against them and their churches by the Armenian Orthodox patriarchs and bishops.

Now, let us look ahead five or six decades what life might have looked like.

> We will "accept whatever Church wielded the biggest club." (A Church of the East priest)[253]

***

Just Imagine you are a member of the Church of the East living in southeast Turkey in the early 1900s. Most of the people in the

---

[252] Ibid p. 324
[253] Joseph, 1961, p. 121

surrounding villages are Kurds, but there are Christian villages as well. Some of your fellow Assyrian Christians[254] (Church of the East) have submitted to the pope and become Catholics. Now they call themselves Chaldeans. Some Protestant missionaries come through your area from time to time. They say they are Christians but they speak strongly against the Catholics. They seem bent on trying to persuade any Christians of the Church of the East to stay away from the Catholic Church. The Catholics are determined, however, to bring you into their church that they claim can be traced back to the first pope--St. Peter. Catholicism does offer a huge advantage because it is better connected to France and other Catholic countries. They might be able to offer better protection and maybe even the possibility of emigration to Europe when the Muslims make life difficult for Christians.

The Protestants have opened up schools and churches, and some of the young people of your village like the way they worship and the special activities for youth. Their holy men do not wear special clothes as the Catholic priests do. In fact, they do not have priests at all. Some Sundays they don't even celebrate the Eucharist (communion). After the sermon, they invite people to give their lives to Jesus. So you have your traditional church, and your priests are telling you to stay faithful to the church you grew up in and honor its traditions. The Catholics are urging you to submit to Rome and be a part of the "one, holy, catholic and apostolic church."[255] The Protestants tell you that the Catholic Church distorts the Gospel by praying to Mary and the saints and by believing in purgatory and other traditions allegedly not in the Bible. The Protestants tell you

---

[254] Remember that the term "Nestorian" is viewed pejoratively by the Church of the East. I have used Church of the East and Assyrian Christians interchangeably in this chapter. Eastern Christians can include Jacobites, Orthodox, Miaphysite, Armenian and other Christians as well as the Church of the East.
[255] From the Nicene Creed. Protestant churches that recite the creed generally point out that the word "catholic" means universal, and does not refer specifically to the Roman Catholic Church.

that the important thing is be "born again" and experience Christ personally.

The Protestants hope that we Assyrian Christians will be what they call "revived" so we will reach the Turks, Kurds, Arabs and Persians of the whole region. Can't they grasp that we have been under the thumb of the Muslims for centuries living as second-class citizens. Now they expect us to share our faith with those who have treated us like second-class citizens for generations.

All of this division among those of us who call ourselves Christians is leaving us very confused. Catholics have connections with Europe, Protestants with America. Even some Russians have come and told us to become Orthodox and the Czars will protect us. What I want to know is what is best for my family and me? Who offers the best protection and benefits for our children?

Curiosity, Commerce, and Conversion

Europeans increasingly began to visit the Ottoman Empire during the 19th century for perhaps three major reasons: curiosity, commerce and conversion. They were curious to visit biblical sites that appealed to their spiritual nature, even as observing the exoticness of Ottoman life, and especially the harems of the sultan, no doubt appealed to the fantasy side for European males. Commerce with trade going both ways increased between Europe and the Ottomans. Converting Muslims to faith in Christ motivated a few Europeans to come to the area. Many more Christian missionaries, both Catholics and Protestants, however, longed for the long-oppressed Assyrian, Coptic, Jacobite, and Armenian Christians to become what each declared to be the truest expression of Christian faith. For Catholic missionaries, the task was to bring the separated eastern Christians under the Bishop of Rome (the pope). Imagine if these long-oppressed Christians could become a part of the universal Catholic Church. How much dignity, strength, and courage it would give them as minorities in the world of Islam!

For Protestants, it meant that if these Christians who spoke Arabic, Turkish, Kurdish and Persian since childhood could be revived, they would be the key to bringing Muslims to faith in Christ! All they needed was to discard "unbiblical" traditions and experience salvation by grace through faith for this to happen.

First, we will examine the Catholic approach and then examine Protestant attempts among the Eastern Christians.

Western Protection of Christians in the Ottoman Empire

After the divide between Orthodox and Catholic in 1054, the Roman Catholic Church endeavored to bring Orthodox and Eastern Christians, especially Miaphysites, into the fold. Pope Origen IV in 1437 had issued a decree that French Catholics should motivate Assyrian Christians to come into the Church. Father Jean-Baptiste, a seventeenth century Capuchin missionary, came to evangelize the Assyrian Christians and bring them into conformity with Rome. The Congregation of the Propagation of the Faith, established by Pope Gregory XV in 1622, sent missionaries to both Ottoman and Persian territories. Eventually more than half of Church of the East joined the Chaldean Catholic Church.[256]

At about the same time, French Jesuit and Lazarist missionaries spread over the Levant[257] and Persia, as did the Capuchin order in Constantinople, Aleppo, and Persia. Carmelites also opened a mission in Aleppo and the Dominicans were established in Syria, Lebanon, Iraq and Anatolia. Missionary orders that enjoyed the protection of France grew in towns and villages that had Christian inhabitants, such as Aleppo, Jerusalem, Libya, Damascus, Mosul, and Baghdad, and in Mardin and Diyarbakir in what is today southeast Turkey. Especially by opening schools, attempts were made to convert Greek Orthodox, Jacobites, Nestorians and Armenians to Catholicism.[258]

---

[256] Ibid, p. 24
[257] The Levant usually refers to what is now the eastern Mediterranean, including, Syria, Lebanon, Jordan, and Palestine. Sometimes Iraq is also included.
[258] Ibid p. 155

Catholic Missions in Iraq

Catholic missions arrived in Iraq, which was still part of the Ottoman Empire, in the early decades of the seventeenth century. The Capuchins arrived first, followed by the Carmelites and the Dominicans. The Carmelites opened the first primary school in Baghdad in 1721, while the Dominicans opened primary schools in Mosul and surrounding villages in 1750.[259]

In Northern Iraq, especially in Mosul and the surrounding villages, including Ahmadiyah, Zakho and Alqosh, those living in villages primarily spoke Syriac while those in towns spoke Arabic. French Dominican nuns arrived in Mosul in 1873 and began to teach young women writing and sewing, The Christians of northern Iraq were under direct Ottoman rule within the *vilayet*[260] of Mosul and had to pay the jizya and follow dhimmi rules. The majority belonged to the Church of the East, but a large minority were Syrian Orthodox Christians.[261]

Eastern Patriarchs React against Rome

There was a firm reaction by the Orthodox, Armenian, and Syriac patriarchs to these Catholic attempts to bring the Christians under Rome. The Muslim Porte[262] was not pleased to see some of his Christian subjects leave the indigenous churches and submit to his traditional enemy, the Pope. The Porte sometimes forbade their Christian subjects to transfer their alliance from one rite to another. Sometimes Miaphysite Christians who had departed to Catholic or Orthodox churches that accepted the ruling at Chalcedon were denounced to the Muslim authorities by their bishops. Those bishops who were willing to report their former members who had changed their alliance to a church connected to Rome were rewarded by the Porte for their resistance to papal rule. In 1700, the

---

[259] Rassam p.103
[260] A *vilayet* is somewhat equivalent to a governorship.
[261] Ibid 106
[262] The central government in Ottoman times under the rule of the Sultan

Armenian Miaphysite patriarch procured a *firman* (legal agreement) forbidding the presence of Catholic missionaries. Armenian Catholics took revenge by abducting the Armenian patriarch. It took the Sultan to settle the strife with a severity that led to martyrdom and apostasy by many. [263]

France's religious protection promoted schisms in every *millet* in the Ottoman Empire, leading to many Christians in the Church of the East, as well as Armenian, Jacobite, Greek and Chaldean Christians, to endeavor to come under the protection of Roman Catholic administration. France had a special relationship with the Maronites, primarily Lebanese Christians who accepted the authority of the pope. Many Armenians also were attracted to Catholicism. Besides its spiritual benefits, it gave them an ally in France and other European countries. This possible connection emboldened their hopes for independence from Ottoman rule one day. In the seventeenth century, France seemed the safest bet to protect Christians. In the nineteenth century, it was the Americans, and in the early twentieth century, it was the Russians that indigenous Christians looked to for protection and other benefits.

The Outreach to the Yezidis

The Yezidis[264], the long-oppressed Kurdish-speaking people who adhere to the alleged indigenous religion of the Kurds before Islam (See chapter 13), showed great interest in converting to Christianity, both Catholic and Protestant branches. Some Armenian Miaphysite clergy who had recently changed their alliance to Catholicism may have feared a loss of financial benefits to their fellow Armenian Catholics and closed the door to further Yezidi evangelization. Furthermore, division between the Carmelite, Jesuit, and Capuchin orders was intense enough that the French council ruled that the all three orders had to approve any missionary endeavor and the

---

[263] Ibid 156-157

[264] Sometimes the line between religion and ethnicity is blurred. The Yezidis are Kurds, but because they are not Muslims, they are often identified as Yezidis despite sharing a common language with Muslim Kurds.

distribution of funds. This led to a virtual full withdrawal of Catholic efforts among the Yezidis.

Ottoman Reaction

With increased travel by Europeans and Americans to visit biblical sites, especially during the nineteenth century, along with increased focus on human rights, there were more calls on the Ottomans to ensure equality among all of its subjects. Both the Church of the East and the Syrian Orthodox Church had learned to some degree to co-exist with their Kurdish and Arab neighbors. The rise of nationalism, as well as contact with traders, travelers, politicians, educators, and missionaries brought a new restlessness to various types of Christians. As their sense of ethnic and religious pride began to grow, the authorities, both regional-and the central Ottoman government, were afraid of the fragmentation of their empire.

> New policies of trade favored Europeans, and benefited the minority Christian populations who had begun to learn European languages and were co-religionists with the Europeans. The Muslims began to feel increasingly threatened by the influence of Europe and the local Christians who profited from European economic control.[265]

As the Ottomans sought to accommodate their Christian populations to some degree at least, the reaction among average Muslims was not favorable. They thought that the Ottomans had sold out to "Christian" powers and denied the Allah-ordained system of dhimmitude of non-Muslim subjects. Subjugated Christians increasingly began to take pride in their ancient heritages before coming under Islam, particularly among people with long and proud heritages, such as Egyptians, Greeks, Armenians, and Assyrians. In some places, Turkish officials tried to implement the "rights" of the former *dhimmis,* but in other places, often out of fear of the reaction they would get from religious Muslims, they did not.

---

[265] Ibid, p. 270

At the highest political level, implementing equality was agreed to, but the problem of implementing it in regional and local areas, where the reaction against it was strong.[266]

Russia also asserted its right to intervene on behalf of Orthodox subjects, especially in the eastern Ottoman Empire where the Armenians were a strong minority. Christians perceived to be connected to Russia or another major European country were generally more secure spiritually, economically, and politically.[267]

The Attraction of being Connected to Western Churches

> *Cases such as these are sufficient to explain why the Greeks and Armenians have been able to make a better stand against the encroachments of Rome than the poor Syrians (Nestorians), whose comparatively small number, their distance from Russia, and geographical position, render them of little importance to the political views of the great Tsar. And added to this, in all their conflicts, they have had to contend single-handed against the powerful influence of France, which arrogates to herself the right of protecting all the "Catholics" in the Turkish empire. George Percy Badger (1842-1844) Reflecting the anti-Catholicism of the Protestant missionaries in the Ottoman Empire.*

Both Catholics and Protestants experienced the eventual resistance of the Eastern Christian clergy who resented and resisted "sheep stealing" by outside missionaries. How could local clergy offer the schools, hospitals and connections with Europe, Russia, or America that the foreign Christians could offer? I do not want to imply that all those who joined the churches connected to the West had impure motives. No doubt, many eastern Christians were drawn to the awe-inspiring liturgy of the Catholics and Russian Orthodox, while others were attracted to the simple presentation of the gospel that the Protestants offered. When we understand the times and pressures that Christians faced as minorities in a much larger sea of

---

[266] Ibid 171-177
[267] Ibid 163

Muslims, it is not too hard to understand why being connected to France, England, and later the USA and Russia, would appeal to Eastern Christians. It is also not difficult to understand why the local clergy felt threatened by those coming from the outside hoping to make converts of their parishioners.

Protestant Approaches to the Church of the East

> With God all things are possible; but humanly speaking there seems little hope of the conversion of these heathen until the native churches shall have risen from sleep, and again trimmed their lamps with a zeal and love such as were exhibited in the early Nestorian missionaries, who carried the glad tidings of the Gospel into the wilds of Tartary, and planted the banner of the cross among the refined pagans of China (George Percy Badger in a first-hand narrative of a mission to Mesopotamia 1842-1844).

I previously mentioned that when Protestant missionaries first encountered the Church of the East, they thought they had discovered some long-lost Protestants. Here were Christians whose beliefs and practices were closer to Protestantism than to Catholicism. After all, they had been declared heretics for refusing to call Mary the Mother of God (*Theotokis*) centuries ago. They did not have statues or pictures hanging in their churches. If I had been a Protestant missionary in those days, I probably would have been as excited as the nineteenth century missionaries were. Imagine that you anticipate years and years evangelizing Muslims with perhaps with few results. Then you discover hundreds of Christians who have not submitted to Rome and who speak the languages and live in near proximity to the very people you hoped to reach!

The Great Experiment

The "Great Experiment" is a phrase that Peter Pikkert, a good friend and a gifted linguist, fluent in Arabic, Turkish and Kurdish, and Bob Blincoe, also a good friend and an incredible motivator and mission administrator, use this term to describe Protestant attempts to revive the indigenous churches of the Middle East. By reviving these ancient churches, it was hoped that they would in turn evangelize the Muslims."[268] In Turkey, Persia, and Arabia, and among the four major ethnic groups that we have focused on throughout this book, the Protestant missionaries saw the Nestorians, Jacobites, and Armenians as the natural instruments of God to reach the Muslim majority in those lands. We should probably be not overly judgmental of these Protestant missionaries, mostly Americans, who bought into the Great Experiment. Sharing the gospel with Muslims is generally a long and arduous process. I know people who have spent many years, even decades, in Muslim countries without seeing any visible fruit. Years of language learning, the study of the Qur'an, and building relationships of trust can be very discouraging.

Bob Blincoe estimates that in the nineteenth and twentieth centuries, perhaps 200 missionaries lived in Kurdistan, but very few spoke Kurdish or even had contact with many Kurds.[269] Their entire focus was on reviving the Eastern Christians whom they hoped would evangelize the Kurds. Those set on evangelizing other major ethnic groups focused on in this book--Arabs, Turks, and Persians— had similar goals. Their focus was on local Christians, not Muslims, believing they were the key to reaching the Kurds, Turks, and Arabs with the gospel.

Looks Good on Paper

Americans especially are generally very pragmatic and want "bang for their bucks." Missionary supporters back home could read stories about schools and hospitals established in places mentioned in their Bibles. David McDowall, the author of a massive historical text on the history of the Kurds, writes that the Nestorians were able to survive because of their seclusion, often blending in with the surrounding Kurdish villages. After the arrival of the well-meaning

---

[268] For a more in-depth study of what I am briefly summarize, I strongly recommend *Ethnic Realities* by Robert Blincoe *and the Church* and *Protestant Missionaries to the Middle East: Ambassadors of Christ or Culture Protestant Missionaries to the Middle East: Ambassadors of Christ or Culture by P. Pikkert*
[269] Blincoe, p. 17

missionaries, however, the Nestorians[270] (and other Eastern Christians as well) received a lot of attention from western-connected outsiders that would lead to their eventual demise. Blincoe points out that within ten years of the arrival of the missionaries, Kurds slaughtered thousands of Armenians and Nestorians.[271] Whereas before there was occasional pogroms and skirmishes, as well as the kidnapping of Christian girls and women, those confrontations between the majority Muslim community and the subjugated Christians paled when compared what happened after the missionaries arrived. In short, the Kurds felt jealous of the empowerment that the local Christians had benefited medically, educationally, and financially from their contacts with missionaries. . Before, the Christians had been to some degree under the thumb of Kurdish agahs (tribal and village leaders). Agahs had collected tribute taxes from Christians, and sometimes agahs sold their Christian serfs along with their land in financial transactions. Now their power over "their Christians" was being threatened.

The American Board of Commissioners of Foreign Missions

One of the leading organizations for missions work was the American Board of Commissioners of Foreign Missions (hence ABCFM). One of their better-known missionaries was Asahel Grant. He was 28 years old and a widower when he volunteered for service in Kurdistan with the ABCFM. He left his two sons with relatives and took his new wife to Kurdistan in 1835. As a doctor, he saw thousands of patients, and he opened a dozen village schools. He later claimed that the Assyrians (the ethnic classification of the members of the Church of the East) were the long-lost tribes of Israel, which caused quite a sensation in that day. We know from the Old Testament that the ten northern tribes were exiled to the lands of the Assyrians along the Habor River (II Kings 17). It is not too hard to understand why Grant was excited. Later his theory was

---

[270] I have used the word "Nestorian" as the authors I am drawing from have used that term.
[271] Blincoe p. 36

discarded, and Grant seemed to have suggested that the Yezidi Kurds were the ten lost tribes. I previously stated why I believe the Kurds (whether Yezidi or Muslim) could well be the ten tribes, but I have stopped short of being dogmatic on the topic![272]

Grant, in his years in Kurdistan, buried his second wife and all four of their children. As mentioned earlier, Grant and other missionaries empowered the Christians and encouraged them not to pay taxes to the *agahs*. By 1945, some 10,000 Nestorians, or about 1/5 of their number, had perished under Bedir Kahn, a major Kurdish tribal leader, who also sold many others into slavery.[273]

From the Middle East to the Ivy League

When Protestants realized that many Eastern Churches were not coming alive spiritually as they hoped and that the local clergy rallied against them, they began to establish Protestant churches for Christians who no longer felt connected to their ancestral churches. Some of these churches grew quite rapidly. Protestant missionaries also established hundreds of schools and hospitals. Many of the schools and universities established by missionaries are still in existence but have been taken over by the governments of the various countries in which they were established. Some are now among the best educational institutions in their respective countries, but seldom is it mentioned that they were founded by Christian missionaries. The Middle Eastern student studying in these institutions today probably has no idea that his or her prestigious school was founded by Christians who wanted to make Christ known and loved among the students.

I suppose it should not surprise us too much that their Christian heritage has been suppressed. After all, many of America's best universities, including most of the Ivy League schools, were established by churches that wanted to give students the best education as well as produce committed followers of Christ. I

---

[272] Brenneman, p. 23
[273] Blincoe, p. 44

wonder how many students at Harvard, Yale, and Princeton, among others, realize the Christ-focused goals behind the establishment of their prestigious universities? The Fire of Purification

In the Ottoman Empire Jewish and Christian craftsmen did much of the jewelry work w (Turkish *kuyumculuk*). In the mid-1980s, I visited the small workplace of an Assyrian Christian goldsmith. His family had been in the jewelry business for generations. I saw him sweep up the dust on the floor of his tiny workplace and put it in a small cauldron. He then placed the cauldron in a blazing fire for several minutes. As he lifted the object out of the cauldron, it looked like a black ball but not perfectly spherical in shape. The blob consisted of the dust particles now glued together by the fire. He placed the blob into a different cauldron and put it back into an even more scorching fire for a time (I cannot remember for how long). He then removed the blob from the fire. Out of the blob of worthless appearing dust particles, a small stream of pure gold came forth. The super intense fire burned up all of the seemingly worthless dust, and in the end, just a few centigrams of gold was produced. How valuable that gold is, however!

Seeing this transformation from dust into gold reminded me of what Saint Peter wrote in his first epistle: "That the trying of your faith being much more precious than gold that perisheth, though it be tried with fire, might be found onto praise, honor and glory at the appearing of Jesus Christ (I Peter 1:7 KJV).

God takes the worthless things of our lives and puts them in the fire of life's tests and trials, which purges and brings forth the "gold" of our lives as they are purified by the fire of His Spirit within us. We can see that beyond the personal application of the Spirit's fire in each of our lives, we can also apply it to the long-suffering church in the Islamic world. It has gone through fiery trials for 1,400 years. It often seemed as though no "gold" would ever come forth. But the Holy Spirit's fire is burning up the dross and impurities of his Church, so that the purifying fire will lead to redeemed people of every other nation (Revelations 5:9) who come forth and give praise, honor and glory to the Lamb of God.

Questions for Discussion and Reflection

- Explain what the "Great Experiment" was and why it sometimes led to disastrous results.
- In most Muslim countries, there is still at least a remnant of historic Christians, though a very small percentage of the population. Do you think Christians coming from outside should work with these Christians, hoping for spiritual renewal, or should they focus strictly on sharing Christ with Muslims?
- Can you identify with the story of how the purifying fire turns dust into gold? Do you see this process in your own life?

18

Christian Minorities and the Decline of the Ottoman Empire

Just imagine that you are an older Armenian in the year 1918. You and your people have been through so much during the last several decades. You saw the final collapse of the Ottoman Empire during World War I, when the Turks made the fatal decision to align with the Germans rather than with the British, French, Russians, and Americans. You saw how many of your fellow Armenians hoped that the Russians, your fellow Orthodox Christians, would liberate you from Ottoman rule, and some of your people took revenge against the Kurdish *agahs* (tribal chiefs) who had oppressed them.

Your fellow Armenians are greatly divided over religion. Proud of your heritage, that you were the first nation to accept Christianity under Great Gregory in 315, you call yourselves the faithful Christians who have refused to convert to Islam when other Christians did so to avoid persecution.

At one time, all of your people were Armenian Orthodox; proud Miaphysites who refused to accept the decision of the Council of Chalcedon. Then Catholic missionaries came to the Middle East and many of your fellow Armenians became Catholics. Several years later the Protestants came and told you not to become Catholic. They preached grace alone though faith alone, and that the Catholics and your historic church both add traditions to the

Gospel. There was quite a three-way battle going on, with your priests telling you to be faithful to your heritage, and the Catholics urging you to join the church that goes back to St. Peter and the Apostles. The Protestants also are pushing you to join their churches, although your priest forbade your people from attending their services. Your bishop even complained to the Ottoman authorities about the proselytizing by these groups, and the government deported some back to their home countries.

In the late 1890s, many of your people were killed by the Ottomans for alleged disloyalty to the Empire. As the empire collapsed, many Armenians thought that the Young Turks, as they called themselves, would unite the people in a secular type of government. Muslims, Christians, and Jews danced and celebrated in the streets, assuming that a new day was dawning. Somehow, the Young Turks became a hyper-nationalist movement. Instead of governance by your own people under Islamic rule as part of the Greek Orthodox millet, identity became based on one's ethnicity, with the Turks being the clear "first among equals."

The tragic mass killing of your people, beginning in 1915, soon after the start of World War I, would end in much death, disease, starvation, and exile. To save their families, many of your people converted to Islam and took on the Turkish identity, at least outwardly.

History and Theology

Armenian Population Estimates

Until World War I, about 40 percent of Istanbul's population was Jewish or Christian. In 1882, the Armenian patriarch in claimed an Armenian population of 2.4 million, however, in 1914, the Ottoman census had given a figure about one-half of that. From the moment the Turkish nation-state was born, the Ottoman Empire's Christians seemed to dissipate despite a population of at least three million in 1914. After World War I, the only reliable census conducted by the Turkish Republic found 77,000 Armenians in 1927.

Destabilizing the Ottoman Empire

Many forces contributed to the destabilization of the *dar-al-Islam* (House of Islam), particularly in the final years of the Ottoman Empire. We previously looked at the Ottoman losses at Lepanto in 1571 and the two failed sieges of Vienna in 1529 and 1683. However, the empire did not collapse overnight. Rather it was known as "the sick man of Europe" as it maintained its hold over much of Eastern Europe, the Middle East and North Africa, but added no new conquests. It was obvious that the overall "energy" of the empire was on the way down and it was nearing collapse. As the empire weakened, the subjugated peoples, especially in the Balkan (eastern European) countries, began to push for independence, looking to the European colonial powers for support.

The battles for emancipation led to massacres in Greece and Bulgaria, the extermination of 20,000 Christians in Syria and Lebanon in 1860, and the deaths of between 200,000-300,000 Armenians in Turkey between 1895-1896. Perhaps as many as 96,000 Jacobites were massacred at Mardin.[274]

To go into detail about the declining days of the Ottoman Empire and the effect on the Jewish and Christian millets is beyond the scope of this book. I have listed some good sources for this in the resource list. The most controversial issue facing the Ottoman Empire in its decline, and the birth of the nation-state of Turkey, concerned the treatment of the Armenians.

The Armenian Struggle

Armenia had always served as a border battleground. Situated between Rome and Persia, the Armenians had declared independence from both Rome and Constantinople and rejected the Council of Chalcedon[275]. Thus, protecting the Armenians was

---

[274] Joseph (1983) p. 98
[275] See chapter 7

not seen as the responsibility of the church authorities in either the west or the east, neither before nor after the advent of Islam.

In the eighteenth and early nineteenth centuries, the Armenians were caught in a three-way struggle among three empires: Ottoman Turkey, Russian under the Czars, and the Persian Safavid dynasty. In 1828, Russia defeated Persia and annexed the area around Erevan (now the capital of Armenia).[276] As a result, thousands of Armenians become a part of the Russian Empire. Other Armenians were educated in schools founded by western missions and were exposed to new ideas. Independent nation-states were being formulated in Europe based on a common sense of ethnic and cultural identity. That was quite a change from the ideology of the Ottoman Empire with its religious millets compelled to submit to the Sultan of the Muslim world.

In the mid-nineteenth century, a movement in the Ottoman Empire called the *Tanzimat* swept through the Empire, and as Esposito points out, social and political reforms were copied from Western Europe in response to internal and external political pressures[277]. The movement sought to centralize the countless fiefdoms, tribes, and small units of local control into a more centralized authority structure. This was not all bad for the Armenians, but with time, the movement became more authoritarian and less tolerant toward minorities. As the Armenians became more self-aware of their history and distinct identity, they appealed to the western powers and Russia for assistance from their Christian co-religionists. The Ottoman Empire's rulers felt very threatened by the western powers, and they countered the growing resistance with the massacre of Armenians.as described above.

The Young Turks

After the first mass killing of Armenians under the Ottomans in 1895, a new movement broke out in 1908 called the Committee of Union

---

[276] http://www.armeniapedia.org/wiki/Armenian_History
[277] Esposito, *The Oxford Dictionary of Islam* p. 314

and Progress, better known as the Young Turks. Most Armenians supported the movement and its promise of fair treatment of the former Christian millets. The movement was initially celebrated by many people in the various millets. The Young Turks adopted an agenda, however, in which Turkish nationalism became dominant. In 1915, as the Russian army invaded Turkey from the north, the Ottoman government began to round up Armenians, killing many and forcing tens of thousands to march toward what is today Iraq with many dying on the way. Estimates of the number of deaths vary between one and two million. Estimates were based on population records that show the number of Armenians living in Turkey before 1915, and the diminished numbers afterwards. Testimonies of the survivors of the genocide are numerous and are very distressing to read.

The alleged genocide of the Armenians in 1915 remains an extremely sensitive issue in Turkey. To this day, Turkey has denied that there ever was a deliberate genocide. During World War I, Turks claim, many Armenians did die, but so did many Turks and people of every other nationality. Some Armenians fought with the Russians against their former Turkish and Kurdish neighbors and were killed in the fighting. Others fought with the Ottomans and remained loyal to the empire.

Whatever the truth is, the suffering of the Armenians probably would not have occurred if World War I had not broken out, which monopolized the Allies' attention. With European armies engaged in massacring one another, and the Marxist-Leninist revolution drawing away the attention of the Russians, there was little outside support for the Armenians.[278]

Much has been said about the apathy of the Western world toward the Armenian genocide, which allegedly emboldened Hitler to believe that Western powers would not oppose his genocide against the Jews. Turks not only deny, that there was a deliberate genocide

---

[278] Hourani, p. 248

against the Armenians, but also say it cannot be compared to the Nazi genocide of Jews, to which some Armenians have likened it. Many Armenians have been strongly appealing to Western governments, including the United States, to commemorate the anniversary of the genocide.[279]

Very recently, U.S. President Joe Biden officially decreed the Armenian genocide. Many other American presidents had refused to do this. Turkey's reaction to this will be interesting to see over the next few weeks and months. Most countries have had shameful chapters in their history and generally have acknowledged their historical national sins and injustices against others. The Turkish official position remains, however, that there never was a deliberate genocide against the Armenian or any other people.

Assyrian Christian Suffering

The suffering of the Assyrians (Suryani) has often been written alongside the suffering of Armenian Christians who were more numerous and hence suffered greater losses. This is not to minimize the suffering that Assyrians have gone through. Assyrian losses in Turkey during the 1915 genocide numbered around 275,000 by some estimates and somewhat lower by others.[280] I know an Assyrian family in Minnesota that had over 60 members of their family killed before immigrating to America many years ago. Assyrians have also suffered greatly in Iraq, and to a lesser degree in Persia as well. The number of Assyrian Christians killed over the last 2,000 years throughout the Middle East is almost beyond comprehension.

The Greeks had a different experience. We will look at that later in this chapter.

---

[279] For a very well-done article on countries and organizations that acknowledge or deny the Armenian genocide, see the following: https://en.wikipedia.org/wiki/Armenian_Genocide_recognition
[280] https://en.wikipedia.org/wiki/Assyrian_genocide

Two Important Treaties

Treaty of Sevres 1920

This was a pact made in August of 1920 between the victorious Allied Powers and the Ottoman Turks. It forced the Turks to renounce all their rights to the Arab regions in the Middle East and North Africa. It also provided for an independent Armenia and an autonomous region called Kurdistan for the Kurds. This was the closest the Kurds ever came to establishing their own homeland. The treaty gave the Greeks a piece of Western Anatolia, including the region where the seven churches of Revelation are located. Armenia's homeland was moved farther north by the Russians, not the Turkish territory that the treaty originally called for. Eventually Armenia combined with Azerbaijan and Georgia to form the Transcaucasian Soviet Federated Socialist Republic (TSFSR).

Treaty of Lausanne 1923

This treaty was negotiated and signed on July 24, 1923. It was very significant for many reasons. As the Ottoman Empire crumbled, western powers sought to divide what is today Turkey and surrounding regions among the British, French, Italians, Russians and Greeks. The founder and hero of modern Turkey, Mustafa Kemal Pasha (generally known now as Ataturk, father of the Turks), rallied the Turkish people to drive out the invaders through a series of brilliant military maneuvers. Most of the European countries that sought to divide Turkey were outside of its geographical borders, but the Greeks had lived in Western Anatolia for centuries. The Treaty of Sevres, which would have given the Armenians an independent state and the Kurds an autonomous Kurdistan, was scrapped, something that many Kurds are still bitter about to this day. A major population exchange took place that involved hundreds of thousands of people, with Muslim Turks in Greece migrating to Turkey and Orthodox Christians in Turkey migrating to Greece.

Greeks and Turks

Just imagine that it is the year 1924 and you are a Greek Christian woman living in Smyrna (now called Izmir) during the emergence of the Republic of Turkey after the fall of the Ottoman Empire. All around your city are the ruins of biblical sites that any Bible reader would know--Ephesus, Colossae, Sardis, Troas, Pergamum, and many more. Some of your fellow Greeks had migrated to the Black Sea coast and they are called Pontian Greeks, but most stayed near your ancestral homeland near the Aegean Sea. Your ancestors have lived in the region for thousands of years, and at one time, Greek was the universal tongue of much of the Western world. It was the language of the New Testament and spoken by the Apostles. Saint Paul spent three years in nearby Ephesus, and every inch of your homeland is holy turf, sanctified by the Apostles and the Fathers of the Church.

The Turks have ruled over your region for centuries, which is painful for your people to accept. Many a discussion occurs among your people about why God has allowed the Muslim Turks to rule over you. You have been haunted by the second and third chapters of the Revelation of Saint John, especially the part that records the words of Jesus to the seven churches. These ancient churches are not far from your city. Over and over Jesus warned them to repent or he would remove their lampstand and bring judgment. In fact, your city of Smyrna is one of only two churches that Jesus did not rebuke. Perhaps that is why there are still some churches left in your city, whereas in most of the other cities mentioned in Revelation there is nothing left of Christian civilization. Some Greeks converted to Islam and married their sons and daughters to Turks. God appears to be on their side, some of them say. Others were just tired of *dhimmi* status. Some of your fellow Greeks do not see it as you do. They attribute the loss of their lands and communities to superior Ottoman military power, not to God's judgment

The Ottoman Empire had been going downhill for a long time. In fact, the Greeks living across the Aegean Sea have been independent of Ottoman rule since the early 1820s. Under the *millet* system, your Orthodox/Christian millet had a fair degree of autonomy. True, you were dhimmis, but many of your community were quite well off financially. During the last couple of decades of the last century, young educated Turks began to challenge the absolute rule of the Sultan Abdul Hamid II. The rebellion was smashed to a degree, but in 1908 the Committee for Union and Progress (CUP), which most people called the Young Turks, finally overthrew the Sultan. The initial days were a grand time. The shouts of jubilant voices rang out as Muslims, Jews, and Christians celebrated in the streets. A new day was dawning.

Sadly, the jubilant times did not last. In 1914 World War I broke out, and the CUP, which had become more nationalist and less favorable to minorities, chose to fight on the side of Germany and the Central Powers against the Allied powers of Britain, France, Russia and the United States. After the defeat of the Central Powers, the Allies wanted to divide the former Ottoman Empire into many pieces. The British, French, Russians, Italians, and your people all wanted a piece. Even the Armenians and Kurds hoped for a piece of the pie. Some treaties were made but a Turkish general named Mustafa Kemal, whom the Turks call Ataturk, rallied the defeated Turkish people and forced the Allies to the bargaining table. The British and their allies agreed to let Turkey become an independent country. Unlike the British, French, and others who came from far away, we Greeks live in the Western part of Turkey. The population exchange of 1923 took place one year ago. An estimated one and one-half million Greek Christians crossed the Aegean Sea and settled in the country of Greece, and about one-half million Muslim Turks crossed the same sea and now live in Turkey. Now there are only a few thousand Greeks left in Turkey. Our Pontian brothers and sisters on the Black Sea Coast have become Muslims whether by force or choice. Our great Aegean civilization that lasted for millennia is no more.

The Turks

Mustafa Kemal

The Turks lost their empire, but under Mustafa Kemal (Ataturk), Turkey became an independent nation-state. Ataturk defeated the armies that sought to divide Turkey, leaving only a small piece for the Turks, and negotiated with the imperial powers to make the borders what they are today. He abolished the Sultanate and proceeded to secularize Turkey and model it after European nation-states. He made ethnic identity rather than religion the glue that held society together. His famous dictum on signs and posters all over Turkey, *"Ne mutlu Turkum diyene"* (How happy is one who can say I am a Turk), redefined the nation's self-identity. Ataturk championed women's rights and gave them the right to vote. Millions of women began to work outside of the home. He outlawed many of the religious practices of the Ottomans, such the requirement that women must wear veils at work places or at universities or schools. He established secular law rather than Shari'a, and replaced the Arabic letters with a Latin alphabet, which made it much easier for Turks to benefit from the writings of western authors, and more difficult to read the Qur'an. Volumes have been written on Ataturk's reforms, and perhaps no people in history experienced such rapid culture change as did the Turks after World War I until Ataturk's death in 1938.

Under current President Recep Tayyip Erdogan, Turkey is becoming more Islamic and conservative in many ways, symbolized by the Hagia Sophia becoming a mosque again. Some Turks (and Kurds) are very happy with the turn back toward Islam, while many educated and urban Turks, in particular, are concerned with Turkey's move away from secularism and the reforms that Ataturk brought to the country.

Application

If you have seen the movie *My Big Fat Greek Wedding,* you might recall the old grandma who is constantly screaming about "the Turks, the Turks." Back in the early 1980s, after speaking at a church about my love for Turkey and admonishing the people to pray for that land and its people, a woman approached me. She said she was of Greek ancestry. She had recently become more spiritually renewed after being a Christian in name only. She told me that her people in Greece and even the Greeks in America are very spiritually dead and few know Christ in a personal way. Then she said, "I don't believe that we will see a spiritual awakening among the Greeks until we forgive the Turks."

To begin to discuss Greek-Turkish relations in any type of detail would fill volumes. The island of Cyprus, our home for almost two and one-half years, is divided into two zones--a Turkish zone to the north and the Greek zone to the south. When we lived there in the late 1980s and early 1990s, there was no passing back and forth between the zones. That has now changed, and Cypriot citizens can go back and forth to a degree. Efforts to bring back the island as one united country have stalled, each blaming the other for the impasse. When you read Greek accounts of the Turkish invasion of Cyprus in 1974, and then the Turkish accounts of Turkey's rescue of its people from an intended Greek genocide against Turkish Cypriots, you cannot help but ponder how the conflict could be perceived so differently. It parallels the complexity of reading both sides of the Israeli-Palestinian conflict.

Disaster Diplomacy

In 1999, a massive earthquake struck Western Turkey, officially killing 17,000 people, with some estimates of double that figure. Greece was the first country to pledge aid and support to Turkey. For a list of Greek contributions, see site below.[281] Less than a month later, an earthquake struck Greece. The loss of life was far less (perhaps 143 deaths), although the structural damage was severe. Turkey rushed aid to the Greeks and the phone lines were jammed with Turks calling to offer help and donate blood. Disaster diplomacy occurs when people rush to aid peoples or countries against whom they have held historical animosity. Thank God that both Greeks and Turks practiced disaster diplomacy despite their centuries of conflict.

Greeks and Turks have much in common in their cuisine, music, dance, ways of expressing emotion, the importance given to family and kinship ties, and a strong sense of national pride in their heritage. Most likely a higher percentage of Turks seriously practice their Islamic faith than Greeks do their Christian faith. For both people, however, religion is often an identity marker as much as it is a faith to be lived out. "I am a Turk; therefore, I am a Muslim." "I am a Greek; therefore, I am a Christian." We hope and pray that the Greeks will be restored to their true Christian heritage and love their former enemies as some of the Armenians have learned to do. (See story below)

A Story of Reconciliation

A Turkish pastor told me an incredible story that demonstrates the grace of God to change hearts. A few years ago, he and other pastors were invited to the country of Armenia for a reconciliation event between Turks (and Kurds) and Armenians. Turkish pastors confessed that they had been told all of their lives that the Armenian genocide never happened. The Armenians confessed to harboring

---

[281]
https://en.wikipedia.org/wiki/Greek%E2%80%93Turkish_earthquake_diplomacy

hatred in their hearts passed down from generation to generation since the alleged genocide. After sharing, prayer and Bible study, Turks and Armenians hugged, wept, forgave each other, prayed together, and washed each other's feet. The following year, a reconciliation conference took place in Turkey in a similar manner. Unless one has lived in Turkey, it may be hard to grasp why that is such an incredible story. It is truly an example of II Corinthians 5:17-19:

> *Therefore if anyone is in Christ, the new creation has come. The old has gone, the new is here! All this is from God, who reconciled us to himself through Christ and gave us the ministry of reconciliation: that God was reconciling the world to himself in Christ, not counting people's sins against them. And he has committed to us the message of reconciliation.*

Questions for Discussion and Reflection

- Do you think foot-washing is a way of bringing healing and reconciliation between oppressors and victims, even if the injustices happened centuries ago? Why or why not?
- Despite Jesus' example of washing his disciples' feet, why do you think most churches no longer practice this?

19

Five Major Events and Increasing Disillusionment

What happened to us?" The question that haunts us in the Arab and Muslim world. We repeat it like a mantra. You will hear it from Iran to Syria, from Saudi Arabia to Pakistan, and in my home country of Lebanon. (Kim Ghattas[282] Lebanese journalist and author)

Just imagine that you are one of a group of Muslim background Believers (MBBs) and Christians from various Middle-Eastern historic churches at a conference taking place in a resort area in one of the more moderate Islamic countries. You have been invited to the conference by a leading satellite channel that broadcasts in several languages throughout the Middle East. In addition to personnel from the satellite station, there are representatives from radio and print ministries as well as some prominent ministry heads and business people. The purpose of the conference is to listen to the Muslim Background Believers and learn from them in order to make the media ministries as effective as possible in ministering to the many types of Christians in the Middle East as well as to those who do not profess Christ.

The Satellite ministry that is the main sponsor seeks to minister to the entire Church, so there are representatives from Roman Catholic, various Orthodox churches, and a wide range of

---

[282] *Black Wave* (2020)

Evangelical and Pentecostal/Charismatic churches and ministries. There are some representatives from the Oriental Orthodox Churches, and even the Assyrian Church of the East has sent a representative as well. There are both men and women ranging in age from early 20s to over 70.

Each morning begins with worship, praise, reading Scripture, a short message from one of the church leaders, and prayer. After breakfast, MBBs begin to share their stories about how they came to faith in Christ. Their stories are incredible! Many common themes emerged throughout each testimony, but each one was also quite different. Some of the MBBs were very devout Muslims; others were Muslim in name only. Some explored the claims of Christ for years; others made the decision to follow Jesus quite quickly. Some talked about the role that Christian friends or foreign workers played in their coming to faith. Still others had a powerful encounter with Jesus through a dream. Several shared about being healed or having their prayers answered after praying for in Jesus' name. They all affirmed the role of satellite television played, whether in their seeking the truth stage or after believing in Jesus as they sought to grow in their faith.

Some of the MBBs related about how they were regarded with suspicion when they began to read the Bible and went to the existing churches, whether Catholic, Orthodox or Protestant, whose members are mostly "birth Christians."[283] The MBBs took the sting out of their statements by stating that they can understand the suspicion the birth Christians had regarding them. After all, for centuries, most of the conversions were from Christian to Muslim. Now, seemingly out of nowhere, Muslims are professing to want to follow Jesus. How can these long-suffering Christians discern their motives? Are they spies for the government or Islamist organizations? Are they hoping that by becoming Christians, their

---

[283] Birth Christians refers to the remnant of Christians whose ancestors have been Christians for hundreds of years, including the Armenians, Assyrians, Greeks, Georgians, etc.

chances of emigration to the west will increase? Are they hoping to marry a Christian girl and convert her to Islam? Even if some of the Muslim enquirers are sincere, will it not bring repercussions against the Christians, and will they be accused of proselytizing Muslims and face yet more persecution? Fortunately, along with some very unwelcoming churches, there have been others that have done all they can to help Muslim enquirers learn about the Savior.

Most of the MBBs now attend small churches in rented buildings or meet in various homes. Some MBBs have joined the historic churches, often after a trial period to test to make sure their faith is genuine. Others have no fellowship with other believers and know no other Christians at all.

As the MBBs shared their stories, one common theme surfaced regardless of whether the person was male or female, young or old, or whatever ethnic background they came from. They had become disillusioned with Islam.

The Former Glory of the Islamic World

There was once a civilization that was the greatest in the world. It was able to create a continental super-state that stretched from ocean to ocean, and from northern climes to tropics and deserts. Within its dominion lived hundreds of millions of people, of different creeds and ethnic origins. One of its languages became the universal language of a large part of the world, and the bridge between the peoples of a hundred lands. Its armies were made up of people of many nationalities, and its military protection allowed a degree of peace and prosperity that had never been known. The reach of this civilization's commerce extended from Latin America to China, and everywhere in between. And this civilization was driven, more than anything, by invention. Its architects, designed buildings that defied gravity, and its mathematicians created algebra and algorithms that would enable the building of computers and creation of encryption. Its physicians examined the human body and found new cures for disease, whilst its astronomers looked into the heavens, named the stars, and paved the way for space travel and exploration. Its writers created thousands of stories-stories of courage, romance and magic. Its poets wrote of love, when others were too steeped in feat to think of such things. When other nations were afraid of ideas, this civilization thrived on them and kept them alive. When the censors threatened to wipe out knowledge from past civilizations, this civilization kept it alive and passed it on to others.[284] *(Ed Hussain)*

The Glory that Was

We feel deeply the humiliation, the marginalization of the whole Muslim world. Muslim countries are so divided, so small, so irrelevant...We are the most backward among nations, and the poorest. Almost the whole of Islam belongs to the Third World. Part of the Middle East may have enormous oil resources, but even there it is the West that ultimately controls them.[285] *(Zaki Badawi)*

The gap between what Muslims once were and where they are now find themselves is at the center of the anger and humiliation driving political violence across the Middle East.[286] *(Shadi Hamid)*

The above citations speak to the despair that many Muslims are experiencing between the perceived gap of what the Muslim world once was and the disillusionment of living in it as it is now. Several events have led to the growing disillusionment that has led to a lack of faith in Muslim leaders and society in general that seems unable to solve the problems facing them.

Five Pivotal Events in the Same Year

In 1979, five major events especially have affected the World of Islam with consequences for the entire world. The fall-out of these events

---

[284] Ed Hussain, pps. 103-104
[285] Dr. Zaki Badawi, cited in Musk, *Kissing Cousins* p. 273
[286] Hamid, p. 12

continues. These are 1) The Peace Agreement between Israel and Egypt; 2) The Iranian Revolution under the Ayatollah Khomeini; 3) The siege of the Holy Mosque in Mecca; 4) The Soviet invasion of Afghanistan; 5) The coming to power of Saddam Hussein. These events are not listed in order of importance, nor are they listed according to the order in which they occurred. Each event not only made a major impact on the world at the time, but also continue to do so in our day.

The First Pivotal Event of 1979

In deference to his age, as the most elderly person at the conference, as well as his years of experience in broadcasting the gospel to the Middle East, Abdullah, an Egyptian, was asked to speak to why many in Egypt and the Arab world are disillusioned with Islam.

In discussing the growing disillusionment in the Muslim World, Abdullah refers back to 1948, when Israel declared its statehood, which was quickly recognized by the United States and many other nations. The next day, a large Arab army marched against the new country, but to the amazement of the world, the Jews came out victorious. Abdullah's parents told him, how the defeat was so humiliating that many Egyptians began to listen more to Hassan al Banna, the founder of the Muslim Brotherhood, and a few years later to Sayyid Qutb, the fiery preacher and influential author, whereas before the defeat many Egyptians were rather lax in their devotion to Islam.

Like many Egyptians of their day, Abdullah's parents idealized the United States after World War II. Its military might, economic prosperity, and individualistic culture as personified in everything from cowboy films to glamorous movie stars, permeated Egypt. Young people emulated what they saw on the big screen and listened to American dance music on radio as nightclubs and drinking establishments multiplied throughout Cairo and other cities.

Sayyid Qutb after returning from Colorado where he completed a Master's degree, preached about a different side of American life. He focused on the racism he experienced as a dark-skinned foreigner, in which he was often mistaken for being a black man. He was very passionate about the moral decay of American society. He went into detail explaining the dancing between unmarried males and females who touched each other while dancing, a practice shocking to traditional Muslims. He somewhat graphically described the sensuousness of American women who accented their sexuality with tight clothes and sensual mannerisms. Furthermore, beyond racism and sex, Abdullah said that most Americans supported the new nation of Israel, and they thought that God gave the Jews victory over the Arab armies. Qutb spelled out both the bankruptcy of atheistic communism in Russia, and the decadence of Western society in his call for Islamic renewal. It was due to the laxness of Muslims in practicing their faith that led to their defeat in battle. The message of the Muslim Brotherhood was "Islam is the solution. "

Abdullah tells how when he was still young, he heard the Egyptian president, Gamal Abdul Nasser, preach fiery sermons about the glory of the Arab people, their long history that dates back to the Prophet Abraham and his son Ishmael, the father of the Arabs. He passionately expounded on the glories of the early caliphates when Arabs were far ahead of the West in every area from medicine to philosophy and education. He proclaimed it is time for Arabs to rise again, but first, Israel has to be destroyed and the Jews thrown into the sea. Even though Abdullah was young, he got caught up in the Nasser's rhetoric and idolized the man as did almost the entire Arab world. In 1967, however, in six days the Jews defeated the united Arab armies again. The Arab armies lost the Sinai Peninsula, the Gaza strip, the West Bank and East Jerusalem to the Jewish victors. The humiliation was so heavy; it felt like a dark cloud descended on Egypt and all Arabs. Nasser, who had arrested hundreds of Muslim Brotherhood members and had Sayyid Qutb executed in 1966, died soon afterwards, broken and discredited.

The call to return to true Islam rang aloud. Islam, rather than the Arab nationalism that had Nasser preached, was the answer to restoring Arab pride and dignity. About the same time, hundreds of thousands of Egyptians went to the conservative Gulf States, particularly Saudi Arabia for work. Upon returning to Egypt, the workers brought with them Salafist/ Wahhabi[287] ideas. Increasingly secular music was replaced by the recitations of the Qur'an in taxis and in shops. More women wore the *hijab* and other forms of conservative dress. Many nightclubs and places that served alcohol were shut down. Mosques were built in every neighborhood.

From Left: Sadat Begin & Carter

Abdullah stated that when Nasser's successor, Anwar Sadat, went to America to make peace with the Jews and signed the treaty between Israeli Prime Minister Menachem Begin, U.S. President Jimmy Carter and himself on Mach 26, 1979, many Egyptians were outraged. Abdullah said he felt both rage and shame that almost consumed him. He had many relatives and friends in the Muslim Brotherhood and he had gone to many of their meetings. In the

---

[287] Salafism/Wahhabism are reform movements focused on restoring the purity of Islam as allegedly practiced during the days of Islam during the days of Muhammad and his successors. Wahhabism arose in Saudi Arabia in the late 18th and early 19th centuries and its literalist interpretation of Islamic Law is still adhered to, although some modernization under the current regime is taking place. Egyptians, influenced by the failure of the wars against Israel, among other factors, hoped that returning to the alleged purity of the past, might give them a much more hopeful future, which unfortunately has for the most part not come to pass.

midst of his anguish, he began reading the Injil that he happened to find in a bookstore. The Message of Jesus was so different from the rantings that he heard from the Muslim Brotherhood, or the cassette tapes of Sayyid Qutb's fiery oratory.

Much of the world rejoiced when Egypt and Israel made peace, and Israel even gave the Sanai peninsula back to Egypt that it had won in what is now called the Six Day War. Sadat and Begin won the prestigious Noble Peace Prize. Most of his friends and neighbors, however, thought the peace agreement was wrong and Muslim radicals assassinated Anwar Sadat in 1981, two years after the Peace Treaty. Muslims trying to understand their terrible defeat in the Six-Day War, often attribute it to the power of the American military that assisted the Jews. However, no foreign troops fought with the Jews. As Abdullah pointed out to his friends, that even if foreign troops had fought with Israel, is not Allah stronger than infidel armies? The reason for their defeat was attributed to people not practicing true Islam.

For Abdullah, the struggle with whether Islam or the way of Jesus was the true path was settled for him by a dream. Jesus appeared to him and took him by the hand and gently admonished Abdullah to follow him. He has been following Jesus ever since. In time, he won the respect of the priests and members of many historic churches. He is also guiding several MBBs in their maturation in the Christian faith. He has made many talks on radio and satellite television, using a different name

During a question and answer time, the topic of the so-called Arab Spring came up, and more recent developments in Egypt, such as the demonstrations against Sadat's successor Hosni Mubarak that lasted for about two and one-half weeks. In the massive protests in Tahrir Square, almost 850 protestors were killed, and over 6,000 injured. In the end, Mubarak resigned. The Muslim Brotherhood then rallied the nation around voting for Mohammad Morsi. However after barely a year in office, a coup d'etat against Morsi, an engineer with a Ph.D. from the University of Southern California, took place. Morsi was arrested and General Abdel Fattah al Sisi became the new President. Many Egyptians felt that Morsi was not given enough time to govern before being replaced. Others felt he was moving Egypt too quickly toward the Salafist type of rigid Islam, and they were glad to see him go.

When asked about the current president, Abdel Fattah al Sisi, Abdullah replied that most Christians seem to be happy with him. He even attended a Christmas Eve mass at a Coptic Church, the first president to ever do so. However, violent attacks still break out against Christians that al Sisi has not been always able to stop.

Egypt remains a deeply divided state. One-half of Egyptians live on two dollars a day or less, and the unemployment or underemployment of 700,000 university graduates does not point to a positive future. There is terrible overcrowding along the Nile River where most Egyptians live because most of the rest of the land is a barren desert. Abdullah cites a World Health Organization survey that showed that 97 percent of Egypt's married women have suffered genital mutilation (FGM) and despite the practice being outlawed since 2007, the majority expect their daughters have it done to them as well.[288] Kilpatrick cites a 2013 Pew public opinion poll, which revealed that the vast majority of Egyptians support the death penalty for apostates from Islam.[289] In other words, most Egyptians can live with their sons or daughters going through a time of agnosticism as many seem to be doing, but they had better not dare become Christians. Abdullah says that Egypt feels like it is ready to explode, yet he has hope, that in its troubles, the people will call out to God, and Jesus will reveal himself to many even as he did to him. Abdullah says that as Egypt goes, so goes the Arab world. He finishes his share of the program by citing from the book of Isaiah:

> *In that day there will be a highway from Egypt to Assyria. The Assyrians will go to Egypt and the Egyptians to Assyria. The Egyptians and Assyrians will worship together. In that day Israel will be the third, along with Egypt and Assyria, a blessing*

---

[288] Goldman, p. 35
[289] Kilpatrick p. 359

on the earth. The Lord Almighty will bless them, saying, "Blessed by Egypt my people, Assyria my handiwork, and Israel my inheritance (Isaiah 1922-25)

The Second Pivotal Event of 1979

The Islamic Revolution in Iran

Hussein and his wife Shireen share their story next. They are about sixty years old and among the oldest of the attendees beside Abdullah. They were students in 1979 when the Ayatollah Khomeini returned from France. They were among the millions that greeted the Ayatollah, whom people hoped would free them from the oppressive, American backed regime of the Shah. It seemed the entire country was excited about the Ayatollah's return from exile from France. Even the Marxist youth were excited about overthrow of the Shah They were confident that they could manipulate the Muslim clerics and bring about a leftist revolution. Wealthy Iranians who worked for oil companies or international businesses were concerned and many fled Iran while they had the chance.

Some people thought Khomeini might be the 12th Imam, the Mahdi,[290] the long awaited savior of the Islamic world, particularly among Shi'a Muslims. In fact, even Sunni Muslims rejoiced in Khomeini's return. Despite centuries of warfare between Sunni and Shia, the Islamic Revolution gave hope to the Sunnis that they too could overthrow the oppressive dictatorships that rule the Muslim world, with some of them having been established by the colonial powers decades ago. They enjoyed seeing Khomeini "sock it to the West" and to take a stand for Islam.

---

[290] Mahdi means guided one, an apocalyptic figure who will return when the corruption of the world reaches its climax. In Shi'a Islam, the Mahdi is often thought to be the 12th Imam who has been in occultation since the 10th century. Among Sunnis, despite no mention in the Qur'an or among the most authoritative of the Hadith, many await his return. Some even say that the Mahdi and Jesus are the same person, while others believe they will work together to build a new world after Jesus kills the *Dejaal* (Antichrist).

Reality Sets in

On November 4, 1979, university students seized the American Embassy and held 52 Americans hostage for 444 days. Hussein and Shireen supported the seizure although they were not directly involved in it. After coming to power in the same year as the Ayatollah returned to Iran, Saddam Hussein attached the country and a bloody war broke out with over one million dead. Most of the world community, especially the Arab Sunnis, supported Saddam under the table because his secular government, although often brutal, was more comprehensible than the Islamic theocracy under the Ayatollah. Tragically, almost every Iranian family seemed to have either lost a son, or had one of their sons be disabled or crippled during the war.

Hussein and Shireen relay how disillusionment with the new regime set in quickly. Persians are well-educated people. They are proud of their cultural heritage and their poetic language. They had refused to be absorbed into Arabic language or culture in the early days of Islam even as most people submitted to Islamic rule (See chapter 10). In the beginning of the Islamic Revolution, people seemed happy to return to a fuller expression of their Shi'a faith, as many felt that too much Westernization was forced on them. With time, however, the regime forced women toward extremely conservative dress, required men to do the daily prayers and fast during Ramadan. Girls were taught that if they showed a little of their hair they would burn in hell. Moral police looked for women who even accidently showed their hair or wore their clothes too tight and best them. Iranian women, generally very fashion conscious, often wearing the latest fashions from Paris, were forced to wear hijab and a tent like garment that loosely fit over their bodies called a *chador*.

It is ironic that religious devotion actually decreased under the Islamic regime. Now Hussein says that maybe two percent of Muslims are in mosque on Fridays. Men and women hold parties with alcohol and drugs flowing freely. The expectations of the Iranian Revolution at its beginning in 1979 to what it has evolved into today can hardly be overstated. On the tragic side, Iran has one of the highest rates of drug addiction in the world. Many women pay for college or their living expenses by prostitution. Millions of Iranians have fled their country and today's children of the great kings and empires of the past are scattered all over the world. On the positive side, many have thrived in their diaspora, and have contributed to the societies wherever they have gone. Hundreds of thousands have embraced Jesus the Messiah as Savior and Lord.

Iranians Thrive in America

As with the Egyptian Copts mentioned earlier, Iran's loss is America's gain. According to the Massachusetts Institute of Technology (MIT) among all immigrant groups, Iranians rank toward the top in income and educational, while contributing the most in taxes and are the most law abiding. One in four Iranians hold a master's or doctoral degree, and one in two Iranian-American households have an annual income over $100,000 compared to one in five among the overall U.S. population. There are 10,000 Iranian-American physicians.

The Third Pivotal Event of 1979

The third major event that took place in 1979 was the siege of the Masjid al Haram in Mecca, the holiest site in all of Islam on November 2. Hundreds of Islamic radicals led bya Saudi preacher Jahavman al-Otabyi, which included men from all over the Muslim world and a handful of American converts, were the intruders. Juhayman al Otaybi declared that his brother-in-law, Muhammed Abdullah al-Qahtani, to be the long awaited Mahdi. The siege was an attempt to purify the modernizing and corrupt Saudi royal family, and a call for a return to purer Islam, including renunciation of western values, expulsion of non-Muslims, abolition of television, and other perceived corruptions of the Saudi royal family. Tens of thousands of worshipers were trapped inside the compound surrounding the Kaaba, the sacred shrine toward which Muslims face in reciting their five daily prayers. The battle for the shrine lasted two weeks, causing hundreds of deaths and ending only after the intervention of Saudi National Guard and French Special Forces. Al-Qahtani, the so-called Mahdi, was killed in the fighting. Juhayman al Otaybi along with 62 other rebels were beheaded in several Saudi cities as the troops of the Royal family again took control. The Ayatollah Khomeini placed the blame on America and international Zionism, and anti-American demonstrations broke out across the Muslim world. The U.S. Embassy in Islamabad, Pakistan and Tripoli, Libya were burned to the ground.

In reaction to the siege, the Saudis reversed their slow move toward modernization, and implemented much of what Juhayman hoped to accomplish in the siege. Women were forbidden to drive, their faces no longer appeared in media, religious police became more rigid in enforcing strict Islamic dress, and places of entertainment were closed. Mosque attendance and fasting during Ramadan was more strictly enforced. Wahhabi Islam spread throughout the Islamic world, and, due to enormous oil wealth, the Saudis built thousands of mosques and Islamic centers and funded many Islamic Studies departments at universities throughout the world, including many at leading American universities, including Harvard and Georgetown. Only recently has there been a gradual decrease in the degree of rigidity in Saudi Arabia, with women being allowed to drive, and some restrictions on various types of entertainment have been lifted.

Another Siege during the Hajj

In 1987, Iranian Shi'ite Muslims demonstrated with large portraits of the Ayatollah Khomeini, shouting, "Death to America", "Death to the Soviet Union" and "Death to Israel." Iranian *hajjis* (religious pilgrims to Mecca) made up 155,000 of the more than two million *hajjis*.[291] The vast majority being Sunnis. Much of the anger concerned Saudi support for Iraq in its long war against Iran.[292] The

---

[291] Hajji is the honorable title for those who have completed the Hajj, one of the five Pillars of Islam. Women who make the Hajj, often are called *Hajjiya*

[292] https://www.nytimes.com/1987/08/02/world/400-die-iranian-marchers-battle-saudi-police-mecca-embassies-smashed-teheran.html

Hajj, one of the Five Pillars of Islam, is supposed to be a place of extreme religious devotion, a once in a lifetime experience that for many required years of sacrifice to make the journey. What a disappointment it must have been as over four-hundred people were killed and an even greater rupture occurred between the two major sects of Islam.

The demonstrations have contributed to ongoing conflicts played out in proxy wars between Shi'a Iran and Sunni Saudi Arabia in the civil wars in Syria and Yemen, and both countries continue to vie for influence in Iraq, Lebanon, Afghanistan, Pakistan and elsewhere.

The Fourth Pivotal Event of 1979

The Soviet Invasion of Afghanistan

The fourth key event in 1979 was the Soviet invasion of Afghanistan. This conflict helped bring about the collapse of the Soviet Union and launched the global jihad movement, especially among Sunnis. Many young Muslims, including Osama bin Laden, left their families and homelands (and in bin Laden's case great wealth) to fight a jihad against the Russian invaders. Up to 100,000 Soviet troops fought in the war, resulting in over three million Afghans fleeing to Pakistan or Iran seeking asylum. The Mujahidin (Islamic warriors) were being cut down by Soviet air power, but after the CIA equipped the Mujahidin with anti-aircraft guns, they were able to send the Soviets packing after nine bloody years. Tragically, the US left Afghanistan in a destroyed state, which helped pave the way for the Taliban and other radical Islamist groups to take over the country. Of course, it was Afghanistan from where Osama bin Laden launched the attacks against the Twin Towers and where America has had its longest war by far in its history. We can only wish in retrospect that if after helping the Afghans defeat the Soviets, the U.S had stayed and helped rebuild Afghanistan. Perhaps the events of 9/11 and the global jihad movement that Osama bin Laden launched might have turned out quite differently.

The Fifth Pivotal Event of 1979

Saddam Hussein Comes to Power in Iraq

The last key event in 1979 we will look at was the coming to power of the brutal dictator Saddam Hussein. Saddam launched a bloody eight-year war with Iran that costs at least 1 million lives of Iraqis and Iranians. After that came the first Gulf War in 1991 when Saddam invaded Kuwait. The U.S. and its allies drove him out of Kuwait and they could easily have put an end to Saddam once and for all. However, President George H.W. Bush did not want to leave a power vacuum in Iraq so he left Saddam in power. He quietly encouraged the Kurds in the north (see chapter 11) and Shi'as in the south to overthrow Saddam assuming he was much weaker than he actually was. As we previously saw, Saddam kept his best troops out of the war to squash any rebellion that might break out after being driven out of Kuwait.

The second Gulf War occurred when the US invaded Iraq in 2003 in response to the terrorist attacks on 9/11. Saddam was captured and executed in 2006. The initial celebrations after Saddam's government was toppled, turned into anger against the U.S. Unfortunately; the U.S. and its allies made many mistakes in the transition after Saddam's fall. One of the main justifications for the invasion was the threat that Saddam had control of WMDs (weapons of mass destruction). Upon not finding the WMDs and over 3,000 American troops have given their lives in seemingly unending chaos, many Americans began to question our role there, and anti-war protests broke out across the US. The majority of Shia (60 percent of Iraq's population) long oppressed under Saddam, increasingly took more power in the new government. Sunnis, in particular, Abu Musab al Zarqawi, a former drug runner, and pimp before his conversion to extremist Islam, helped establish Al Qaeda in Iraq, which later evolved into ISIS. Zarqawi was killed by an American missile in 2006, but by then the foundation for ISIS was firmly in place. Much of the appeal of ISIS was its anti-Shia and anti-

American ideology, which was rooted in apocalyptic imagery.[293] When the caliphate began to collapse, it led to much disillusionment, although a remnant of ISIS jihadists have regrouped and still pose a threat.

Many books have been written about these events. Violence, deep division between Muslim sects, lagging behind in human rights, women's rights, education, poverty, and overall living standards for the majority of the world's Muslims, and millions of displaced peoples have contributed to the despair that I mentioned earlier. The gap between how Muslims once ideally perceived their world, and the disarray that it finds itself in now, has led to much soul-searching an anguish. Well-known Turkish author, Mustafa Akyol, asks question: Are Islamists Ruining Islam? He goes on to say:

> *It just doesn't look convincing to say, "Islam is a religion of peace," while adding, "but we will kill anyone who apostatizes from it." Similarly, it doesn't make much sense to insist, "Islam shows great respect to women," while we have authoritative texts on how to beat your wife in appropriate ways.*

While much of the disillusionment is against Islamism (radical Islam) rather than with the type of somewhat nominal Islam that the majority of Muslims practice, the results are telling. Akyol cites that Iraqis who do not trust Islam-based political parties has risen from 51 to 78 percent. In the six Arab countries where the poll was taken-Algeria, Egypt, Tunisia, Jordan, Iraq and Libya, pollsters found that mosque attendance has dropped by more than 10 percent on average, and Arabs who described themselves as not religious has gone up from 8 to 13 percent since 2013.[294]

Muslim academics speculate about whether the degree of secularization that has occurred in Europe and the western world

---

[293] There are obscure hadith that point to an invasion of the Romans (generally thought to represent Christianity) into the sacred lands of Islam, which include Iraq and Syria. Some even say Raqqa would be the center of resistance, the city which ISIS made its capitol.

[294] https://www.hudson.org/research/16131-how-islamists-are-ruining-islam

could ever happen in the Islamic world. Akyol, in addition to the rise among non-religious Arabs cited above, quotes one Lebanese born Middle East commentator, Karl Sharro, who attributes the decline to disappointment in the social and political manifestations of the Islamic awakening. These manifestations include, "disappointment with the Muslim Brotherhood in Egypt, the shock of ISIS, fatigue with sectarian parties in Iraq and Lebanon, and anger at the Islamist regime in Sudan." [295] Akyol, as a devout Muslim, fears that disillusionment with Islamism may lead to disillusionment with Islam itself.

Radicalism is Not Dead!

> "If they (Muslims) had gotten rid of the punishment (usually death) for apostasy, Islam would not exist today"[296] (Yusuf Qaradawi-Head of the Muslim Brotherhood and one of the most respected Islamic scholars today).[297]

We must not think, however, that radicalism among Muslims is dead by any means. Dr. Tawfik Hamid, a physician and a former radical Muslim who has often spoken to high levels of government to the U.S. Congress and on major news channels, recalls several incidents that have stirred up Muslim protests that have turned violent. As he points out, we might wish they were protesting honor killings, forced marriage of young girls, or jihadism in general. Instead, in 2006 there were violent demonstrations against Pope Benedict XVI because he cited a historical text critical of Islam. The same year many cities erupted into chaos because of a Danish

---

[295] https://www.nytimes.com/2019/12/23/opinion/islam-religion.html

[296]https://www.gatestoneinstitute.org/3572/islam-apostasy-death

[297] Cited by Monie Darwish, the founder of Former Muslims.org, and who has authored many books and spoken to large crowds, facing much opposition from Muslims whenever she speaks, points out that the above citation is not said with a sense of shame, but rather in a quite matter of fact way. Qaradawi justifies the death penalty for apostasy (riddah). How many Muslims would leave Islam and search for another faith if there was not such a harsh penalty for apostasy, is anyone's guess.

newspaper printing a cartoon of Muhammad with a bomb on his head. There was also a murder of Theo van Gogh. Then there was the more recent example in 2015 of the French satire magazine Charlie Hebdo, when two brothers killed twelve and injured eleven others in retaliation of the magazine's mocking of Muhammad.

Hamid says there are seven key issues that distinguish Salafist type radical Muslims from those with a modern outlook. He lists these tests to cut through layers of deceit by those who claim to be moderate but in reality hold to Salafist views. He uses the phrases "passive terrorism, passive support, and passive denial" in discussing those who would not personally engage in suicide bombing or related events, but agree with the ideology that fuels those who do carry out the acts.[298]

Dr Hamid's litmus test to distinguish between Muslims with Salafist views from those with moderate views are as follows:

1) Do you believe that those who leave Islam should be killed?
2) Do you believe that beating women is acceptable and that women accused of adultery should be stoned to death?
3) Do you believe that Jews are pigs and monkeys?
4) Do you believe that it is right to offer non-Muslims the options of submitting to Islam, paying the jizya or to be killed? (Sometimes fleeing can be an option often having to leave all possessions behind).
5) Do you support the enslavement of female war prisoners and the right to use them as concubines?
6) Do you support perpetual war against the Jews to exterminate them?
7) Do you believe that homosexuals should be killed[299] (as ISIS has done in Iraq and Syria by throwing them off rooftops)?

---

[298] Hamid, pps. 87-90
[299] Ibid p. 105

A Moroccan Scholar's Disillusionment

Several months ago, I met a Moroccan man whom I will call Osman (not his real name) who knows Islam very well. He has large portions of the Qur'an committed to memory and has studied his faith at a high academic level. He has totally renounced his former faith, and while he is not yet a Christian, he is reading the *Injil* and books related to the Christian faith. He says emphatically, that ISIS and al Qaeda are practicing the Islam that the Qur'an advocates, not the watered-down version that is practiced by the majority of Muslims in the world. Osman believes that as more Muslims explore what the Qur'an and the Hadith really say about jihad, women, and treatment of non-Muslims, millions will leave their religion in droves. The Internet has enabled Muslims to examine their faith and hear why many are becoming agnostic.

Deism in Turkey

In Iran, forced Islamization after the 1979 Islamic Revolution turned millions of Iranians off from the rigid Islam forced upon them. Turkey, considered the model Islamic country by many where Islam has been primarily a privatized faith like Christianity is in the West, has often found people longing for a return to days of the Ottoman Empire, when Islam was the rule of all aspects of life. Successive governments after Ataturk died in 1938, have been mostly corrupt and have failed to provide solutions to the problems the average Turks feels. Secularism has left a spiritual vacuum in peoples' lives leading to many longing for a faith that addresses society's needs and is practiced more overtly. A few years ago, I was a reader of a Turkish woman's Master's thesis on the topic of the prosecution of women in Turkish academia because they dared to wear hijab! In the student's interviews with these fired women, most of them stated the irony of being allowed to wear hijab in America where many did their graduate work, but could not wear it in their home country despite it being over 99 percent Muslim.

President Recep Tayyip Erdogan, however, seems bent on re-Islamizing Turkey and has stated the goal of raising up a generation of pious youth. This is quite contrary to the secular, western looking Turkey established by Ataturk. Citing Akyol again:

Under the leadership of President Recep Tayyip Erdogan, Turkey's formerly marginalized Islamists have become the new ruling elite. This allowed them to make their faith more visible and assertive— but it is a fig leaf for their insatiable lust for power. The disillusionment is often only with Islamism as a political instrument, but it can turn against Islam, the religion itself. In Turkey, the latter is manifested in a social trend among its youth that has become the talk of the day: the rise of "deism" or belief in God, but not in religion.[300]

A Turkish sociologist who is a practicing Muslim states that, "Turkish religiosity has been put to the test, and while it succeeded politically, it has failed spiritually."[301] Some Turkish journalists have blamed the rising agnosticism as a western conspiracy to shake the Turks from their faith in order to "Christianize" them. This accusation seems ridiculous in that there are only a few thousand Turks from a Muslim background who have professed faith in Christ.

We must be careful not to overstate the growing agnosticism throughout the Muslim World. One survey revealed that 80 percent of Egyptians believe that those who are declared apostates from Islam should be killed. Many surveys have pointed out that in Europe many second-generation Muslims are more religious than parents. Thousands of European Muslims joined ISIS much to the agony of their parents.

It is hard to say whether the new agnosticism will increase. It may be viewed as a fad that young people will pass through but will return to their faith upon marriage and in wanting to instill religious values in their children. Becoming a Christian, however, is an entirely different matter than going through a time of skepticism.

---

[300] https://www.hudson.org/research/16131-how-islamists-are-ruining-islam
[301] https://www.nytimes.com/2019/12/23/opinion/islam-religion.html

The world of Islam is a long way from allowing the freedom of choice that would allow its citizens to follow the religion of their choice. A period of agnosticism may be viewed as a stage that many young people pass through. Becoming a Christian, however, is often perceived as a betrayal of one's religion, culture, family, and heritage.

Could there be a major loss of faith in the Islamic world comparable to what has happened in Europe and increasingly in the United States? The big question for Christ-followers is what will replace the spiritual vacuum if the loss of faith continues.

The young people of the Muslim world desperately need our prayers and the good news of the gospel!

Questions for Discussion and Reflection

- The author mentions five pivotal events that all took place in 1979 but the repercussions are still being felt today. In what ways do you see the fall-out of these events being played out on the world stage?
- How might the growing agnosticism in parts of the Muslim world compare to agnosticism that seems to be growing in the Western World?

20

Truth, Power and Love in Action

We put no stumbling block in anyone's path so that our ministry will not be discredited. Rather, as servants of God we commend ourselves in every way: in great endurance, in troubles, hardships and distresses; in beatings, imprisonments and riots; in hard work, sleepless nights and hunger; in purity, understanding, patience and kindness; in the Holy Spirit and; **in sincere love, in truthful speech and in the power of God;** *with weapons of righteousness in the right hand an in the left; through glory and dishonor, bad report and good report; genuine yet regarded as imposters; known yet regarded as unknown; dying, and yet we live on; beaten and yet not killed; sorrowful, yet always rejoicing; poor yet making many rich; having nothing, and yet possessing everything (II Corinthians 6:3-11).*

Previously, I have told the story of some precious Iranians coming to faith. Below are three stories of people who came to faith during our ministry in the Middle East through encounters with truth, power and love. I first introduced this these words in the introduction. In this chapter, I share a specific story that demonstrates each element at work in the lives of three people from the ethnic origins focused on in this book.[302] The first story is about a Kurd who encountered truth. Another is about an Arab who

---

[302] I told these stories in a chapter in another book under a different name for security reasons. The stories are slightly reworded, but similar in content.

experienced Christ through an awesome power encounter. Finally, there is an account of a Turkish man, who by experiencing practical expressions of love by Christ-followers opened his heart to salvation through Christ. In each story, the other dimensions also played a role, however. Few Muslims will ever come to faith in Christ without a supernatural divine intervention, whatever form it takes. The vast majority of people will need a human instrument as well, if not in their initial encounter with Jesus, certainly in the discipleship process. Thank God for satellite television, radio programs, the Internet, and Bible correspondence courses, which certainly can all play a major role. I am sure there will be Muslims who have met Jesus and grown in faith, and will be in heaven one day, without ever having met another follower of Christ face to face. Without a doubt, there are unknown thousands of people who have encountered Christ in many ways, particularly through satellite television or radio, or even in a dream, who are known only by God. How much greater it is, however, when those who follow Jesus can meet with like-minded brothers and sisters for mutual encouragement and growth.

A Kurdish Truth Encounter

After living in a city that was 99 percent Muslim, with pockets of Christians both local and international, I felt the Lord speak very clearly to move my wife and three children across the country to a city that as far as I knew had no local or international believers in Christ. In fact, the closest fellowship with Western Christians of any denomination was 1,000 kilometers (over 600 miles) away. The city was in the midst of a bloody ethnic conflict that had claimed the lives of hundreds of victims. It was full of displaced people from other cities and even other countries.

There was an ancient church in the city that traced its origin back to the third century when the city was a center of Eastern Christianity. Through persecution and emigration, the church had dwindled down to just a few families. The church practiced a liturgy dating back to the fourth century. Tts priest wore special clerical robes, chanted all prayers and scripture readings, and burned incense.

People lit candles representing their prayer intentions and reverently kissed icons. On their way out of the church, they kissed the priest's hands. As a former Evangelical/Pentecostal pastor, none of these liturgical rituals was a part of my way of practicing my faith. Nevertheless, I felt impressed by the Spirit to attend the church regularly.

It was a challenging time for all of our family. I taught English until 9:15 each night during the week and on Saturdays and Sundays until 6:30. Only on weekday mornings before office hours, and in the afternoons before evening classes, did I have any time to meet people and share the gospel. The local people could not understand why we moved to that city in such a troubled region of the country. They wondered why I would move my family to a city in a war zone when there were so many cities that were much more westernized. Furthermore, why move into a city known for violence rather than one near the beautiful beaches for which the country is famous?

We saw no spiritual breakthrough for several months. My wife and children all got hepatitis. I had caught hepatitis the previous year, so at least one of us was healthy. I knew that plain-clothes police were monitoring my classes. I was really questioning whether God had truly spoken to me about moving to this city. There was nothing to confirm that the Lord was in the move.

It was Christmas Eve, but there was no Christmas atmosphere, let alone celebration, in a totally Muslim city. I bought cheap toys for the kids, and my wife and I tried to help them remember the true message of Christmas without any of the glitter of an American Christmas. Upon awakening on Christmas morning, there was snow on the ground! That just does not happen in this city in December. If it snows at all, it would be in late January or early February and it usually does not accumulate. This time, there was enough snow to make a snowman and have a snowball fight. By the next day, all the snow had melted. Our family will never forget that day! God cared enough to send us a white Christmas in our loneliest hour.

After many months, the priest of the ancient church took me into his confidence. He told me about a man named Davud (not his real name) who had been meeting with him for several months. Davud was a businessman who had a reversal in his business and went bankrupt. He had not been a devout Muslim. He was a womanizer and a heavy drinker. Going bankrupt caused him to begin searching for a deeper meaning in life. He read the Qur'an cover to cover several times, but it did not satisfy the hunger in his heart. He read in the Qur'an about the *Tawrat* and the *Injil,* so he went to the priest mentioned above and asked for a copy of those books. The priest was initially reluctant to give him a copy. Remember, this was a long-suffering community, and perhaps Davud's aim was to get him in trouble by accusing him of spreading Christian propaganda. He somewhat reluctantly gave Davud an *Injil,* and Davud read it from cover to cover several times. Then he began to read the Old Testament as well. He desired baptism but the priest could not baptize him legally.

The priest told me that when I first visited the church, he thought my goal might be to "Protestantize" his small flock as some Protestants had tried to do in times past. When I demonstrated respect for their ancient church, attended worship, and stayed in their monasteries, he changed his tune and he introduced me to Davud.

Over the course of the next year and a half or so, I met with Davud many times and eventually baptized him and one of his sons. Others also came to faith and we met in different homes at least once a week. I thought it best, however, to leave the city and visit from time to time as I drew so much attention from the authorities to the local believers.

A few years later Davud was killed. There are different accounts of what happened. One account was that he was drinking and fell off the roof of a hotel where he had been staying for a business trip. Others said it was work-related, due to jealousy by others in his line of work. Some said he was murdered because of his Christian faith. Nevertheless, Davud's legacy lives on through his children. One of his daughters is a pastor's wife and an author. One of his sons is a faithful member of a local church along with his family. Some have not yet come to faith.

In that city there is now a church pastored by a MBB (Muslim background believer) that is full of MBBs who have encountered Christ in a powerful way. I do not take credit for establishing the church, as it was those who came after my time there that discipled a key person who is now the pastor, and whom the Lord has greatly used. Davud and some of his family played a role as members of the church. The church building was mostly paid for by the sacrificial gifts of its members. It had many battles in court to get its building, and there have been many threats against it. Nevertheless, the church has persevered and has had an opportunity to distribute many *Injils* and share the Gospel with thousands of people in the city and the surrounding areas.

As we see in Davud's story, it was primarily through **truth** that Davud discovered Jesus. He read the Bible many times and compared it to the Qur'an. Davud encountered the Spirit's power as well, in making the Living Christ real to him, and making him a bold witness. The love of the priest after his initial suspicion of Davud certainly played a major role. By God sending us all the way from America to his city in the middle of a civil war helped convince Davud of God's great love for him in a special way.

Davud was convinced that Muslims need to read the Qur'an in their own language. Most Muslims, because they do not know Arabic, simply have no idea what Islam is really about. Davud believed that Christians before sharing the gospel should encourage Muslims to read the Qur'an for two reasons. One is to see that *Isa* (Jesus) is mentioned many times in the Muslim's holy book, which might lead them to be curious to learn more about him. Second, is for them to see for themselves what the Qur'an really says, and not just the parts that the Imam wants them to hear at Friday prayers.

An Arab Power Encounter

In another city in our family's Middle East journey, we encountered a man named Nuri (not his real name). Nuri looked like a Middle East version of a Mr. Universe, with bulging muscles across his body. He earned his living by doing incredible feats of strength. He used to lie on the street and place his stomach under the tire of a jacked-up truck. Then the jack would be lowered and he would bear the weight of the truck upon his stomach. He would collect money from the crowd for doing this and other feats of strength as well as demonstrate his skills in karate. He would ask for more money, promising an even more daring feat, as he passed around a bucket for the collection. Nuri would then proceed to place his Adam's apple on the tip of a sword placed in a vise-like object that gripped it tightly. Then someone would strike him on the neck with a bat-like club, and break the club without the sword penetrating his throat.

Not all of his muscles could save him from cancer, however. He was twenty-six years old when my partner and I met him. He was dying in a hospital, and according to the doctors, he had at most only a few months to live. Nuri needed several thousand dollars to be transferred to a hospital in a much bigger city for a last moment surgery at one of the best hospitals in the country. My partner and I raised the money for the operation, but before he went to the bigger city, we prayed for him in Jesus' name. We had also given him an *Injil,* which he seemed to enjoy, but he did not see much relevance with so little time left to live. When Nuri arrived at the big city hospital, the doctors took X-rays again and saw no sign of the cancer. Nuri was then released from the hospital. He came back to us not knowing what to do. Previously, every X-ray had shown that Nuri's body was full of cancer, but after he began reading the Injil and was prayed for in Jesus' name, he was told he has no cancer. When Nuri told my partner and me about his experience, we told him that Jesus healed him. Nuri said that it was impossible because he had killed people and Allah will not forgive murder. We pointed out that David and Paul had both killed people, and yet God forgave them.

As we prayed for Nuri to receive Christ, we also had to cast out some demonic powers that had enabled Nuri to do some of his incredible feats of strength. This powerful man had encountered a power greater than any he had ever known before in the person of Jesus.

In Nuri's case, **power** was the most important dimension. Love also, as my partner and I visited Nuri many times and raised money for him to have an operation even though it turned out that it was unnecessary. Truth did not play as big as a role as it did in Davud's conversion because Nuri was too ill to wrestle with theological issues. After receiving Christ, however, Nuri began to read the Scriptures to be able to give an answer to those who challenged his faith.

A Turkish Love Encounter

Muhammad had lived a hard life. He lost his mother when he was only a year old. His father remarried a woman who never cared for Muhammad or offered a mother's love. He grew up in a poor village, but later he moved to a tough neighborhood in a large city. He became a chain smoker and an alcoholic. He married a woman with whom there was little marital harmony. He was a truck driver by profession, spending days and weeks on the road, smoking and drinking the years away. One day Muhammad saw an advertisement in a newspaper about how to receive a free *Injil*. He was curious and ordered the *Injil*, but he could not break the habits that he realized were killing him.

My partner and I met Muhammad and he told us about getting an *Injil* years before. My partner was deported from the country, but I continued to work with Muhammad, visiting him often at his place of work. We began to pray together and the Lord raised up a fellowship of believers. Their stories about the changes that Christ had made in their lives were very exciting. Within the group were diverse ethnicities and people from all over the political spectrum, from extreme left-wing groups to right-wing factions. It reminded me of how among Jesus' disciples there was Matthew, a tax collector and collaborator with the Romans, and Simon the zealot revolutionary who fought to bring the empire down. They were far apart ideologically, yet brought together by Jesus, as were people from such opposite political views in our fellowship.

The Lord set Muhammad free from chain-smoking and alcoholism. His son is a dynamic believer and the joy of Muhammad's life. His life is still hard in his retirement. He has very little fellowship, as the fellowship we had started eventually dissolved when we too had to depart. Some of the believers moved to other places for work and others fell away from the faith. Muhammad has had some major health problems, including cancer, but he gives thanks to God every day. The doctors have told him repeatedly that he should have died long ago due to the severity of his cancer.

For Muhammad to follow Christ was not a major truth issue, as he never really was a practicing Muslim. He has seen wonderful miracles in his life. About twenty years ago, several local doctors said his leg would have to be amputated. A German doctor said the same thing. However, he still has both of his legs, and cancer that should have killed him years ago has not done so. However, for Muhammad, it was **love** that drew him to faith in Jesus and kept him in the faith even when many have fallen away.[303] Growing up in a home without love, Muhammad loved coming to our home for meals and playing with our then-young children. One time a number of years ago, Muhammad and I tracked down some of the people who came to faith in the late 1980s and early 1990s and who had not had much fellowship since then. We asked them what stood out about our times when we were fellowshipping together, mostly outside in a forested area in a range of low mountains when the weather was good. When it was too cold or rainy, or for prayer

---

[303] Sadly, many MBBs fall away from faith in Christ for many reasons. Jesus' parable about the sower and the seed (Matt 13) gives us insight into why this occurs, not just among Muslim converts, but also even in the West where persecution is not an issue. Several times a week I pray for the spiritual restoration of people whom I know, both Muslim and non-Muslims, to come back to faith in Christ. I think often of how Jesus lovingly restored Peter after the Apostle denied knowing our Lord three times (John 21:15-22).

meetings, we often met in our home or the home of one of the believers. I was somewhat hoping that the believers might say, "We remember your sermons or that teaching you gave." After all, I had spent hours working on sermons in another language. However, what they said they were most nostalgic about was not my sermons, but the times we met in our home. They remember the meals my wife made (they still remember the exact dishes she prepared!). They ate and played with our kids and still remember their names from so long ago. They also remember the singing of hymns and discussion about the Bible on the side of the mountain overlooking the sea.

Muhammad strongly believes that love is the key to the Middle Eastern heart, because beneath the friendly and hospitable surface, there are many obstacles to real friendship (as there often are in the West). There are layers of social stratification, pressure to conform, issues of trust, and many other hindrances that make it challenging to bring people together in that country for regular fellowship. People are terrified of being ostracized for seemingly small infractions of social rules that will lead to gossip and alienation. How often I have heard Muhammad introduce me as a professor. This shocks people who know Muhammad as a former truck driver with limited education. Then he goes on to say that we are closer than natural brothers. He says it is almost impossible to imagine a similar relationship within the society with such a major gap in educational and social status. (I honestly believe Muhammad is smarter than I am, but has not had the opportunities I have had.)

The often-superficial relationships with people we call "friends" in American culture generally will not cut it in Muslim culture. Friendship demands much greater levels of time commitment than often we are prepared to give. This topic alone deserves much greater depth than I can give it in a short chapter, but those who seek to point Muslims to Jesus must be prepared to give much more time and energy in building relationships with Muslims than they might be used to in Western culture.

Muhammad and I have traveled tens of thousands of kilometers by bus together visiting people interested in the gospel. In his later years now, Muhammad has had many health issues but I stay with him in his apartment every year. We talk on WhatsApp several times a week. For Muhammad, it was not primarily about truth or even miracles. It is about a consistent relationship that has stood the test of time.

Examples of Divine Encounters in the Bible

Divine encounters (some prefer to say "divine appointments") are numerous in the Scriptures. A divine encounter occurs when the Lord brings a seeking person and a follower of Jesus together in adverse circumstances.

The Woman at the Well

In the life of Jesus, the story of the woman at the well comes to mind.[304] Here was a woman who had been married five times and was living with a man not her husband. She was shunned by her community, which is why she was drawing water by herself, rather than with other women. Probably most of the women in the community were worried their own husbands would fall under the woman's ability to seduce. At just the right moment Jesus meets her and reveals he is the Messiah, and she tells the entire town about a man who knew her entire sordid life and ministered grace despite it.

Cornelius

I alluded to the example of Cornelius before. Here was a Roman centurion who was drawn to Judaism and learned to pray, give alms and teach his family to fear the Lord. He was highly spoken of by the Jews; a very unusual way for a Gentile to be regarded by God's chosen people. He has a vision to send for Peter, and Peter was given a dream that revealed that he was no longer to keep the gospel from non-Jews, the Gentile nations. The result is that the Church was

---

[304] The full story can be found in John 4.

birthed among Gentiles. It was the first of tens of thousands of people groups around the world who have been led to faith by Jesus-followers who obeyed the Lord and were led to a key person[305] or group that God had prepared to receive the message of salvation. (See important footnote below)

The Ethiopian Eunuch

The story of the Ethiopian Eunuch is a great story of a divine appointment. A eunuch for the queen travels to Jerusalem on the queen's business. A spiritually hungry man acquires a scroll of the book of Isaiah, and while riding in a chariot is trying to figure out what the portion of Scripture means. In the middle of the spiritual breakthrough in Samaria (see Acts 8), an angel of the Lord tells Philip to go south to the desert road that runs from Jerusalem to Gaza. Philip approaches the man and asks him, "Do you understand what you are reading?" The eunuch asks how he can understand if he has no one to instruct him. Philip proceeds to demonstrate from Isaiah 53 how Christ fulfilled the words that he was "led like a lamb to the slaughter, was humiliated and received no justice." Philip went on to explain the story of Jesus, and as they rode along, the Ethiopian sees water and asks to be baptized.

This Ethiopian Eunuch is among the first of the hundreds of millions of African believers now and throughout history.

Conclusion

For those of us who have given years and decades of our lives to make Christ known among all people, and Muslims in particular, the Lord grants us a divine appointment with people prepared for the gospel. We seek to make Christ known so the Lord brings

---

[305] Many people sharing the gospel with Muslims call Cornelius and the Ethiopian eunuch as examples of a "person of peace" based on Luke 10:6. The idea is that in midst of a non-Christian community; the Lord has prepared people to receive the gospel, and will direct the servant of Christ to the interested non-Christian often in miraculous ways. The person of peace, who is respected by his /her community, can act as a mediator between the Muslim community and the person bringing the Gospel.

seekers like the Ethiopian Eunuch, the Roman Centurion, or the shunned Women at the Well across our path. Next, we will devote a chapter to each of the roles that truth, power and love play in bringing Muslims to discover the Savior who navigates divine encounters for his servants who are willing to place themselves at his disposal.

Question for Discussion and Reflection

- Can you think of a time in your life when God arranged a divine encounter between you and another person?
- Peter needed to see a dream before he realized that the Lord had a divine appointment lined up for him. Phillip, on the other hand, seemed to be ready to obey immediately. How can we prepare ourselves better to be open for divine encounters?

21

Truth and Five Issues that Cause Muslims to Stumble

(This chapter has not been written for those who regularly engage Muslims or have entered into debates with Muslim scholars. Each of these issues has been addressed in much fuller detail in other writings, some of which I have included in the bibliography. My purpose is to introduce the major obstacles that Muslims face when considering the Christian faith so that the reader can do further study on each of these objections).

Just Imagine you are a young Muslim girl who has grown up hearing repeatedly that Christianity is false and Islam is the only true faith. You have heard that the reason that Christians and Muslims do not share a common faith is that the Christian's Holy Book has been corrupted.

You have been taught that Christians claim to believe in one God, but then they say that God is three in one, something they call the Trinity. So how can God be one and three? Who was in heaven controlling the universe while God was Jesus living on earth? How can God have a son? What a tragedy that the Christians believe that Jesus is God! As for Jesus being crucified, there is no way that God would allow one of his holy prophets to die such a shameful death. What really happened is that the Jews came to arrest Jesus, and God tricked them by making Judas look like Jesus. God took Jesus to himself without dying, and Judas was the one who was crucified.

Then one day you see an advertisement for a free *Injil* in a newspaper. You are a little curious about a book that your family, friends, and even schoolbooks say has been corrupted, and that Jews and Christians no longer have the holy books that Allah revealed to Moses and Jesus. You wonder why Allah would allow the *Tawrat* and *Injil* to become corrupted if He revealed them to the great prophets, Moses and Jesus. Why would Allah allow two billion Christians to be deceived? You went ahead and ordered the *Injil,* and you watched for it in the mail to make sure you collected the mail before your father and mother see it. If they know you are reading the holy book of the Christians, you are afraid of how they might react.

As you read the Injil in your room while pretending to read novels, you are gripped by the person of Jesus. His teachings and miracles are fascinating. So much of the book is about love. You have been taught that the Qur'an is authoritative only in Arabic and so you have never read it. You only know what the Imam at the mosque and your family tell you about what it says. Now you go to a bookstore and buy a Qur'an in the language of your country. As you compare the two books, you are surprised at how much more you enjoy reading the Bible than the book everyone around you says is the uncorrupted word of Allah. What if the Bible is true? What if everyone you know is wrong by believing the Bible cannot be trusted. What if Isa is really more than a prophet?

Speaking the Truth in Love

The teachings of Islam differ from the other declared heresies that we discussed in previous chapters. Arianism does not deny the crucifixion. Nestorianism and Monophysitism do not deny the divinity of our Lord. Islam, on the other hand, denies the essential core doctrines of Christianity as stated in the Nicene Creed. While Christians may debate fellow Christians about the rapture, predestination, speaking in tongues, whether women pastors are biblical, and thousands of other issues that have arisen over the centuries, most Christians who accept the Bible as inspired, at least agree on the essentials of the divinity of Christ, the Trinity, and the cross and resurrection. (I realize there are skeptics in all denominations that question even the core doctrines of historic Christianity.) Christians that seek to engage Muslims with the Gospel, however, will encounter at least five major issues and many minor ones related to the "Big Five" that totally challenge the essence of historic Christianity. These are (not necessarily in order of importance) 1) The alleged corruption of the Christian Scriptures; 2) The Trinity; 3) The Divinity of the Lord Jesus Christ; 4) Jesus as the Son of God; 5) The crucifixion of Jesus on the cross and his resurrection from the dead.

Some Christians hope to simply co-exist with their Muslim brothers and sisters. Many liberal theologians have advocated for separate ways to salvation. In other words, the Jews look to Moses and the Torah, Christians find eternal life through belief in Jesus' death and resurrection, while the Muslim path is through submission to Allah as revealed to Muhammad, the final Messenger of God as revealed in the Qur'an.

True followers of Christ can never accept error and falsehood for the sake of just getting along. We are commanded to walk in love and speak the truth in love. When I examine the history of debates between Christians and Muslims, they do not seem to have led many people to change their minds to accept the faith of the other. That is not to say that there is no place for debate. Paul debated with Jewish scholars in the book of Acts several times. Much of the talk today, however, focuses on interfaith dialogue, which seeks to find common ground rather than focusing on areas of disagreement. For many, this is a positive development because they feel that debate has its origins in intolerance. I personally have been a part of an ongoing Christian-Muslim dialogue for many years. In our dialogue, we have found that Christians of a more liberal persuasion are generally more willing to downplay the historic teachings of our faith than Muslims are willing to soften theirs for the sake of mutual accommodation. Occasionally, on the other extreme, a Christian joins the dialogue, but argues for "truth" without demonstrating love or respect for the Muslims in the meeting. Speaking the truth in love can be challenging when discussing issues like the Trinity and the crucifixion of Jesus!

A Brief Examination of the Major Muslim Objections

> *But in your hearts revere Christ as Lord. Always be prepared to give an answer to everyone who asks you to give the reason for the hope that you have. But do this with gentleness and respect (1 Peter 3:15).*

I have listed one or two verses in the Qur'an that have shaped how Muslims perceive the faith that Christians hold dear. We will look at the major five objections that are frequently raised. There are others to be sure, but these are the "Big 5."

Does the Qur'an Teach the Corruption of the Tawrat and the Injil?

And in their footsteps We sent Jesus, the son of Mary, confirming the Law that had come before him: We sent him the Gospel: therein was guidance and light, and confirmation of the Law that had come before him: a guidance and admonition to those who fear Allah. Let the People of the Gospel judge by what Allah has revealed therein. If any fail to judge by the light of what Allah has revealed, they are no better than those who rebel. (Qur'an 5:46-47)

> *If you are in doubt as to what we have revealed to you, then ask those who have been reading the Book from before you. The Truth indeed has come to you from your Lord; so be in nowise of those in doubt. (Quran 10:94)*

Perhaps the most cited verse in the Qur'an that hints that the Bible has been corrupted:

So for the breaking of the covenant We cursed them and made their heart's hard. They distort words from their proper usages and have forgotten a portion of that of which they are reminded. And you will observe deceit among them, except a few of them (Qur'an 5:13).

This verse seems to be referring more to changing or distorting words rather than the text itself being corrupted. No one would deny than many have distorted the words of the Bible (and the

Qur'an for that matter) and have used it to say what they want it to say. To say, however, the text itself has been corrupted is a different matter. One would think that if Jews and Christians had corrupted the text itself, than the Qur'an would strongly admonish Muslims to avoid and even destroy the corrupted texts.

So if the Bible was corrupted before Muhammad who lived 600 years after Jesus, why did Muhammad not clearly say so and forbid his followers to read it? If it was corrupted after the Prophet, then are we to assume that thousands of copies in numerous languages were gathered, and every copy changed in the exact same way, and then redistributed around the world? Furthermore, why would Allah allow his previous word to Moses and Jesus to be corrupted in the first place? As Don McCurry, a veteran of over 50 years of working with Muslims, says, it was not until 90-150 years after Muhammad that Muslims began to accuse Christians of corrupting scripture when most Christians clearly did not accept his prophethood.[306]

It is amazing that when Muslims actually read one of the Gospels, they are often absolutely gripped by the person of Jesus. The Gospel of Luke is the gospel most often recommended for a Muslim to read at the beginning stage. However, the hearts of many Muslims are also enraptured by the Gospel of John despite the fact that the incarnation, a doctrine so contrary to what Muslims believe, is stated in the very first verse of the first chapter. Matthew's gospel, particularly the Sermon on the Mount (Matthew 5-7), also seems to grip Muslim readers. Matthew clearly states that prayer, fasting and almsgiving should be done in secret so only God sees the action. This is contrary to the oft-Muslim practice of fasting and praying for others to see, or in order not to be shamed.

Stories of Muslims reading the Injil and being overwhelmed at the person of Jesus are numerous and exhilarating to read or hear in person. One thinks of the stories of Mark Gabriel and Nabeel

---

[306] McCurry, p. 239

Qureshi[307] as two prominent examples. I gave the example of Davud in the previous chapter. It is not surprising that Satan has worked so hard to blind Muslim eyes to the Bible by claiming it has been corrupted.

Do Christians Worship Three gods?

> *Those who say that Allah is Christ, the son of Mary, have disbelieved. Christ himself said: "Children of Israel, serve Allah who is my Lord as well as your Lord." Allah will ban the Garden to anyone who associates anything else with Allah; his lodging will be on fire. ...Those who say: "Allah is the third of three" have disbelieved. There is no deity except Allah alone. (Qur'an 5:72-73).*

> *People of the Book, do not exaggerate in your religion and tell nothing but the truth about Allah: Christ Jesus, the son of Mary, was merely Allah's messenger and His <u>word</u> which He cast into Mary, and <u>a spirit</u> proceeding from Him. Believe in Allah and His messengers and do not say: Three! Refrain; it will be better for you. Allah is one Allah alone; glory be to Him beyond having any son! He owns whatever is in Heaven and whatever is on earth. Allah suffices as a trustee. (Qur'an 4:171).*

The Trinity remains the hardest of the foundational teachings of Christianity for Muslims to come to grips with. When I was still quite new in Turkey, in order to improve my Turkish, I read a book that contained 42 testimonies by former Christians who had converted to Islam. Every single one mentioned the Trinity as one, if not the major, reason why they rejected Christianity in favor of Islam. They all expressed their frustration at not hearing a clear explanation of the Trinity, whereas Islam's strict monotheism was very understandable.

---

[307] Both of these men have written best-selling books about their journey to Christ and the role reading the Scripture played in their conversions.

I believe we have to acknowledge that the Trinity is a mystery. At the same time, we need to do the best we can to explain the mystery in understandable terms.

We must always explain to our Muslim friends that we believe that God is one. Jesus said, "Hear O Israel, the Lord your God is One" (Mark 12:29). Then he goes on to cite the Great Commandment about loving God with all of your heart, mind, soul and strength, and your neighbor as yourself.

The Athenasian Ceed states, "We worship one God in Trinity, and Trinity in unity; neither confounding the persons; nor dividing the essence." To illustrate what the Creed says for the non-theologian, I cite a former Muslim friend of mine who now follows Christ. He explains the Trinity like this: "Suppose you are talking to a Muslim friend and they accuse you of *shirk*.[308] You can ask them, 'friend, am I talking to your body, mind, or spirit now?' He or she will probably reply that you cannot divide people that way as he or she is one person but also has a body, mind and spirit."

In their excellent book, Norman Geisler and former Muslim Abdul Saleeb, illustrate it as the Father planned salvation, the Son accomplished it by the cross, and the Holy Spirit applies it to the lives of believers. The Son submits to the Father and the Holy Spirit glorifies the Son.[309] They further illustrate it by drawing on a well-known analogy of St. Augustine who stated that love has three dimensions—the lover, the beloved and the love that they share. In the Trinity, the Father is the lover, the Son the beloved, and the Holy Spirit is the spirit of love.[310]

The Trinity took the church a long time to figure out as we saw in earlier chapters. It will take time for Muslims to figure it out as well. Be patient! Once Muslims have really experienced Christ, they

---

[308] *Shirk* is the unforgivable sin in Islam and refers to attributing partners to God or polytheism.
[309] Geisler & Saleeb, p. 272
[310] Ibid, p. 275

usually get the theology right. If fact, they will find ways to express the Trinity, and how Jesus can be both fully God and fully man, better than most of us can!

Citing former Muslim Daniel Shayesteh:

> There is therefore an exact revelation of the Trinity when the Qur'an mentions the words, "God," "Spirit" (or "Word") and "Jesus". The Trinity is not three gods. It is the three persons of the One God revealed as part of the plan of salvation to redeem us in all the dimensions of human life...When we invite God into our lives, and let His Spirit and Word and Love express His Oneness to us, only then will we be able to understand that the Trinity of the Bible is something that stands for One God, not three.[311]

How can Jesus be God?

They indeed disbelieve who say; Surely Allah—He is the Messiah, son of Mary. (Surah 5:17)

And Allah will say, O Jesus, son of Mary, didst thou say to men, 'Take me and my mother for two gods besides Allah'?" He will say "Glory be to Thee! It was not for me to say, what I had no right to say." (Surah 5:116)

Jesus is called a Spirit from God (*Ruhun min Allah*) and Word of God (*kalimatu-Allah*) (Qur'an 4:171). This is not to say that the Qur'an verifies the Trinity or the divinity of Jesus by any means, but it does use terminology that makes it easier for Muslims to understand that Jesus is the Word of God (John 1:1) and sends the Holy Spirit to those who believe (John 14:16,17).

We saw how difficult it was during the first five centuries of Christian history to sort out how Jesus could be fully God and fully man. Even after all of the divisions and councils, Christians could not reach an agreement after the Council of Chalcedon. It should probably be not too surprising that Muslims struggle with the issue

---

[311] Shayesteh, p. 79

of the divinity of Christ. However, if God is God and can do anything he wants, why could he not take on human form for the sake of redeeming humankind? As Paul said, "God was in Christ, reconciling the world to himself" (2 Corinthians 5:19).

The issue of the divinity of Christ cannot be separated from the doctrine of the Trinity. The important thing is for Muslims to experience the living Christ in their lives. Like with Trinity, Muslims can explain why they believe Jesus is more than a prophet of Islam better than we can once they experience his grace.

The Son of God

> They say: "The Merciful has adopted a son." You have brought something monstrous. The heavens almost burst apart with it while the earth splits open and the mountains fall down with a crash for they should ascribe a son to the Merciful. It is not fitting for the Merciful to adopt a son." (Qur'an 19:88-92)

> It beseems not Allah that He should take to Himself a son. Glory be to Him! When He decrees a matter He only says to it, "Be," and it is. (Surah 19:35)

We have all seen "John 3:16" written on signs between the goal posts at football games. I have never understood the purpose of these signs, because most people probably do not know the verse those numbers represent. If they do know it, they probably do not need to be reminded of the verse in the first place! Sometimes I ask my students what it means when we say that God so loved the world that He gave his only begotten son? Then I ask them to think how the idea of God having a son must sound to Jews and Muslims. One cannot have a son without a sexual act, so are we implying that God had relations with Mary? They are quick to affirm that it does not mean that God had sexual relations with Mary. It is ironic that Muslims have no trouble believing that Mary was a virgin. The virgin birth of Jesus is a dogma that some modern liberal Christians stumble over, but not Muslims. For Muslims, Allah simply said for it to be and so it was. However, the idea that Jesus was begotten in any way, as the verses above show us, is regarded as a monstrous claim that splits the heavens and earth!

In trying to help my students understand what "son" means, I have pointed out that we can use "son" in both in a physical and a metaphorical way. In fact, in Arabic the word *ibn* can be used in a figurative sense, whereas the word *walad* refers to a physical son. We can say that someone is a son of his time, or a son of his generation. We obviously do not mean that he is a physical son. It means that the person personifies or embodies the values and reflects the times of his generation. Among Muslims, you might ask, what would they would call a person who personifies the core values of their culture and generation in a special way? Would you ever call that person a "son" in a figurative way? [312] Remember that Jesus *said,* "He who has seen me has seen the Father" (John 14:9).

The Crucifixion

> *Allah has stamped them (the Jews) for their disbelief. They only believe a little, because of their disbelief and their uttering such terrible slanderer about Mary, and also for their saying, "We killed Allah's messenger Christ Jesus the son of Mary." They neither killed nor crucified him, even though it seemed so to them (Qur'an 4:155-157).*

Mustafa Akyol in his book, *The Islamic Jesus* summarizes three ways that Muslims have understood the crucifixion of their Prophet Isa.

1) Jesus was crucified but did not die. Despite alll that he went through, including the scourging, the crown of thorns, being nailed to the cross, the cross falling into the hole making his bones dislocate, and the spear thrust in

---

[312] To clarify this for my students, I have used the examples of Kurt Cobain, the rock star, which after his death from a drug overdose, was said to have been the "son of Generation X." Another rock star, Bruce Springsteen, has been called a "son of the working class." We can use examples from within Muslim culture or more generic terms such as a "true son of the Kurds, Turks, Somalis, Afghans, etc. to illustrate that son can be understood metaphorically.

his side, somehow Jesus did not die, but after they put him into the tomb, he got up and convinced people that he conquered death when he rose from the dead.

2) Someone else was crucified. Somehow, God made someone like Judas, or possibly all the disciples were changed to look like Jesus, so it was someone else who was actually crucified.[313] This is the substitution theory that the majority of Muslims in the world believe.

3) The Jews should not boast that they crucified the Messiah.

Akyol seems to think that number three above is a real possibility, which is contrary the view of most Muslims. Aykol cites the late Montgomery Watt, "since the crucifixion was the work of Roman soldiers...(and) since the crucifixion was not a victory for the Jews in view of (Jesus') resurrection[314] that Christians could agree with the Qur'anic statement. However, Aykol goes on to say the Qur'an gives no room to accept the theology of the cross that Jesus's death was an atonement for the sins of humankind[315].

We could wish that more Muslims would accept the third interpretation, however, it is deeply ingrained in their understanding that it was Judas, or possibly Simon of Cyrene, who was crucified, and God took Jesus directly to Paradise without dying. It must be pointed out that even if the historicity of the cross became the predominate view among Muslims, it will take a divine work of the Holy Spirit to reveal to them the vicarious nature of the death of Jesus on the cross. As John the Baptist, whom Muslims call *Yaha*, declared, "Behold the Lamb of God who takes away the sins of the

---

[313] Most Muslims believe that it was Judas Iscariot that was crucified. Simon of Cyrene is another popular candidate as he was the one who carried Jesus' cross. The false Gospel of Barnabas, written in the 16th century, most likely by an Italian convert to Islam, says that all of the disciples were made to look kike Jesus and the Romans picked one of them to crucify.

[314] Akyol, p. 154

[315] Ibid p. 154

world" (John 1:29). Muslims believe that no one can atone for the sins of another, and that all people will stand before Allah and give an account, and hope that he will have mercy on them. When Allah weighs their deeds on the scale that determines paradise or hell, *inshallah*[316] their good deeds will outweigh their bad ones. Ultimately, however, it is up to Allah to determine the eternal destination of each person.

The Passion of the Christ

One of the clearest examples of spiritual warfare concerns Mel Gibson's movie *The Passion of the Christ*. Muslims by the millions watched the film and were deeply moved by it. Considering that Muslims generally say that Jesus was not crucified, it was surprising that they were flocking to a film that is contrary to what they believe. What is even more surprising is that Muslim governments allowed the film to be shown in cinemas and the film was widely promoted. Probably the major reason for the positive publicity is that the film was allegedly anti-Semitic and portrayed the Jews in a bad light.

Just when it looked like millions of Muslims might rethink what they have been taught about the cross, the devil stole the seed of God's Word out of their hearts. How? At the time the movie was at its peak, a picture on the Internet went viral. It showed American soldiers, including a female soldier, laughing at a nude Iraqi man on his knees at the notorious Iraqi prison Abu Ghraib. Nothing could be more offensive to Muslims than to be laughed at by a woman, especially one from a perceived occupying force.[317]

You may ask, what does a stupid act by an American soldier have to do with Jesus on the cross? The problem is that the film was produced by an American film company. The anger across the Islamic world at that shameful act by a female American soldier was

---

[316] *Inshallah*, God willing.
[317] This event was brought to my attention by Dr. Douglas Clark

so great that many Muslims were blinded to the message of the film.[318]

One final note about the crucifixion. If crucifixion did not happen, then obviously the resurrection of our Lord from the dead did not occur. Muslims believe in the ascension in the sense that God took Jesus to heaven. By faith in Jesus' physical resurrection from the dead, the certainty that Jesus delivered us from the fear of death (Hebrews 2:15) and triumphed over death itself, assures us that "because he lives we will live also" (John 14:19). When one goes to a Muslim funeral, there is none of the celebration that can be observed at a funeral of a true Christ-follower. The Muslim funeral is about a vague hope that the good works of the deceased outweigh the bad, and *inshallah* he or she might go to Paradise. That is a far cry from the certainty that Jesus gives his followers when he took the sting out of death by rising from the dead after his crucifixion (1st Corinthians 15:55-57).

Conclusion

Peter tells us to always be ready to give an answer for the hope that we have with gentleness and respect (1st Peter 3:15). This implies to me that we should live in such a way that people, ask why we have so much hope in a world that seems to be falling apart. Each of us must study our faith and learn how to defend it through the proper use of apologetic reasoning that address the five major issues above and other issues that often surface. However, let me state again that without genuine loving relationships and a life that models the life of Jesus and is full of the Holy Spirit, even the best arguments for the Christian faith may fall on deaf ears. That is why love, which we will look at soon, and supernatural confirmation by the Holy Spirit, have

---

I want to point out that many American soldiers went to Iraq and did their best to represent Christ to the Iraqi people. Whether we agree with the war or not, I in no way want to disrespect the thousands who died or were severely injured in the invasion, or the many troops who did much good work. That is what makes what happened at Abu Ghraib so tragic[318]

to be working in a Muslim's life for him or her to desire to learn about our Lord and Savior.

Questions for Discussion and Reflection

- Which of the "Big 5" objections do you think is the hardest to explain to Muslims? How might you better prepare yourself to be able to give a good answer to that objection?
- Speaking the truth in love presents a great challenge. Many of us are inclined to argue for the truth and not speak in love, while for others, the temptation may be, for the sake of maintaining friendship, to downplay the truth, especially about the claims of Jesus. In your own life (not necessarily only with Muslims in mind), which are you more inclined toward?

22

What are Crypto-Christians?

Just **Imagine** you are living in the northeast of Turkey. Your village is about as picturesque as can be imagined. Due to much rainfall, everything is a deep shade of green. Tree-covered mountains majestically arise as far as the eye can see. From your home, you can view the Black Sea stretched out before you. You grow tea as your livelihood, because your village is in the tea-growing region for both local consumption and for export. You have a Muslim-Turkish name, your wife wears conservative Islamic clothing, and you go to mosque on Fridays. Unlike some of your neighbors, you do not pray five times a day, but you generally keep the fast during Ramadan. Actually, if the truth were told, due to your hard work as a tea grower, there are times you eat and drink a little before the fasting ends at *iftar*.[319] Especially during the long days when the sun does not set until late evening. Nevertheless, for all appearances, you are a good Muslim.

Inside your mind, however, there is a battle going on. You know that your great great-grandmother's family was Christian. They converted to Islam in the terrible days after World War I, during a time of much upheaval. In order to save her children, your great great-grandmother converted to Islam after the killing of her

---

[319] *Iftar* is the breaking of the fast at sundown during the month of Ramadan.

husband by the Ottoman soldiers. Since that time, the subsequent generations have been raised as Muslims.

You love your homeland, and you have your family and work with which to be concerned. Your neighbors are kind to you. Some of them no doubt also have Christian ancestry, but they have been Muslims for over one hundred years. You wonder if any of them are curious about the faith of their ancestors.

There is a curious streak in you that is growing. There are some ruins in your village of an old church. This building has the remains of an altar, and the very faded frescoes of religious figures that must have meant something to the Christians of your ancestor's day. You wonder what your great great-grandmother might have believed. Why did she convert to Islam? Would she have been killed if she had not? Did she believe Jesus really was the Son of God and secretly perform Christian practices? How can you find out more about your Christian heritage without your neighbors, and even some of your relatives, finding out? Their attitude is that it is best not to bring up the ghosts of the past.

History and Theology

One day a Turkish friend and I had lunch in the Black Sea area of Turkey. This region was the last area to convert to Islam slightly over one hundred years ago. One of the waiters caught our eye and we began to engage him in conversation while he was not serving other customers. When the lunch crowd tapered off, we had tea with him. We went back to the same restaurant the next day and again during a lull in customers, we drank tea and spoke with him again. Later we met the waiter away from the restaurant and my friend asked him if had ever heard of the *Hamsheen* people. My friend, whose story I have told in chapter 27 under the name Muhammad, said he had heard about the Hamsheen in this area and wanted to meet some. The Hamsheen are Armenians who had converted to Islam after World War I. Our waiter friend, looking around to make sure no one was listening, told us that he was Hamsheen, and although he knew very little about his ancestral faith, he and some of his relatives were curious about it.

The *World Christian Encyclopedia* defines crypto-Christians as "secret believers in Christ not professing publicly, or publicly baptized, nor enumerated or known in government census or public opinion polls, hence unknown to the state or public or society (but usually affiliated and known to churches.)" The WCE estimates there are perhaps 120 million hidden believers in the world today, with millions more who practice aspects of two faiths. Earlier we looked at crypto-Jews and crypto-Muslims during the Reconquista. Remember that these people were outwardly Catholic, but in secret performed Jewish or Muslim religious acts. In this section, I am using the term "crypto-Christian" not to refer to secret or hidden believers, however. Secret or underground believers are numerous throughout the Muslim world, and it is impossible to estimate their numbers. In this chapter, I use the term crypto-Christian to refer to people who are aware that their ancestors converted to Islam under conditions of great stress. They have a curiosity about their ancestors' former faith, and may even maintain Christian ritual practices that they may not fully understand.

An Example from Japan

In the 17th century in Japan, during the Shogun era, there was a large turning in Japan toward the Catholic faith. Tragically, it was almost wiped out by the Buddhist and Shinto majority who said that converting to Christianity was a denial of their cultural identity. Nevertheless, nearly 400 years later, some descendants of these people still can recite their Catholic prayers in Portuguese, and they take the Eucharist (communion) with rice, fish, and sake. They have no contact with the wider church and assume they are the only believers in the world.[320] Today, perhaps one-half of all Christians in Japan are descendants of these crypto-Christians.

---

[320] Jenkins (look up source)

During the Ottoman Empire

In Turkey, the Islamic Turks pushed their way east after the pivotal battle of Manzikert in 1071 and over the next almost four hundred years fought, invaded and settled throughout Anatolia until they took the grand prize of Constantinople (Istanbul) in 1453. Due to the Ottoman reaction to the humiliating military defeats at Lepanto (see chapter 22) and Russian aggression (and the association of Russians with Christianity), many Christians outwardly converted to Islam when the Ottomans retaliated harshly toward their Christian minorities. F.W. Hasluch. records the conversion of 8,000 families to Islam while others fled to the Crimea and surrounding areas at the end of the seventeenth century. Many Christian Greeks, Armenians, and Assyrians, converted to Islam during this time. Many, however, reconverted to Christianity around 1860 [321].

There is little doubt that hundreds of thousands of Turkish and Kurdish people have ancestors who would have identified themselves as Armenians, Greeks, Georgians, or Assyrians centuries ago before the coming of the Seljuk Turks. Many girls from these backgrounds converted to Islam after their fathers or brothers were exiled or killed. Then they eventually married Turkish husbands and raised their children as Muslims. In the turbulent years of World War I, in addition to Armenians and Assyrians, Greek Christians were also in a difficult position. Professor Vasileisos Meichanetsidis claims that 250,000 Pontus Greeks (remember Pontus was one of the areas mentioned on the Day of Pentecost; see chapter one) were forced to convert to Islam and speak Turkish rather than Greek. Some of the young boys were trained in the *devshirme* system and became Janissaries (chapter 15). Girls were married off to Turks further depleting the Greek population.[322] In addition to the quarter of a million Greeks who Islamized, another quarter of a million migrated to the Caucasus and the Black Sea

---

[321] F.W. Hasluck: *Journal of Hellenistic Studies Volume 41. No. 2:* pps. 199-202
[322] https://www.gatesonteinstitute.org/15321/turkey-isalmized-christians

areas under Russian control, and their descendants are mostly Orthodox Christians.

There are still ruins of monasteries and churches in the Black Sea region that remind the local people of the Christian heritage of the region. A friend of mine who has spent much time in the area tells the following story. In a beautiful mountain village on the border of Turkey and Georgia, a woman shared the gospel with the queen. She received the message, but her husband the king, was very opposed to it. He was struck blind and lost in the woods so in his desperation, he promised that if the Christian God would heal him, he would believe in the God of his wife, the queen. The Lord healed him, and the conversion of the Georgian people began. In the sixth or seventh century, the Georgian king sent people to witness about Christ to the Lazori king. Many of his subjects placed their faith in Christ. Centuries later, the Ottomans rounded up the priests, beheaded 300 people, and rolled their heads in the town square. That event caused the Laz people to convert to Islam. The Laz are known as sea people who speak Turkish with a funny accent, and are often the brunt of jokes. The Laz today are probably unaware of these historic stories. They continue to make their living by fishing, farming, and increasingly, migrating to the larger cities in Western Turkey.

Richard and Jewel Showalter, whom I mentioned previously, in their journey retracing footprints of the Church of the East along the ancient Silk Road, tell how one night they sat down at a Kazakh family's *yurt* (tent-like home). They were served a wonderful meal, and their host told them how his ancestors used to eat from a common platter and always served the head of the sheep to the guest of honor. What stood out to the Showalters, however, was that they made a sign of the cross over the head of the sheep before serving it. Their host said that they did not know why they made the sign of the cross, except it was a custom. Now after coming to Christ, the host realized that his ancestors must have been Christians.[323] It

---

[323] Showalters,. p. 66

is true that before Islamization, many Kazakhs were Christians, but they have been predominantly Muslims for centuries before coming under Communist oppression for many decades. Now many of these Turkic people have come back to Christian faith, although the majority are still Muslims.

Summary of Crypto Christians

What would happen if there is an awakening by the Holy Spirit directed toward the tens of millions of Muslims who want to learn about the faith that their ancestors embraced before Islam? There is already evidence of this happening among many Arabs, Iranians, Turks and Kurds. Some have discovered that their ancestors were Greek, Armenian, Assyrian, or another Christian people before being absorbed into Turkish, Kurdish, or Arab identity, and into the Islamic religion. Imagine if in response to Christians around the world interceding in prayer for them, millions of these people would become curious about their ancestry before Islam. (This is not to say that their ancestors were necessarily avid Christ followers. Many of them no doubt were quite nominal in their allegiance and may have been quite ignorant of the gospel).

You have probably been around a fire roasting hot dogs or marshmallows while heating hot chocolate and trying to keep warm. The fire had blazed brightly for a while, became just right to roast marshmallows over, but gradually was on the verge of going out with only a few embers still glowing. Then someone who wants to roast another hot dog or marshmallow, blows lightly on the coals and the fire springs forth again.

I hope many of the readers of this book will pray for a rekindling of the fire that may appear to have almost died out. With the fresh breath of the Holy Spirit falling on them, however, millions of crypto-Christians will again blaze with the divine fire of the Spirit and be a light once again to the darkness surrounding them.

Questions for Discussion and Reflection

- Can you think of some customs that people practice without knowing the origin of the custom, like the example of Kazakhs making the sign of the cross over the head of a sheep?
- How can followers of Christ today reach out to people whose ancestors may have had a Christian heritage? How might we discern if there is any latent curiosity about their ancestor's faith?

23

Muslims Encounter Spiritual Power

Just imagine that you are a recently married Muslim woman from a traditional family. Your family arranged your marriage to a fellow employee of your father. You do not have any strong feelings for the man because you barely know him, but neither are you repulsed by him. He is only a few years older than you, makes a decent living and seems to be a nice person. Your wedding night went fine. You were a virgin and it was obvious to your husband that there was no one before him. You both continue to work but after for a couple of years your husband's family are beginning to wonder when the grandchildren are going to come. You have been married four years now and your husband is wondering what is wrong with you. You are sensing that his family is beginning to pressure him to divorce you.

A doctor examined you but the results are not conclusive. Barrenness is always assumed to be the woman's fault in your culture, a woman's worst nightmare. You make vows to Allah that you will be more faithful in doing your five prayers a day. You will fast at Ramadan this year despite it being in the hot summer months, and you will not cheat and drink, and eat a little secretly as you have in the past. You will give more *zakat* (alms) to the poor. Another year passes and still no pregnancy. Talk of divorce is more out in the open now. You know that as a divorced woman you have little chance of marrying again as the reason for your divorce will be obvious. You are nearing your thirtieth birthday and still no children.

One day you are not feeling well and you stay home from work. As you flip through the television channels, you come across a woman who is speaking about Isa's (Jesus')power to do miracles even today as he did long ago. As a Muslim, you know Jesus was a great prophet who healed the sick and even made clay pigeons come to life. When this woman prays, you pray with her and hope that Allah does not strike you down for praying in Jesus' name. A couple of nights later you have a dream in which Jesus in a snow-white robe tells you not to be afraid and that he has heard your request. A few days later, you notice that your monthly period is late. You wait a few weeks but still no period. You had yourself tested, and it is confirmed. You are pregnant! Your husband and his family are rejoicing and praising Allah.

You continue to watch the Christian satellite station whenever your husband is not home. Everything in you wants to learn more about Jesus but you are sure all hell will break out if you tell your husband and his family.

Flaw of the Excluded Middle

Professor Paul Hiebert opened the eyes of many missionaries and theologians with his diagram that he calls the "flaw of the excluded middle." He argues that the worldview that Western Christians generally operate under, even if unconsciously, does not give enough attention to the unseen forces that are being played out in the realm between God and humans.

In the Bible we see a supernatural world full of the paranormal, a world of angels and demons, blessings and curses, miracles and unexplainable events. When people study Islam in an academic setting, they most likely will study the Five Pillars, learn about the life of Muhammad, and examine some surahs of the Qur'an. They will probably learn something about Islamic history and its relationship to the previous Abrahamic faiths of Judaism and Christianity. They will most likely not study what goes on in real life among average Muslims who have to cope with very adverse struggles that distress their lives. Those who have lived among Muslims for an extended period will likely encounter what has been called folk Islam, which is practiced by folk Muslims[324] and quite different from what is written in textbooks about "pure" Islam based on the Qur'an. I have adapted the diagram below from Hiebert's to make it more particular to the Islamic world. Picture a world with Allah above and human beings below. In the secular worldview, there may be or may not be a higher power, but there are natural laws that govern the universe. In the world of folk Muslims, there are many forces and beings between Allah and the frail world of human beings. This is illustrated in the diagram below, which shows many of the beliefs and practices that make up the "excluded middle."

Allah

Curses, witchcraft, sorcery, evil eye, ghosts, ancestors, occult, magic potions, *jinn*[325], divination, charms, amulets, angels, demons, impersonal forces, casting spells, *baraka*[326], tombs of saints, pirs[327]

Human Beings

In between Allah and human beings is the "flaw of the excluded middle." Rick Love has decades of experience in the topic of folk Islam. He says that more than three-fourths of the Muslims in the

---

[324] Folk or popular Islam/Muslims are those who may submit to Islam, but at the same time hope to manipulate unseen forces that seem to be stacked against them. Even after embracing one of the world's religions, animistic practices can continue being practiced along with the required rituals of the world religion. For example, Jews, Christians and Muslims may all claim their respective faith, but still wear an amulet to protect against the evil eye or seek advice from a fortune-teller.

[3] Jinn are unseen spirit beings created from fire rather than dust, like humans. They generally are evil and cause mischief, but are not as evil as the Bible portrays demons. The etymology of the word *genie* most likely comes from this word.

[326] Baraka means blessing, referring to spiritual power that some people possess that enables them to heal or perform miracles.

[327] Pirs are living people thought to have spiritual power

world practice folk Islam, with beliefs and practices sometimes seemingly the opposite of Qur'anic Islam, which is based on submission to Allah. [328] Love goes on to explain some key differences between formal Islam and folk Islam.[329] Notice his diagram below, which I have adapted between formal and informal or folk Islam closely before reading on.

Formal Islam	Folk Islam
Cognitive, Truth-oriented	Heart-felt, Emotional
Legalistic	Mystical
Ultimate Issues of Life	Every day Concerns
Origins, heaven, hell, purpose	Health, guidance, success, prosperity
The Qur'an	Supernatural Power
Sacred Traditions	Spiritual Revelations
Institutional	Inspirational
Supplicative	Manipulative

The Evil Eye

> "Two thirds of mankind die from the attacking influence of the evil eye upon them; the remaining third dies because it is careless in protecting itself against the evil eye." A proverb from Palestine (cited in Musk.)[330]

---

[328] Love p. 2
[329] Ibid p. 22
[330] Musk, *The Unseen Face of Islam* p. 22

The concept of the evil eye permeates many Middle Eastern societies (and Christian and Jewish ones as well). Every newborn baby in many Muslim societies has a blue bead pinned onto his clothing to protect the infant from a jealous glance that may bring harm to the child. This is especially true for male infants, who are generally seen as more desirable than female babies. (This preference may not be as true among modern westernized Muslims.) Suppose you have a new healthy baby boy. Your neighbor, however, has not been able to conceive. She may unconsciously look with envy upon your baby and cause it harm because of her jealousy. If someone compliments the parents of the new baby son, the parents will almost always say, "Mashallah" (May God protect him), and knock on wood or pull on their ear lobe as well. These expressions are in addition to wearing a blue bead, which serves as an amulet to ward off evil.

Urine in Tea and Reading Coffee Grounds

Some women Christ-followers who have been invited into a network of Muslim women have reported watching women place a small drop of their urine in their husband's tea. The idea is that magical power will be released because the urine is a part of them. They hope by doing this, the husband will stay attached to his wife and not to go astray by chasing after other women. Women also give importance to reading coffee grounds to predict the future. Others (including men) will seek ways to place a curse on someone by whom they feel threatened. One cannot help but feel for the women in any culture who have stuck with their husbands through difficult years, and finally, after he begins to earn some real money, they fear he might be seduced by a younger fortune-hunting woman.

Women who cannot have children often seek remedies outside of merely submitting to Allah's will. They may ask someone to make a magic potion for them. Others pray and make vows to deceased Muslim holy men who were known to possess *baraka*. Not only dead saints, however, are consulted. Many women will go to anyone, male or female, Christian or Muslim, if they have *baraka* and can offer possible supernatural assistance. In one city we lived in, the

Christian priest told of long lines of women, in full Islamic conservative garb, lining up to ask him to write an amulet[331] or pray a blessing on an object that belongs to someone they want to bless or curse.

Once I took a group of students to one of Istanbul's largest mosques to observe the Friday prayer time. There must have been close to 1,000 men at the mosque. After the final prostrations, we visited a shrine to a dead Muslim "saint" next to the mosque. The shrine was full of mostly women making pledges to the long-deceased saint. One could see the seriousness and sometimes pain in their faces. I can visualize them praying, "Ya Allah, if you will give me a child so my husband does not divorce me, I will be the most faithful of Muslims." Or, "Ya Allah, if you help my son or daughter win the university exams, or help my daughter find a good husband, I will vow to do 'such and such'." The irony is while the men at the mosque were submitting themselves to Allah and leaving the rest to *kismet* (fate), their wives were next door, hoping to change their *kismet* by performing folk Muslim practices. This is not to say that men do not practice folk Islam. Muslim women, however, often feel powerless and at the mercy of forces stacked against them. Folk practices may give them a sense that someone or something out there has their backs.

The Hunger for Spiritual Power in Folk Islam

Drawing on Rick Love's work again for defining six components of folk Islam:

- Power(s) are in supernatural beings and forces, such as demons, angels and *mana* (unseen force)[332];
- Power persons include imams, shamans, anyone who is thought to have *baraka*;

---

[331] An amulet is a charm that is worn to protect against evil forces such as the evil
[332] *Mana* is generally like an unseen force behind reality. In the Star War films, you often heard the phrase "May the force be with you." That would be an example of *manna*. One could say "May the *manna* be with you."

- Power objects include charms and amulets;
- Power places can be saint's tombs or a particular place said to have *baraka* (see story below about St. Theresa);
- Power times include the hajj (pilgrimage to Mecca), Muhammad's birthday, or the birthday of deceased Sufi saints;
- Finally, power rituals such as chanting of verses from the Qur'an in a magic way, or verses from the Qur'an that are often cited magically as if the words themselves contain spiritual power.[333]

It is interesting that St. George, the saint famous for killing a dragon in Christian lore, is known as *Khidir* to Muslims, and his assistance is often sought in exorcisms from demonic powers. St. George is especially noted for exorcisms. If a Muslims has a child on death's doorsteps, despite being good Muslims, they may ask a Coptic priest to baptize their child.[334]

In Turkey, in the month of April, the St. George Orthodox monastery on an island in the Marmara Sea about an hour boat ride from Istanbul, is visited by many seeking miracles. Catholic, Orthodox and Protestants offer to pray for both Christians and Muslims who bring every type of prayer request to the island of that special day.

Cave Church in Cairo

In Cairo, Egypt, there is a remarkable church, known as the Cave Church, constructed within caves by the loving, sacrificial gifts of its

---

[333] Love, p. 24
[334] Albera & Courucl *Sharing Sacred Spaces in the Mediterranean*, P. 161

members, most of whom are the poorest of the poor who work in the area where garbage is collected and sorted. Yet God works powerfully in that church, and during most services, many people, mostly Muslims, are set free from demonic power through exorcisms performed by the priests in the name of the Jesus.

The Importance of Dreams and Visions

If anyone of you sees a dream that he likes, then it is from Allah, and he should thank Allah for it and narrate it to others, but if he sees something else, i.e. a dream he dislikes, then it is from Satan, and he should seek refuge from Allah from its evil, and he should not mention it to anybody for it will not harm him. (Hadith recorded by al Bukkari) [335]

Dreams carry much weight among Muslims. If the Qur'an was revealed through angelic dreams and visions, it should not be surprising that dreams and visions are seen as ways that God communicates with people. Another verse from the Hadith states, *Whoever sees me in a dream will see me in his wakefulness and Satan cannot imitate me in shape. (al Bukkari)*[336]

Dreams are one of the major ways that the Lord is speaking to Muslims today. One can read online of numerous accounts of Jesus revealing himself to Muslims through dreams. Better yet is to hear an exciting in-person account of how a dream influenced a Muslim! An excellent DVD[337] tells the story of five people from various parts of the Islamic world for whom dreams played a major role in their lives, pointing them to Christ. One of the stories involves someone I know quite well who has become a powerful Christian leader.

For Christians, dreams and visions should be familiar ground. In the Bible, we read of Jacob's dream of the ladder from earth to heaven and the angels go up and down the ladder with the Lord at the top looking down. In the dream, the Lord renews his promise that Jacob's descendants will be as numerous as the dust of the earth and

---

[335] Summarized Sahih Al Bukkari p. 1014 (9:119-O.B)
[336] Ibid p. 1015
[337] *More than Dreams.* The DVD is available in many languages.

all nations will be blessed through him and his offspring (Genesis 28:10-15). Joseph dreams of his brothers' bundles of grain bowing to his bundle. In another dream, even the sun, moon and eleven stars bowed to him (Gen 37:5-9). Later he interprets Pharaoh's dreams and becomes the Prime Minster of all of Egypt! (Gen 41). We think of Daniel interpreting many dreams and becoming a witness of the God of Israel to both the Babylonian and Persian Empires, greatly influencing their rulers toward faith in the Yahweh (Jehovah) Furthermore, Isaiah, Jeremiah, and several of the so-called Minor Prophets also had dreams and visions. Even Balaam's donkey saw a vison which saved Balaam's life (Numbers 22).

In the New Testament, we see Joseph responding to a dream that instructed him to take Mary as his wife even though she was pregnant. Without that dream, Joseph would have put Mary away quietly so she would not be publicly shamed (Matthew 1:19) and face probable severe punishment. God warned the Magi in a dream not to return to Herod after seeing the Christ child (Matt 2:12). In a dream, Joseph was ordered to flee to Egypt during Herod's slaughter of babies under two years of age (Matt 2:13). Dreams are prevalent throughout the book of Acts, as we have seen. In Peter's sermon on the Day of Pentecost, when 3,000 people repented of their sins and believed on Christ, Peter quoted the Prophet Joel who prophesied that in the last days, *I will pour out my Spirit upon all people. Your sons and daughters will prophesy, your old men will dream dreams, and your young men will see visions* (Joel 2:28).

Morton Kelsey in his book, *Dreams: A Way to listen to God* states:

There is a difference between knowing something through deduction and reason, and knowing it through experience and confrontation. Deduction and reason can teach us a great deal, but they alone cannot give our lives meaning. Only a direct experience of the spiritual can do that. I know of no better way to achieve this experience, this confrontation with God, than through the dream.[338]

In another book, Kelsey states that[339]

In the Christian tradition, until the 17th century, dreams were significant because they revealed something beyond the human experience that gave purpose and meaning, or warning where spiritual disaster impended. In Jung's terminology, dreams can express the reality of the collective consciousness of the objective psyche. In religious terms, they kept the people in touch with the purpose and direction of spiritual reality.

Rick Kronk, a veteran in making Christ known to Muslims, confirms that every church father, from Justin Martyr to Origen and Cyprian, during the first 500-600 years of Christian history, believed that it was natural for Christians to have supernatural encounters with Jesus, mostly through dreams[340]

The late Nabeel Qureshi, in his excellent *book Seeking Allah, Finding Jesus*, reveals how over a five-year period, in medical school in debate and dialogue with his roommate, David Wood, he explored the claims of Christ against the counter-claims in the Qur'an. Even though Qureshi came to accept the claims of Christ through reasoning and research (he was after all a scientist) it still took at least three dreams to persuade him to make the decision to follow Christ, knowing what pain it would place on his family. [341]

Real Life Stories

In the book, *The Unseen Face of Islam* by Dr. Bill Musk tells ten stories of people who had important needs in their lives and sought solutions in ways that go outside the borders of Qur'anic-based Islam.

---

[338] Kelsey (1978), p. 100
[339] Kelsey (1991) p. 24
[340] Kronk, p. 79
[341] Qureshi pp. 260-283

In one story, Musk tells of a Muslim woman named Hoda who lives with her husband in Cairo, Egypt. Hoda and her husband had finally conceived a seemingly healthy boy they named Ismet, but after about a year, Hoda became concerned. While other mothers talked about their children's first steps, Ismet was not even able to sit up. Hoda and her husband became more and more frantic as they took Ismet to doctor after doctor seeking a cure. Hoda had to carry him everywhere even after Ismet turned five and then six years old.

Hoda has searched her heart and soul many times about why this tragedy had happened to them. How had she displeased Allah? Had she violated some taboo or done some other sin that brought this on their heads? Then a friend named Samia told her to take Ismet to the Shrine of St. Theresa of Avila in Cairo. Hoda at first says she cannot take her baby to a Christian shrine. Samia, however, tells her that many Muslims go to the shrine and shares with her how her brother's wife could not conceive. After going to St. Theresa's shrine, she got pregnant and now has four children.

Hoda and Samia go to the shrine while their husbands go to Friday prayers at the mosque. At the shrine, they saw hundreds of notes, mostly written by Muslims, thanking St. Theresa for her assistance. St. Theresa died in 1582 and was canonized, the first woman to be named a Doctor of the Roman Catholic Church. None of this mattered to Hoda. What mattered was whether St. Theresa has *baraka*, and if so, would she grant Hoda her request for Ismet's healing?

The answer to both was yes. Ismet, although initially weak from muscular atrophy due to not using his muscles for six years, was fully healed! Hoda promised that at every Christmas and Easter she would come to the shrine and honor the blessed saint.[342]

Did Hoda become a Jesus-follower as a result? I do not know. Did she even pray in Jesus' name? How could a 16th century Catholic saint heal a Muslim boy 500 years later? These are all valid

---

[342] Musk, *The Unseen Face of Islam* pps. 87-91

questions. I cannot answer why Ismet was healed, while many fine Christians have a disabled child who has not been healed. Perhaps our Lord just wanted to bless Hoda and did this miracle out of his grace. Did everyone that Jesus healed become a dynamic Christian afterward? We do know that Jesus told a story about ten lepers and the only one who came back to thank him was a Samaritan. Hoda at least comes back to thank St. Theresa twice a year. For all we know Jesus might have revealed himself to her since the book was written.

St Theresa of Shubra in Cairo gets many Muslim visitors as mentioned in the story above, especially with those with children needing healing.[343] With urbanization, the village culture of shared shrines of Christian and Muslim holy people are not as full as it used to be, especially due to the rise of Islamic fundamentalism that sees folk practices as un-Islamic. Many Muslims however still pray to icons and light candles at Christian sites.

Thousands of people claim to have been healed at shrines dedicated to Mary. This fact may make some readers uncomfortable. Yet the Bible is full of stories that defy our natural reasoning. There is the story about the person who fell into Elisha's tomb and came back to life? (II Kings 13:20-21). We might think of the woman who just wanted to touch the hem of Jesus' cloak to be healed, which reflects a worldview based on magic? (Luke 8: 43-48) How about the Pool of Bethesda where the blind, lame and paralyzed came for healing? (John 5:3) Perhaps we need to see that the compassion and mercy of the Savior goes beyond our logical categories, and realize that Jesus touches people who, despite not having perfect theology, have experienced his grace and mercy.

A Dream and a Divine Encounter

Author and popular speaker Sherry Weddell [344] tells a story about a man with an obvious charism of evangelization named David. He was reading his Bible at an airport and a young man from a Muslim

---

343 Albera & Couci p. 164
344 Weddell, pps. 131,132

family kept staring at him but looked away when David smiled at him. When David slipped out to go to the restroom, the young Muslim followed him in and asked David to tell him about Jesus. David invited the young man to receive Jesus into his heart and life, which he did more than willingly. He explained to David that every night for a month he had a dream about a man named Jesus who was hanging and bleeding from a cross while gazing at him and telling him that he loved him. The young Muslims slipped the Bible secretly into his bag, telling David that his father must not know about this. Only God knows how many other stories similar to this have occurred around the world.

A Spiritually Hungry Woman and a Blanket

In a previous chapter, I told Ishmael's story. He tells of a woman and her husband from Iraqi Kurdistan who had just immigrated to a Western country. The husband was a doctor who had secretly believed in Jesus but had not told his wife. She had heard that their friend Ishmael had become a Christian, and she told her husband that the first thing she would do when she got to their new country was to bring Ishmael back to Islam. While at prayer, Ishmael sensed the Spirit telling him not to directly evangelize the doctor's wife but rather to just demonstrate Christ's love for her. Upon arriving at the airport, the wife quickly rips into Ishmael for leaving Islam. Ishmael does not respond but offers her incredible hospitality (being hospitable is probably the most important Kurdish value but Ali and his family went even beyond what culture dictates). Ishmael and his wife continued to reflect on the joy and peace of the Lord without saying anything about the source of their joy.

One night the woman's husband came to their room after she was already in bed. Not wanting to awaken her, he laid down on the floor near the bed. She woke up the next morning and told her husband that a white sheet was covering him when she woke up. Her husband replied, "I did not have any sheet covering me. I slept without a sheet."

Then the Lord spoke to her heart that her husband was clothed in the righteousness of Isa and that she needed to be also. Neither Ishmael nor the husband knew that the wife had been crying out to Allah and pleading, "O Allah, I have served you for many years as best as I can and I do not have the peace that Ali the *kafir* (infidel) has. Please show me the truth. Is Islam the right path, or is Jesus the way?" That night Jesus revealed himself to her. Ishmael says that the woman was so overcome with joy that she became "drunk in the Spirit," and desired to go out and hug every person and tell him or her that Jesus loves him or her. She remains glowing Christian many years later.

Hindu and Muslim Demons?

A final story comes from outside of the Middle East. In Rajasthan, West India, I was with a team of our students. As I was preaching in a church, a woman let out a blood-curdling scream. She could not be quieted as she screamed and shrieked and thrashed about on the floor, causing the people seated near her to flee. Continuing with the service was pointless, so the elders gathered around her and brought her up for prayer. We prayed for her for at least half an hour or so before she finally quieted down and left. A few days later, she came back to the church and let out the same blood-curdling screams. She was probably not even five feet tall and weighed less than 100 pounds. Yet several grown men, including me, and I am a big guy, could hardly hold her down. We continued praying in Jesus' name, and she kept falling asleep as we rebuked the devil and prayed for her. It was frustrating as we wanted to see her set free, but she kept going to sleep!

She came a third time and once again manifested ugly hissing sounds and demonstrated supernatural strength. This time, however, the power of Jesus set her free. She was delivered from demonic power and gloriously saved. I asked the Indian brothers why it took three times of prayer, over several hours, to see her finally freed. They said that the first demons they encountered entered the woman when she was abused as a child at Hindu temples in a tragic practice called *devadasi*[345] The final demons possessed her when she went to a Muslim folk practitioner who tried to free her using Muslim folk practices, which only led her deeper into demonization.

A couple of days later, we went to her family home. The family of six lived in a single room with a shared toilet with others in the neighborhood. The next day, after months of unemployment, the husband found work. Their daughter is now in Bible school.

Without question, many Muslims who have been involved in folk practices will need deliverance from demonic powers and spirits that have sought to control and ultimately destroy them before they can be set free by Jesus. Western Christians in particular have to be prepared to transition from focusing on presenting Muslims with cognitive truth alone, to ministering in power through the Holy Spirit to set the captive free.

Colossians 2:15 *In this way, he disarmed the spiritual rulers and authorities by his victory over them on the cross.* (NLT).

Questions for Discussion and Reflection

- Often Western Christians study Islam academically but have never dealt with the power aspect of folk Islam. How can those who want to make Jesus known among Muslims be better equipped to minister to folk Muslims?
- Which of the stories did you enjoy the most and why—Hoda and Ismet at the Shrine of St. Theresa; the woman who had a vision of her husband being covered by a sheet of righteousness; or the demonized Indian woman?
- Dreams play a major role in bringing Muslims to Christ. Have you ever had a dream that deeply impacted you spiritually?

---

[345] Devadasi is illegal, but often families sometimes innocently give their daughters to the temple thinking they are serving the gods, when in actuality they are sexual slaves to Hindu priests.

24

How Mary Keeps Showing Up among Muslims

Just **imagine** you are a teenage Egyptian girl from a religious but not overly strict Muslim family. Your grandmother has told you this story before, but now as you approach your later teen-age years, you are more interested in what she witnessed in 1964 in Zeitoun, a suburb of Cairo. She tells you how hundreds of thousands of people saw a strange light and the image of Mary above a Coptic Church. If only Christians had seen the vision of Mary, she would not have believed it. Thousands of other devout Muslims, however, saw it as well. She wonders why Mary did not appear at a mosque rather than a church, but since both religions believe in Mary; maybe it does not matter.

You share with a close friend what your grandmother has told you. She says that in 2009, her mother saw a vision of Mary above a Coptic church in Giza, near the famous pyramids. A few days later, tens of thousands of Muslims and Christians saw the vision. 2009 was not so long ago. You are eager to talk to your friend's mother without appearing too eager. She too is a religious Muslim, and she points you to the Qur'an, the 19th Surah called *Maryam* (Arabic for Mary). You eagerly read the account and other verses related to Maryam.

Next, you begin an Internet search whenever you can access a computer, because you do not have one of your own. One article states that there is more about Maryam in the Qur'an than there is in the Bible. So you ask yourself, then why does Maryam show up at churches rather than mosques? After all, the Prophet Muhammad said that his daughter was the most blessed of all women after Maryam. As you continue to search, you read about Maryam appearing in Syria and Bosnia. Outside of the Muslim world, she also appeared in Lourdes, France and Guadalupe, Mexico.

You believe that Isa was a great prophet and did miracles. You even know good Muslims who have gone to the Christian shrine of St. Theresa in Cairo and had their prayers answered (See previous chapter). However, Christians believe Jesus is the Son of God, which to you is absolute blasphemy. At least, it was until quite recently. You continue to research online whenever you can access a computer. You try to find more people who have seen either the first apparition in Cairo or the second one of Maryam in Giza. You have even talked to some Christians about it. They are generally afraid to talk with Muslims about faith, as they might be accused of proselytizing, but you have met a couple of Christians who have tried to answer some of your questions about Maryam and Isa. They also invited you to attend the Cave Church in Cairo. It is a church built inside a cave, where miraculous healings occur and many people are delivered from demons. You plan to visit the church as soon as you can do so without your family learning about it.

> She (Mary) said: My Lord, how can I have a son and man has not yet touched me? He said: Even so Allah creates what he pleases. When he decrees a matter, He only says to it, Be, and it is (Qur'an Al Imran 3:46).

History and Theology: Is Mary a Missing Bridge to Muslims?

Mary has been perceived as both a bridge and a barrier in the evangelization of Muslims. In 1965 at the second Vatican Council, the Catholic Church declared that Christians and Muslims share a devotion to Mary. In fact, an entire Surah in the Qur'an is named for her. However, Mary is acknowledged as the mother of Jesus, and although honored in both faiths, Islam denies Jesus' divinity. There is a limit, therefore, to how far Muslims can go in revering Mary.

Historically, at times Mary has been perceived as a warrior on the side of Christians against pagans and Muslims. Byzantine Christians saw her as a powerful barrier against Islam, almost like a Deborah or Jael type figure (Judges 4) who battled on behalf of the people of God. In the celebrated victory at Lepanto, devotion to Mary as expressed through the rosary was seen as pivotal for the Christian victory over the Turks in 1571 (See chapter 16). Although the Ottomans remained powerful for another one hundred years, it was the beginning of their decline.

Narratives of Jesus' Birth

The angel Gabriel was sent from God to a town of Galilee called Nazareth, to a virgin betrothed to a man named Joseph, of the house of David, and the virgin's name was Mary. And coming to her he said, "Hail, favored one! The Lord is with you (Luke 1:26-28 NAB).

Behold, you will conceive in your womb and bear a son, and you shall name him Jesus. He will be great and will be called Son of the Most High...But Mary said to the angel, "How can this be, since I have no relations with a man?" And the angel said to her in reply, "the Holy Spirit will come upon you, and the power of the Most High will overshadow you Therefore the child to be born will be called holy, the Son of God. (Luke 1:31-35 NAB)

From now on all generations will call me blessed (Luke 1:48 NIV)

It is especially in the Gospel of Luke, which gives us the story of the annunciation, the visitation of Mary to Elizabeth, the Angel Choir, the Magnificat, and other details about birth of our Lord. Matthew's Gospel also tells us how the Magi honored the Christ child and the holy families' flight to Egypt.

Besides the New Testament, the Proto-Evangelium of James, not included in the canon of Scripture, has interesting insights into the birth narratives, including the Annunciation, the birth of Mary, and the birth of Jesus. This chapter does not intend to be an entire study of Mary in the Bible, but rather where the story intersects with the Muslim understanding of it.

Mary in the Qur'an

Of the 114 surahs (chapters) in the Qur'an, only one is named for a woman. That woman is *Maryam* (Mary) in Surah 19. She is also mentioned prominently in Surah 3 (Al Imran), and there are scattered references in other surahs. Let us examine what one prominent Muslim writer says in an article entitled *Mary, the Virgin, in Christianity and Islam*.[346] The author, Abdul-Rahman Mojahed, argues that Mary is more honored in Islam than in Christianity. That is debatable. That she is mentioned more frequently in the Qur'an than in the Bible is true. That many Protestants, in particular, hardly ever mention Mary except in Christmas nativity plays, is also true. Many Protestants, in reaction to perceived Catholic Mariolatry often go to the other extreme and seldom acknowledge Mary.

In the Qur'an Al-Imran 3:33-37, Mary's birth is mentioned. The wife of Imran says, 'My Lord, indeed I have pledged to you what is in my womb, consecrated for your service, so accept this from me...My Lord, I have delivered a female.' ...And I have named her Mary, and I seek refuge for her in you and for her descendants from Satan, the expelled from the mercy of Allah (Al-Imran 3:33-37)."

An often-cited Hadith[347] says, "I heard the Messenger of God saying, there is none born among the offspring of Adam, but Satan touches... A child, therefore, cries loudly at the time of birth because of the touch of Satan, except for Mary and her child" (Hadith of al Bukhari). It can be pointed out that the Bible does not mention the birth of Mary but the Qur'an does.

Later in the same surah in the Qur'an, it says, "And mention when the angels said, 'O Mary, indeed Allah has chosen you and purified you and chosen you above the women of the world. O Mary, be

---

[346] https://www.islamforchristians.com/mary-virgin-christianity-islam/
[347] *Hadtih* are the words and deeds of the Prophet Muhammad complied long after his death. Next to the Qur'an in authority.

devoutly obedient to your Lord and prostrate and bow with those who bow in prayer" (Imran 3:41- 43).

Surah 19, which is named after Mary, tells of the birth of John (Yaya) to a couple well past their years of childbearing. The Qur'an says that Zechariah would not be able to speak for a time (three nights) as a sign (Qur'an: Maryam 19:5-10). Then an angel represented herself to Mary and tells Mary that she will give birth to a pure boy. Mary asks, "How can I have a boy while no man has touched me and I have not been unchaste?" (19:20).

It is interesting that the Qur'an states, "And (We cursed them) for their disbelief and their saying against Mary a great slander." Then in the next verse the Qur'an states, "And for their saying: We have killed the Messiah, Jesus son of Mary, the messenger of Allah, and they killed him not, nor did they cause his death on the cross, but he was made to appear to them as such" (Al- Nisa 4:156-157). The verse appears to refer to Jews who are cursed for slandering Mary. Many of the Jewish townspeople assumed that Mary had committed adultery and so Jesus as a baby speaks from the crib and defends his mother against malicious attacks (Qur'an 3:45-46).

Surah 66:12 also mentions that Mary, the daughter of Imran, guarded her chastity, as does 21:91. Surah 3:42 not only mentions her purity but says that she is chosen above the women of the world, "O Mary, indeed Allah has chosen you and purified you and chosen you above the women of the world. In Surah Maryam 19:29 we see again the child speaking from the cradle. The stories of Jesus speaking as an infant and making a clay pigeon come to life are found in *The Infancy Gospel of the Thomas*, which predated Islam but are not found in the canonical Gospels in the Bible.

Turkish writer Mustafa Akyol cites a well-known legend that when Muhammad smashed hundreds of idols in the Ka'aba in 630, he spared only the frescoes of Jesus and his mother. Over 500 years later, in 1187, the Muslim leader Saladin[348] reconquered Jerusalem and destroyed the churches built by the Crusaders but not those built by Eastern Christians. One Crusader relic that Saladin did not destroy was the Church of St Anne, believed to be the childhood home of the Virgin Mary (St Anne is the legendary mother of Mary). Akyol cites a Catholic source that notes "the Muslims' great reverence for Our Lady (Mary) precluded them from destroying her birthplace."[349]

There is much more in this chapter that I will not address for space concerns. It must be pointed out however there is another side to the honor of Mary. Surah 19: 35 states, "It is not befitting for Allah to take a son; exalted is He! When he decrees an affair, He only says to it, 'Be, and it is.' Many verses later this surah says, "And they say, 'The Lord most merciful has taken for himself a son. You have done an atrocious thing. The heavens almost rupture therefrom and the earth splits open and the mountains collapse in devastation that they attribute to the Most Merciful a son" (19:88-92). In summary, the Qur'an is very affirming of Mary as a virgin who supernaturally gave birth to the Prophet Isa. The Qur'an, however, forbids the over exaltation of Mary very strongly. "And beware of the day when Allah will say, 'O Jesus, Son of Mary, did you say to the people, 'take me and my mother as deities besides Allah?' He will say, 'Exalted are you! It was not for me to say that to which I have no right' (Al Ma'ida 5:116) Scholars have speculated that Mary seems to be part of the Trinity in this verse. Perhaps the Prophet came across a heretical Christian group that assumed that if Jesus was divine, then his mother must be also. As we have seen, however, she is to be honored and to be held in high regard, but not worshipped.

Bishop Fulton Sheen on Mary and Muslims

In 1952 Bishop Fulton Sheen, perhaps soon to be Saint Sheen, wrote a book entitled, *The World's First Love*. Long before there was much

---

[348] Remember Saladin, the leader of the Muslim army that retook Jerusalem from the Crusaders (See chapter 17)
[349] Akyol, *The Islamic Jesus,* (p. 105)

about Islam in the news, and most Muslims were just coming out from under colonial powers, Bishop Sheen made some interesting points in the chapter "Mary and Moslems." He rightfully writes, "If Moslemism[350] (Islam) is a heresy...it is the only heresy that has never declined...There was never a time in which it declined, either in numbers, or in the devotion of its followers."

If Muslims are to be converted to Christianity, according to Sheen, "It is our belief that this will happen not through the direct teaching of Christianity, but through a summoning of the Moslems to a veneration of the Mother of God." Bishop Sheen goes to cite from Surahs 3 and 19, especially the verse "Oh, Mary, God has chosen you and purified you, and elected you above all the women of the earth." Mary, then, for the Muslims is the true *Sayyida,* or Lady. The only serious rival to her in their creed would be Fatima, the daughter of Mohammed himself. But after the death of Fatima, Mohammad wrote: "Thou shalt be the most blessed of all the women in Paradise, after Mary." [351] He mentions that in parts of Africa and India, the Pilgrim statue of the Lady of Fatima has been used in religious processions and has led to the conversions of Muslims and others.[352]

In addition to Bishop Sheen, two men whom we examined earlier, Nicolas of Cusa and William of Tripoli, wrote positively about the way that Muslims understood Mary, and that she could be a bridge to the Muslim heart.

The story of the shrine of Our Lady of Fatima

Muslims occupied what is today Portugal for centuries. When they were driven out during the Reconquista, the last Muslim chief had a beautiful daughter named Fatima, no doubt named after the daughter of the Prophet. A Catholic young man fell in love with her, and instead of escaping with her people, Fatima stayed behind and embraced the Catholic faith. Fatima died young, and the young man

---

[350] Moslemism and Mohammadism are out of date way to say Islam.

[352] Sheen, p. 208

named their town Fatima, which is interesting in the light of the fact that no other Portuguese city or town has an Arabic name.

The story of three Portuguese children who saw apparitions of Mary at Fatima in 1917 is well-known in Catholic circles. The children were shown visions of events that were going to happen soon. Young children who had little knowledge of the world predicted these events, including World War II, the rise and fall of Communism, and many others.

Apparitions of Mary

Requests for Prayer at House of Mary

The Shrine of Fatima, as far as I know, has not led to massive numbers of Muslims acknowledging Christ at this point in history. Portugal is hardly a common destination for Muslim pilgrims. Other Marian shrines do draw large numbers of Muslims, however. Rita Gerge-Tvrtkovic says that the shrine of Our Lady of Africa in Algiers draws about 40,000 visitors per year, and the vast majority are Muslims. About one million visitors a year visit Maryam Ana Evi near Ephesus, the alleged home of Mary after Jesus' resurrection and ascension. It is ironic that Ephesus was the place where Mary as *Theotokos* was defined at the Council of Ephesus in 431 (see Chapter 5). It was also her place of residence after the Apostle John took Mary under his care as Jesus had instructed him to do from the cross (John

19:27). One can see hundreds of thousands of prayer requests stuffed into every crack of the wall that lies outside of the alleged home of Mary in Ephesus, Turkey. There is a Christian room where Christians light candles and drink holy water, and a Muslim room that contains verses from the Qur'an about Maryam, especially Surah 19. For most Muslim women, barrenness is the worst thing that can happen to a woman. Many women come to Ephesus to beseech the Virgin Mary to have a child. There are other Marian shrines in Muslim countries, including Syria, Lebanon, Pakistan, Iraq, Jordan and especially Egypt. Gerge-Tvrtkovic also mentions other shrines where Muslims often go that are not in the Muslim world.[353]

What Happened at Zeitoun?

In 1968, the ancient country of Egypt was experiencing an economic, political, social and spiritual crisis. In the midst of the upheaval, the image of the Virgin Mary was seen above St. Mary's Coptic Christian church in the Cairo suburb of Zeitoun by two Muslim security guards at a garage across the street from the church. This was not a one-time appearance of the blessed mother. The apparitions continued for five months for hours at a time to millions both Muslims and Christians, who claimed to have seen the Virgin. Prominent Catholic and Protestant church leaders verified the apparition. It is quite possible that this church was on the very path where the holy family passed through as they fled to Egypt.[354]

---

[353] Rita Gerge-Tvrtkovic, p. 45
[354] Cruz, pp. 209-213

Apparition of Mary at Zeitoun

In December of 2009, a Muslim neighbor of a Coptic Church in Giza, home to the Pyramids and Egypt's third largest city, claimed to have seen a light over the church from a coffee shop across the road. Over the next few days, 200,000 people, both Christians and Muslims, witnessed to seeing strange light, as had previously occurred in the church in Zeitoun. This seemed to happen at a time when Egypt's unity was under threat. Not long before, several Coptic Christians had been shot and murdered. Mary has been a shared symbol that transcends religious differences. Joan Carroll Cruz tells of two other apparitions in Egypt, that were witnessed to by millions.[355] Egyptians claim their church was founded by St. Mark, the author of the second Gospel. They are justifiably proud that the family of our Lord sought refuge in Egypt at a time when Herod sought to kill all children under age two in Judea.

Apparitions in Syria

In another hot spot in the Arab world, the Virgin has appeared as well. In 1982, the Syrian regime was ruled by Hafiz al Assad, the father of the current dictator Bashar al Assad. That year saw what has been called the Hama massacre when the Alawite government put down a Muslim Brotherhood revolt. Evidently, Mary appeared in an ordinary house in the old city of Damascus. Other manifestations preceded the apparition of Mary that drew

---

[355] Ibid, 239-244

thousands of people over a period of years, in which she pleaded for unity and peace among Christians and between Christians and Muslims.

Our Lady of Lebanon

Our Lady of Lebanon is visited by millions of Muslims and Christians yearly. During the month of May, a month especially focused on Mary for Catholics, this shrine receives about a million visitors. Throughout the year, many from Muslim countries, especially from Iran, visit the shrine and pray for Mary's intercession. The Catholic News Service reports a Muslim woman who did not disclose her real name, fearing a reaction from her parents, wearing a *hijab,* who stated, "Honestly, I came here to pray and to ask many things of Maryam al Aadra (the Virgin Mary). I asked her to protect the people I love and to make clear to me the way I should go. I prayed at her feet." [356] Saint John Paul II visited the shrine in 1997 and prayed "Our Lady of Lebanon who had watched over the agonizing suffering of the Lebanese people could help all those who were suffering in the world." His successor, Pope Benedict XVI, invoked an appeal for peace and protection among the various communities in Lebanon, a country often torn apart by internal conflict between its peoples. [357]

---

[356] https://www.catholicnews.com/services/englishnews/2016/in-lebanon-muslims-and-christians-visit-marian-shrine-at-harissa.cfm
[357] https://en.wikipedia.org/wiki/Our_Lady_of_Lebanon

The Miracle of Medugorje?

Medugorje in Bosnia and Herzegovina has been the center of much controversy but also much blessing to hundreds of thousands of pilgrims. This apparition site has not yet been either authenticated or rejected by the Vatican. Some things about this apparition are particularly intriguing. One reason is that the apparitions, which began on June 24, 1981, were like at Fatima, given to children. At Medugorje, it was six children rather than three who began to experience apparitions of the Virgin Mary. As with Fatima in Portugal, however, because it was children who experienced the apparitions, it led to many doubting their authenticity even among some clergy. Bosnia and Herzegovina was part of the former Yugoslavia, a communist country as well as at the crossroads between Orthodox Serbia, Catholic Croatia, and Muslim Bosnia. One of the six visionaries, Mirjana Dragicevic Soldo, now 55 years of age, has been the primary spokesperson and writer. Her book is a fascinating account of the apparitions, the impact they have had, and the trials and tribulations that resulted from them.[358] In addition to the suspicions about whether or not the apparitions are real, at the time, Bosnia-Herzegovina was a communist country, part of the former Yugoslavia. The six visionaries paid a price for their faith. There were mocked and discriminated against at school. Marijana describes the persecutions she went through in high school, and in particular at university, as all professors had to swear allegiance to the atheistic Communist party. She was eventually forced out of the university.

In her book, Marijana Soldo discusses how a Muslim woman named Paasha was especially interested in her apparitions. As we saw earlier in this chapter, Mary (Maryam) is the only woman mentioned by name in the Qur'an. Other titles for Mary that Paasha confirmed are *Saimah* (she who fasts) and *Siffiqah (she who confirms the truth)*.[359] Other Muslim imams (religious leaders) also have

---

[358] *My Heart will Triumph* by Mirjana Solda (2016)
[359] Soldo, p. 119

visited the Marian Shrine and do not see it as contrary to Islam, but others have not been so affirming. Could some imams or regular Muslims, have secretly embraced Jesus as a result of seeing the apparition? That is a question that needs to be carefully researched.

Saint John Paull II's Embracing of Medugorje

John Paul II was according to Marijana a firm believer in the apparitions at Medugorje. He asked the pilgrims there to pray for his intentions and states how he followed the messages from the beginning. He called Medugorje the "hope for the entire world."[360] On a note which might relieve some who worry about Mary being exalted over Jesus, a pilgrim asked Marijana should not the apparitions focus on Jesus. She replied, "Our Lady has never said, "Come to me and I will give you..." On the contrary she has only said, 'Come to me and I will lead you to my Son and he will give you...) [361]

Evidently, according to the Catholic News Agency, the Vatican has been tracking Medugorje very closely. As there have been many false apparitions, there is much caution before the Church gives its official approval. Without question, tens of thousands of people have been converted and made much stronger in their faith. Some has said that Medugorje is like a continuation of Fatima calling the world to conversion. Most of the prayer is directed toward the conversion of sinners. Marijana has evidently said that as of March 18, 2020 the virgin will no longer appear to her every month as he has done monthly since 1987.In 2014, the Vatican commission concluded a "four year-long investigation on the doctrinal and disciplinary aspects" (Catholic News Service). Pope Francis believes that much good fruit has come out of the apparitions, and he has approved Catholic pilgrimages there, but he has not made a final deliberation on their authenticity.

---

[360] Ibid p. 197
[361] Ibid p. 200

As of now, thousands of pilgrims continue to visit the site. Watching some of the You Tube clips taken at Medugorje remind me of the days when Charismatic renewal swept through churches from Catholic to Assemblies of God, and in many churches of varying theological and denominational backgrounds. There was much joyful singing, dancing, testimonies of conversion and healing, and people glowing with the love of Jesus.

Because this apparition is quite recent compared to many others, it has gotten more media attention. Full-length documentaries can be found on You Tube[362] along with many others, some very favorable and some not so. The impact that these apparitions have made on Muslims could be an important topic for further research.

Jesus has many ways of drawing Muslims to himself, and we saw in the previous chapter the way he powerfully uses dreams to reveal himself to searching hearts. God has left a witness in the Qur'an that, despite its denial of the full divinity of our Lord, and its denial that Mary is the *Theotokos*, it gives enough information about Mary and her Son to wet the appetite of Muslims to learn more. Can we rejoice when a Muslim discovers Jesus, whether through encountering him in a dream, through reading the *Injil*, or through an apparition of his mother? As is often cited by Catholic and Orthodox Christians, "Mary always points people to her Son."

Questions for Discussion and Reflection

- How might Maryam (Mary) be a bridge to Muslims? Why do you think many Christians, in particular Catholic and Orthodox, perceive Mary playing a much more active role in salvation, protection, and answering prayer than Protestants tend to do?
- What do you think about apparitions? It is one thing to believe in the historic Mary, another for people to "see" her

---

[362] https://www.youtube.com/watch?v=c9dQYRQXbXc

today. Have you ever made a pilgrimage to a Mary shrine like Fatima, Lourdes, or Guadalupe? If not, would you like to?

25

Daring to Love

Just imagine you are a young girl named Aisha from a small city. Your family is quite devout, at least on the surface. Your high scores on university entrance examinations earned you a place at a prestigious university in a big city several hours from your hometown. It is an elite university, full of students from prominent, wealthy families. Your father is not from that world and sees little need for a girl to be educated when he sees your future as one of an early marriage and having many children.

Your mother supports you. She was married at 16 and had three children by twenty years of age. She understands why you want to do something different than she did with her life. She really had no choice when she married so young, but she knows that winning a place at a leading university would be an open door for you. She pushed you to study hard from primary school through high school, and sacrificed financially so you could attend special classes on the weekends to improve your foreign language, math and science scores. The hard work paid off, as you were accepted into law school in one of the top universities.

During your first year at university, students primarily study academic English as most of the courses are taught in that language. It is a huge advantage to know foreign languages well for future job prospects. One of your teachers especially stands out to you She has an inner joy about her that seems genuine. She cares about her students and often goes with them to outdoor tea gardens where women are free to sit and drink tea and socialize. One day you linger after class and ask her a question about English grammar, but your real purpose is to get to know her better. After answering your questions about grammar, she invites you for a cup of tea at the tea garden.

For some reason even though your English is still limited and her Turkish is not yet fluent, you have opened your heart to her. You tell her how your father wants you to come home to get married and forget about university. He says the son of one of the leading families in your town wants to marry you. Even now, your family and the potential groom's family are making the preliminary arrangements. The young man's family is willing to marry their son into your family despite his family being higher than yours on the social scale. For some reason, their son wants to marry only you.

The teacher says, "Aisha, you are exceptionally beautiful. It is not surprising that he would desire you. How well do you know this man?" You answer her that you barely know him. You talked to him in high school a few times surrounded by other students, and that was it. You sensed he liked you, but you never encouraged it.

You tell the teacher that you want to finish your education and become a lawyer. You want to help women who are forced into marriage at young ages, and to work for there to be greater criminalization for those who commit honor killings.[363] Your dreams will come to nothing if you have to return home and get married before you even begin to study law.

Now you nervously share with your teacher what happened to you a couple of months ago. It was very hard to talk about it, but you know no one else to tell whom you think you can trust.

---

[363] Honor killings occur when some is perceived to have violated a family's or a unit of society's collective honor. It tends to most happen when a girl-woman has been accused violating sexual mores. Often the father, older brother, uncle or whoever carries out the killing of the alleged violator, is not penalized to the degree he would if he had committed a murder that is not "honor" related.

You were invited to a party with some of the most popular students at the university. Many were children of prominent families. At that party, a handsome young man flirted more with you than with other girls. "Most of the girls showed far more skin and danced much more suggestively than me but the young man seemed to have eyes only for me." The rest of what happened is a bit of a blur. The man offered you a drink and when you looked away for a moment to greet someone, he must have slipped something into your drink. What you do know is that several hours later when you woke up in a strange bed, you realized you are no longer a virgin.

You have no money like some of the girls do to get a surgery to sew your hymen and attempt to fool their husbands on their wedding night. Soon it will be your wedding night. When your husband discovers you have been with someone else, he will denounce you to the entire community. Your family will so ashamed that your father or brother may kill you or have someone else do it. Honor killings are still occur in your town even in these days.

You find yourself going to your teacher several times over the next few weeks before your father is demanding that you come home and marry the young man from your hometown. The teacher tells you she cares for you and is asking God what is the best thing to do. She reads to you beautiful sounding words form the Bible, especially about how much Jesus valued women. She told you the story of the woman caught in adultery and how Jesus intervened for her, saved her life and told those who wanted to stoner her, "Let he who has no sin throw the first stone" (John 8:1-11). You like the story, but will Jesus step in and save you from your family? The teacher wonders what is the ethical thing to do. Is it right for her to give money to Aisha to deceive her family? What if Aisha was not really raped and wants to cover up her promiscuous life style as many rich girls do in her country?

History and Theology

When Brothers (those in the Muslim Brotherhood) tell the stories of why they joined, there's usually that one person with exceptional charisma and character who showered them with attention at the mosque or school, introducing them to Banna's (Hasan al Banna-founder of the Muslim Brotherhood) writings and bringing them into a circle of friendship and solidarity (Tewfik Hamid) [364]

Doing Life Together

The above citation should challenge us as Christians. The Muslim Brotherhood, practices what the Apostle Paul demonstrated to the Thessalonians.

> *...Just as a nursing mother cares for her children, so we cared for you. Because we loved you so much, we were delighted to share with you **not only the gospel of God but our lives as well** (1st Thessalonians 2:7-8).*

For those who have given their lives to make Christ known among Muslims, the above verses especially ring true. We not only share the gospel as glorious as it is. We also must share our lives in loving relationships that go far beyond a one-time presentation of the gospel. The point could be made that the Apostle Paul was addressing believers here, not unbelievers. But we do not know when the Thessalonians actually came to the understanding of who Jesus was. No doubt many were still trying to figure it all out when Paul shared his life with them as well as the gospel. We often hear the phrase today, "doing life together." Doing life with Muslims that the Lord brings into our path, goes way beyond the verbal presentation of the key components of the gospel message. It involves doing life with them in the midst of life's joys and sorrows, ups and downs. Foreign Christian teachers as in the story of Aisha have found themselves in similar situations. Muslims, as do most people, struggle with employment related issues, personal relationships, marriage, raising children, and in trying to understand adverse things that have happened to them that they do

---

[364] Hamid, p. 103

not understand. Sometimes we just need to listen and be there even if we do not verbalize the gospel every time.

What Leads Muslims to Accept the Way of Jesus?

In the citation above, we can see the importance of relationship even in recruiting young men into the Muslim Brotherhood, an organization often accused of terrorism. In 2008, Professor Dudley Woodbury published the results of interviews and surveys of 750 MBBs from around the world. The survey was directed toward examining the key factors that led Muslims to embrace Christ, despite the price that they know they will most likely pay. There were a number of reasons, but the most cited one was the lifestyle of Christians, demonstrated in their love for even non-Christians and their treatment of women as equals. In addition to the "love factor," what drew Muslims to accept the Christian faith was 2) the power of God in answered prayers and healings, as well as seeing dreams and visions of Jesus; 3) dissatisfaction with Islam, especially radical expressions of it; 4) the truths in the Bible spoke to them; 5) Biblical teachings about the love of God expressed through the life and teachings of Jesus.

The Apostle Paul tell us that three things remain-faith, hope and love and the greatest of these is love (1st Corinthians 13:13) Reading the Bible, dreams, visions and answers to prayer all played a major role in Muslims coming to faith in the Woodberry survey. We, who hope to reach Muslims with the Good News, should study apologetics vigorously, and know well what we believe and why we believe it. We should also be people of faith, ready to pray for a healing or a deliverance from demonic powers. Even dynamic encounters with truth and power, however, can only go so far unless undergirded by love.

Allah: A Master to Obey or a Father to Love?

Islam is about submission and obedience to the alleged will of Allah. Islam is not about a relationship with a loving Father who loved us so much that he sent his only Son to die for us. God is often portrayed as merciful in the Qur'an, but he only loves those who love him. The God of Islam is not love as the Bible states (1st John 4:8) and certainly his love is not unconditional. That is why Muslims who really sought to submit to Allah before they came to Christ, imply that they believed in Allah and tried to obey the Qur'an by praying five times daily, keeping the Ramadan fast, giving *zakat* (alms) etc. but it was never enough to please Allah. After encountering Jesus, however, they now no longer feel far from God and know Him as a loving Father.

The story of the Prodigal Son in the Bible (Luke 15:11-32) is especially applicable to Muslim culture. The son disrespects his father, and by demanding his inheritance, he is basically saying he does not want to wait until his father dies to get what is coming to him. He goes to a foreign land and lives like a king for a time but then runs out of money. To survive, he has to feed pigs, which is about the lowest job a Jewish boy (the same is true in Muslim culture as pork is totally forbidden) can do. The son comes to his senses and tells himself that if he goes home, he can be a slave to his father since he lost his right to be a son. As he approaches his home, his father sees him coming from afar and immediately takes off running toward him. Why the urgency? Because the people of his village knowing how the young man treated his father, were probably going to kill the son, which according to the Law of Moses, rebelling against one's parents was a capital crime (Deuteronomy 21:21). The father not only prevents his son from being harmed, bur embraces him, declares a celebration feast upon his return, and restores him to his place of being a son. God in the Bible is a Father who loves his children, even when they go astray. He is not a slave master to be feared, but a Father who is to be lovingly obeyed.

Wounded Healers

Most Muslims are hungry for love and are drawn to people who do as the Lord commanded us "to walk in love" (2nd John 6). On the surface, it may not appear that Muslim society is as broken as the West is. In reality, sin is more hidden and not as open. Once trust is established with a Muslim, however, he or she may open up and share that they have suffered from terrible abuse within their family or community. They feel that they cannot share what happened to them with others in their own culture. I often use the deceased Dutch priest, professor, and popular author Henri Nouwen's phrase "wounded healers" to encourage my students to go out into the world as wounded healers. If they have been wounded and have felt guilt and shame but have been or at least in the process of experiencing Jesus' love healing their wounds, they can be used by Jesus to bring healing to others, in particular Muslims. Muslims often feel they have no one with whom they can share what happened to them as the story of Aisha illustrates.

Fearing Muslims

I am convinced that Satan has worked overtime to make Christians fear Muslims. The Bible says that perfect love drives out fear (1st John 4:18). I have been asked in churches about the dangers of Muslims posing outwardly as normal Americans but have been secretly radicalized. While I do not deny there are very evil Muslims in the world who want to harm the infidels, the vast majority are people like most of us who have been wounded. Unlike those of us who have been transformed by the love of Jesus, they do not know where to turn to find healing for their wounds. Would to God that thousands go forth in Jesus' name, not to kill as the Crusaders did, but to bring healing--physical, mental and spiritual--to the wounded Muslims of the world. To do this, however, will demand a commitment to learn new languages, live a life beyond reproach, and give of our time and energy to a task that may not show results for a long time. Red martyrdom is possible, but white martyrdom is certain! (See chapter 3)

Examples of Encounters with Love

A wonderful couple moved out to a Middle Eastern city with no other Christian fellowship, and no known believers in Jesus, much like we did near to same time. This family of five really walked in love, holiness and the power of the Spirit. I shared earlier how the Lord brought people into our path by divine appointment who were open to the gospel. A similar thing happened to our friends. They knew no one in the city who was a Christian or who was interested in learning about the Christian faith, but God supernaturally brought people who were spiritually hungry across their path. In several months, a loving fellowship of believers was established.

A young man joined the fellowship and seemed to sincerely want to be a follower of Christ. In reality, he was reporting to the police the activities of the group. Evidently, the young man was part of a hyper-nationalist movement that perceived that Western Christians only came to their country to cause division, with the goal of weakening the state by dividing people over religion. Not long afterward, the foreign family was arrested and were deported a few weeks later, and some of the believers were arrested. The young man, however, began to regret what he had done, confessed to my friends what he had been an informer to the authorities, and deeply regretted what had happened to the family and the local believers. When it was time to say goodbye to the family just before they were deported, he told them he had never seen the kind of loving relationship before between a husband and a wife, and the reciprocal love the parents had for their children and the children had for their parents. It went beyond duty and obligation to something that the informant had never seen before. It is what the Bible calls *agape* love. That love spilled over to all whom they met. While it was too late to undo the damage that had led to their deportation, he went on after going abroad to Bible school in another country, to become a pastor of a local MBB church until he passed away a few years ago.

The Story of Azad

I learned a valuable lesson about how much value the Lord places on one life as you will see in the story of Azad (not his real name).

I had the change to teach at North Central University (NCU) in Minneapolis, Minnesota for two years during a time of transition for our family before we went to Central Asia after almost fifteen years in the Middle East, I had been interested in the Muslim countries of the former Soviet Union since the 1970s. Finally, it seemed to be the right time to go another area of the world. I was increasingly burdened in prayer for the Turkic peoples of Central Asia, including the Uzbeks, Turkmens, Azerbaijanis, Kazakhs and Kyrgyz. After finishing my two-year commitment at NCU, they offered me a permanent job to teach and be the department chair of what we now call the Global Studies program. I turned the position down because I wanted to serve in Central Asia. We left our two sons in the States and we sent our daughter to boarding school in Germany.

The language in our new country was relatively close to Turkish, so my wife and I could survive in the language for our daily needs, but I wanted to learn the dialect of this new land so I could speak more clearly to peoples' hearts. I hired a teacher with whom I met with almost every day. We became good friends and eventually I accompanied him to his village about three hours away by bus. The village was one of hundreds of a former Soviet era forced *kolkhoz* (forced collective villages). The natural setting was quite beautiful, but most of the people were impoverished. My teacher introduced me to his brother whom I have called Azad.

Azad suffered from a terrible disability. It was painful to watch him walk. Every step must have been agonizing for him. His teeth were rotted out and he was all skin and bones. His house had neither electricity nor an inside toilet. It was cold in the winter and hot in the summer. His only real diversion was smoking, and he chain-smoked, as cigarettes were cheaper than quality food.

His brother told me how Azad got to be in this condition. He drove a tractor for the collective village, and one day, in the cold winter, the tractor tipped over and he was trapped underneath it with no help nearby. He yelled out for help repeatedly, but no one could hear him. Eventually he was discovered, but by that time, his legs were frozen and he never physically recovered. He lost his livelihood, his physical strength and his wife. She began regularly cheating on him with a government official in the region, and she eventually left him destitute in his broken down condition.

Azad was very friendly to me but he was a man who had lost every reason to live. His brother, my language helper, had never been a devout Muslim and had become a Christ-follower a few years previously. Together we shared the gospel with Azad. I also offered to help him with his physical needs. His teeth had rotted out so he could not eat solid food, which is one reason why he smoked so much. I offered to pay for false teeth if he gave up smoking. He successfully quit, and with his new teeth be began to gain weight and no longer looked like a skeleton. His walking also improved, and although not perfect, it was far less painful than it used to be. Azad too, placed his faith in Jesus.

After about five months in our new country, my wife and I came back to the Twin Cities to teach a January term and to visit our sons who were attending (NCU). Surprisingly, one of the professors had resigned and I was offered the assistant professorship position again. I told the university I would pray about it, and we went back to a different Central Asian country to teach a one-month course at a recently established Bible school. After teaching every morning, I spent the afternoons in the country pouring out my heart to God in prayer. Should I stay in Central Asia and continue to be one of the few foreign workers devoting their lives to reaching Muslims, or take the position at NCU and teach and perhaps be able to inspire many young people to go to the Muslim world?

As we were new in Central Asia and still in language study in yet another language, I thought after consulting with my wife Sherry, that maybe we would take the post at NCU. There were so few of us in those days laboring to make Christ known, maybe we could multiply our efforts.

Still I was baffled why if the Lord wanted us at NCU, I did not sense that when I was offered the position two and a half year previously. I could have bought a house in the Twin Cities rather than pay rent with nothing to show for it for thirty months. I could have begun working on my Ph.D. earlier. My daughter would not have had to go to boarding school alone while only in the ninth grade which was very hard for her. It just not make sense. Then I sensed the Holy Spirit whisper the word "Azad" into my heart. It was as if the Lord said, "If I want to jerk your lives around and inconvenience you for a couple of years, what is that compared to Azad's soul? You were the right person to reach him and he is precious to me." I learned first-hand what the Lord would do to show his love to someone! That is a lesson I hope I never forget.

A True Pioneer of Relational Evangelism

Lilias Trotter (1853-1928) stands out as one of the first apostles to Muslims who advocated friendship evangelism for Muslims. She is a model to emulate for the hundreds of unmarried women who have followed her tracks in the male-dominated Muslim world and made a huge contribution despite facing many obstacles. The physical, spiritual, and cultural obstacles she had to overcome in Algeria to make Christ known put most of our efforts today to shame. A good amount has been written about Lilas' life, so I am only going to present a few highlights that are especially relevant for this book.

Totter was born in London, England to a family well off financially. They encouraged Lilas to read and especially to excel in art. She suffered from poor health for most of her life. She developed a heart for the poor early and learned to use the famous evangelist D.L. Moody's *Wordless Book*[365], and received training in sharing the Gospel from the evangelist himself. She was involved in inner-city ministry in London for years before she ever thought about going abroad. She was gifted artistically, and she had the special privilege to be tutored under John Ruskin, one of the most famous artists of his day. She had no real training but enjoyed such an extraordinary natural gift in painting with watercolors that Ruskin delighted in taking her under his wing. Lilias spending so much time in inner-city ministry in London that he felt should have been given to her art frustrated him at times. Much more could be said, but in the end, she made missions her first priority, which Ruskin never understood.

---

[365] Evidently this was a book without any writing that explained the gospel in pictures that especially was helpful in explaining spiritual truth to the illiterate.

When Trotter was thirty-four she applied to the North Africa Mission board for full-time service, but because of her weak heart, she was turned down. The board allowed her to be somewhat unofficially affiliated with them. She sailed for Algeria with Blanche Haworth, who was her co-worker for thirty years, and one other woman. The three would never have passed a health exam, did not have financial backing and did not know a word of Arabic.

There were no language schools to learn Arabic, and furthermore, most Algerian women were secluded behind closed doors. Simply going out on the streets to practice learning a new language was impossible for a woman in Algeria in 1888. Although most women were illiterate, Lilias prepared literature in Arabic for the day women would be able to read. Noel Piper points out that:

> Lilias was not daunted by the traveling conditions. Each journey was risky for two women traveling alone with an unfamiliar guide through territories where Europeans were targets for desert bandits, scorpions, disease, and ferocious dogs. ...Within hours, the air could sear the lungs and sunburn the traveler.[366]

When Lilas Trotter moved into the Arab quarter after living in the French Quarter for several years, she encountered every kind of demonic and occult power imaginable. There probably were not the workshops on spiritual warfare in those days as there are now, and it must have been quite a shock. Noel Piper cites a letter by Trotter stating, "All the outward ways in which the powers of evil are invoked—the spells, the sorceries, and witchcraft—come to light more and more as we get contact with the people"[367].

I suppose I could have written about Lilias in the chapter about power encounters as well as in this chapter. Quoting Helen Kooiman Hosier:

---

[366]Piper p. 55.
[367] Ibid, p. 57

Lilias Trotter was at least a century ahead of her time in developing ways to reach Muslims with the Gospel. She realized that Algerians would not receive the gospel through traditional evangelism tools of proclamation and persuasion. Instead, she employed a combination of literature and art, undergirded by a lifestyle of love and encouragement. [368]

Lilias Trotter kept a daily journal and in one of the quotes she says, "Take the hardest thing in your life-the place of difficulty, outward or inward, and expect God to triumph gloriously in that very spot. Just there he can bring your soul into blossom."[369]

Lilias Trotter

Certainly one can see evidence of truth and power in Lilias' life. She had to learn to communicate to women who had no education and somehow find a way to share the gospel in a way they could grasp. She had to stand down demonic powers that tried often to destroy her already poor health, as well strongholds that held the Algerians in bondage. She especially, however, a model for us of love. No other reason but love for the Savior and the people of Algeria would have

---

[368] Hosier, p. 290.
[369] https://www.pinterest.com/pin/153685406012596693/

pushed her to never give up in the face of little outward fruit, deplorable conditions, demonic powers, and constant illness.

Raymon Lull in the 12th century and Lilas Trotter in the 19th and early 20th centuries are no doubt rejoicing in heaven, where they can look down on what the Spirit is doing in Algeria today. Lull who died as a martyr, and Trotter who was an example of white martyrdom, are no doubt celebrating the thousands of Algerians who have believed in the One whom they proclaimed so faithfully long ago.

Conclusion

I would like to put a Bible into every Muslims' hands and have them read about Jesus for themselves. If we could pass out a Bible to every Muslim in the world, however, the vast majority of them would probably be placed on a shelve and unread. I can wish that every Muslim would see a dream or vision of Jesus. However, if the Lord's main way were to communicate primarily through dreams and visions, he would not need to use human messengers in the first place. Most people, and in particular Muslims who have been taught that the Bible is a corrupted document, will not read it unless it is given to them by someone they know and trust. Paul wrote about the Corinthians, "You yourselves are our letter, written on our hearts, known and ready by everyone" (II Corinthians 2:2-3). No doubt, most Muslims will read us before they ever read the Bible For whatever reason, the Lord chooses to use imperfect people like you and me to do his work. I cannot cause a Muslim to have a dream of Jesus or read the *Injil.* But what I can do with God's help is to show him or her that God loves them and I do too.

Questions for Discussion and Reflection

- In the "just imagine" story of Aisha and her Christian teacher, what do you think you would have done if Aisha had come to you with her story?
- The author mentioned how God "jerked" their lives around for two and one-half years primarily for the sake of Azad. Can

you think of a time when the Lord inconvenienced you for the sake of someone else that you did not understand at the time?

- What stood out to you about the short story of Lilias Trotter?

26

Persecution and Refugees: Both at all Time Highs

T *here are many who say, 'Why don't the Christians just leave Iraq and move to another country and be done with it." To this question we would respond, "Why should we leave our country—what have we done?" The Christians of Iraq are the first people of the land. You read about us in the Old Testament of the Bible. Christianity came to Iraq from the very earliest days through the preaching and witness of St. Thomas and others of the Apostles and Church Elders.*[370]

Syrian Refugees

In this chapter, we will examine the global refugee crisis. The world is experiencing the largest refugee crisis since World War II. For Christians in particular, persecution at the hands of Muslims has led to them having to flee their homes and countries to find a safe

---

[370] Minority Report: Christian Persecution in Muslim-Majority Countries

refuge. Perhaps at no time in history have more Christians faced persecution than they are now currently. In this chapter, we will examine the statistics surrounding both the refugee crisis and the persecution of Christians, what the Bible has to say about both these issues and hear some stories of persecuted refugees whom I have encountered.

Please kill our Son and his Wife

In a city full of refugees last year, my students and I met a man and his wife who had both become Christians within the last couple of years. The wife, whom I will call "Dara" is as sweet a person as one could ever meet. Her husband also is a man one cannot help but like. They are bubbling over with the joy of the Lord. They exude kindness, hospitality, and love.

Dara was a Yezidi and her husband "Mustafa" was a Sunni Muslim. Mustafa's parents were so shocked that their Muslim son would marry a Yezidi woman, that they had a leading imam (religious leader) issue a *fatwa* (an authoritative legal opinion by a qualified religious leader) that anyone who could find and kill their son and his wife would honor Allah. They would also give them a monetary gift. The shame that Mustafa and Dara's marriage brought on the family could only be cleansed by an honor killing. The couple and their children were forced to flee across the nearest border to another Muslim country. Living in much fear that someone could report their new location to their families and that someone might fulfill the *fatwa,* they recently fled to an unwelcoming, but non-Muslim country, hoping to get asylum to somewhere they can life safely.

It would be nice to think that Dara and Mustafa's story is unique and there are few like them. Although the details change with each story, their experience is far from isolated. Millions have and are continuing to experience what this chapter focuses on: religious persecution leading to life as refugees.

Refugees in the Bible

> The Hebrew word **ger** translated variously into English as foreigner, resident alien, stranger sojourner, or immigrant— appears ninety-two times in the Old Testament. "Welcoming the stranger... is the most often repeated commandment in the Hebrew Scriptures, with the exception of the imperative to worship only one God[371] (Theologian Orlando Espin)

Biblical Characters who were Refugees

When we examine the biblical characters who were refugees, it reads like a Who's Who of important characters. We might immediately think of Joseph driven into exile by his brothers. Moses has to flee Egypt or face death under Pharaoh. David is forced to escape from the jealousy and wrath of Saul. Elijah has to flee to a neighboring land after King Ahab and Queen Jezebel sought his life. Daniel and the three Hebrew young men are forcibly taken from their homeland and exiled to Babylon. Queen Esther and her uncle Mordecai are refugees in Persia. Not only individuals, but, entire tribes and even nations are exiled. The Israelites of the Northern Kingdom are forcibly removed to Assyria in the eighth century B.C. The Babylonians forcibly exiled the people of the southern Kingdom of Judah almost two hundred years later. These exiles are the settings for several biblical books, particularly the books of Esther and Daniel.

In the New Testament, most of the Apostles, especially Paul, are driven from their homes for the sake of the Gospel. Peter addresses his first epistle to God's elect as exiles scattered throughout the provinces of Pontus, Galatia, Cappadocia, Asia an,d Bithynia." (1 Peter 1:1). God's only begotten Son experienced life as a refugee when his earthly family had to flee from the wicked Herod bent on killing in infants under two years of age. (Matthew2:13-15). I wonder if most Christians today think about the Lord they profess was once

---

[371] Bauman, Stephen, Soerens, Matthew, Smeir, Issam p. 30

a persecuted refugee fleeing an evil ruler in a scenario somewhat similar to what millions of Christians in Iraq, Syria, Iran, and in many other places in our world today have gone through.

The gods of the Nations versus the God of the Bible

The God of the Bible is unique from the gods of the other nations worshipped by the pagan neighbors of the Israelites. Their gods were usually on the side of the rich and powerful. After all, that is why the elite were rich and powerful because the gods ordained it! Therefore, everyone had to be subservient to those who were in authority. In contrast, the God of the Israelites cared about the poor, the widow, the orphan, and the refugees, even those who were not Israelites. The gods of the surrounding nations did not show concern for the foreigners or strangers among them. In the Old Testament, foreigners were to be protected from abuse and oppression (Lev 19:33), from unfair treatment in the courts (Deuteronomy 1:16-17; 24: 17-18), and they were to be included in the Sabbath rest (Deut 5:12-15). Furthermore, employers were commanded to treat Hebrew and foreign workers equally (Deut 24:14-15); they even had the right to seek asylum (Deut 23:15-16), and the mighty and awesome God would defend them. The Lord commanded his people to love the fatherless, the widow, and foreigners residing among them, and that they must never forget that they too before the Exodus, were once slaves, foreigners, poor and oppressed (Deut 10:17-19). [372]

There are many verses that could be cited outside of the first five Books of Moses (the Pentateuch) but one in particular especially stands out:

> *Does it make you a king to have more and more cedar? Did not your father have food and drink? He did what was right and just, so all went well with him.* **He defended the cause of the poor and**

---

[372] Das, Rupen & Hamoud Brent ((2017) *Strangers in the Kingdom* pps.37-39

> *needy, and so all went well. Is that not what it means to know me? declares the Lord. (Jeremiah 22:15-16).*

In the New Testament, the 25th chapter of Matthew is particularly convicting when we look at how Jesus separates people and nations into two groups-the sheep and the goats at the when he returns and sits on his glorious throne. Jesus tells the sheep on his right to

> *Come and be blessed by my Father, take your inheritance, the kingdom prepared for you since the creation of the world. For I was hungry and you gave me something to eat, I was thirsty and you gave me something to drink, I was a stranger and you invited me in, I needed clothes and you clothed me, I was sick and you looked after me, I was in prison and you came to visit me.*

In this well-known text, the righteous will ask him,

> *Lord when did we see you hungry and feed you, or thirsty and gave you something to drink. When did we see you a stranger and invite you in or needing clothes, and clothe you. When did we see you sick or in prison and go to visit you. Jesus answers by saying, "when you did it to the least of these brothers and sister, you did it for me.*

> *Then Jesus tells those on his left to depart from me into the eternal fire prepared for the devil and his angels. Then he states in the negative that those on his left did not feed, clothe, or visit the sick or imprisoned. (Matthew 25:31-46).*

We can rightfully define the word "stranger", to include refugees as among those with whom our Lord is especially concerned. We might also recall Jesus' oft-told parable of the Good Samaritan (Luke 10:25-37). The Apostle Paul says something quite similar, but rather than taking revenge against our enemies, he admonishes us to, "if you enemy is hungry, feed him; if he is thirsty, give him something to drink. In doing this you will heap burning goals on his head. Do not be overcome by evil, but overcome evil by with good" (Romans 12: 19-21).

James says that "Religion that God our Father accepts as pure and faultless is this: to look after orphans and widows in their distress and to keep oneself from being polluted by the world" (James 1:27). There are many widows and orphans among the refugees of today.

The Refugee Crisis

A Brief Look at the Numbers

> Refugees are people who have fled war, violence, conflict or persecution and have crossed an international border to find safety in another country...someone who is unable to unwilling to return to their country of origin owing to a well-founded fear of being persecuted for reasons of race, religion, nationality, membership of a particular social group or political opinion[373]

According to the 2019 UNHCR (United Nations High Commissioner for Refugees) statistics, there are 79.5 million displaced people in the world today. Twenty-six million are refugees, defined as those who have had to cross an international border, while 45.7 million have been forced to flee their homes but are still within the borders of their country of origin. People in that category are referred to as internally displaced people (IDP). Another 4.2 million people are seeking asylum, but have not been officially approved as refugees yet[374]. There are also economic migrants or those who primarily seek to leave their homes and country for economic reasons rather than on grounds of persecution. The tens of millions of people facing severe economic hardship are NOT included in this number. To be considered an official refugee who qualifies for humanitarian assistance, the person or family has to be able to prove they are in serious bodily harm due to religious, political or socio-cultural reasons.

One oft-cited fact is that the world is currently in the midst of the biggest refugee crisis with more displaced people than at any time

---

[373] https://www.unhcr.org/en-us/what-is-a-refugee.html
[374] https://www.unhcr.org/en-us/figures-at-a-glance.html

since World War II. About 1 percent of the world's people have been forced to abandon their homes, communities and in many cases, their countries of origin.

Refugees among the People of Pentecost

Syrian IDPs and refugees are by far the largest group. In Turkey alone, there are at least 3.6 million Syrian refugees and hundreds of thousands more in other Middle Eastern countries. Almost a million Syrians were accepted as refugees in Germany and tens of thousands more in other European countries. By far, however, much greater numbers reside in nearby countries. There are massive numbers of internally displaced peoples (IDPs) who have fled their homes but are within Syria's borders. At least one-half of Syria's population is displaced.

Thousands of more refugees from many countries had their hopes raised when Turkey opened its border for refugees to leave for Europe, as Turkey complained that the European Community did not keep their pledge of six billion Euros to look after the refugees within Turkey. European governments hoped to keep refugees in Turkey, thinking that they might be able to eventually return to their country of origin when conditions improved. When the door appeared to open for refugees to be able to get to Europe, thousands went to Greece and are now living in no man's land. One morning I witnessed busloads of refugees being loaded onto buses at 5:00AM. They looked excited, dazzled, fearful, anxious, and sleepy all at the same time. They know they are not wanted in Greece, but Turkey does not want them to stay either. The path to Europe is uncertain and the vast majority will not make it to the West. They will face more years of living in poverty, face much discrimination, their children will lose years of schooling, and be forced to be dependent of the aid of humanitarian agencies. Many of the refugees were successful people in their homelands—doctors, engineers, teachers, and entrepreneurs. They do not want to rely on aid, but they are not allowed to work in their countries of exile.

Syria and the Refugee Crisis

According to UNHCR, 68 percent of the world's refuges are from five counties. Syria has almost double the number of refugees of any other country.

1) Syria 6.6 million
2) Venezuela 3.7 million
3) Afghanistan 2.7 million
4) South Sudan 2.2 million
5) Myanmar 1.1 million

By a large margin, Turkey is hosting the most refugees with 3.6 million from Syria alone. Before we look at other refugee situations, let us examine the situation in Syria, which has created the largest number of refugees.

Like Father Like Son

It is ironic today that Bashar al Assad, the brutal dictator of Syria whom many see as responsible for the death of hundreds of thousands of its citizens in the long brutal civil war, has generally treated Christians relatively well. Like his brutal father, Hafez al Assad, before him, Bashar's minority Alawite [375]community has ruled over a large majority of Sunni Muslims since about 1970. The irony is that Bashar al Assad was an eye doctor, his wife dressed very fashionably, and he was touted as the new type of Middle Eastern ruler—educated, western looking, and progressive. Bashar, however, cracked down very harshly against the protesters during the quite recent Arab Spring[376] As protests broke out across the

---

[375] The Alawites are a minority religion containing elements of Druze, Shi'a Islam and Christianity. They only make up 110-15 percent of Syria's population, but have controlled the government for decades. They tend to be secular in orientation, and Christians have generally done well under their rule.

[376] Arab Spring broke out in 2010 when a Tunisian fruit seller set himself on fire to protest the inhumane treatment he had often received at the hands of the police. From Tunisia, the uprising spread to many other Arab nations. Sadly, much of the good that might have come from it was high-jacked by Islamists.

Arab-Muslim world, Assad, no doubt by being a member of a minority community reigning over a much larger majority Sunni Muslim community, felt very insecure about holding on to his power. The tragic result is millions of Syrians are internally displaced, and millions more Syrians have sought asylum in other Middle Eastern countries or in the West. It must be remembered, however, that as a member of a minority community, Assad knows that if the majority Sunnis, especially those shaped by Islamist thinking, come into power, it could lead to massive slaughter of his people. Even many Sunni Muslims have supported the regime who also fear an Islamist takeover if Assad falls.

When the civil war broke out in 2011, perhaps up to 40 percent of the first refugees were Christians, who were afraid if Assad fell, radical Sunni Muslims would take over the country, and they would face much oppression. Syria's Christian population once was as high as 16-20 percent before the civil war. It is uncertain what the percentage is now and what percentage of the refugees are Christians.

There are also accounts of Muslims coming to faith in Christ in parts of Syria, but for now exact numbers will be difficult to ascertain with any degree of accuracy.

Refugees among other the other Peoples of Pentecost

Especially in the 1980s, thousands of Iranians sought refugee status even as Afghans fled to Iran for asylum from the Russian invasion. It is estimated that after the peak refugee years (1980-1991) about 1.5 million Iranians became refugees in Turkey.[377] There are still tens of thousands of official Iranian refugees in Turkey but many more have come as tourists and are staying without being official refugees. Across the world, about ten percent of Iranians make up the Iranian diaspora. Los Angeles, California has is sometimes

---

[377] https://en.wikipedia.org/wiki/Turkey%27s_migrant_crisis

referred to as "Tehrangeles[378], because of the large number of Iranians residing there.

In 1991, at least two million Kurds fled Iraq across the borders of Iran and Turkey seeking safety as previously described in chapter fifteen. More recently, Christians, Yezidis, and Muslim refugees sought protection in the Kurdish region of Iraq.

There are about 2.6 million displaced Afghans within Afghanistan, and 2.7 million in other lands, with the vast majority (88 percent) in neighboring Iran and Pakistan.[379]

ISIS Reinstitutes the Coercion

It was especially after the American invasion of Iraq to oust Saddam Hussein in 2003, that the Christian minority of around 5 percent were put at great risk. Many Sunni Arabs, with whom Saddam shared a common identity, perceived Iraqi Christians as collaborators with the Americans. Many Muslims took their animosity out on Christians after the American invasion, including long-time neighbors who sometimes betrayed them for their possessions. The actor Jim Caviezel, who portrayed Jesus in the Mel Gibson film *The Passion of the Christ,* tells the story of a Christian boy who was kidnapped from his family. The ransom demand was high and the family was trying to borrow the money from everyone they knew. There was a knock on the door and according to Iraqi custom; some neighbors of the Christian family gave a big platter of rice with meat on top. As they sat down to eat the rice, they discovered that the "meat" was their little son.[380] (This is not to say there were no Muslims who stood up for their Christian friends and neighbors). It is tragic though to hear how their neighbors often betrayed Christians and Muslims, who had lived side by side for a thousand years. There are many stories of Yezidis who in some places also

---

[378] Tehran is the capitol and largest city in Iran

[380] The Story was taken from the DVD *Facing Extinction: The Christian of Iraq* narrated by Jim Caviezel

lived side by side with Muslims, reporting that their neighbors cheered when ISIS jihadists took the Yezidis by force knowing that they were doomed.[381]

A further blow to Iraq's people, including Christians occurred after ISIS assumed power in parts of Iraq, including Mosul, the third largest city in Iraq and the modern name for the biblical city of Nineveh. In total 6 million people fled from their homes during ISIS' peak years. Fortunately, 4 million have returned to Iraq, but 1.6 million still displaced in camps. Iraq's Christian community is believed have been reduced to about one percent after being around 5 percent before the American invasion and the coming of ISIS. For the Christians of Mosul and in other areas, the choices were; 1) pay the *jizya*; 2) convert to Islam; 3) face execution. ISIS reinstituted what had been a historical practice from the early days of Islam.

A report concerning the Iraqi Assyrian Christian community that has been exiled in Turkey, says it is one of the largest Catholic communities in Turkey. In November 2010, there were 5,235 Iraqis in Turkey registered by UNHCR. ... In January 2011, there were 6,600 registered Iraqi refugees and 1,700 registered Iraqi asylum seekers in Turkey, mostly women.[382]

On a brighter side, while both the American invasion and ISIS were harmful in that the number of Iraqi Christians was severely reduced, it also has led to many Iraqi Christians being renewed spiritually, whereas before many were Christian in name only. It has also led to Muslims coming to faith in the Savior.

Turkish Asylum Seekers

In addition to being the largest receiver of refuges in the world, a number of Turks have fled from their homeland to seek asylum in Europe. After the failed 2016 coup in Turkey and the harsh

---

[381] Farida Khalaf tells of this in her book, *The Girl who Beat ISIS: My Story*
[382] https://www.google.com/search?q=Christian+IRaqi+Refugees+in+Turkey&rlz =1CiGCEU_enUS821US821&oq=Chr&aqs=chrome.1.69i57j69i59j69i61l3j69i65j5l2. 6749j0j7&sourceid=chrom

crackdown of President Erdogan against any type of dissent, tens of thousands of Turkish journalists, academics, military, and human-rights advocates have been detained and thousands more have fled to Europe seeking asylum.

Three Interesting Facts about Immigrants and Refugees in America

In their insightful book, *Seeking Refugee* by Stephen Bauman, Matthew Soerens, and Dr Issam Smeir, several things challenge the thinking of many Americans. The idea that the United States accepts mostly Muslim refugees is not true. Even Iraq which is near 99 percent Muslim, out of a total of 125,000 Iraqi refugees admitted since 2007, more than 35 percent have been Christian, many more times than the percentage of the Christian population. [383] The Pew research center reports that 61 percent of the refugees who entered the U.S. in 2016 are Christians and only 22 percent are Muslims. [384]

Many assume that refugees and immigrants get generous financial benefits without having to contribute anything to the US. Economy. In reality, the average immigrant paid more in federal, state, and payroll taxes ($7,826) than they received from governmental services ($4,422) in terms of food stamps welfare assistance etc.[385]

Rick Stearns, President of World Vision, says more American have been killed by dog attacks than by Islamic extremists, and of 200,000 Americans murdered after 9/11, only 60 have been by Jihadist terrorists.[386]

Persecution and the Refugee Crisis

Persecution leads to the majority of people fleeing from their homes, communities and even countries to face an uncertain life in unfamiliar places among strangers, with no certainty about their future. Victims were Muslims of the wrong sect, Yezidis, and

---

[383] Bauman, Soerens, and Smeir p. 38
[384] Pew Research Center
[385] Ibid p. 67
[386] Ibid p. 81

Christians. Let us now examine the scope of the global persecution of Christians statistically before finishing the chapter with some inspiring stories.

Stories of the persecution of Christians, which has resulted in many of them becoming refugees, has been told in many well-written books, on the Internet, and in the publications of Christian ministries to the persecuted church. As powerful and often heart-retching as these stories often are, I have limited this chapter to a few stories of people whom I have personally met whose stories I have heard firsthand over the last few years.

The Bible and Persecution

There is an intriguing couple of verses in the book of Revelation that are challenging to interpret. The context is the Lamb's breaking of the seven seals. The first four seals are the well-known white, red, black, and pale horses. What the white horse represents has been interpreted in many ways, a topic I do not wish to enter! The red, black and pale horses usher in terrible calamities of war, economic collapse, famine and plague. Of course, the entire book of Revelation can be interpreted in many ways. Some respected commentators see it primarily through a historic lens, while others see from chapter six to the end as futuristic. There are other interpretive streams as well. It is the fifth seal that is especially relevant for the topic of this chapter that is difficult to understand.

> *When the Lamb broke the fifth seal, I saw under the altar the souls of all who had been martyred for the word of God and for being faithful in their testimony. They shouted to the Lord and said, "O Sovereign Lord, holy and true, how long before you judge the people who belong to this world and avenge our blood for what they have done to us?" Then a white robe was given to each of them. And they were told to rest a little longer until the full number of their brothers and sisters—**their fellow servants of Jesus who were to be martyred**—had joined them (Revelations 5:9-11 NLT).*

The NIV words the last sentence as, "...they were told to wait a little longer, until the full number of their fellow servants, their brothers, and sisters, were killed just as they had been." Is there some number, known only to the Lord when he finally says, "enough?" According to Open Doors, 260 million Christians face high levels of persecution. Many have been, continue to be, and will be martyrs, paying the ultimate price for their faith. When will our Lord say, "Enough?" Matthew 24:14 says, "The Gospel of the Kingdom will be preached as a witness to all nations (people groups) and then the end will come." Are these the two best indicators that determine when the Lord will return? The Gospel of the Kingdom going forth to the remaining unreached people groups without a witness, which will no doubt lead to many more people being martyred for the sake of Christ. These two prophecies seem to be the clearest signs to determine when the Lord returns..

How many Christian Martyrs?

David Barrett, probably the world's leading statistician in all matters related to Christianity in the world, estimates that 70 million Christians have been martyred for their faith since the beginning of Christian history until current our day.[387] He states that more Christians have been killed since 1900 than in the other 1,900 years of church history combined.

It is important to point out that tens of millions of Christians were killed in Communist regimes and in other types of totalitarian systems throughout history besides Islam. There are many excellent authors and organizations that focus on the persecuted church that I recommend readers to consult, to aid us in informed, focused, and passionate intercession. Raymond Ibrahim,[388] Paul Marshall,

---

[387] https://www.christiantoday.com/article/70-million-christians-martyred-faith-since-jesus-walked-earth/38403.htm

[388] Raymond Ibrahim's *Crucified Again* and *Sword and Scimitar* are excellent accounts by this leading Egyptian scholar, who also writes regularly for *Gatestone Institute*, which among other issues, gives accounts of Jewish and Christian persecution under Islam. Gatestone Institute <list@gatestoneinstitute.org>

Elizabeth Kendal[389], Thomas Doyle, and organizations including Open Doors, Voice of the Martyrs, and Christian Concern are all excellent sources among others. *Fleeing ISIS Finding Jesus* tells the accounts of Christians under ISIS.[390] Some very recent graphic accounts of what Christians have suffered under ISIS has been done by Voice of the Martyrs.[391] Voice of the Martyrs recent book *-n, i-am* contains many stories of Christians suffering under ISIS. When ISIS warriors informed Christians that their options 1) submit to Islam; 2) pay a *jizya* that few could afford; 3) or be killed. Some fled, leaving their entire life's possession behind them. The ISIS jihadists marked Christian homes with a red "N" which stands for *Nazrani* (Arabic for Nazarene, a slang word for Christians).

Open Doors, established by Brother Andrew, publishes each year the World Watch List (WWL) of countries where Christians suffer the most persecution. The list can be downloaded easily and prayed over each day.[392] Elizabeth Kendal also posts regular updates for focused prayer for persecuted Christians.[393]

For those who want to read a story about an American who suffered imprisonment in a Muslim land, and which involved the highest levels of our government getting involved in setting him free, Andrew Brunson tells his story of two years of imprisonment in Turkey in a very honest way in his recent book. [394] He tells his story

---

[389] *After Saturday Comes Sunday* by Elizabeth Kendal, is an excellent work of not only telling gripping stories, but also going deep into the ideology of the persecution of Christians under Islam. The title refers to Saturday being the holy day for Jews and Sunday the holy day for Christians, whereas the holy day for Muslims is Friday. Radical Muslims believe that they, the Friday people, will triumph over the Saturday and Sunday peoples.

[390] *Fleeing ISIS Finding Jesus* Charles Morris and Craig Borlace

[391] I-am-n is a collection of stories of Christians suffering under ISIS and other Islamist groups by Voice of the Martyrs

[392] https://www.opendoorsusa.org/wp-content/uploads/2020/01/2020_World_Watch_List.pdf

[393] http://rlprayerbulletin.blogspot.com/

[394] *God's Hostage* by Andrew Brunson

in a very humble manner, sharing his inner struggles with faith and trying to fight off despair.

Three Sources of Persecution

In the Muslim world, in particular, there are three sources of persecution. One is the persecution of Christians by Islamic governments. Examples of this would be Iran, Saudi Arabia, some of the Gulf and North African states. The second type is vigilante-type groups that are not official government-sanctioned but may operate with a degree of government compliance. These groups would include Boko Haram, Al Shahab, Muslim Brotherhood, and many others. The third type is the kind of persecution that comes from the MBB's own family, workplace, community, and "friends." This can be the most insidious when one's enemies are of their own household much like what Jesus told his followers to be prepared for. *Do not suppose that I have come to bring peace, but a sword. For I have come to turn a man against his father, a daughter against her mother, a daughter-in-law against her mother-in-law—a man's enemies will be the members of his own household. Anyone who loves their father or mother more than me is not worthy of me, Whoever does not take up their cross and follow me is not worthy of me. Whoever finds their life will lose it, and whoever loses their life for my sake will find it* (Matthew 10:34-39).

It is hard to imagine any more straightforward words than what Jesus said about the realities of persecution. While the persecution from government and vigilante groups probably leads to more martyrdoms, persecution within the family or society is probably the most difficult for believers to endure. It is one thing when a government persecutes those who follow Christ. It is another when members of one's own family, seek to kill the a family member who has chosen to follow Jesus.

Another haunting verse, while in the immediate context refers to persecution of Jews who embraced Jesus as Messiah, it seems particular fitting to those who accept Jesus in the Islamic world. *They will put you out of the synagogue; in fact, the day is coming when anyone who kills you will think they are offering a service to God* (John

16:2). I think of how brutal Communism was and the millions of Christians who were killed in Eastern Europe, the former Soviet Union, China, and in other Asian Communist countries. Yet in Communist regimes, no one claimed to be doing it in the service of God. Yet many Muslims believe they are serving Allah when they kill even one of their own family members who have left Islam to follow Christ.

A Look at the Scope of Persecution

Fifty-six million Christians live in Muslim majority countries or 2.6 percent of global Christian population.[395] I do not know of any place in the Muslim world that when someone leaves Islam and follows Christ it does not lead to at least one of the forms of persecution mentioned above. Even if the government is relatively lax, there will be vigilante type groups that will take it upon themselves to carry out Allah's wrath against apostasy. Within the family of the MBB, it is often a father against his own children, or sibling against sibling, that makes choosing Christ such an all or nothing decision.

Where is the Persecution?

Open Doors gives the global church the World Watch List of persecution, listing the 50 Countries where persecution is the most severe[396]. The top 20 for 2020 are as listed:

1. North Korea
2. Afghanistan
3. Somalia
4. Libya
5. Pakistan
6. Eritrea
7. Sudan

---

[395] Minority Report: Christian Persecution in Muslim majority countries
[396] https://www.opendoorsusa.org/christian-persecution/world-watch-list/?initcid=20SRP&initpkg=20SRP-0&cid=7010b000001YkjbAAC&pkg=a150b000004P00wAAC&gclid=EAIaIQobC hMIx_mbkpLv7AIVCNbACh3MHg0ZEAA

8. Yemen
9. Iran
10. India
11. Syria
12. Nigeria
13. Saudi Arabia
14. Maldives
15. Iraq
16. Egypt
17. Algeria
18. Uzbekistan
19. Myanmar
20. Laos

The list focuses on both *squeeze* and *smash* factors. Squeeze factors include the pressure that Christians face in each area of their lives at home, at work, in the community, at worship, and in other spheres of life. Smash factors are about the actual violence that Christians may face.[397] Notice that fifteen of the top twenty countries with the greatest degree of persecution of Christians are Muslim majority nations.

Iraq and Syria are graphic examples. Iraq's Christian population has decreased from 1.5 million to under 300,000 Christians in the last ten years. BBC News reports that in Syria hundreds of thousands of Christians have been displaced by fighting or have fled from the country.

Persecution of Yezidis

In addition to the persecution of Christians, I have included the terrible oppression that the Yezidi have experienced especially at the hands of ISIS. The following has been compiled by the Yezidi

---

[397] https://www.opendoorsusa.org/christian-persecution/world-watch-list/about-the-ranking/

Affairs Directorate.[398] Their numbers show that 18 Yezidi temples have been destroyed, and that twelve massacres in their ancient homeland in the mountains and villages of Sinjar province have occurred. The kidnapping of 5,838 Yezidis with 3,758 remaining in captivity somewhere by Islamic State jihadists, demonstrates that we cannot wash our hands of ISIS by any means. How many of the captives, mostly girls and young women, who were used as sex slaves, are still living is uncertain. Jihadists killed most of the men and many boys were brainwashed into radical Islam as described previously.

A Personal Account

A few years ago when ISIS was still frequently in the news, I had a chance to speak in a church in Iraqi Kurdistan. I heard many tragic stories of Yezidi girls who had been raped and used as sex slaves by ISIS fighters. Some of them, even after escaping or being ransomed, feel that they will no longer be considered marriageable. For Yezidis, as is true among most Muslims as well, virginity is non-negotiable. I pleaded with the church to receive these girls as Christ would, and regard them as victims not compliant in any way with what has happened to them. Several of the new followers of Christ from a Yezidi background said they appreciated my words, and that they would do all they can to integrate the girls back into the community.

We see the example how Jesus regarded women whom society held in contempt such as the woman at the well (John 4) and the woman caught in adultery (John 8). He restored their dignity and worth so lovingly and graciously, that I often pray that the Yezidi people, especially those who now profess to know Christ, will find the grace to receive their traumatized and abused daughters and wives back into their community. We hope that they will be willing to give their sons to these girls who have been horribly defiled but not by their own choice. This would be totally contrary to traditional culture, but

---

[398] https://www.yazda.org/ is an organization that tracks the suffering of the Yezidi people in many locations

what strong evidence it would be to the one who declared, *The Spirit of the Lord is on me, because he has anointed me to proclaim good news to the poor. He has sent me to proclaim freedom for the prisoners and recovery of sight for the blind, to set the oppressed free, to proclaim the year of the Lord's favor* (Luke 4:18-19).

Muslims also Suffer from Persecution

Muslims have also suffered persecution in many parts of the world. Uighur Muslims in China, Rohingya Muslims in Myanmar, and some Sunni Muslims in Syria are three current places. Muslims suffered in Bosnia under the Serbs, and especially in Afghanistan under the Soviets. Both of these wars drew many young Muslims from around the world into the global jihad movement. Christians mostly suffer persecution without fighting back, whereas the oppression of Muslims often leads to many Muslims joining in the battle against the oppressors. One might say the Christian way is through spiritual warfare rather than physical jihad as employed by the many, including Osama bin Laden, who fought against the Soviets.

Inspiring Stories of Persecuted Refugees

As I mentioned previously, many powerful stories of refugees and what they have endured have been recorded in several books and websites. I will tell you a few stories of people whom I have met in my more recent travels in the Middle East often with students from North Central University.

At the beginning of this chapter, I told the story of Mustafa and Dara. In a city not far from Mustafa and Dara, we met a wonderful Iraqi family. The husband is a principal of a high school and his wife is a physician. They have two wonderful children. This well-educated joyful Christian family would be an asset in any country in which they reside. There were forced to flee Iraq when ISIS jihadists gave them twenty-four hours to either convert to Islam or be killed. After years of surviving in camps, the Canadian government finally received them as refugees. Iraq's loss is Canada's gain. However, few among even very qualified professional refugees are allowed to practice their professions without years of study to upgrade their qualifications to practice the same professions in the West as they did in their home countries. Among refugees, you might meet someone holding a rather low-skill job but who in their home countries were high up on the social ladder as doctors, lawyers, engineers, or successful businesspersons. Few complain, however, as they feel lucky to be alive and realize that thousands of their fellow refugees are still languishing in refugee camps.

A couple of years ago, my students and I hosted a picnic for Iraqi Christian refugees. We met at a park and of course, made kebabs, the food item offered at almost every picnic or gathering. The young usually circle dance, sing and play football (soccer) and volleyball. Despite some language barriers, our students had a wonderful time with the Christian refugees. They have endured many years of lost education, faced very uncertain futures (I do not know how many of them have made it to the West) and even if allowed to work, would generally be grossly underpaid with no recourse to appeal to higher authorities because refugees usually have no rights. Yet for several hours at least, these young people could forget about what they suffered in the past, take their minds off their bleak future, and celebrate the moment.

Iraqi Christian Refugees

We met some refuges from Afghanistan from the Hazara ethnic group discrimination in Afghanistan both because of being Shi'a Muslims in a country that is overwhelmingly Sunni, as well as their Asian appearance where that sets them apart from the majority. They share the same ethnic background that one of the main characters in the well-known book *The Kite Runner*.

Across the region, we met many believers from an Iranian background. Often churches that may have only a few local believers, have scores of Iranian refugees who are joyfully singing, praising, and giving testimony to the grace of Christ in their lives. In one city, around two hundred Iranians gathered to celebrate Jesus. That was almost the entire Iranian refugee community! It is remarkable how despite what they have suffered in the past, and facing an uncertain future, how they can celebrate their new lives in Christ so fervently. Some refugees we encountered are not Christians. Some are Kurds who fled from ISIS and Sunni Arabs who feared death at the hands of the Assad government.

In addition to refugees, we met some real heroes who are ministering to the refugees in the name of Christ. There is a former Afghan refugee woman who ministers to the oppressed Yezidis. Her own story inspires the women and children even as her team of volunteers helps the women to learn new skills to be able to survive when they leave the refugee camps.

A Yezidi Refugee Camp in Northern Iraq

There is a faithful pastor who ministers to the displaced Christian community there and meets those with the greatest needs. Many refugees have come to personal faith in Christ because of his and his wife's efforts. I could tell many other stories of God's faithful servants serving the displaced and suffering in difficult situations.

A Ministry to Yezidi Children by a Former Afghan Refugee

Conclusion

Persecution and refugees. A story that could be told repeatedly throughout the 2,000 years of Christian history. The settings and circumstances may change, but the story remains the same. Those who follow Jesus must be ready to lose everything for his sake. Today millions of our brothers and sisters in Christ are persecuted, and tens of thousands are refugees or IDPs. Millions more are refugees who do not know Christ. Their situation is far worse. Imagine being a refugee or IDP because you practice a different type of Islam, or follow a religion that other than Islam but without the hope that the gospel gives to those who are persecuted. After all Jesus said, *blessed are those who are persecuted because of righteousness, for theirs is the kingdom of heaven.* (Matthew 5:10). May God help us all to practice the words as stated in the book of Hebrews:

Keep on loving one another as brothers and sisters. Do not forget to show hospitality to strangers for by so doing some people have shown hospitality to angels without knowing it. Continue to remember those in prison as if you were together with them in prison, and those who are mistreated as if you yourselves were suffering (13:1-3).

Questions for Discussion and Reflection

- Which of the three sources of persecution do you think would be hardest to endure: persecution from the government, from vigilante groups, or from one's own family and community? Why?

- If you had to leave everything behind and flee to a strange country, what would you miss the most?

The Conclusion of the Journey

We are almost to the end of our journey of 2,000 years. Two millennia have passed since the fire of Pentecost burned so brightly. We are inspired by those disciples who had recently witnessed the resurrection of our Lord, and in the power of the Holy Spirit, as they spread the message of the risen Savior to the known world both in and outside of the Roman Empire.

The great Apostle Peter boldly preaching to many of those who had recently shouted for the crucifixion of Jesus, proclaimed that the Lord made this man whom they crucified Lord and Christ. On that glorious day when the 120 worshipped in languages they had never learned, 3,000 people believed in Christ and were baptized in the Holy Spirit and in water. Soon afterwards, Peter preached and thousands more believed after a lame man was healed. Sometime later, Peter through a divine appointment goes to the home of a Gentile military commander and his family, and the first Gentiles are added to the church. How astonished Peter must have been to witness the Holy Spirit come upon these Gentiles who like the 120 spoke in tongues.

As Peter was primarily the Apostle to the Jews, the Apostle Paul, the former persecutor and chief enemy of the early Christians, became the primary Apostle to the Gentiles in the Roman Empire. His exploits cover more ground in the New Testament than even Peter's do, as the Lord transformed this persecutor of the early Christians into the man who argued the strongest that the gospel belonged to all people.

Thomas and several of the other apostles took the gospel outside of the Roman Empire. The so-called "doubting Thomas," planted churches in what is today Iraq, Iran, parts of Central Asia, and on into India. He was probably the most traveled of all the Apostles.

Even after the Holy Spirit descended on the believers, people are still human, and it did not take long before divisions occurred. Paul addressed divisions several times in his epistles. Persecution to a degree, however, at least seemed to have kept the believers relatively united over the first three centuries. Suddenly, however, in the midst of the worst persecution at the hands of the Romans, Emperor Constantine converted to Christianity. From persecution to privilege, Christians had quite the change in status!

We encounter several major doctrinal controversies, especially over the identity of the Lord Jesus Christ throughout the next few centuries. How can Jesus be both God and Man? Out of the bitter Arian controversy came a creed that is still recited each week among Roman Catholics and other Christian bodies. It was not long, however, until the phrase *Theotokos* (God-bearer or mother of God) which Nestorius refused to confess, led to his excommunication. What became known as the Church of the East, the great missionary church, derogatorily called Nestorian, took the gospel throughout the Middle East, Central Asia, India, and even to China.

Then came the controversy led by Eutyches who denied the humanity of Christ after the incarnation. Nicene was supposed to be the council that solved the issues of Jesus' divinity and humanity. Then the Council of Ephesus was thought to have solved the problem of the *Theotokos*. Twenty years later, however, the Council of Chalcedon due to so much internal conflict was conducted to address the nature of Christ after his taking on of human flesh in the incarnation. The Council of Chalcedon settled Christological issues for most of the Christian world, but a large faction believed that the Chalcedonian agreement was too similar to the beliefs of the Nestorians and refused to accept the 451 ruling. Despite all of the divisions, name-calling, excommunication, and other ugly incidents that happened among the Body of Christ in the Middle East, the

Church evangelized not only the peoples of the Middle East and parts of Asia and Africa but most of Europe. As Saint John Paul II stated:

> The Christian faith has shaped the culture of the continent and is inextricably bound up with its history, to the extent that Europe's history would be incomprehensible without reference to the events which marked first the greatest period of evangelization and then the long centuries in which Christianity, despite painful division between East and West, came to be the religion of the European peoples.[399]

Today, countless millions of Europeans no longer practice the faith that was the backbone of their civilization. Most non-Europeans however still perceive of Christianity as a European religion despite the fact the first Christians were Middle Eastern and the Gospel went to Asia and Africa before it went to Europe.

Muhammad Changes the World

Out of Arabia, a man named Muhammad began to preach what first appeared to be a message similar to what Jews and Christians read in their holy books. Not before long, however, it became apparent that Muhammad's grasp of the Torah did not satisfy his Jewish listeners, leading to a massive killing of Jews and a rift that is still being played out on the world stage today. Muhammad spoke highly of Jesus and his mother but Christ-followers realized before too long, that Muhammad was not preaching the same faith that had been handed down to them. He denied the divinity of Jesus and his vicarious death on the cross for the sins of humankind. Christians were forced to flee from Arabia, and within a few decades, Islam dominated most of the Middle East and worshippers of Jesus were reduced to *dhimmi* status.

The majority of Arabs embraced Islam, thrilled to have Muhammad, as one of their own kin. They invaded much of the

---

[399] Ratzinger & Para, p. 35

known world, including the lands where Christians once were a majority. Most Persians and Kurds submitted to Islam but maintained their own languages and culture, keeping alive their own identity The recently converted Turks in the 11th century, become Islam's chief warriors, and dominated much of the former New Testament world where the Apostles lived and preached. None of this happened overnight, but over several centuries, North Africa, the Middle East, Central Asia, parts of Europe, chunks of Africa south of the Sahara, and large portions of Asia came under the domain of Islam. As Pope Benedict XVI pointed out, "it was not until the triumphal advance of Islam in the seventh and early eighth centuries that a border would be drawn across the Mediterranean, subdividing what had been a single continent into three: Asia, Africa, and Europe."[400]

Christendom and Islam often battled militarily, something that was allowed for Muslims, but seemingly contrary to the teachings of Jesus. The Crusades, the battles for Constantinople, Lepanto, and Vienna show how difficult discerning the will of God is if we judge whom God favors by their military victories. Does a victory in battle mean that God is on one side and the loss of the other to be understood as God's punishment for heresy, immorality, or laxness in the practice of faith? Both Christians and Muslims have interpreted events in this way. The severe persecution of Christians throughout Islamic history is terribly disturbing, but we also need to remember that the vast majority of the Muslim world came under European colonialism by the time of the Second World War, which continues to affect the Muslim world today. It also needs to be remembered that what we might call Western imperialism, to most Muslims was Christian domination.

The Reassertion of Islam

The repeated defeats of the Muslim armies against Israel, served as a catalyst to call Muslims back to a more rigorist practice of Islam,

---

[400] Ibid pps. 52,53

after decades of westernization and secularism had engulfed the Islamic world. The reassertion of Islam has led to much division over the question of what is true Islam. Is it the Islam of Rumi, the widely read 14th century Persian poet who speaks much about love and acceptance? Or is true Islam the Islam of Al Qaida and ISIS? Is it true what one author wrote in *Jihad Watch*. "The many interviews showed that Islam is distinguished by being the only religion that makes people more prone to violence the more religious one becomes?"[401]

The Internet has allowed Muslims to ask questions and debate about their faith, even allowing them in the privacy of their own homes to question the less glorious side of their Prophet's life and what their holy book says about jihad and the treatment of women. Web sites and books abound with variant positions about what is the TRUE Islam. Will the Dar al Islam triumph over the Dar al Harp, and bring peace and justice to the world?[402] Will Muslims stay faithful to Allah even as they confront a world of television, films, and Internet that show the Dar al Harp seemingly to be triumphing in health, education, and quality of life over the Dar al Islam? How can Muslims borrow from the best of the West without losing their souls? Do not sincere Christ-followers face a comparable struggle today as they try also to live holy, God-pleasing lives in a world increasingly dominated by moral relativism, selfishness, materialism, and apathy? In both the Islamic world as well as the Western world, many people are disillusioned with religion and the number of agnostics is rapidly growing.

The Real Battle

For Christ-followers, the important battle is the battle for eternal souls. We must not allow negative images of Islam, to make us

---

[401] Kilpatrick, p. 298.

[402] The phrase *dar al harp* versus dar al Islam, meaning the house or abode of war (not under Islam) versus the house of or abode of Islam. Some Muslims say that only when the entire world submits to Islam will there be any peace and justice in the world.

angry, antagonistic, or indifferent toward Muslim peoples. For probably the first time in history, probably more Muslims are becoming Christ-followers rather than former Christians converting to Islam. There are encouraging signs, but the signs still point to a long journey ahead.

Truth without love

There are some politicians, preachers, talk show hosts, and authors who constantly warn against the threat of Islam, resulting in fear and Islamophobia. That is not to say that their warnings are invalid, but it is not the whole side of the story. There is certainly a need for those who warn the complacent West as Robert Spencer, William Kirkpatrick, Raymon Ibrahim the Gatestone Institute and many others do, by demonstrating how radical Islam poses a threat to the West. It is especially distressing how little focus there is in the average Western church on praying for their persecuted brothers and sisters in the Islamic world and beyond. Speaking the truth about some of the dangers of extremist Islam without calling on Christians to love their Muslim neighbors as some conservatives have done, is contrary to the teachings of Jesus, however.

"Love" without truth

Political correctness, the hesitancy of being accused of Islamophobia, accepting the oft-repeated clichés that Islam is at heart a peaceful religion that has been hijacked by terrorists, have led some to the other extreme. Dialogue and understanding are often advocated as the end in relations between Christians and Muslims. Is dialogue without evangelization enough? Why would any true Christ-follower not want Muslims to know their heavenly Father, who loved them enough to send His Son to die for them? Tolerance is not synonymous with love. Love wants the best for people, and the best thing we can give anyone is to know Jesus Christ and his gift of abundant and eternal life through him. Dialogue and building loving relationships with Muslims are essential, but it is not an end in itself.

Loving Muslims versus Loving Islam?

Christians who desire Muslims to know Jesus often discuss and debate much about approaches to sharing the gospel. Some call for confrontational approaches that highlight the differences between the two faiths. Others suggest conciliatory approaches trying to ways to bridge the theological gaps. One this is sure: Encounters with truth, power and love are the trinity that all people, including Muslims desperately need.

Intercessory Prayer for Muslims

I have been a part of an international prayer effort since 1984 to pray for Muslims every Friday at the noon hour for an hour and a half for God's grace, mercy and love to be poured out on the entire Muslim world. Among various denominations and fellowships, prayer for Muslims is also taking place. There have been prayer movements that focus on special prayer during the month of Ramadan. One worldwide prayer meeting for Muslims has pledged itself to ten years of 24/7 prayer. As far as I know, there has not been a gap in time when the Muslim world is not being brought before the Father for his blessing and mercy since this prayer meeting began several years ago. When I was in Bible school in the early 1970s, my school maintained a twenty-four hour, seven days a week prayer meeting for several years. Dick Eastman a prominent missions leader, challenged us with verses from Ezekiel about how the Lord sought for someone to stand in the gap, but he could find no one so he destroyed the land (22:30-31). May there never be a time when someone is not earnestly seeking the Father to make his Son known among hungry Muslims! All of these prayer efforts focus on prayer for Muslims to come to know the love of Christ. They desire to bless Muslims with the greatest gift of all--salvation through Christ.

David Garrison recently in an article in *Christianity Today* tracked the movements to Christ that contain at least 1,000 baptized believers over a ten-year period. I have referred to his excellent work several times. As Garrison points out, there were very few movements to track until the last few decades. After traveling through much of the Muslim world, and interviewing thousands of Muslims who are now following Christ, he realized that the movements to Christ began about when the *Muslim World Prayer Guide* was published around thirty years ago. This was not long after the *Juma'a* (Friday) intercessory prayer movement that I mentioned above began in 1984.

The Holy Spirit is drawing Muslims to Jesus in an unprecedented way. God alone knows how many Muslims believe in Jesus as Lord and Savior but are not counted in any statistics. Garrison estimates that less than one-half of one percent of the world's Muslims follow Christ.[403] For three reasons that statistic does not overly discourage me. One, compared to forty years ago, that is very significant growth! Two, as stated above, there could be countless Muslims who have believed in Jesus but no one knows about them. We pray for the day when they can all declare their allegiance to Christ openly as his redeemed people. The third reason is that there are over 600 Million Spirit-filled Christians in the world who transcend denominational boundaries. Most of these children of Pentecost are in the "developing world of Africa, Asia, and Latin America. Many of these Christians are now engaged in sharing their faith with Muslims in their homelands and in the heartlands of Islam. We also pray for spiritual renewal in Europe and the United States. Despite the overall decline of Christianity in the West, there are also hopeful signs of renewal among Catholics, Orthodox, and Protestants. The Spirit has not given up on the West yet!

Getting Muslims into the Jesus Boat

A while ago, I was sharing my passion to see the entire Body of Christ, not just one branch of it to take on the task of reaching Muslims with the Good News with a priest. I have often thought about what he said:

We need to get Muslims into the Jesus boat. Some Muslims will climb into the Evangelical boat. Some will get into the Orthodox boat. Some will get

---

[403] Garrison, p; 232

into the Catholic boat. What is important is getting them into the Jesus boat (Fr. Cloutier, pastor and priest at Maternity of Mary Church in St. Paul, Minnesota).

Many servants of Christ through the ages and in our day have poured out their hearts in love for the people to whom the Lord called them. In many cases, the fruit of their sacrifice and prayer may not be evident on the surface. We see through a glass darkly, but when Christ returns and we are united at the Marriage Supper of the Lamp, the fruit of our labors of love be will be revealed. May there be people from every tribe, kindred, nation and tongue around the throne, worshiping the Lamb of God who has redeemed us with his own blood. May God help us persevere in prayer and in making Christ known through truth, power and love to those who do not know His Son. May the prayer of Jesus be answered that, "they may be one as we are one" (John 17: 11).

Appendix A: Glossary of Foreign Words

Arabic, Turkish, and Kurdish Words	
Agah (Kurdish?)	Tribal and village leaders
Amazigh	Free people
Aslan	lion
baraka	Blessing, referring to spiritual power that some people have to perform healing or other miracles.
Caliphate	Administrative head of the Islamic world, both politically and spiritually
Chador	A tent-like women's garment that loosely fits over the body
Dar-al harp	Literally "House of war"
Dar-al Islam	Literally "House of Islam"
Davud	David
Dawa	Literally "call me to Islam"
Dejaal	Antichrist
Dervish	Sufi Muslims who live ascetically
Devshirme	Turkish practice of taking sons of Christians and making them into Islamic warriors.
dhimmi	Non-Muslims living under Islamic rule and "protection"

Firman	Legal agreement
Hadith	Sayings and deeds of the Prophet Muhammad, second only to the Qur'an in importance to govern the lives of Muslims
Hafiz	Memorizer of the entire Qur'an
Hajj	Pilgrimage to Mecca
Hajjis	Religious pilgrims to Mecca
Hanifs	Arabs who believe in one God but are neither Jew nor Christian
hijab	Scarf like head covering for women
Hijra	Muhamad's journey from Mecca to Medina
houris	Dark-eyed beautiful virgins who inhabit Paradise.
Iftar	Breaking of the fast at sundown during the month of Ramadan
Imam	Prayer leader in a mosque, often a head of a community
Iman	Core beliefs of Islam
Inshallah	God willing (said when making statements about the future)
Injil	Gospel
Isa	Jesus
Isa al-Masih	Jesus the Messiah
Islam	Peace or submission
Jabril	Angel Gabriel
Jihad	Holy war
jihadi	Person who fights in a jihad
jinn	Unseen spirit beings created from fire rather than dust. They generally are evil and cause mischief, but are not as

	evil as the Bible portrays demons. The etymology of the word *genie* most likely comes from this word.
Jizya	Poll tax paid by Christians to Muslims administrators
Kafir	Infidel
Kalimatu-Allah	Word of God, referring to Jesus
Kamil Adam	Perfect man, a model for all of humanity
Khidir	St. George
Kismet	Fate
Mahdi	Long-awaited savior of the Islamic world (more detail in footnote)
Mana	Unseen force
Maryam	Mary; the title of the 19th Surah
millet	Religious-political community defined by its adherence to a religion
Muezzin	Person who calls Muslims to prayer
Mujahidin	Islamic warriors
Musa	Moses
Nuh	Noah
pirs	Men and women who others look to for spiritual guidance, often displaying a degree of supernatural power.
Qiblah	Direction Muslims face when they perform their five daily prayers
Ruhun min Allah	Spirit from God, referring to Jesus
Salat	Five-times-a-day ritual prayers that Muslims are required to do
Sayyida	Lady

Shahada	"There is no God but Allah," one of the five pillars of Islam.
Shari'a	Islamic law
Suam	Fasting from food, liquid, smoking, and sexual relations, from sunup to sundown, especially during the Holy Month of Ramadan
Surahs	Chapters in the Qur'an
Tanzimat	Movement within the Ottoman Empire to combine small units of local control into a more centralized authority structure
Tawhid	"God is one," the core belief of Islam
Tawrat	Torah
Tespih	Muslim prayer beads that somewhat resemble a rosary
Ummah	Muslim community
Zakat	2.5 percent of what a person owns that is given to the poor or to advance the cause of Islam
Zebur	Psalms of David

Appendix B: Ancient and Current Churches of the Middle East Mentioned in Book

Chalcedonian Churches (accepted the ruling of the Council of Chalcedon in 451)

Eastern Orthodox Churches

Patriarch of Alexandria

Patriarch of Damascus (Antioch)

Patriarch of Istanbul (Constantinople)

Patriarch of Jerusalem

Church of Cyprus

Melkite Greek Orthodox

Catholic Churches

Armenian Catholic Churches

Chaldean Catholic Churches

Coptic Catholic

Eastern-Rite Catholic

Greek (Melkite) Catholic

Latin-Rite Catholic

Maronite Catholic

Syrian Catholic

Non-Chalcedonian Churches (did not accept the Council of Chalcedon)

Oriental Orthodox Churches (Miaphysites, Monophysites)

Armenian Apostolic Church

Coptic (Egyptian) (Orthodox) Church

Ethiopian Orthodox

Syrian Orthodox (Jacobites)

Accepted neither the Council of Ephesus or Council of Chalcedon

(Assyrian) Church of the East (Nestorians)

Protestant

Many denominations and fellowships (See individual denominations or World Christian Encyclopedia, Operation World or Internet sites for recent background and statistics)

Muslim Background Believer Churches

Mostly made up of converts from Islam. Mostly Protestant but generally try to not to focus on denominational identity. Range from churches that resemble western churches except for use of the local language, to fellowship of believers whose worship resembles Islamic worship. Generally try to fit with the general culture of its surrounding as not to appear overly foreign, but rather to demonstrate that one can be a true Arab, Turk, Iranian or Kurd and be a follower of Christ.

Appendix C: Timeline of Events

(In some cases, exact dates are uncertain. The most often cited dates are used here. All are A.D.

30-33: Jesus Crucified and resurrected

30-33. Day of Pentest

33-34 Conversion of Paul

38 The Conversion of Cornelius

38 Thomas and other Apostles begin take Gospel out of the Roman Empire

46-57 Paul's Missionary Journeys

70 Roman capture of Jerusalem and destruction of the Temple

296-628 Off and on wars between Rome and Persia

303 Diocletian persecution of the church

312 Constantine's Conversion and Edict of Milan: Christianity becomes legal

325 Nicene Creed

431 Council of Ephesus

451 Council of Chalcedon

610-632 Muhammad's Revelations

622 The *Hijrah:* Muhammad and followers flee from Mecca to Medina

624 The *Qibla* (direction Muslims face when they pray) is changed from Jerusalem to Mecca

622-632: Early battles and Spread of Islam in Arabia

630 Muhammad takes Mecca and is accepted by most Arabians as a prophet

631 Battle of Tabuk against the Byzantines: Many Arab tribes and many Jews and Christians accept Islam

632 Death of Muhammad

633-7 Arabs conquer Syria and Mesopotamia

634 Fall of Jerusalem

637 Beginning of conversion of the Persians (Iranians) and Kurds

639-42 Conquest of Egypt

643-44 Jews and Christians ordered out of Arabia and *jizya* established by Caliph (Omar (Umar)

661-750 Umayyad Caliphate with its center in Damascus

670 Conquest of North Africa

680 Battle of Karbala and (Hussein's martyrdom (Sunni and Shite spit deepens and continues on to today)

691 Construction of the Dome of the Rock in Jerusalem

711 Berbers convert to Islam and Muslims take Spain

718 Muslim army defeated by Byzantines

732 Charles Martel defeats Muslim armies, halting the conquering of Europe by Muslims

781 Caliph Al-Mahdi and Patriarch Timothy of the Church of the East (Nestorian) engage in dialogue

800-1100 Many works of philosophy, science and medicine translated into Arabic by *dhimmis* and Abbasid Empire experiences Golden Age

909-1170 Fatimid Caliphate in Egypt destroys Tomb of the Holy Sepulcher 1009

970 Conversion of Seljuk Turks begins, as they enter Caliphate from the East

988 Conversion of Slavs to Christianity

1054 The Eastern Church (Orthodox) and Western Church (Roman Catholic) divide

1055-1080 Seljuks take Baghdad and occupy Syria and Palestine including Jerusalem

1071 Battle of Manzikert-Seljuk Turks begin conquest of Anatolia (Turkey) over next 400 years

1095 Pope Urban II calls for Crusades at Council of Clermont

1099 Crusaders capture Jerusalem

1187 Saladin defeats Crusaders at Battle of Hattin and retakes Jerusalem

1219 St. Francis preaches to both sides during the Crusades and is invited into Sultan's Tent

1225-74 Thomas Aquinas acknowledges debt to Muslim scholars Avicenna and Averroes, although disagreeing with key points of Islamic theology

1235-1316 Raymon Lull learns Arabic, preaches in North Africa, advocates preaching rather than Crusades and is martyred

1258 Mongols invade and destroy Baghdad, ending the Abbasid Caliphate

1281-1918 Seljuks give way to Ottomans who rule much of the Middle East, North Africa and parts of Eastern Europe until World War i

1295 Ghazan becomes the first Mongol ruler to convert to Islam

1370-1404 Tamerlane conquers Central Asia and well beyond-virtually destroying Church of the East

1389 Ottomans take Kosovo in Serbia and control Eastern Europe

1438 Devshirme, the forced conversion of Christian youth to Islam and turning them into Islamic warriors called the Janissaries begins

1453 Mehmet II leads Ottomans to take Constantinople, change Hagia Sophia into a mosque

1492 Granada, the last Muslim stronghold in Spain, falls during Reconquista

1514-1747 Frequent wars between Ottomans and Persians

1517 Protestant Reformation

1517-1922 Establishment of self-governing non-Muslim religious groups

1520-1566 Rule of Suleiman the Magnificent-Ottoman Empire at its peak

1529 First Ottoman attempt to conquer Vienna turned back

1565 Ottoman siege of Malta

1571 Battle of Lepanto halts Ottoman advance into the Mediterranean

1683 Jan Sobieski of Poland defeats Ottomans during the 2nd attempt to conquer Vienna

1745 Beginning of Wahhabi movement in Arabia

19th Century-much of Islamic world falls under European domination, particularly by Great Britain and France

19th Century Catholics and Protestants establish schools, hospitals and compete for converts from the historic churches. Catholics try to bring them under submission to Rome while Protestants seek to revive the church so it will evangelize Muslims.

1895-Perseuction of Armenians and other Christians under Ottomans

1908 Young Turk Revolution Turkey moves from the Millet system to Turkish nationalism

1914 Ottoman war on Germany's side in World War I

1915 Slaughter and displacement of Armenians and Assyrians

1918 Collapse of the Ottoman Empire. Ottoman rule ends on Arab lands

1919 Greeks land in Izmir (Biblical Smyrna)

1920 Treaty of Sevres Homeland promised to Kurds and Armenians out of the collapsed Ottoman Empire

1923 Treaty of Lausanne Forms modern nation-state of Turkey without homeland for Kurds and Armenians

1923-24 Kemal Ataturk founds and then secularizes Turkey after Ottoman Empire disintegrates

1924 Many Greeks killed and population exchange: Greek Christians in Turkey settled in Greece, Turkish Muslims in Greece settle in Turkey

1932- Much of Arab world declared independence from British and French

1948 Establishment of the State of Israel

1952-Nassar seizes power and tries to unite Arabs against Israel

1962-1965 2nd Vatican Council

1965 Crackdown against Muslim Brotherhood in Egypt

1966 Martyrdom of Sayyid Qutb, the godfather of Islamic radicalism

1967 Six-Day Arab-Israeli war ending with Jerusalem coming under Jewish control

1979 Peace agreement between Israel and Egypt; Iranian Islamic Revolution; Soviet Union invasion of Afghanistan; Siege of Mecca; Saddam Hussein comes to power

1981 Anwar Sadat assassinated

1982 Israel invades Lebanon

1988 Saddam Hussein's Anfal Operation against Kurds

1991 First Gulf War; Iraqi Kurdistan gains a measure of autonomy

1994-Jordan-Israel Peace Treaty

2001 The events of 9/11 against USA. USA invades Afghanistan

2003 U.S. invasion of Iraq

Current Refugee Crisis with the majority of refugees either Muslims or minorities persecuted in Muslim Lands

Persecution: Ongoing from earliest days of Islam, varying in intensity

1980s-Current: Earnest Prayer for Muslims around the World

2000-Current: Increased Number of Muslims Coming to Faith in Jesus

Appendix D: Bibliography and List of Sources

Akyol, Mustafa (2017). The Islamic Jesus. New York: St. Martin's Press.

Albera, Dionigi & Courci, Maria. (2012). *Sharing Sacred Space in the Mediterranean.* Bloomington, IN: Indiana University Press.

Ali, Daniel & Spencer, Robert (2003). *Inside Islam: A Guide for Catholics.* West Chester, PA Ascension Press.

Axworthy, Michael (2008). *A History of Iran.* New York: Basic Books.

Badger, George Percy (1852). *The Nestorians and Their Rituals.* London

Bailey, Betty Jane & Bailey, J. Martin (2003). Grand Rapids, MI Eerdmans Publishing

Barrett, David, Kurian, George, & Johnson, Todd. (2001). *World Christian Encyclopedia.* Oxford, UK: Oxford Press.

Bauman, Stephen, Soerens, Matthew, & Sheir Issam (2016). *Seeking Refuge,*

Chicago: Moody Publishers.

Bell-Fialkoff, Andrew (1996). *Ethnic Cleansing.* New York: St. Martin's Press.

Bennett, Clinton (2008). *Understanding Christian-Muslim Relations.* London: Continuum.

Blincoe, Robert (1998). *Ethnic Realities and the Church: Lessons from Kurdistan* Pasadena, CA: Presbyterian Center for Mission Studies.

Bokenkotter, Thomas (1990). *A Concise History of the Catholic Church.*

New York: Image Books.

Brad, Chad, Draper Charles, & England, Archie (2003). (Eds). *Holman Illustrated Bible Dictionary.* Nashville, TN Holman

Brenneman, Robert L. (2016). *As Strong as the Mountains: A Kurdish Cultural Journey.* Long, Grove, IL: Waveland Press

Brunson, Andrew (2019). *God's Hostage* (Kindle eBook)

Bulliet, Richard (1979). *Conversion to Islam in the Medieval Period.* Cambridge, MA: Harvard University Press.

Burgess, Stanley (Ed) (2011). *Christian Peoples of the Spirit*. New York: New York University Press.

Chadwick, Henry (1993). *The Early Church*. London: Penguin Books.

Courbage, Yousef, & Farues, Phillipe. *Christians and Jews under Islam*. (1997). London: I.B. Tauris Publishers.

Cragg, Kenneth (1991). The Arab Christian: a History in the Middle East: Louisville, KY: Westminster/John Knox Press.

Crocker, H. W. (2001). *Triumph: The Power and Glory of the Catholic Church*. New York: Three River Press.

Cruz, Joan Carroll (2012). *She How She Loves Us: 50 Approved Apparitions of our Lady*. Charlotte, N.C. TAN books

Cumming, Joseph (2011). Toward Respecful Witness in *Fruit to Root*. Woodberry, Dudley Ed. Pasadena, CA: William Carey

Davis, Leo Donald (1983). The First Seven Ecumenical Councils (325-787) Collegeville, MN: The Liturgical Press.

Dinno, Khalid, S. (2017). *The Syrian Orthodox Christians in the Late Ottoman Period*. Piscataway, NJ: Gorgias Press.

Duffy, Eamon (1997). *Saints and Sinners: A History of the Popes.* New Haven. Yale University Press.

Durie, Mark (2010). *The Third Choice.* Deror Books.

Elwell, Walter A. (1984). *Evangelical Dictionary of Theology.* Grand Rapids, MI: Baker

Esposito, John (2003). *The Oxford Dictionary of Islam.* Oxford University Press.

Foltz, Richard (1999). *Religions of the Silk Road.* New York: St. Martin's Press.

Frankopen, Peter, (2017). *The Silk Roads.* London: Bloomsburg

Gabriel Mark. (2003) *Islam and the Jews.* Lake Mary, FL: Charisma House

Gabriel Mark. (2004) Jesus and Muhammad. Lake Mary, FL: Charisma House.

Garrison, David (2014). *A Wind in the House of Islam.* Monument, CO: WigTake Resources.

Geisler, Norman L. & Saleeb, Abdul (2002), *Answering Islam*. Grand Rapids, MI Baker Books

George, Timothy (2002). *Is the Father of Jesus the God of Muhammad?* Grand Rapids, MI Zondervan

Ghattas, Kim (2020). *The Black Wave*. New York: Henry Holt and Company.

Glasse, Cyril (2008). *The Concise Encyclopedia of Islam*. London. Stacey International.

Goddard, Hugh (2020). *A History of Christian-Muslim Relations*. Edinburgh: University Press.

Goldman, David, P. (2011). *How Civilizations Die (And Why Islam is Dying Too)*. Washington, Regnery Publishing.

Gonzalez, Justo L. (2010). *The Story of Christianity Vol 1* New York: Harper One.

Guillaume, A. (2000 14th edition). *The Life of Muhammad* translated from Ibn Ishaq's *Sirat Rasul Allah*.Oxford, UK: Oxford University Press.

Hamid, Shadi (2016). *Islamic Exceptionalism*. New York: St. Martin's Press.

Hamid, Tawfik (2015). *Inside Jihad.* Mountain Lake Park, Maryland. Mountain Lake Press.

Hardon, John A. (1981). *The Catholic Catechism: A Contemporary Catechism of the Teachings of the Catholic Church.* New York: Image Books.

Hausefeld Mark & Lynda (2005). *Silk Road Stories.* USA: Onward Books.

Holcomb, Justin S. (2014). *Know the Creeds and Councils.* Grand Rapids, MI Zondervan

Hosier, Helen Kooiman (2000). 100 Christian Women Who Changed the 20th Century: Grand Rapids, MI: Fleming H. Revell

Hourani, Albert (1991). *A History of Arab Peoples.* New York: Warner Brothers Press.

Hussein, Ed (2018) *The House of Islam.* Kindle eBook

Ibrahim, Raymond (2013). *Crucified Again* (Kindle eBook).

Ibrahim, Raymond (2018). *Sword and Scimitar.* New York: Da Capo Press.

Irvin, Dale T & Sunquist, Scott W. (2004) *History of the World Christian Movement.* Maryknoll, New York: Orbis Books.

Izady, Mehrdad R. (1992). *The Kurds: A Concise Handbook.* Washington D.C. Crane Russak.

Jabbour, Nabeel. (2008). *The Crescent through the Eyes of the Cross.* Colorado Springs, CO: Navpress.

Jenkins, Philip (2010). *Jesus Wars.* New York: Harper Collins.

Jenkins, Philip (2008). *The Lost History of Christianity.* New York: Harper Collins.

Johnson, Paul. (1976) *A History of Christianity.* New York: Simon & Schuster

Joseph, John (1983). *Muslim-Christian Relations and Inter-Christian Rivalries in the Middle East.* Albany, NY: State University of New York Press.

Joseph, John (1961). *The Nestorians and Their Muslim Neighbors.* Princeton, New Jersey: Princeton University Press.

Karsh, Efraim. (2006). *Islamic Imperialism.* New Haven, CT: Yale University Press.

Keener, Craig (1993). *The Bible Background Commentary*: New Testament. Downer's Grove, IL IVP

Kelsey, Morton 1978. *A Way to Listen to God*. New York: Paulist Press.

Kelsey (1991) *God, Dreams and Revelation*. Augsburg, Fortress Press

Kendal, Elizabeth (2016). *After Saturday Comes Sunday* (Kindle eBook)

Kennedy, Hugh (2007). *The Great Arab Conquests*. London: Weidenfeld & Nicolson.

Khalaf, Farida. (2016). *The Girl who Beat ISIS: My Story*. UK Penguin Random House.

Khan, Muhammad Muhsin (1994), Summarized Sahih al Bukkari: Ridyadh, Saudi Arabia

Kilpatrick, William (2020). *What Catholics Need to Know about Islam*. Manchester, NH: Crisis books.

Kreeft, Peter (2017). *Catholics and Protestants*. San Francisco: St Ignatius Press.

Kronk, Rick (2010). *Dreams and Visions.* Italy: Destiny Image.

Latourette, Kenneth, Scott (1976). *A History of the Expansion of Christianity: The First Five Centuries.* Grand Rapids, MI: Zondervan.

Ibid: (Volume 2) *The Thousand Years of Uncertainty.*

Ibid (Volume 3). *Three Centuries of Advance.*

Lewis, Barnard (1995). *The Middle East:* Great Britain Simon & Schuster.

Lewis, Bernard (2004). *The Crisis of Islam:* New York: Random House.

Little, Derya 2017). *From Islam to Christ: One Woman's Path through the Riddle of God.* San Francisco: Ignatius Press.

Longenecker, Dwight & Gustafson David (2003). *Mary: A Catholic— Evangelical Debate.* Grand Rapids, MI: Brazos Press.

Love, Rick (2000). *Muslims, Magic and the Kingdom of God.* Pasadena, CA: William Carey Press.

Maalouf Tony, (2003). *Arabs in the Shadow of Israel.* Grand Rapids, MI Kregel Books.

MacCulloch, Diarmaid (2009). *Christianity: The First Three Thousand Years.* New York: Viking.

McCurry, Don (2011) *Healing the Broken Family of Abraham.* Colorado Springs, CO: Ministries to Muslims.

Mandryk, Jason (2010). *Operation World.7th Edition).* Biblica Publising: Colorado Springs, CO.

McDowall, David A. (1996). *A Modern History of the Kurds.* London: I.B. Tauris

Meyendorff, John (1979). *Byzantine Theology.* New York: Fordham University Press.

Moffett, Samuel Hugh (2003). *A History of Christianity in Asia:* Maryknoll, New York Orbis Books.

Morris, Benny & Ze'evi Dor. (2019). *The Thirty-Year Genocide.* Cambridge MA: Harvard University Press.

Morris, Charles & Craig Borlace. (2016). *Fleeing ISIS, Finding Jesus.* Kindle eBook.

Moucarry, Chawkat (2001). *The Prophet & the Messiah:* Downers Grove: IVP

Musk, Bill (2005). *Kissing Cousins? Christians and Muslims Face to Face:* Oxford, UK. Monarch

Musk, Bill (2003). *The Unseen Face of Islam.* London: Monarch Books.

Noll, Mark A. 1997). *Turning Points.* Grand Rapids, MI. Baker Books.

Olson Roger E. (1999). *The Story of Christian Theology.* Downers Grove, IL IVP

Omar, Irfan Ed. (2007). *A Muslim View of Christianity: Essays on Dialogue by Mahmoud Ayoub.* Maryknoll, N.Y. Orbis Books.

Pikkert. P. (2008). *Protestant Missionaries to the Middle East: Ambassadors of Christ or Culture.* Amazon.

Pincot, David (2018). *The Crucifix on Mecca's Front Porch.* San Francisco Ignatius.

Piper, Noel (2005). *Faithful Women and Their Extraordinary God.* Wheaton, IL Crossway Books.

Quash, Ben & Ward Michael (Eds) (2007). *Heresies and How to Avoid Them:* Grand Rapids, MI Baker Academic

Qureshi, Nabeel (2014). *Seeking Allah, Finding Jesus* Grand Rapids, MI Zondervan

Rassam, Suha (2010). *Christianity in Iraq.* Victoria, Australia: Freedom Publishing.

Ratzinger, Joseph (Pope Benedict XVI) & Marcello, Pera (2007). *Without Roots.* New York: Basic Books.

Robinson, Neal (1991). *Christ in Islam and Christianity.* New York: State University Press.

Rowe, Paul S. (Ed). (2019). *Routledge Handbook of Minorities in the Middle East.* London: Routledge.

Rupen, Das & Hamoud, Brent (2017). *Strangers in the Kingdom,* Langham Global Library.

Shayesteh, Daniel (2010). *Islam and the Son of God.* Sydney, Australia: Talesh Books.

Sheen, Fulton (1952) *The World's First Love.* New York: McGraw-Hill Book Company.

Shelton, Brian (2018) *The Quest for the Historical Apostles,* Grand Rapids, MI: Baker Academic.

Showalter, Richard & Jewel (2009). *A Silk Road Pilgrimage.* Scotsdale, PA: Herald Press.

Soufan, Ali (2017). *Anatomy of Terror.* New York: W.W. Norton and Company.

Spickard, Paul & Cragg, Kevin (2001) *A Global History of Christians.* Grand Rapids, MI: Baker Academic.

Tejirian Eleanor, & Simon, Reva Specto (2012). *Conflict, Conquest and Conversion.* New York: Columbia University Press.

Stark, Rodney (2009). *God's Battalions.* New York: Harper One

Tilley, Allan, Rodney (2020). *Finding Christ in Muslim Lands.* Kindle Direct Publishing

Turtkovic, Rita George. (2018) *Christians, Muslims, and Mary*: New York: Paulist Press.

Volf, Miroslav (2011). *Allah: A Christian Response.* New York: Harper One

Warraq, Ibn (2003). *Leaving Islam.* Amherst, NY: Prometheus Books.

Weddell, Sherry (2017). *Fruitful Discipleship.* Huntington, IN: Our Daily Visitor

Wheatcroft, Andrew (2004). *Infidels: A History of the Conflict between Christianity and Islam.* New York: Random House

Wilson Mark. (2020) *Biblical Turkey.* Istanbul, Turkey: Yayinlari.

Weigel, George (2013). *Evangelical Catholicism.* New York: Basic Books

Woodberry, Dudly (2011). *From Root to Fruit.* Pasadena, CA: William Carey

Wright, Robin (2008). *Dreams and Shadows: The Future of the Middle East.* London: Penguin Books.

Yamauchi, Edwin (1990). *Persia in the Bible.* Grand Rapids, MI Baker Book House

Ye'or Bat (1996) *The Decline of Eastern Christianity under Islam: From Jihad to Dhimmitude.* Cranbury, NJ: Associated University Presses